State and Society in Twentieth-Century America

State and Society in Twentieth-Century America

ROBERT HARRISON

Longman
London and New York

Addison Wesley Longman Limited
Edinburgh Gate,
Harlow, Essex CM20 2JE,
United Kingdom
and Associated Companies throughout the world

*Published in the United States of America
by Addison Wesley Longman Inc., New York*
© Addison Wesley Longman Limited 1997

First published 1997

ISBN 0 582 267722 PPR
ISBN 0 582 270006 CSD

British Library Cataloguing in Publication Data

A catalogue record for this book is available from the British Library

Library of Congress Cataloging-in-Publication Data

Harrison, Robert.
  State and society in twentieth-century America/Robert Harrison.
    p. cm.
  Includes bibliographical references (p.) and index.
  ISBN 0-582-27000-6. — ISBN 0-582-26772-2 (pbk.)
  1. United States—Politics and government—20th century.
2. Social problems—United States—History—20th century. 3. Social conflict—
United States—History—20th century. 4. Progressivism (United States politics)
5. New Deal, 1933-1939. 6. United States—Social policy. I. Title.
E743.H277   1997
973.9—dc21   97-14180
                                                              CIP

Set by 7 in 10/12 ITC New Baskerville
Produced by Longman Singapore Publishers (Pte) Ltd.
Printed in Singapore

Contents

List of Figures and Tables

Acknowledgements

Parts of Chapter 2 draw on the author's article 'The Weakened Spring of Government Revisited: The Growth of Federal Power in the Late Nineteenth Century', published in Rhodri Jeffreys-Jones and Bruce Collins, eds., *The Growth of Federal Power in American History* (Edinburgh, Scottish Academic Press, (1983), p. 62–75. We are grateful to Scottish Academic Press for their kind permission to reproduce sections of this article.

Preface

'We regard the state as an educational and ethical agency whose positive aid is an indispensable condition to human progress', proclaimed a group of young American economists in 1885. Nearly a century later, President Ronald Reagan told the nation that, 'In the present crisis, government is not the solution – it is the problem'.[1] These two statements frame the outer limits of the period to be covered by this book. They also indicate its central subject-matter. For much of the twentieth century, progressives and liberals believed, like the founder members of the American Economic Association, that the powers of the modern state could be harnessed to resolve social conflicts, alleviate social injustice and promote social progress. By the 1970s and 1980s, not only conservatives like Reagan but many who called themselves liberals had come to doubt whether the exercise of government power could ever provide solutions for America's mounting social and economic problems. The liberal project that lasted for a better part of a century seemed to have lost its way.

Two central themes run through this book. One is the development of the tradition of liberal reform, from progressivism to the New Deal and beyond, which has long preoccupied historians of twentieth-century America, such as Richard Hofstadter in his classic *The Age of Reform*. The other is the growth of the state, which has more recently occupied the attention of historically orientated social scientists like Stephen Skowronek and Theda Skocpol. These political developments, which form the thematic spine of the work, are set against the dramatic changes in American society that occurred during the twentieth century. Although the book focuses

1. Quoted in George E. Mowry, *The Era of Theodore Roosevelt and the Birth of Modern America, 1900–1912* (New York, 1958), p.22; *Guardian*, 21 Jan. 1981.

particularly on two principal eras of reform, the Progressive Era and the New Deal, pointing out both the continuities and the differences between them, attention is also paid to the 1920s, in order both to challenge the conventional image of a period of unmitigated reaction and to show how the politics of the decade reflected the conflicts and tensions of a society in change, and to the post-Second World War period, in which the New Deal tradition was both reinvigorated and challenged. It closes with an examination of the problems of contemporary American government and considers whether recent political developments foreshadow 'The End of Liberalism'. A number of themes are kept in the foreground throughout, including the control of big business, social and urban policy, labour relations, and the problem of civil rights.

List of abbreviations

AAA	Agricultural Adjustment Act
AABA	American Anti-Boycott Association
AALL	Association for the Advancement of Labor Legislation
ACW	Amalgamated Clothing Workers
ADC	Aid to Dependent Children
AFBF	American Farm Bureau Federation
AFDC	Aid to the Families of Dependent Children
AFL	American Federation of Labor
AMA	American Medical Association
ASL	Anti-Saloon League
CAP	Community Action Program
CES	Committee on Economic Security
CIO	Congress of Industrial Organizations
CORE	Congress of Racial Equality
COS	charity organisation society
CP	Communist Party
CWA	Civil Works Administration
EEOC	Equal Employment Opportunities Committee
FBI	Federal Bureau of Investigation
FERA	Federal Emergency Relief Administration
FHA	Federal Housing Administration
FSA	Farm Security Administration
FTC	Federal Trade Commission
GDP	gross domestic product
GNP	gross national product
GFWC	General Federation of Women's Clubs
ICC	Interstate Commerce Commission
IWW	Industrial Workers of the World
NAACP	National Association for the Advancement of Colored People

NAM	National Association of Manufacturers
NCF	National Civic Federation
NCL	National Consumers' League
NCLC	National Child Labor Committee
NIRA	National Industrial Recovery Act
NLB	National Labor Board
NLRB	National Labor Relations Board
NRA	National Recovery Administration
NWLB	National War Labor Board
OAA	Old Age Assistance
OAI	Old Age Insurance
OASI	Old Age and Survivors' Insurance
PAC	political action committees
RA	Resettlement Administration
RFC	Reconstruction Finance Corporation
SCLC	Southern Christian Leadership Conference
SEC	Stock Exchange Commission
SPA	Socialist Party of America
STFU	Southern Tenant Farmers' Union
TVA	Tennessee Valley Authority
UAW	United Automobile Workers
UMW	United Mine Workers
WCTU	Women's Christian Temperance Union
WPA	Works Progress Administration
WTUL	Women's Trade Union League

CHAPTER ONE

Introduction

State and society

'It is not always necessary, though better, to make an engagement to see the President', a Washington correspondent suggested in 1900.[1] Such was the informality with which President McKinley's White House, with its minuscule staff, operated. It was not unknown for his predecessor, Grover Cleveland, to answer the telephone himself or to open the door to callers. In contrast, any reporter, never mind a casual visitor, wishing an audience with President Bill Clinton might, even if successful, have to wait days for the briefest of appointments. Layers of bureaucracy separate the president from the people whom he serves, while the whole apparatus of government has become almost unfathomably massive.

At the simplest level the growth of the American state can be measured in terms of the expansion of the federal government (see Table 1.1). Whereas in 1900 federal outlays amounted to $521 million, three-quarters of which were accounted for by defence, military pensions and the postal service, the sum expended in 1994 was no less than $1,460,914 million, an increase, even allowing for inflation, by a factor of 132. The latter sum absorbed 21.7 per cent of the gross national product (GNP) of the United States (and nearly 5 per cent of the gross domestic product of the entire globe), as against 2.8 per cent in 1900. To express the figures another way, whereas at the beginning of the century the federal government spent $28, at 1958 prices, for each citizen, in 1994 it spent $1,086. The United States does not carry out all the responsibilities of

1. Walter Lord, *The Good Years: From 1900 to the First World War* (New York, 1960), p. 5.

1

TABLE 1.1   *Outlays of United States Government, 1900–1994*

Year	At current prices (x $1 million)	At 1958 prices (x $1 million)	At 1958 prices per capita ($)	As percentage of GNP
1900	521	2 144	28.17	2.8
1905	567	2 172	25.92	2.3
1910	694	2 361	25.55	2.0
1915	946	2 324	23.12	1.9
1920	6 358	9 722	91.29	6.0
1925	2 924	5 634	48.65	3.1
1930	3 320	6 734	54.66	3.7
1935	6 497	15 251	119.71	9.0
1940	9 468	21 567	163.26	9.5
1945	92 712	155 296	1 110.05	43.8
1950	42 562	53 070	349.37	14.9
1955	68 444	75 296	456.06	17.2
1960	92 191	89 246	495.81	18.3
1965	118 228	106 608	550.95	17.3
1970	195 649	144 711	709.37	19.4
1975	332 332	177 149	822.04	21.7
1980	590 947	205 690	905.33	21.8
1985	946 391	252 236	1 060.26	23.4
1990	1 252 705	274 897	1 102.23	22.6
1994	1 460 914	282 685	1 086.00	21.7

Sources: US Bureau of the Census, *Historical Statistics of the United States: Colonial Times to 1970* (Washington, D.C., 1975), Series F1,5, A7, Y457, 462–3; *Statistical Abstract of the United States, 1980* (Washington, D.C., 1980), nos 2, 436, 531, 725; *Statistical Abstract of the United States, 1995* (Washington, D.C., 1995), nos 2, 517, 699.

government. Thus a more complete measure of the growth of the public sector would incorporate state and local, as well as federal, spending (see Table 1.2). In 1902 governments of all kinds spent $1,660 million, that is 7.7 per cent of GNP; in 1990 they spent $2,219,000 million, or 40.0 per cent of GNP. Even allowing for inflation, that represents a 73-fold increase. Whereas in 1902 government spent $84.29, at 1958 prices, for every American, in 1990 it spent $1952.46. Over the same period public employment rose from 1,129,000 to 18,745,000, that is from 4.0 to 15.2 per cent of the civilian labour force.

The growth of the state is not measurable solely in terms of the number of dollars spent or officials employed by government departments, but also by the extent to which government rules and regulations direct and restrain the actions of individual Americans.

TABLE 1.2 *Federal, State and Local Government Expenditure, 1902–1990*

Year	Expenditure per capita in 1958 dollars			Expenditure as per centage of GNP		
	State/Local	Federal	All govt.	State/Local	Federal	All govt.
1902	55.25	29.04	84.29	5.0	2.7	7.7
1913	76.73	33.16	109.89	5.7	2.4	8.1
1922	100.42	68.28	168.70	7.4	5.1	12.5
1927	129.19	59.38	188.57	8.1	3.7	11.8
1932	162.87	85.03	247.90	14.1	7.3	21.4
1938	162.39	148.27	310.66	10.9	10.0	20.9
1942	141.29	500.92	642.21	6.7	22.5	28.9
1946	140.97	712.00	852.97	8.9	29.3	38.2
1950	209.60	367.74	577.34	9.0	15.7	24.7
1955	248.38	489.36	737.74	9.4	18.4	27.8
1960	290.44	523.20	813.64	10.7	19.3	30.0
1965	456.19	606.08	1 062.27	11.0	19.0	30.0
1970	452.46	754.84	1 207.30	13.1	21.8	34.9
1975	540.22	845.21	1 385.43	14.3	22.3	36.6
1980	522.96	946.22	1 469.18	12.6	22.8	35.4
1985	614.09	1 157.14	1 771.23	13.6	25.5	39.1
1990	726.78	1 225.68	1 952.46	14.9	25.1	40.0

Note: The figures in this table are drawn from different series to those in Table 1.1. and therefore do not correspond exactly. In particular, the figures for federal expenditure include grants-in-aid to subnational governments that are not included in the federal outlays enumerated in Table 1.1.

Sources: US Bureau of the Census, *Historical Statistics of the United States: Colonial Times to 1970* (Washington, D.C., 1975), Series Y522, 590–1, 671; *Statistical Abstract of the United States, 1980* (Washington, D.C., 1980), nos 480, 490; *Statistical Abstract of the United States, 1990* (Washington, D.C., 1990), no. 455; *Statistical Abstract of the United States, 1995* (Washington, D.C., 1995), nos 474, 478.

In the words of the historian Bernard Wishy, the daily lives of American citizens are 'diffused with the state'.[2] With the home she lives in purchased by means of a mortgage guaranteed by the Federal Housing Administration, her children educated in schools assisted by federal funds and subject to federal anti-discrimination legislation, her savings guaranteed by a federal deposit insurance scheme, her weekly pay protected by federal minimum-wage laws, and perhaps by the bargaining power of a trade union operating

2. Bernard Wishy, *Good-bye Machiavelli: Government and American Life* (Baton Rouge, La., 1995), p. 251.

under federal labour relations law, but eaten into by federal income tax assessments and by contributions to compulsory federal old age and unemployment insurance schemes, the roads she drives on constructed with the help of federal funds for interstate highways or urban renewal, the food she eats, the drugs she takes, the cosmetics she applies regulated by the federal Food and Drug Administration, and even the air she breathes covered by federal emission standards, the typical American citizen confronts the national government in almost every part of her existence. Were she to become a single mother, fall into poverty, start a business or operate a farm, her contact with government would be still more extensive. Compare this with the experience of her grandmother at the start of the century, who was only likely to encounter the federal government in the guise of postmaster or letter-carrier. There is no doubt that, for better or for worse, in a multitude of ways, both fundamental and trivial, the hand of the state is far more intrusive at the end of the twentieth century than it was at the beginning.

What do we mean by the 'state'? According to Max Weber, 'states are compulsory associations claiming control over territories and the people within them'.[3] They include those individuals and agencies that have authority to make decisions that are binding upon members of society and possess the coercive power to enforce their decisions. A broader definition would go beyond that to incorporate the organisation and process of governance and the structure of decision-making, the means by which conflict is handled and social relations are regulated. The state is embedded in a 'governing system' which incorporates not only those persons possessing formal authority but a penumbra of institutions, ranging from political parties to foundations and think-tanks, and including the broader class of what are now called policy intellectuals, which contribute to that process. The democratic state is subject to a variety of influences. Nevertheless, while recognising this, it is helpful, for analytical purposes, to hold to a working definition which confines itself to those agencies entrusted with formal power.

Renewed interest in the 'state' in recent decades stems from a number of different sources: a debate within Marxism about the autonomy of the state in relation to class power; a reaction within political science against the 'behavioral turn' of the 1950s and 1960s and towards a renewed appreciation of the role of institutions and the determining importance of historical process; a similar interest

3. Theda Skocpol, 'Bringing the state back in', in Peter B. Evans *et al.*, eds, *Bringing the State Back In* (Cambridge, 1985), p. 7.

among historical sociologists in the influence of historical contingency; and a growing awareness among historians of the limitations of the 'new social history', which, with its concentration on the immediate lived experience of men and women, neglected the wider framework of political power which framed their lives. As William E. Leuchtenburg reminds his fellow historians, paraphrasing Trotsky, 'While you may not be interested in the State, the State is interested in you'.[4] In each case, scholars have gravitated from a 'society-centred' approach, in which the state is seen as having a secondary, or epiphenomenal, impact on social development, to a 'state-centred' approach, in which the state is regarded as an explanatory variable in its own right. Whether they have moved too far in that direction is something which we will have to explore with particular reference to the political history of the United States.

The study of the state necessarily involves a comparative perspective. Interest in the subject in recent decades is informed by a sense that the experiences of different nations have much in common. The 'modern state' emerged in response to the development of an urban-industrial society since the nineteenth century, growing at similar rates in different nations, performing certain common functions, such as the regulation of large-scale business, the mediation of labour relations, and the provision of welfare, and displaying certain common structural features, such as the growth of bureaucracy. State-making was a common response to the problems of modern society. It is equally apparent that there are enormous cross-national differences in the process of state formation and in the size and structure of the state. For example, wide variations manifest themselves in the nature of the welfare state – the extent of government intervention, the type of risks covered – and the timing of its arrival, with Germany establishing social insurance programmes in the 1880s, while the United States waited until the 1930s before installing any systematic coverage at a national level.

There is, in political terms, no universal 'response to industrialism'. The state does not merely reflect society but is, at least to some degree, autonomous. The actions of government are not determined by the logic of economic development, the balance of social forces or the dynamics of class conflict, as pluralist political

---

4. William E. Leuchtenburg, 'The pertinence of political history: reflections on the significance of the state in America' *Journal of American History* 73 (Dec. 1986), p. 600.

scientists and orthodox Marxists have, in different ways, assumed. The state is not a 'cash register' which merely aggregates the outcome of social pressures. Governments are, in Theda Skocpol's words, 'authoritative and resourceful organizations . . . sites of autonomous action', while government officials are partly autonomous actors, with ideas and interests of their own.[5] The growth of the state is influenced by the pre-existing configuration of political ideas and institutions: the informal traditions and practices that guide political actors, as well as the formal constitutional structure; the ideological presuppositions that, consciously or unconsciously, frame the boundaries of political possibility; and the established areas of governing experience and expertise. A state's existing 'political capacity', including its formal powers, fiscal resources and administrative expertise, constitutes a major constraint on policy formation. Like a river in flood, the authority of the state tends to flow down channels that have already been opened up for it. It prefers to solve problems that it is already equipped to solve, rather than tackle new ones. Furthermore, notes Skocpol, 'policies, once enacted, restructure subsequent political processes'.[6] Bureaucracies are created and interest groups and expectations are adjusted in ways which, by a process of feedback, influence the course of future policy-making. In other words, the development of the state can only be understood historically.

The United States has often appeared to be something of an exception to general assumptions about the growth of the 'modern state'. To European visitors like Alexis de Tocqueville, nineteenth-century America had the appearance of a 'stateless society'. There was no 'state' in the European sense of a clearly defined and self-conscious bureaucratic class with a sense of common responsibility for governance, no hereditary monarchy, no great standing army, no national corporations or formal estates representing major interests in society, no ruling class – in short, no 'establishment'. Americans, to H.G. Wells, lacked a 'sense of the state'.[7] Even in the late twentieth century the public sector, though massively enlarged, is smaller in the United States than in most comparable industrial nations. This is evident in the relatively small number of sectors of the economy subject to government ownership or control, as well as

5. Theda Skocpol, *Protecting Soldiers and Mothers: The Political Origins of Social Policy in the United States* (Cambridge, Mass., 1992), p. 42.
6. Ibid., p. 58.
7. Stephen Skowronek, *Building a New American State: The Expansion of National Administrative Capacities, 1877–1920* (Cambridge, 1982), p. 3.

in the relative underdevelopment of the American welfare state. Despite its vertiginous growth during this century, public spending in the United States, as a percentage of GNP, remains lower than in most other Western democracies.

Of course, in an American context the concept of the 'state' is problematic in another way. In many European countries, like France or the United Kingdom, the state is a unitary formation, in effect corresponding to the national government. In America 'state' is the name given to the subnational units which form the Union. Each of the fifty American states has its own government which enjoys a measure of sovereign power. The Constitution adopted in 1787 left important areas of governmental responsibility to the states, including most matters of domestic policy, while the national (that is 'federal') government concerned itself with matters of common concern like foreign relations and interstate commerce. Federal power has, of course, increased enormously in the twentieth century, and the United States government has intervened in many areas of policy that were formerly the exclusive preserve of the states. Indeed, there are few areas of governance in which federal money and federal regulations do not now intrude. Nevertheless, the continuing importance of state and local governments is visible in the figures for government expenditure (see Table 1.2). In 1902 state and local governments combined spent nearly $2 for every $1 spent by the federal government. Even after the explosive growth of the federal government during this century, subnational units still accounted for 37.2 per cent of all government spending in 1990. Indeed, since much federal expenditure takes the form of grants-in-aid to the states, amounting to $135,377 million in 1990, the government agents with whom the public comes into contact are still more likely to be state or local than federal employees. In 1990 they accounted for 83 per cent of total public employment. The activity of the states, though relatively diminished, has expanded greatly in absolute terms over the course of the century. The states have remained jealous of their prerogatives, nourished by a 'states' rights' tradition that goes back to the earliest years of the Republic. Thus the American 'state' cannot be wholly comprehended without closely considering the role of the states.

Another distinctive feature of the American state is the system of 'checks and balances' that is built into the constitutional fabric. Anxious to prevent the concentration of power in the hands of any one individual or agency, whether it be a tyrannical chief executive or a popularly elected legislature, the framers of the federal

Constitution, and likewise of the several state constitutions, distributed authority among the various branches of government, furnishing each with power to check the initiatives emanating from its counterparts. Rather than being concentrated, as under the British Constitution, power is dispersed. The machinery of government is engineered to ensure that the separate components of government act as checks upon each other, rather than moving in unison. In the words of James McGregor Burns, 'our system was designed for deadlock and inaction'.[8] The different parts of the 'state' act in different ways and pursue different objectives, sometimes objectives which are diametrically opposed. When President Bill Clinton and Speaker Newt Gingrich engage in their ritual dance of mutual accusation, they are doing no more than re-enacting a series of similar confrontations – between Andrew Jackson and Henry Clay, Andrew Johnson and Thaddeus Stevens, Harry Truman and Robert Taft. Their oppositional relationship follows as much from their respective institutional positions as from any personal or ideological antagonism. Thus we have a twofold separation of powers: a vertical separation between state and federal governments; and a horizontal separation within each sphere between the several branches of government. Furthermore, the demarcation disputes that arise from so pronounced a dispersion of powers give an important, sometimes a determining, role to the federal judiciary, which assumes the responsibility of arbitrating questions of constitutional authority and, in effect, of legislating upon a variety of major substantive issues. Thus the constitutional structure of the United States confers exceptional decision-making powers on the courts.

The American governing system is one of almost baffling complexity. The American state is a complex entity, in which authority is fragmented and policy-making sometimes incoherent. The political parties, with their decentralised structure and heterogeneous composition, can only partly mitigate its centrifugal tendencies. The peculiar structure of what Samuel Huntington has described as a 'Tudor polity' has contributed significantly to the way in which American government has responded to the challenges of the twentieth century.[9]

---

8. James M. Burns, *The Deadlock of Democracy* (Englewood Cliffs, N.J., 1964), p. 6.
9. Samuel P. Huntington, *Political Order in Changing Societies* (New Haven, Ct., 1968), p. 98 and pp. 93–139 passim.

Liberalism

Those who have most enthusiastically advocated the growth of the state during the twentieth century have been known as liberals, and earlier as progressives. 'Progressives', said Theodore Roosevelt, the first of the reforming presidents of the twentieth century, sought 'to use the government as an efficient agency of and for the practical betterment of social and economic conditions throughout the land'.[10] For a variety of reasons and in a variety of ways, progressives and liberals called on the power of the state to achieve a limited measure of social change within the framework of a capitalist society. They engaged in a succession of attempts to find non-socialist solutions to problems of economic concentration, social injustice and class conflict. 'It has been the function of the liberal tradition in American politics', wrote Richard Hofstadter, whose *Age of Reform* offers a starting-point for any historical study of twentieth-century American reform, 'from the time of Jeffersonian and Jacksonian democracy down through Populism, Progressivism, and the New Deal, at first to broaden the numbers of those who could benefit from the great American bonanza and then to humanize its workings and help heal its casualties.'[11] Inevitably lacking the ideological clarity of either right-wing or left-wing alternatives, the approach of liberalism to the use of government power has been at best pragmatic, at worst merely expedient, according to the demands of time and circumstance. Nevertheless, American liberals in the twentieth century shared a strong sense of common purpose, believing themselves to be enlisted in an ongoing struggle to redeem America from selfishness and injustice.

There have been several periods of liberal reform, several liberal moments when for various reasons the bounds of possibility appeared to open up. The Progressive Era, roughly from 1900 to 1917, saw the first widespread recognition of the need for government intervention to cope with the problems of a modern industrial society, resulting in a profusion of regulatory legislation, at state and national levels, to control business corporations and to eradicate a variety of social evils, ranging from slum housing and

10. Quoted in Sidney Fine, *Laissez Faire and the General Welfare State: A Study of Conflict in American Thought, 1865–1901* (Ann Arbor, Mich., 1956), p. 388
11. Richard Hofstadter, *The Age of Reform: From Bryan to F.D.R.* (New York, 1955), p. 18.

child labour to intemperance and 'white slavery'. The Progressive Era culminated in American intervention in the First World War, which can be seen as a final progressive crusade, an apotheosis of progressivism, both overseas, in the form of Wilson's programme for a new liberal world order, and at home, in the shape of the 'war welfare state'. But in war progressivism also found its nemesis. Popular disenchantment with wartime restrictions and Wilsonian internationalism resulted in something of a reaction against the reforming impulse in domestic politics.

The 1920s appear in the textbooks as a decade dominated by a crass and atavistic conservatism (contrasting sharply with the innovative character of the social and cultural life of the 'Roaring Twenties'). The 'Age of Normalcy', the era of Harding and Coolidge, is set out in stark contradistinction to the era of Theodore Roosevelt and Woodrow Wilson. Yet this is only partly true. A variety of progressive reform movements maintained their vigour during the 1920s, while, as Tables 1.1 and 1.2 make clear, the overall volume of government activity continued to grow.

The critical moment in the development of the American state came in the 1930s in the form of the New Deal. In the wake of the economic collapse that followed 1929, the Administration of Franklin D. Roosevelt set in motion a series of spectacular and innovative reforms, including a suite of relief and public works pro-grammes, a system of agricultural price supports that has, in essence, remained in place ever since, extensive government supervision of banking and the stock exchange, fundamental changes in labour relations law, and the establishment, somewhat belatedly, of an American welfare state. This, above all, came to represent the heart of the New Deal legacy and the core of the liberal tradition which emerged from the 1930s. The Second World War consolidated many of the policy innovations of the previous decade, while checking moves towards a more comprehensive welfare state. The Second World War was not succeeded by a conservative reaction, despite the grandstanding of right-wing Republicans like Robert Taft and Joseph McCarthy, so much as by a steady, incremental expansion of New Deal programmes supported by a modestly liberal cross-party consensus.

The liberal tradition reached its apotheosis in the 1960s with John F. Kennedy's New Frontier and particularly Lyndon B. Johnson's Great Society, which took the programmatic liberalism of the New Deal to its uttermost limits. 'Enacting the post-World War II liberal agenda practically in toto', as John J. Broesamle notes,

Johnson 'left liberals groping for a new one.'[12] The greatest test came in campaigns to use the power of government to remove inequalities of access and opportunity on the basis of race and gender, which proved both problematic and politically divisive, and in the grandiose attempt to eradicate poverty, which aroused hopes and expectations that the rather limited suite of programmes that went to make up the War on Poverty could not possibly fulfil. The failure of Big Government to live up to the extravagant claims made for it during the 1960s did much to erode the credibility of the liberal project itself. It appeared, even in the eyes of sympathetic critics, to have reached a dangerous condition of hubris, in which it was believed that the state could solve any problems, redress any grievances, correct any inequalities, and in which government bureaucracies had become hopelessly overextended. To conservative critics, from Goldwater to Gingrich, the events of the 1960s and early 1970s demonstrated the bankruptcy of liberalism. Since the 1970s conservatives have been in the political ascendancy, while liberals appear apologetic, unsure of themselves, and reluctant to associate themselves with what in the 1988 campaign was gingerly alluded to as the 'L-word'.

There is therefore a strong sense that, in talking about liberalism in twentieth-century America, we are dealing with a political, intellectual and cultural phenomenon whose history is virtually closed. Just as liberalism arose as a way of thinking about the problems that American society faced at the turn of the century, it now seems to offer a less convincing guide to the problems of the new postindustrial society that is arising at the close of the millennium.

---

12. John J. Broesamle, *Reform and Reaction in Twentieth-Century American Politics* (Westport, Ct., 1990), p. 69.

CHAPTER TWO

State and Society in Late Nineteenth-Century America

The 'lengthening arms of government'

The modern American state did not spring, like Athene, fully formed into existence. It emerged from a nineteenth-century political tradition which was far more interventionist than is commonly supposed. An examination of the political world of the late nineteenth century – the so-called 'Gilded Age' – will serve not only to place the state-building projects of the twentieth century against their historical background but also to set out some of the features of the political institutions and political culture that Americans took with them into the twentieth century.

The late nineteenth century often features in textbooks as the golden age of *laissez-faire*, a period in which prevailing social theories, in particular classical economic theory and a conservative reading of Social Darwinism, affirmed what Herbert Spencer called 'the principle of letting all people take the benefits and evils of their own acts' and condemned government interference with the natural operation of social and economic laws.[1] By such standards most practical businessmen and most politicians were regrettably heterodox. *Laissez-faire* may have been the prevailing theory among economists, sociologists and the editors of journals of opinion, but American citizens showed little hesitation in calling upon government for assistance, and American legislators frequently obliged. 'Our statute book is filled with provisions which utterly disregard the let-alone theory of government', admitted Congressman Henry

---

1. Quoted in Sidney Fine, *Laissez-faire and the General Welfare State: A Study of Conflict in American Thought, 1865–1901* (Ann Arbor, Mich., 1956), p. 32.

12

Cabot Lodge, 'and every time we dredge a harbor or deepen a river or open a canal we set it at naught.'[2]

Numerous studies have revealed the extent of government support for business development during the nineteenth century, especially at a state level. This included the grant of liberal corporate charters and special privileges, such as the right to take private property for public use without the owner's consent (eminent domain), the right to charge tolls on public highways, and the provision of capital for businesses such as railroads which were said to be 'affected with the public interest'. The federal government, too, furnished generous assistance to the transcontinental railroads during the 1860s and 1870s, donating in excess of 100 million acres of public land and close to $100 million in cash subsidies and loans. To the jaundiced eye of Gideon Welles, Andrew Johnson's Secretary of the Navy, 'The granting of acts of incorporation, bounties, special privileges, favors, and profligate legislation of every description [was] shocking'.[3] Although the enormous cost of the railroad subsidies, and the flagrant corruption which attended them, brought such generosity into disrepute, Congress continued to appropriate large sums for the improvement of rivers and harbours, a project always dear to its members' hearts, and it became increasingly committed to a generous programme of government-financed agricultural research. The high protective tariffs imposed during the Civil War continued throughout the period, averaging 47 per cent in 1867, 49.5 per cent as a result of the McKinley tariff of 1890 and dipping only slightly below those levels in the intervening years.

Economic policy, according to Richard L. McCormick, was primarily 'distributive' in character: it involved the allocation of resources and privileges to certain favoured individuals, groups or localities – whether it be a grant of land, a tax exemption, a direct subsidy, a legal privilege such as eminent domain, or tariff protection for a specific commodity. Two assumptions were necessary to justify such liberality. The first was that distributive policies were capable of an almost infinite 'disaggregation', so that aid to one locality or group need not preclude similar benevolence to others. Potential conflicts of interest could be at least partially resolved by a process of 'log-rolling' in which legislative majorities were assembled by parcelling out aid to as many localities as was

2. Quoted in John A. Garraty, *Henry Cabot Lodge: A Biography* (New York, 1953), p. 138.
3. Quoted in Matthew Josephson, *The Politicos, 1865–1896* (New York, 1938), p. 52.

necessary to get the package through. River-and-harbour and tariff bills were commonly sewn together like a traditional patchwork quilt. Secondly, it was assumed that there existed among the various elements of society a 'harmony of interests' such that policies benefiting one group would redound to the advantage of all. Advocates of the protective tariff, for example, promised security for American manufacturers, protection for American workers against the 'pauper labour' of Europe, and a guaranteed 'home market' for American farmers. It was, proclaimed a Republican spokesman, 'a policy broad enough to embrace within the scope of its beneficent influence all our population'.[4]

It has to be admitted that such laws did not meet with universal approval. They were, in fact, ideas closely associated with the Republican Party. Republicans proclaimed the virtues of an energetic government which pledged its resources to protect and promote the development of industry and agriculture. In contrast, Democrats, in language inherited from Jefferson and Jackson, warned that government favouritism to private enterprise, with its 'unwholesome progeny of paternalism', would, by creating artificial distinctions in society, jeopardise the moral integrity of the Republic itself. These ancestral ideologies retained their meaning with reference to the distributive issues that for so long had provided the substance of economic policy. That is why the tariff did such yeoman service as a defining issue for both parties. As Morton Keller points out, it accorded well with 'the traditional Republican stress on the active state'.[5] By the 1880s tariff protection had become the central item in Republican appeals to the national electorate, while to the Democratic Party it offered a standard around which to rally its disparate and discordant elements. Nevertheless, much as party standard-bearers like Grover Cleveland might condemn protective duties as an indefensible extortion from the people on behalf of special interests, Democratic legislators found it difficult, on tariff bills, as on subsidy or internal improvement bills, to resist the special interests lodged within their own constituencies.

Government spending during the Gilded Age showed only a slight increase relative to the growth in population and none at all relative to the growth in incomes. In 1896 federal expenditure was,

---

4. Quoted in R. Hal Williams, *Years of Decision: American Politics in the 1890s* (New York, 1978), p. 11.

5. Morton Keller, *Affairs of State: Public Life in Late Nineteenth-Century America* (Cambridge, Mass., 1977), p. 379.

in real terms, 91 per cent higher than it had been twenty-five years earlier, during which period population increased by 71 per cent and GNP nearly doubled. The civilian employment of the federal government more than quadrupled, reaching 240,000 in 1901. Most of the additional officers were employed in extending postal services to a growing population spread over a larger area. Throughout the period the Post Office Department accounted for around 60 per cent of federal employees. Apart from that, the major items of expenditure related to past and future wars. The military establishment, the servicing of the national debt generated by the Civil War and the provision of military pensions consumed 74 per cent of the federal budget in 1871 and 71 per cent in 1896. The chief objects of expenditure were related to traditional functions of government and, in the case of post offices and pensions, were intimately linked to the system of patronage and favours which lay at the heart of nineteenth-century party politics.

There was nothing novel about the distribution of pensions to the veterans of America's wars. What was novel about Civil War pensions was their generous coverage and their extraordinary cost. By the end of the century the annual pension bill was over $140,000,000, engrossing nearly 30 per cent of the federal budget, while close to a million ex-soldiers and their dependents were in receipt of benefits. The original pension law of 1862 promised pensions to Union soldiers who had incurred permanent injury or disability as a direct consequence of military service and for the widows and other dependents of men who had died in action or from causes traceable to wounds or sickness contracted while in service. This law was somewhat liberalised by later legislation and still more by the generous attitude of the Pension Bureau and of congressmen, who spent much of their time energetically pursuing individual claims. A Republican Congress in 1890 removed the confining requirement that disabilities be demonstrably traceable to military service and granted pensions to all veterans incapacitated from the performance of manual labour, whatever the cause, and to all dependent widows, thereby greatly enlarging the number eligible. Although critics inveighed against the massive expense of the programme, Republicans promised, in the words of their 1888 platform, to 'provide against the possibility that any man who honorably wore the Federal uniform shall become the inmate of an almshouse, or dependent upon private charity'.[6] There was a strong public disposition to be liberal in the treatment of veterans, a

6. Donald B. Johnson, ed., *National Party Platforms* (Urbana, Ill., 1978), p. 82.

disposition fortified by the diligent efforts of numerous pension agents and the organised influence of veterans themselves, effectively marshalled in the Grand Army of the Republic. From the point of view of the Republican party leaders who were among its chief advocates in 1890, more liberal pension legislation formed part of a wide-ranging package of distributive measures the centre-piece of which was the McKinley tariff bill.

Pensions fitted easily into the distributive politics of the Gilded Age, but they also prefigured the twentieth-century welfare state. Pensions went to disabled veterans, including those suffering from old age, since, even before the practice was formalised in 1904, the Pension Bureau tended to regard old age as a source of disability in itself. They became in effect a disability and old age pension programme for the benefit of a particular class – Union veterans and their dependents – but a very large class, larger and more generously provided for than the beneficiaries of the early European pension schemes. It took the federal government into thousands of homes, offering pensions not as a charity but as a right, in a fashion quite without precedent and, until the 1930s, without successor. That what Theda Skocpol describes as 'an analogue to noncontributory old-age pensions' did not become the model for a more general social insurance system may be attributed to the more general reaction against distributive policies around the turn of the century. The 'precocious social spending state' that emerged fortuitously from the Civil War and the distributive politics of the nineteenth century had no immediate progeny.[7]

The development after the Civil War of a complex and integrated national economy gave rise to a variety of clashes of interest that were difficult to resolve within the traditional frame-work of nineteenth-century politics. They included the increasingly troubling confrontation between capital and labour, but also conflicts between competing business groups, for example between railroads and the shippers whose goods they carried, between dairymen and the manufacturers of margarine, or between the producers and refiners of petroleum. As the market system became 'far too remote and massive to be influenced by individuals', notes Samuel P. Hays, many such groups organised to advance their common interests.[8] They naturally turned to government to redress

---

7. Theda Skocpol, *Protecting Soldiers and Mothers: The Political Origins of Social Policy in the United States* (Cambridge, Mass., 1992), p. 132.

8. Samuel P. Hays, *American Political History as Social Analysis* (Knoxville, Tenn., 1980), p. 252.

their grievances, forcing it, in McCormick's words, 'to take explicit account of clashing interests and to assume the responsibility for adjusting them through regulation, administration, and planning'.[9]

Railroad policy offers a clear illustration of this process. By the 1870s the discriminatory pattern of rates had created conflicts of interest that made railroad regulation a major political issue. Intense competition between the recently established trunk-line systems forced down rates over competitive long hauls, sometimes to unremunerative levels, leaving the carriers to recoup their losses on shorter routes where they did not have to compete. Shippers complained of rates unduly favouring their competitors. 'It is in effect letting one man steal another man's business', as one protested.[10] Merchants in the Iowa river towns complained of low through rates on grain shipments to Chicago, while the independent oil producers of Western Pennsylvania criticised the rebates enjoyed by Standard Oil, and New York City merchants resented the preferential rates granted by the trunk lines to their competitors in Baltimore and Philadelphia. The Hopkins and Reagan bills of 1876 and 1878, direct ancestors of the federal Interstate Commerce Act, were introduced on behalf of the Petroleum Producers' Union, while the New York merchants, if not necessarily, as Lee Benson claims, 'the single most important group behind the passage of the Interstate Commerce Act', were among its most influential and persistent advocates.[11] The demand for regulation was not merely a product of the aggregation of business pressures but reflected also a public opinion aroused by widespread suspicion of corporate power, which at that date was most potently exemplified by the railroads. Most congressmen by 1885 had come to sense a 'general desire' that Congress should exert its authority in this field.

Already by 1887 twenty-six states had passed laws regulating the railroads, but their scope was greatly limited by the interstate character of most railroad business. Even before the Supreme Court decision in *Wabash, St Louis and Pacific Railway Company* v. *Illinois* (1886) withdrew interstate traffic from state control, these limitations were becoming clear. 'This species of regulation', pronounced Justice Samuel Miller, 'is one which must be, if established

9. Richard L. McCormick, *From Realignment to Reform: Political Change in New York State, 1893–1910* (Ithaca, N.Y., 1981), p. 255.

10. Edward A. Purcell Jr., 'Ideas and interests: businessmen and the Interstate Commerce Act' *Journal of American History* 54 (1967), p. 567.

11. Lee Benson, *Merchants, Farmers and Railroads: Railroad Regulation and New York Politics, 1850–1887* (Cambridge, Mass., 1957), p. 212.

at all, of a general and national character, and cannot be safely and wisely remitted to local rules and local regulations.'[12] The *Wabash* decision brought the long rumbling movement for federal regulation to a head and gave a renewed urgency to demands for congressional action.

The need to accommodate so many different interests and points of view resulted in legislation which contained serious ambiguities and inconsistencies. The Interstate Commerce Act of 1887 required that rates be 'just and reasonable' but did not stipulate precisely how 'just and reasonable' rates were to be determined. The act prohibited various forms of discrimination in rates but also prohibited the sort of pooling agreements between railroads that might have mitigated it. As Charles Francis Adams Jr., railroad president and former Massachusetts Railroad Commissioner, explained, 'uncertainty and fluctuation in rates and discrimination between shippers' were caused by 'the struggle to secure business when competition is unchecked'.[13] Indeed, the prohibition of pooling in the law reinforced those very competitive forces. The railroad historian Albro Martin attributes the ultimate failure of this first stab at federal regulation to Congress's insistence on imposing an unrealisable competitive ideal on an industry which was essentially a natural monopoly. However, that is to ascribe too definite a purpose to the law's authors, who wished merely, in this preliminary stab at railroad regulation, to eradicate the most blatant abuses, such as granting rebates to favoured shippers and charging more for a short haul than for a long haul over the same route, rather than to establish a detailed and comprehensive system of federal supervision.

The Interstate Commerce Commission (ICC) created to enforce the act exerted, in its early years, a fairly broad discretion, permitting certain forms of collusive rate agreement and assuming the right to set rates in place of those which it found, on complaint, to be unreasonable. For a while at least, the new law had a discernible effect in reducing personal and place discrimination. However, the authority and influence of the ICC were drastically curtailed by a series of adverse court decisions, particularly that of the Supreme Court in the Maximum Rate Cases of 1897, which denied that the Commission had been empowered to set rates.

---

12. Quoted in Loren P. Beth, *The Development of the American Constitution, 1877–1917* (New York, 1971), p. 146.
13. Quoted in James E. Anderson, *The Emergence of the Modern Regulatory State* (Washington, D.C., 1962), p. 101.

Equally damaging was the Court's insistence on a full judicial review of ICC rulings, meaning that hearings before the Commission became a mere formality. The prospect of the Commission's acting as a quasi-judicial agency in transportation matters was firmly quashed. By 1900 its impotence was frankly admitted. Its troubles stemmed largely from the reluctance shown in the language of the Interstate Commerce Act to vest wide discretionary powers in the hands of an administrative commission, still a novel governmental device. Adams had noted in 1887 that the movement to regulate the railroads threw into question 'the very principles upon which the government was established', especially the reliance on judicial surveillance over economic affairs.[14] The failure of Congress to create the instrumentalities that were needed to carry out this task and a jealous defence of their prerogatives by the courts left the old governing arrangements substantially intact and the issue of how best to meet the challenge of the new industrial economy substantially unresolved.

Several other aspects of interstate business became subject to federal regulation during this period. To protect the interests of dairy farmers, Congress in 1886 imposed a tax on the manufacture of margarine. A series of laws regulated interstate shipment of livestock, and in 1890, to protect overseas markets, a system of federal inspection was introduced covering meat bound for export. Congress also enacted national trade-mark and bankruptcy laws and, in a spate of moral enthusiasm, barred lottery tickets from interstate commerce. In response to a sudden burst of industrial combinations, Congress in 1890 passed the Sherman Antitrust Act, which made illegal 'every contract, combination . . . or conspiracy in restraint of trade or commerce among the several States or with foreign nations'. This was a general declaratory law which did little more, than write the 'old and well-recognized principles of the common law' into the federal statute-books so as to make them enforceable in the federal courts.[15] The Sherman Act seemed much less significant to contemporaries than it did in retrospect; little public attention was paid to its passage. It was left to later decades to struggle with the legal ambiguities embedded in the language of the

14. Quoted in Stephen Skowronek, *Building a New American State: The Evolution of National Administrative Capacities, 1877–1920* (Cambridge, 1982), p. 121.

15. Henry S. Commager, ed., *Documents in American History* (2 vols, New York, 1949), II, p. 136; Senator John Sherman quoted in William Letwin, *Law and Economic Policy in America: The Evolution of the Sherman Antitrust Act* (New York, 1966), p. 96.

act and the extreme practical difficulties involved in its enforcement.

Judges showed little reluctance to assume jurisdiction over complex questions of economic policy, such as industrial relations or the structure of railroad rates. 'The great body of judges are as well versed in the affairs of life as any', claimed Justice Brewer, and as well equipped to unravel the 'scholastic verbiage . . . of expert witnesses.'[16] A feature of the developing pattern of regulation, in its early stages, was a dependence on judicial procedures to adjust conflicts of interest. The uncertainty and hesitancy of legislators, and in some cases their failure to legislate at all, left large areas of discretion to the courts, which, in the absence of a developed tradition of public administration, filled the resulting 'void of governance'.

Both state and federal governments passed a great volume of regulatory legislation during this period. Indeed, as William Brock has comprehensively demonstrated, many of the most extensive and innovative exercises of authority came from the states. But in certain crucial areas federal power was expanding at the expense of the states. The Supreme Court increasingly tightened the reins governing state legislation which impinged upon interstate commerce. Interstate commerce, declared Justice Stephen J. Field in *Welton* v. *Missouri*, 'is of national importance, and admits and requires uniformity of regulation'.[17] The attitude of the federal courts, along with the practical difficulty of state regulation of national businesses, contributed to a steady augmentation of federal power at the expense of the states.

'New causes are at work in the world', observed James Bryce in 1895, 'tending not only to lengthen the arms of government, but to make its touch quicker and firmer.'[18] Both Congress and the state legislatures passed a variety of measures regulating private business activity, many of minor significance, many ineffectual, but constituting in aggregate what Keller describes as 'a gradually thickening system of government supervision' – one which carried important precedents, and important lessons for the future.[19] The further elaboration of the 'system of government supervision' was, however, inhibited by the absence of a strong tradition of public

16. Quoted in Anderson, *Emergence of the Modern Regulatory State*, p. 150.
17. Quoted in James Willard Hurst, *Law and the Condition of Freedom in the Nineteenth-Century United States* (Madison, Wis., 1956), p. 46.
18. James Bryce, *The American Commonwealth* (2 vols, New York, 1895), II, p. 539.
19. Keller, *Affairs of State*, p. 409.

administration, which left responsibility for regulation largely in the hands of the courts, and the existence of political institutions which were geared primarily to the expression of local interests and the articulation of more traditional forms of economic policy.

A 'stateless society'?

The demands placed upon government in the late nineteenth century, transformed in both scale and character, were not easily accommodated within the 'established modes of governance'. What Stephen Skowronek calls 'the state of courts and parties' lacked the administrative capacity to handle the problems posed by the clash of interests in an industrial society.[20]

Starting at the top, the presidents of the era subscribed to a limited view of their office. Like Grant, they regarded the president as a 'purely administrative officer', responsible for little more than the smooth running of the departments of state. Lacking other than a rudimentary staff, presidents were, according to the administrative historian Leonard D. White, 'immersed in the particulars of Administration'.[21] Patronage matters, in particular, took up much of their time. A succession of chief executives from Hayes to McKinley doggedly defended the prerogatives of their office against congressional interference, but this did not entail any claims to broader national leadership.

The relatively small number of federal civil employees consisted predominantly of post office officials and revenue collectors, with only around 10 per cent located in the capital. Before 1883 there was no professional civil service. Government offices were distributed on the basis of political services to faithful party members every time a different party, or even a different faction of the same party, won the presidency. The 'spoils system' was by no means conducive to an efficient or conscientious, or sometimes even an honest, management of public affairs. It was still less conducive to forethought or planning, to any considered reflection on the nation's problems. In 1883 Congress set in motion a process of civil service reform. The Pendleton Act of that year created a professional civil service to which admission would be by competitive examination and promotion on merit. The new system

---

20. Keller, *Affairs of State*, p. 289; Skowronek, *Building a New American State*, p. 24.
21. Leonard D. White, *The Republican Era, 1869–1901: A Study in Administrative History* (New York, 1958), pp. 23, 93.

applied at once to clerks in the Washington departments and in the larger post offices and custom houses, and it could be extended by presidential order. However, both the creation and extension of the system were inspired more by partisan advantage than an interest in efficient administration, as politicians sought both to propitiate the reform vote and to save their own appointees from being turned out of office when their opponents came to power. The politicians ensured that reform did not entrench too deeply on their established ways of doing things. Although the number covered by civil service rules increased from 13,924 (out of 131,208 civilian employees) in 1883 to 94,839 (out of 208,000) in 1900, the overall expansion of federal employment left the number of patronage appointments largely unchanged. The absence of a sensible personnel system and the fact that merit rules applied only very loosely to promotion made the civil service unattractive as a career for able and ambitious persons. Thus, while it almost certainly did make for more efficient administration of the larger post offices and custom houses, civil service reform reduced only slightly the patronage resources available to party leaders, and it did not lead to the creation of a permanent administrative class responsible for the long-term development and application of policy.

Nineteenth-century politics was pervaded by the spirit of localism. Political activity involved communities and grew out of their interests and preoccupations. This was reflected in the behaviour of Congress, and equally of state legislatures. 'The members of the Senate and the House', observed Senator Thomas Bayard in 1881, 'are the advocates and representatives of different local interests all of which naturally seek to influence the transactions of the government on their own behalf.'[22] Their constituents' views were most clearly expressed with reference to local interests in the narrowest sense, and it was to these that many congressmen devoted their time and attention. Federal expenditure on the improvement of rivers and harbours, the construction of federal buildings, the enhancement of postal services and similar raids upon the Treasury composed a large part of what constituents expected from their congressmen, and congressmen from the government. Congressmen were expected also to attend to their constituents' more personal demands for patronage, pensions and other claims against the government. The later President James A. Garfield commented that two-thirds of his time as a congressman

22. Quoted in David J. Rothman, *Politics and Power: The United States Senate, 1869–1901* (Cambridge, Mass., 1966), p. 81.

was spent going round the departments as a claim agent or looking for jobs for his constituents. Since few could expect to spend more that one or two terms in Washington – the average service was 2.05 terms – or think in terms of a career in national politics, their standing at home mattered much more to them than their standing on Capitol Hill. Indeed, given such limited expectations regarding the office of a congressman, it was hard to resist demands that the office be subject to rotation, as was indeed the practice in much of the rural North.

The profusion of essentially administrative business that came before Congress, including such matters as private pension claims, patents, the location of mail routes and the detailed supervision of public spending, tended to crowd out the consideration of questions of general policy. That Congress devoted so much time to such matters, however, was not so much a distortion as a true expression of its function in the political world of the nineteenth century. Much of its business was highly distributive in character, consisting not so much of general policies as an accumulation of 'highly individualized decisions' catering to the needs of specific groups which, in the disarticulated society of the nineteenth century, were also highly localised.[23]

Allan Nevins describes the House of Representatives in 1875 as 'a Laocoön struggling against the serpentine constrictions of bad rules, organized obstruction, and lack of responsible leadership'. The rules offered immense scope for dilatory tactics. They were, said William P. Frye of Maine in 1880, 'a body of rules calculated better than anything else to disturb the legislator and to obstruct legislation'.[24] Party leaders lacked the authority to plan strategy or determine the order of business. What organisation there was was provided by the committee system, but this made for a dispersion of power and responsibility. There was, observed Congressman George F. Hoar, nowhere a 'responsibility for securing due attention to important measures, and no authority to decide between their different claims'.[25] Hence any form of permanent and comprehensive policy was virtually unattainable. The same lack of party organisation hampered the legislative efficiency of the Senate,

23. Theodore J. Lowi, 'Public policy, case studies, and political theory' *World Politics* 16 (1964), p. 690.

24. Quoted in Allan Nevins, *Abram S. Hewitt: With Some Account of Peter Cooper* (New York, 1935), p. 401; William A. Robinson, *Thomas B. Reed: Parliamentarian* (New York, 1930), p. 65.

25. Quoted in Margaret Susan Thompson, *The 'Spider Web': Congress and Lobbying in the Age of Grant* (Ithaca, N.Y., 1985).

where neither party caucus nor guillotine impaired the individual senator's freedom of action.

It is true that congressional procedures were tightened up considerably during the last two decades of the century. The archaic and anarchic rules of the House of Representatives were substantially revised in 1890, reducing particularly the scope for obstructive tactics by the minority. These changes created at least some of the conditions for responsible party government. David Rothman has traced a similar tightening of party discipline in the Senate around 1890. The aim in both cases was to enable small Republican majorities to enact an ambitious legislative programme. But that programme was decidedly traditional in its composition, including tariff legislation, generous appropriations for rivers and harbours and a dramatic liberalisation of pension laws, as well as a proposal to prevent the intimidation of Southern Republicans at the polls. The achievements of what became known for its extravagance as the 'Billion Dollar Congress' (1889–91) may, in fact, be seen as an apotheosis of the distributive politics of the Gilded Age.

In short, nobody was responsible for taking a national view, for the development of policy over the long term – neither presidents, nor top civil servants, nor congressional leaders. Indeed, as we have seen, much policy-making was left to the federal judiciary, which filled the resulting vacuum of authority. By the very nature of the judicial process, policy was laid down in a reactive and piecemeal fashion which was by no means conducive to considered policy-making. Such a response, however, was all too typical of the late nineteenth-century American polity.

Popular politics

The Gilded Age came at the end of what McCormick calls the 'party period' in American politics, a period in which political parties offered the major forum for mass public involvement in political life.[26] Parties were largely instrumental in generating the massive electoral turnouts of the period. During the period 1876–92, the average turnout at presidential elections (which may admittedly have been inflated a little by instances of electoral fraud) was 79.6 per cent, while in many Northern states, such as New York, the

26. Richard L. McCormick, 'The party period and public policy: an exploratory hypothesis' *Journal of American History* 66 (1979), pp. 279–98.

figure was nearly ten points higher. But that is only one measure of the extent of popular involvement in politics. Election campaigns drew large numbers of people away from their daily pursuits, not only to vote on election day, but to attend rallies, parades and other spectacular events. For example, in 1876 we read of a torchlight procession 1½ miles long that wound its way through the streets of the modest-sized town of Erie, Pennsylvania, while a whole buffalo was barbecued for the benefit of the faithful at a rally in Reading. Assemblies of 50,000 or more were common in larger cities. Each campaign featured a series of spectacular meetings, parades and rallies, with lavishly decorated floats, brass bands, glee clubs, marching companies, often lavishly attired in quasi-military uniform, flags, banners, and cheering crowds.

At the simplest level, electioneering offered itself as pure entertainment. Politics might be compared to a spectator sport, with its excitement, its unpredictability and its ability to sweep men, women and children out of the routines of their everyday existence. Yet contemporaries would perhaps have found such an analogy uncomprehending and unflattering. The thousands who attended election rallies were not attracted solely by the noise, the colour and the excitement. They paid serious attention to speeches that went far beyond the bounds of what a late twentieth-century audience would consider either reasonable or bearable. This was a society which relied predominantly on verbal communication and which relished public speaking both as a medium of expression and as an art form. The rallies and the parades, moreover, had a serious significance in themselves. They grew out of a continuing tradition of popular involvement in politics that went back to the Revolution. They were a kind of 'vital democratic theater' which expressed the involvement of all citizens in the process of government, made visible the convention that American government depended on the consent of the governed, and reminded citizens that voting was therefore a public duty.[27]

At the same time, the street theatre of campaigning underlined the fact that political activity for nineteenth-century Americans grew out of their membership of communities. Voting was not regarded as a private act to be carried out in the secrecy of a polling booth, which is why for a long time Americans resisted the introduction of a secret ballot. Often voters would march up to the polls in groups – of workers from a factory, residents of a nearby village or members

27. Michael McGerr, *The Decline of Popular Politics: The American North, 1865–1928* (New York, 1986), p. 6.

of a political club – proudly bearing the favours of their chosen candidate and flourishing the distinctively coloured ballot-papers of their chosen party, register their votes to the cheers of fellow supporters, then, having voted, remain on the scene to greet later delegations, as appropriate, with shouts of derision or acclaim, before finally adjourning, where it was legal and sometimes where it was not, to a neighbouring saloon. The whole exercise was conducted in public. It gave men an opportunity to register their allegiances, to display their loyalties, before the community to which they belonged.

The hoopla of campaigning invested voting with additional meanings. It drew people into political action, made it easier, more natural, for individuals to bear the opportunity costs that such activity entailed. Not only men of voting age were sucked into the excitement. Women participated in campaigns in a variety of ways, whether representing Liberty, marching in companies, sewing flags and uniforms or merely lining the streets at election parades. Young people, too, participated, whether formally or informally. The exhilaration and the drama of campaign meetings, by making politics more exciting to boys and youths, made it more likely, more natural, that they themselves would become politically active as adults. Thus the mass parades and rallies were not merely an expression of the political enthusiasm of late nineteenth-century Americans; they in themselves contributed to its perpetuation by initiating new generations into the vibrant political culture of the age.

Political participation for most nineteenth-century Americans was expressed through membership of one of the two major political parties. Partisanship was deeply embedded in American culture. It served as the lens through which people viewed the world of public affairs. Most of the newspapers that they read, dependent as their publishers were on patronage in the form of official advertising and public printing contracts, were attached to one party or the other, and thus they offered a highly coloured reading of political events. The party press made the political world look simpler, less nuanced, and presented issues in a sharper, less ambivalent way, making participation, for the average citizen, all the easier. A highly partisan political universe was one in which most citizens found it easy to find a place. In a society characterised by extraordinary rates of population turnover, political parties made it possible for newcomers to locate themselves politically in a new community, thereby maintaining high rates of turnout at a time of continual demographic flux. Moreover, the party organisations actively encouraged voting: they helped new voters to register, in the case of immigrants providing advice on naturalisation procedures and even paying the fees; they enlisted men and boys in political clubs; they organised parades and rallies which sustained public interest throughout the campaign; and on election day they provided transport and inducements, sometimes liquid, sometimes even monetary, to get voters to the polls. An immense amount of labour was devoted to the task of simply 'getting out the vote'.

Party loyalty was, for most Americans, intensely felt. Unflinching loyalty was a matter of principle, to desert one's party an act of dishonour, in effect a form of apostasy. The woman who asked if it was possible for anybody to be both a Christian and a Democrat expressed by implication an almost universal sentiment. In the absence of polling evidence we cannot, of course, be sure, but all the evidence suggests that the great majority of voters were firmly attached to one party or the other. Voting returns down to a precinct level display great stability in the distribution of the vote between the parties over a long period, providing a basis for estimates that about 90 per cent normally voted for the same party in successive elections.

Precisely what the sources of party loyalty were has been the subject of heated debate over the last twenty or thirty years. It is clear that, outside the South, a majority of the business community and the professional classes were Republican, while the Democratic Party in urban areas, with its largely immigrant vote, was coming to take on something of a blue-collar complexion. A generation of 'new political historians' has emphasised ethnic and religious affiliations, rather than social and economic circumstances, as the prime determinants of party identification, and a number of local studies, like those by Richard Jensen and Paul Kleppner, have found high correlations between ethnicity and party allegiance. In fact, ethnocultural differences can only explain so much. Most voters, after all, were native Protestants. In a state like Indiana, which harboured few immigrants or Catholics, only a fraction of party allegiance can be attributed to ethnic or religious identifications. Here less tangible factors, like historic settlement patterns and local rivalries, may have influenced voting, but even the most detailed studies have failed to uncover unambiguous general relationships.

The structure of politics in the nineteenth century was highly decentralised. Its roots were firmly embedded in the soil of local

communities. In this structure political parties played a crucial role.
They provided linkages between individuals and their government,
between the periphery and the centre, between localities and the
political life of the nation. They established working relationships
between individuals at different levels of government and in
different parts of the country, thereby linking the disparate
elements of the political system. Political parties therefore brought
a measure of cohesion to public life. In that way, Theodore J. Lowi
has argued, they played a 'constituent' role in American politics.
While they have been much less responsible for the formulation of
policy and have not often offered the electorate clear programmatic
alternatives, American parties have operated in important ways, by
offsetting the formal separation of powers, to make the political
system workable. Thus those Mugwump reformers who, like their
later twentieth-century equivalents, condemned the major parties
for their lack of ideological or programmatic clarity, largely
misinterpreted their function in American political life.

While politics absorbed a surprising amount of attention from
most citizens of the nineteenth-century Republic, for a substantial
number it formed their life's work. These were the professional
politicians, the men who devoted themselves to operating the
complex machinery of American democracy. The system was, in
fact, highly labour-intensive. The work of campaigning absorbed a
great deal of effort: organising speakers, marshalling supporters for
political rallies, printing and distributing campaign literature, canvassing voters and finally, on election day, manning the polls and
transporting voters to the ballot-box. But the process of nominating
candidates was hardly less laborious. In order, in theory at least, to
provide rank-and-file voters with an opportunity to influence the
party's choice of candidates, local caucuses or primary elections
were held to choose delegates to county or city conventions, which
in turn nominated candidates or delegates to further state and
national conventions. These meetings were organised by an
elaborate hierarchy of committees, from national down to precinct
level. The result, according to Matthew Josephson, was 'a colossal
elective pyramid, a vast mechanical structure of primaries,
conventions, committees, whose workings, wheel within wheel,
whose numerous details, committee business, advance arrangements, were far too complex to remain subject to the casual will or
decisions of the masses of busy workaday citizens'.[28] This structure,

---

28. Josephson, *Politicos*, p. 69.

notionally designed to make the parties responsive to the will of the people, in practice proved relatively invulnerable to public control.

Ordinary citizens had neither the time nor the inclination to attend the preliminary caucuses, still less to run as delegates to party conventions or serve on party committees. Those who did perform these tasks were, of course, the professional politicians, the recipients of government patronage, the 'postmasters, revenue officers, custom tide waiters and peripatetic government agents' who, for example, regularly packed Republican conventions in Pennsylvania.[29] And such men were naturally beholden to the state and city bosses who controlled the patronage on which they depended for their daily sustenance. The conjunction of so labour-intensive a pattern of party organisation with the 'spoils system' established in the Jacksonian Era and still, as we have seen, substantially intact at the close of the century, tended to produce hierarchically structured party 'machines' which had a commanding influence over nominations and sometimes, especially in the cities, over government.

Yet we must not, as some contemporaries did, overstate their cohesion or their power. To some extent the 'machine' is a construct located in a rhetoric of opposition. Intraparty rivals, political adversaries and 'good government' reformers naturally resorted to overstatement in an effort to discredit powerful political leaders. Even apparently well-organised city machines such as Tammany Hall were riven by internecine squabbles and beset by local rivalries. Successful state bosses like Matthew S. Quay of Pennsylvania and Thomas C. Platt of New York retained their positions by a careful strategy of negotiation and compromise and by being careful not to overstep the limits of their power. Above all, their power was localised. As Robert Marcus has shown, Republican state bosses found it virtually impossible to translate their local power into national influence. Although party leaders came together every four years to nominate a president and then to elect him, they were signally unable to forge any durable national organisation. The 'constituent' political parties, therefore, were incapable of providing the national leadership that was lacking in the formal structure of government.

There was a fair degree of correspondence between American political institutions as they operated in the late nineteenth century

29. Philadelphia *Times*, 5 Sept. 1877, quoted in Robert Harrison, 'Blaine and the Camerons: a study in the limits of machine power' *Pennsylvania History* (July 1982), p. 61.

and American society. Both were dominated by the spirit of localism. Both were highly decentralised. Allan Nevins described American society before the Civil War as 'invertebrate'; the same might be said of the American polity. What skeleton it possessed was provided by the federal judiciary, which was entrusted with wide discretion in many crucial areas of policy-making, and political parties, which linked the various components of the system together. It was significant that the United States lacked, until the 1880s, a professional civil service but did support a very large number of professional politicians. They were dedicated primarily to the pursuit of office and had no broader responsibility for government; they were in no sense a governing class. The skeleton that held the 'state of courts and parties' together was a very fragile one indeed.

Gilded Age reform: Mugwumps and Populists

The Gilded Age generated a multitude of reform movements varying widely in their provenance and purpose, from the devoted armies of men and women who toiled for the cause of temperance to isolated bands of committed anarchists and Marxian socialists. However, two sets of reformers require special attention. The small elite groups who variously called themselves Liberals, Independents and Mugwumps could not differ more markedly in their background and beliefs from the numerous but ephemeral farmers' movements that ranged across the Great Plains and the South, of which the most spectacular and significant was the Populist Party of the 1890s. Yet, although they approached the task of reform from very different perspectives and from different ideological positions, each contributed important ingredients to the complex and fluctuating *mélange* of twentieth-century liberalism.

The self-styled Liberals (so-called by analogy with the Liberal followers of Gladstone) were a faction of disaffected Republicans. Having loyally supported it during the crusade against slavery and secession, they came to feel that the Republican Party had lost its way. Instead of a party moved by high ideals, it had become a political organisation whose sole purpose was the attainment and exploitation of office. Corrupt 'spoilsmen' like Ben Butler and James G. Blaine held power at the expense of men of intelligence and integrity. The result was a woeful decline in the standards of public life, marked by a series of disgraceful political scandals. Many

Independents supported the Liberal Republican candidacy of Horace Greeley in 1872, and more would have done so had they been able to stomach the candidate; they toyed with insurgency in 1876 and 1880; and in 1884 a number of so-called Mugwumps bolted from the party to support the Democratic candidate Grover Cleveland, a man of unimpeachable probity and modest reform leanings, rather than the prototypical 'spoilsman' Blaine, the 'Tattooed Man' of Thomas Nast's cartoon. Thereafter, about half the Mugwumps retained an uneasy association with Cleveland's party, while most of the others remained suspended between the two major parties, at least until the free silver campaign of 1896 described in the following section.

A 'Mugwump', in popular parlance, was a man who sat with his Mug on one side of the fence and his Wump on the other. In a political world where intense partisanship was taken for granted, the Mugwumps refused to allow party loyalty to guide them in their choice of men and measures. Spurning party discipline, they jealously guarded their political independence. It was because the mass of voters blindly followed the call of party, they believed, rather than exercising the cool deliberate reflection that was required of a republican citizenry, that unscrupulous and self-seeking politicians were able to clamber into office. It was because the public had allowed the public service to be prostituted to the spirit of party, in the form of the noxious 'spoils system', that powerful political machines had been constructed which denied the voters a voice in the selection of candidates or the articulation of policy.

The solution offered by the Liberal reformers – and, indeed, what they understood by the term 'reform' – was civil service reform, a cause which appeared 'no whit inferior in dignity or worth' to the abolition movement that had absorbed the energy and enthusiasm of the preceding generation. Reform was obviously necessary to create an honest and efficient public service – 'a Government', as Carl Schurz put it, 'which the best people of this country could be proud of'.[30] But it would also undermine the party machines, which depended for their sustenance on government patronage and which, deprived of their life-blood, would wither away, allowing the restoration of 'responsible' party organisations. Therefore, argued Charles Bonaparte, civil service reform was 'the prerequisite to all other reforms, whether legislative

30. Quoted in John G. Sproat, *The 'Best Men': Liberal Reformers in the Gilded Age* (New York, 1968), pp. 257, 81.

or administrative'.[31] Furthermore, by restoring the standards of statesmanship that had prevailed in the Republic before the 'spoils system' worked its corrosive effect on the fabric of public life, reform would permit the 'best men', currently pushed aside by 'spoilsmen' and 'ward heelers', to play their rightful part in government. Evidently, a merit system would open government service to young men of education and talent. In a politics devoted to principle and animated by high standards of public service, the 'natural leaders' of society would be able to compete successfully against 'inferior men' whose sole talent was the appropriation of patronage and the manipulation of party machinery.

These self-styled 'best men' were drawn, with few exceptions, from backgrounds of wealth and privilege. Their strength, such as it was, was concentrated mainly in the metropolitan centres of the East and Midwest. Born to an at least modestly wealthy and well-established family, educated in a college or university at a time when only about 2 per cent of Americans entered higher education, engaged in a professional or mercantile career offering a comfortable subsistence, and eminently clubbable, the typical Mugwump enjoyed unusual advantages. He was typically an Anglophile, with wide-ranging intellectual and cultural interests, who regarded himself as part of a transatlantic community of knowledge and ideas.

The Mugwumps, it has to be said, were self-consciously elitist. They believed that the 'best men' should govern, men of intelligence and breeding like themselves. Their elitism and their wilfully skittish political behaviour brought down upon them the wrath of professional politicians, who characterised them as dudes and dilettantes, the 'man-milliners' and 'carpet-knights' of politics, 'political hermaphrodites' incapable of participating effectively in the rough-and-tumble politics of the age.[32] 'The civil service reformer's political impotence accurately reflected his loss of social and economic power. He was out of step with the rest of society', observes Ari A. Hoogenboom.[33] Historians like Hoogenboom see the reformers as politically isolated, their ambitions thwarted by their incapacity to come to terms with the political currents of the age. The unfavourable opinion of historians, mostly sympathetic to

31. Quoted in Skowronek, *Building a New American State*, p. 54
32. Keller, *Affairs of State*, p. 248; Geoffrey Blodgett, 'The Mugwump reputation, 1870 to the present' *Journal of American History* 66 (March 1980), p. 883.
33. Ari A. Hoogenboom, 'Civil service reform and public morality', in H. Wayne Morgan, *The Gilded Age* (revised edn, Syracuse, N.Y., 1970), p. 86.

the twentieth-century liberal tradition, was confirmed by evidence that most Mugwumps were highly conservative in their social and economic views. Convinced of the eternal validity of classical economic theory, devoted to the gold standard, highly censorious towards protective tariffs, business regulation, eight-hours laws or any other interference with the inexorable laws of trade', hostile towards trade unions and agrarian organisations, unsympathetic to social reform, they appeared to cling to the principles of nineteenth-century liberalism in defiance of the evidence around them. That is why the literary historian Vernon Parrington, himself raised in the heartland of agrarian protest, described them as 'ethically bankrupt'.[34]

This representation is, however, incomplete. In the first place, while it is true that the Liberals were typically drawn from the ranks of established families identified with an older social and political regime, they were also heavily involved in the formation of a new one. They participated in the establishment of a newly invigorated university system; they played a part in the institutional development of professions like law and medicine; and they belonged to cosmopolitan networks of academic and professional specialists, with a vision that far transcended the local horizons of most politicians. Used to working in an environment in which decisions were made on a rational and impersonal basis, they identified themselves with 'new values of professionalism, self-discipline and science'.[35]

Secondly, while the civil service reformers no doubt had personal axes to grind in their campaign against the 'spoils system', they saw more clearly than anybody else the incapacity of American governing arrangements when confronted with the new problems of a complex, interdependent industrial society. They championed, in Skowronek's words, 'a fundamental reconstruction of the mode of governmental operations'. They sought to overcome the impasse between the demands of governance in an industrial age and existing governing arrangements. 'The goal of the dominant element in the civil service reform movement was, then, nothing less than a reconstitution of the American state in its organizational, procedural and intellectual dimensions.'[36] Negative though their views of the functions of government often were (although many

34. Vernon Parrington, *The Beginnings of Critical Realism in America, 1860–1920* (New York, 1930), p. 179.
35. Skowronek, *Building a New American State*, p. 53.
36. Ibid., pp. 42, 55.

younger Mugwumps did advocate a more positive use of government power), they grasped the structural problem that confronted the American state at this critical juncture. 'Snivel-service reform', as its enemies called it, was not an ephemeral project; it was a necessary prerequisite for any significant adjustment in the size and functions of the state. Furthermore, in their efforts to bypass existing political channels, they created a new 'political style' which was to be immensely influential in the decades to come. Instead of working through the medium of party, they explored the possibilities of independent voting, using their willingness to 'scratch' the party ticket at a time when such behaviour was relatively rare, to force both parties to take their views into account in the selection of candidates and policies; they explored the possibilities of education, correspondence, press campaigns, and other pressure-group tactics. Despite their small numbers, they were much more successful in achieving their goals than their image of elegant futility would suggest. Not only was substantial progress made in the fields of civil service and electoral reform, but their 'political style' of independent voting and pressure politics greatly influenced the behaviour of both voters and party leaders in the following century.

Like the Mugwumps, the Populists have received disproportionate attention from successive generations of historians, who have long debated their place in American political history. The first historian of Populism, John D. Hicks, writing in 1931, interpreted it as a precursor of the reform movements of the twentieth century, which shared the fundamental objective of social and economic justice and, in time, adopted many Populist policies. To Richard Hofstadter, writing in 1955, Populism was a basically irrational movement of confused and ignorant ('credulous') farmers who shared a paranoid view of the world, attributed their economic problems to conspiracies by remote enemies, and were prone to outbursts of xenophobia and anti-Semitism. In the 1960s Populism received more sympathetic treatment from historians loosely affiliated to the New Left like Norman Pollack, who, discounting the elements of irrational prejudice, described it as a radical movement which offered 'an extraordinarily penetrating critique of industrial society', a valid American alternative to Marxism.[37] In a rather different vein, Lawrence Goodwyn depicted Populism as the culmination of a series of attempts to free the farmer from the toils of the financial system that increasingly

37. Norman Pollack, *The Populist Response to Industrial America* (Cambridge, Mass., 1962), p. 9.

entrapped him, through the formation of cooperatives and, when that failed, by calling on the action of government, through reform of the monetary system. Populism, he believed, was essentially a movement of ordinary Americans to regain control over their lives in the face of an increasingly impersonal industrial society. While critics have questioned both the centrality of the cooperative movement in Populist thinking and its viability as the basis for an alternative ordering of society, most recent interpretations agree with Goodwyn in placing Populism squarely in the republican tradition.

Clearly, how historians interpret a movement like Populism depends on their own political perspective – on where they are looking from. It also depends on what they are looking at, since the movement contained a number of very diverse elements. But what makes Populism especially difficult to characterise is its transitional status in the history of American reform. It can, on one hand, be located at the end of a Jacksonian anti-monopoly tradition which distinguished producers from non-producers, the 'people' from the 'interests', and sought to keep alive a republican vision of a society of small independent producers. On the other hand, we can identify Populism, in Hofstadter's words, as 'the first modern political movement of practical importance in the United States to insist that the federal government had some responsibility for the common weal'.[38] In the words of the Populist governor of Kansas, 'It is the business of the government to protect the weak, because the strong are able to help themselves'.[39] Despite the Jacksonian rhetoric that Populist orators indulged in, theirs was in many ways a very modern reform movement.

The background to agrarian protest was a protracted, though erratic, secular decline in the prices of staple crops between the 1870s and the 1890s. Wheat, which averaged around a dollar a bushel on the Chicago exchange between 1878 and 1881, by the mid-1890s was selling for around 60 cents. Likewise, cotton fell from 9.5 cents to 5.8 cents a pound. Still more violent fluctuations might occur in the short run, with prices sometimes falling to such an extent that crops were hardly worth taking to market. Deflation hit farmers by increasing the real value of their indebtedness. Farmers, by the nature of their calling, are chronically prone to indebtedness, but there were two regions where debt posed special

38. Richard Hofstadter, *The Age of Reform: From Bryan to F.D.R.* (New York, 1955), p. 61.
39. Pollack, *Populist Response to Industrial America*, p. 18.

problems. One was the Great Plains, from Texas to the Dakotas, the last agricultural frontier, where in the 1870s and 1880s settlers had poured in to exploit the fertile virgin soil and the uncharacteristically generous rainfall, willingly mortgaging land, horses and machinery at high rates of interest, but where after 1887 a decade of drought and declining crop-yields forced thousands off the land and left many others stranded with debts they could not pay. The other was the South, where most of the productive land was cultivated by small farmers, operating under a bewildering variety of tenancy agreements and dependent for working capital on provision merchants, who were often also landlords, to whom they were forced to mortgage their crops. At the high rates of interest which prevailed in the capital-starved postbellum South, the resulting burden of indebtedness was desperately hard to shake off and, though rarely amounting to genuine debt-slavery, severely constrained the economic opportunities of tenants and share-croppers, both black and white, leaving them mired in a wretched poverty and a humiliating dependency which only the economic transformation of the region after the Second World War would bring to an end.

The People's Party grew out of the National Farmers' Alliance and Industrial Union, one of a succession of organisations created by farmers since the 1860s. The Farmers' Alliance, as it was generally called, originated in Texas, at the intersection of the Great Plains and the Cotton Belt, and spread rapidly during the late 1880s. In many localities Alliancemen set up cooperatives through which they could buy and sell at more advantageous prices and, in the South at least, free themselves from the shackles of the crop-lien system. These cooperative experiments invariably failed because their members lacked the financial resources to make them viable and because local merchants, naturally hostile to the enterprise, refused to trade with them or extend credit. This failure drew the Alliances into politics. Their leaders concluded that the cooperative movement could only succeed, and their members secure the social and economic autonomy that they sought, if fundamental changes were made in the nation's financial system. Therefore, Alliance radicals were converted to 'greenbackism', which became, says Goodwyn, the 'centerpiece of Alliance doctrine'.[40] Rather than currency being issued by national banks, in the interest of bankers and speculators, the government should issue its own inconvertible

---

40. Lawrence Goodwyn, *Democratic Promise: The Democratic Moment in America* (New York, 1976), p. 140.

legal tender notes, or 'greenbacks' as they were known when issued during the Civil War, a 'people's currency' freely available to all and adjusted to the needs of the people. To this was added C.W. Macune's subtreasury scheme. Macune proposed that the federal government should establish a system of warehouses in agricultural counties where farmers could store their crops, which would serve as security for low-interest loans, rather than marketing them at once, at unfavourable prices, in order to pay off their debts. For Southern farmers in particular the subtreasury scheme offered freedom from the 'bondage' of the crop-lien system. Instead of mortgaging their crop to the 'furnishing man', they would mortgage it to the government. To store crops and provide cheap credit for farmers was a very novel use of government power.

It was a use of government power which was too novel for most Democratic and Republican politicians to contemplate. By 1892 many Alliancemen had become convinced of the need for independent political action. In that year a national Populist Party met at a convention at Omaha, Nebraska, which attracted an array of unkempt agrarians and congenital reformers. It was a chaotic body, periodically possessed by wild enthusiasms, its members given to hymn-singing, horseplay and intermittent firing of pistols, quite unlike the controlled excitement of a major party convention. After a preamble which conjured up an apocalyptic vision of American society ('From the same prolific womb of governmental injustice we breed the two great classes – tramps and millionaires'), the party's platform turned to consider the financial question. The Populists believed that since the Civil War the money supply had been deliberately curtailed, by removing the legal tender status of the 'greenback' dollars issued during the war and by demonetising silver, thereby shackling the currency to the gold supply (which was growing at a slower rate than the economy), with the result that the value of money rose and prices fell. Creditors clearly gained from the enhancement of the value of their assets, while debtors, such as farmers, correspondingly suffered. But there was nothing inevitable about this; it was not to be interpreted as the outcome of inexorable economic forces. It was the result of 'unwise and pernicious legislation', enacted at the behest of the 'money power', which enabled the hard-earned income of the many to be expropriated by a privileged few: 'the supply of currency is purposely abridged to fatten usurers, bankrupt enterprise, and enslave industry'. The Populists therefore called for 'a national currency . . . issued by the General Government only', in place of that issued by the banks; free coinage of silver at the former legal ratio in relation to gold; and enactment of the Alliance's subtreasury plan.[41]

The second principal plank in the Omaha platform was national ownership of railroad, telephone and telegraph companies. Transportation was, of course, a major component in the eventual price of farm products, which were bulky relative to their value, and western farmers felt themselves to be especially subject to rate discrimination and at the mercy of transportation monopolies. Western farmers had long been in the forefront of the movement for railroad regulation. In view of the evident debility of state and federal regulation of the railroads, Alliance radicals turned to government ownership as the sole remaining recourse.

Most Populists were wholeheartedly committed to the ideals of private property and equality of opportunity in a capitalist society. But they also offered a far-reaching critique of the contemporary industrial system, which, they believed, was 'working the hopeless pauperization and degradation of the toiling masses'.[42] The trouble lay with government favouritism to certain groups. In particular, monopolies of credit and transportation, both critical to any form of enterprise, permitted a privileged few to expropriate the earnings of the actual producers of wealth, ultimately forcing them into tenancy and 'serfdom'. Hence the Populists called upon government to take control in these crucial areas. In this respect Populism anticipated the direction of twentieth-century reform movements like progressivism and the New Deal, but it went much further than either in its insistence on government control of the monetary system and government ownership of the railroads. Hofstadter has described Populism as a kind of 'entrepreneurial radicalism', a movement of small agrarian businessmen who, while clothing themselves in the language of radicalism, in actuality sought only to adjust certain economic parameters to their own advantage – something achieved much more effectively by later farm pressure groups.[43] But, rightly or wrongly, most Populists sought more than this: they sought ways to give ordinary men and women a greater degree of control over their lives in the face of an impersonal industrial society. They wished to regulate the developing system of corporate capitalism so as to enable small producers to make an independent living. There could, they believed, be no 'political freedom' without 'industrial freedom'. As

41. Johnson, *National Party Platforms*, pp. 89–91.
42. Pollack, *Populist Response to Industrial America*, p. 27.
43. Hofstadter, *Age of Reform*, p. 58.

William F. Holmes has noted, 'Populism represented the century's last major expression of the republican tradition' which linked freedom to the ownership of productive property.[44] Twentieth-century reform movements, in contrast, started from the assumption of the inevitability of corporate capitalism and the decline of individual enterprise and worked to achieve a measure of social justice within that framework.

Despite its claim to represent the voice of 'labour', of the 'industrial classes' in town and country, the People's Party made few inroads into the electoral strength of the major parties in industrial areas. Nor did it make a significant impression in rural counties of the Northeast or the settled regions of the Old Northwest, with their more stable and diversified agricultural economies. Even in the Populist heartland of the Plains, the South and the Mountain West the third party won only a plurality of votes, depending on fusion with the weaker of the major parties to attain power. Its strength was concentrated in areas of acute discontent, character-ised by one-crop agriculture and transportation monopolies, and even there it was the more geographically remote and socially isolated counties that most consistently lined up majorities for Populist candidates

After its modest success in 1892, the Populist Party continued to advance at a state level, despite the depredations suffered by its Southern wing from intimidation and electoral fraud and the ever-disruptive impact of racial differences. The more general depression that hit the country after 1893 seemed to offer a golden opportunity for the new party to make still further inroads. Instead an ill-fated fusion with the Bryan wing of the Democratic Party brought about its demise. Although historians since Hicks have pointed to the Populist proposals that were adopted by later reform movements, its central policies were not. Indeed, if Populism had an heir it was not progressivism but the Socialist Party of America (SPA), founded in 1900, which flourished in areas of Populist strength like Oklahoma and Kansas and whose titular leader, Eugene Debs, was a former Populist. Thousands of Populists who did not join the SPA or revert to their former allegiances seem to have drifted out of politics altogether or, in the case of Southern blacks and a large number of Southern whites, been simply disfranchised. Rather than constituting a new beginning for American reform, Populism disappeared into a void.

44. William F. Holmes, 'Populism: in search of context' *Agricultural History* 64 (1990), p. 44.

Epilogue: the 'crisis of the 1890s'

The fate of Populism was sucked into the politics of depression that followed the financial panic of 1893. Not only did the depression itself cause a great deal of suffering and discontent, but it drove home to Americans the momentous character of the social and economic changes that the nation was undergoing. The result was not only a political crisis of some magnitude but also a broader crisis of confidence in American institutions that was a necessary prerequisite for more fundamental changes in the functions and organisation of the American state in the Progressive Era.

The depression that began in 1893 was the most severe of the nineteenth century. Hundreds of banks closed their doors, railroads were taken into receivership and factories closed down. As a result, millions of workers were unemployed – nobody knows how many, but the president of the American Federation of Labor (AFL), Samuel Gompers, estimated 3 million, and it could well have been more. Bread-lines appeared with alarming suddenness in the nation's major cities, and thousands of tramps roamed the country in search of work. Some, like the so-called Coxey's Army, congregated in large numbers to petition the government for public works projects to generate employment. Pathetic, even ridiculous, though this ragged host may have seemed, it offered a clear expression of the level of popular discontent. A series of bitterly fought labour disputes heightened the atmosphere of crisis. Most significant in its effects and in its implications was the Pullman boycott of 1894, which for a time paralysed the nation's railroads, until it was broken by a federal court injunction against the leaders of the American Railway Union and the ruthless application of military force.

What is striking is the alarm with which social elites reacted to such manifestations of discontent. Coxey's tatterdemalion army provoked fears of revolution and anarchy everywhere it went. 'We have, in fact, come dangerously near to the condition of things at the time of the French Revolution', declared *Nation* editor Edwin L. Godkin, with unforgiveable exaggeration. 'We have been brought to the ragged edge of anarchy', warned US Attorney-General Richard Olney when confronted with the Pullman boycott.[45] The movement of tramps and the militancy of industrial workers evoked

---

45. Quoted in Sproat, *'Best Men'*, p. 258; Alan Nevins, *Grover Cleveland: A Study in Courage* (New York, 1944), p. 622.

fears of an uprising of the 'dangerous classes', on the model of the Paris Commune, that explosion of destructive violence that still haunted the minds of respectable Americans. Society, it appeared, was becoming dangerously unstable.

From the point of view of the middle and upper classes, the Democratic President Grover Cleveland, whose strict Jeffersonian principles had become indistinguishable from a coldly dogmatic adherence to *laissez-faire*, was wholly dependable. 'Though the people should support the Government, the Government should not support the people', he declared in vetoing a bill appropriating money to provide seeds for drought victims in drought-stricken areas of Texas.[46] He adhered firmly to the principle of 'honest money', that is the gold standard, in the face of popular enthusiasm for free coinage of silver, which, it was hoped, by augmenting the supply of money would give the economy a salutary inflationary stimulus. Southern and Western Democrats repudiated Cleveland and, on taking control of the party's national convention in 1896, nominated William Jennings Bryan on a platform which called for free coinage of silver, railroad regulation and tougher antitrust laws. When Bryan, in his famous 'Cross of Gold' speech, urged the convention to fight on the side of 'the struggling masses against the idle holders of idle capital', he not only evoked the Jacksonian traditions of his party but also pointed forward to the liberal activism of the twentieth-century Democracy.[47] The Democratic Party of Bryan, who acted as titular leader of the party for about a decade and a half, was not the Democratic Party of Cleveland. Instead of a party which mingled the Jeffersonian/Jacksonian belief in limited government with an increasingly conservative *laissez-faire* philosophy, it began to acknowledge the need for a measure of government intervention which anticipated, however distantly, the party of Franklin D. Roosevelt and the New Deal. Bryan, then, led the Democratic Party into a new political era.

The election campaign of 1896 was fought with an intensity unparalleled since Reconstruction. This was the 'Battle of the Standards' – between the inflationary claims of free silver and the security of gold. The Republicans nominated William McKinley on a platform which came out 'unreservedly for sound money', that is the gold standard. Gold and silver stood for more than mere forms

46. Quoted in Sproat, *'Best Men'*, p. 166.
47. Bryan, 'Cross of Gold Speech', in Richard Hofstadter, ed., *Great Issues in American History: From Reconstruction to the Present, 1865–1969* (New York, 1969), p. 172.

of currency. They were invested with great significance as symbols of a wider sectional division: between periphery and core; between the small-town community values represented by Bryan and the values of the new urban-industrial society represented by McKinley, and still more by his campaign manager the industrialist Mark Hanna. Republican speakers raised the standard of class conflict in a campaign which by no means divided the electorate along class lines. They accused Bryan of seeking, by inflating the currency, to repudiate debts and undermine property rights, of inviting anarchy and plunder. 'Beyond his feeble and ignorant presentation of his monetary heresy lies the deep abyss of socialism', warned *Harper's Weekly*. To Theodore Roosevelt, who became at times quite hysterical about the threat that Bryan posed, his was 'a semi-socialistic agrarian movement'.[48] In fact, urban workers evinced little enthusiasm for a candidate whose political style was so redolent of the agrarian hinterland and whose platform was designed to raise farm prices. Silver inflation held no appeal for those who had to go into the market to buy their food. This was reflected in the election results. Bryan and the Democrats swept the agricultural states of the South and West but won few of the states north of the Ohio or east of the Missouri which held the largest populations and carried the largest electoral votes, and therefore went down to a heavy defeat.

The election of 1896 was what some political scientists and historians have defined as a 'critical election'. To a limited extent at least, it broke the mould of late nineteenth-century politics. The Democratic Party, debilitated in the industrial East and Midwest by the nomination of Bryan, by a deep-rooted division between its urban and rural wings, and, above all, by its association with the economic distress of the 1890s, was reduced to the status of a near-permanent minority at a national level until another, still harsher, depression in the 1930s. An intensely competitive party system was replaced, at a national level, by a protracted Republican hegemony. The wider significance of this is highly problematic, especially as it coincided, as we shall see, with other, more fundamental changes in American electoral behaviour.

The 1896 campaign formed part of a series of alarming events that in aggregate engendered a broader crisis of confidence. The upsurge of agrarian discontent, the mass strikes, the armies of tramps that roamed the country – the 'sandwich-men of poverty,

48. Quoted in Paul S. Coletta, *William Jennings Bryan: Political Evangelist, 1860–1908* (Lincoln, Neb., 1964), pp. 185, 194.

the peripatetic advertisers of social misery', as the journalist W.T. Stead called them – and the bitterly divisive election of 1896 alarmed many Americans.[49] They seemed to expose fundamental economic and social divisions, suggesting that the social order was seriously askew. These fears were echoed by many of the writers of the time, ranging from the grave warnings of Henry George and Josiah Strong to the dystopian visions of Ignatius Donnelly. In a real sense, then, the 1890s constituted an important 'watershed' in American history, separating the more optimistic and confident world of the nineteenth century from the troubled century that we live in.

49. Stanley P. Caine, 'Origins of progressivism', in Lewis L. Gould, ed., *The Progressive Era* (Syracuse, N.Y., 1974), p. 21.

CHAPTER THREE

Capital, Labour and the State, 1890–1920

The second industrial revolution

At the end of the nineteenth century the American economy went through what could be described as a 'second industrial revolution'. Of course, the economy had been industrialising at an extraordinary rate for much of the century, but in the closing decades it seemed to undergo a fundamental change of state. Industrialisation around the turn of the century entailed more than increases in manufacturing output and a series of technological innovations; it involved fundamental changes in the structure of the economy. In the first place, the completion, and more importantly the integration, of the railroad network drew what Robert Wiebe has usefully called the 'island communities' of mid-nineteenth-century America into a national economy.[1] Secondly, by the 1900s important sections of the economy had come to be dominated by a relatively small number of giant corporations. In the words of John Tipple, 'The impact of the newborn corporation on American society was almost cataclysmic. ... Its size alone was sufficient to change fundamental social and economic relationships.'[2] Thirdly, the reorganisation of industrial production brought with it a major transformation of labour relations whose consequences unleashed a level of class conflict unprecedented in the history of the Republic. As an employers' representative noted in 1901, 'By the side of the labor problem all other worldly problems are secondary. ... Here it seems everything in the industrial world begins and ends.'[3]

1. Robert H. Wiebe, *The Search for Order, 1877–1920* (New York, 1967), p. 44.
2. John Tipple, 'The Robber Baron in the Gilded Age', in H. Wayne Morgan, ed., *The Gilded Age* (revised edn, Syracuse, N.Y., 1970), p. 14.
3. Quoted in Melvyn Dubofsky, *The State and Labor in Modern America* (Chapel Hill, N.C., 1994), pp. xvii–xviii.

The 'transportation revolution' which commenced in the generation before the Civil War was completed in the thirty years after 1865. By 1900 the United States had 258,784 miles of track, sufficient to bring railroad communication within reach of all but the most thinly populated regions of the country. By 1900 gaps in the network had been substantially filled, major rivers bridged, a uniform gauge established, smaller lines consolidated, and arrangements made to expedite the passage of through freight. At the same time, the use of steel rails, faster and more powerful locomotives, and electric signals and telegraph messages to track the movement of trains had contributed to a substantial fall in freight rates. In their aggressive efforts to drum up business, freight agents offered a variety of special rates, especially on long-distance routes. According to one railroad president, the policy was to adjust tariffs so that, 'regardless of distance, producers . . . in every part of this country, shall to the fullest extent possible, have equal access to all parts of this country'.[4] Such a rate-making strategy went a long way towards eliminating distance as a consideration in producers' marketing decisions.

In 1893 the Interstate Commerce Commission noted that a national market had taken the place of the local market. Partially independent local economies were now brought into the orbit of the national economy, in some cases rather suddenly. The national market offered exciting possibilities for manufacturers, but it also brought more intense competition. In the context of a secular fall in prices between the 1870s and the 1890s, those who prevailed were the producers who could pare their costs to the bone. Successful manufacturers, like Andrew Carnegie and John D. Rockefeller, were obsessive about cutting costs, adopting all possible innovations to improve productivity. In the steel industry, for example, economies of scale, such as the conservation of heat through the construction of larger furnaces or by moving the molten metal directly from blast furnace to Bessemer converter and from converter to rolling mill, using electric trolleys and cranes to expedite the transfer, enabled Carnegie to reduce steel prices at his J. Edgar Thomson Works by two-thirds between 1878 and 1898. As the apostle of scientific management Frederick Winslow Taylor observed, the most advanced methods could only be applied 'at a

---

4. Quoted in William Z. Ripley, *Railroads: Rates and Regulation* (New York, 1916), p. 133.

large volume of output'.[5] Thus the scale of operations grew inexorably. Whereas the J. Edgar Thomson Works cost $1.25 million to build during the 1870s, the integrated plant opened by United States Steel in 1907 at Gary, Indiana, also representing the state of the art for its day, cost $75 million.

The capital needed to finance operations on such a scale was beyond the resources of all but the wealthiest individuals. While railroads, whose capital demands far exceeded those of any other enterprises in mid-nineteenth-century America, had from the start been forced to apply to the public for funds, manufacturing companies were until the 1890s, with few exceptions, either family firms or partnerships. Even Carnegie Steel was a partnership until 1901. But when Carnegie retired, his holdings were absorbed into a vast conglomerate: United States Steel. By that date most large industrial firms had also become public joint-stock corporations, which in 1904 accounted for 74 per cent of American manufacturing output.

Companies with massive investments in plant and machinery had a powerful incentive to secure greater control over their economic environment. They had too much at stake to leave their fortunes to the vagaries of the market. Therefore they combined with other firms in the same industry, usually during a period of intense cut-throat competition, as in the steel industry during the 1890s, in order to stabilise prices. Alternatively, like Carnegie, they expanded vertically to secure control of supplies of raw materials, such as iron ore and coking coal, and to control the market for their goods, by investing in the manufacture of finished steel products. In either case the object was to escape the tyranny of the market, to replace the 'invisible hand' of the market with the 'visible hand' (the phrase is Alfred D. Chandler's) of managerial control.[6] Decisions which were once external to the firm were now taken internally. The aggregate result was a massive consolidation movement which transformed the American industrial landscape around 1900. In the boom years that followed the depression of the 1890s, between 1898 and 1902, 3,653 separate mergers took place involving nearly a third of the total capital invested in manufacturing, giving rise to such behemoths as United States Steel, International Harvester and American Tobacco. The rise of the big business corporation had

5. Quoted in Edward C. Kirkland, *Industry Comes of Age: Business, Labor and Public Policy, 1860–1897* (New York, 1962), p. 173.

6. Alfred D. Chandler Jr., *The Visible Hand: The Managerial Revolution in American Business* (Cambridge, Mass., 1977).

wide-ranging implications for the orientation of American culture, patterns of opportunity, labour relations and, above all, the relationship between state and society.

The remaking of the American working class

The reorganisation of industrial production had profound consequences for the lives of industrial workers. Indeed, a transformation of working practices was central to that process. Between the Civil War and the First World War several industries underwent a comprehensive reorganisation of production, involving the introduction of machinery and the minute division of labour. For example, in the packinghouses that stood alongside the giant Union Stockyards in Chicago the job of a butcher was minutely subdivided, involving in one plant as many as seventy-eight separate operations. The carcass was brought to the men on pulleys so that each could detach his allotted portion. This 'disassembly line' supposedly inspired Henry Ford to introduce the assembly line proper in the production of his Model T Ford in 1913. The work was broken down into simple tasks which could be easily learned, enabling not only greater mechanical efficiency, but also the employment of unskilled workers who were cheap to hire and easily replaced, in place of the more expensive and troublesome skilled craftsmen. By 1917 62 per cent of Ford workers were operatives and assemblers. Skilled workers, once central to the production process, now played an ancillary role: supervising machine-tenders, making tools and repairing machinery. The assembly line, rather than a new departure, was the logical culmination of this development. In the metal-working industries, which were less amenable to mechanisation and continuous-flow production, employers were also paying increasing attention to the details of the work process in order both to increase productivity and to increase managerial control. The techniques of 'scientific management', whose most enthusiastic prophet was Frederick Winslow Taylor, included '*enforced* standardization of methods, *enforced* adoption of the best implements and working conditions, and *enforced* co-operation of the employees under management's detailed direction'.[7] Along with the technological changes, then, went a revolution in management.

7. David Montgomery, *Workers' Control in America* (Cambridge, 1979), p. 26.

What contemporaries called the 'drive system' involved, then, the employment of highly specialised machinery, a highly developed division of labour, clearly set-out work routines, and detailed supervision of workers by foremen and managers wielding almost dictatorial powers. Not only the subjection of workers to a new set of factory disciplines but the host of indignities, injustices and petty tyrannies suffered at the hands of foremen and managers bred resentment at what workers condemned as 'industrial slavery'. Workers' resistance, through labour organisations and sporadic industrial action, in turn encouraged management to tighten its control over the work process and eliminate competing sources of authority. The history of industrialisation in America was one of a continuing struggle for control of the workplace. This conflict was a major source of friction between employers and employees and a critical element in the labour struggles of the period.

American workers worked long hours and at what foreigners regarded as a 'killing pace'. The reorganisation of production frequently required a more continuous and unremitting effort on the part of workers, while employers found speeding up the production line to be one of the easiest ways to increase productivity. Mechanisation and the 'speed up' made accidents all the more likely. Such incidents as the Cherry Hill disaster in the Illinois coalfield, in which 256 miners died, or the Triangle Fire in a New York clothing factory, in which 146 women and girls were incinerated or shattered as they threw themselves from the burning building, stood out only by virtue of the scale of the tragedy. In the closing years of the nineteenth century the average death rate from industrial accidents was 35,000 a year, the average rate of injuries sufficient to cause loss of a working day 536,000, a casualty rate comparable to that produced by the Civil War. The casualty rate for railroad trainmen was one in eleven, for immigrant workers at Carnegie Steel one in four. Conditions in the mines, in the steel mills and, as Upton Sinclair vividly demonstrated in his novel *The Jungle* (1906), in the packinghouses resembled images from Dante's *Inferno*.

To some extent, American workers were compensated for the dangers and discomforts of industrial life by relatively high wages. However, the rewards of industrial progress were most unevenly distributed. A New York survey in 1910 of over 100,000 workers found that skilled workers like printers and building tradesmen earned typically between $30 and $40 a week, whereas employees in the garment industry and other 'sweated' trades ranged between $5 and $10. Peter Shergold's study of the 'American Standard' of living reveals similar discrepancies between the wage-rates of skilled and unskilled workers in Pittsburgh. Skilled workers could enjoy a reasonable standard of living, including decent, well-appointed accommodation, an adequate diet and the occasional purchase of new clothes, furniture and household utensils, without in most cases requiring wives or older children to work. On the other hand, unskilled workers lived close to the margin of subsistence. Few unskilled male workers in the first decade of the century earned the $15 a week which Pittsburgh social workers believed necessary to support a family. Such families could only survive with the support of more than one income. Therefore women and older children joined the workforce in large numbers. Unskilled workers could only afford accommodation in the tenement districts of a city like New York or the shanty towns that clustered around the steel mills in the Pittsburgh region. They had little surplus cash for luxuries or, more importantly, to set aside against the emergencies that were endemic to working-class existence: industrial accidents, sickness and the regular bouts of unemployment which only the most fortunate workers could avoid. The difference between skilled and unskilled workers, therefore, was a difference not just in standard of living but in style of life.

Equally significantly, in industrial America the difference was also one of ethnic origins. Whereas by 1900 skilled workers were typically either native Americans or older immigrants, from Britain, Ireland, Germany and other Western European countries, unskilled workers were mostly recent immigrants, the great majority of whom came from Southern and Eastern Europe. In 1910 81 per cent of the unskilled workers in Carnegie Steel were immigrants; in one plant 48 per cent did not even speak English.

The 'ethnic recomposition of the American working class' in the late nineteenth and early twentieth centuries had dramatic repercussions for the development of working-class culture.[8] A distinctive artisan culture had developed among native workers before the Civil War. It incorporated the belief that those who laboured with their hands were worthy of respect and a 'just' return for their labour and that members of a trade were linked together, as Sean Wilentz explains, by a web of reciprocal obligation, a code of unselfish 'brotherhood' quite different to the developing middle-class ethic of possessive individualism. In the factories of

8. David Montgomery, *The Fall of the House of Labor* (Cambridge, 1987), p. 174.

post-Civil War America work was still largely controlled by skilled craftsmen, whose knowledge and skill were indispensable to the process of production. They retained much of the autonomy of earlier artisans, enabling elements of the antebellum artisan culture to survive. 'The ethical norms governing workplace behavior' formed the basis, according to David Montgomery, for a 'collectivist counter-culture in the midst of the growing factory system'.[9] It was in defence of such norms, and in defence of the autonomy and dignity of skilled workers, that early trade unions were formed during the second half of the nineteenth century.

Various working-class institutions developed in factory towns like Lynn, Massachusetts, where working associations were reinforced by residential proximity and a strong sense of neighbourhood. Lunch-rooms and cafés catered to industrial workers, providing, like the saloons, a source of news, job information and social contact. Poolrooms, bowling alleys, theatres, baseball teams, volunteer fire companies, political clubs, benevolent societies and lodges also provided a focus for working-class sociability. So, in Lynn, did trade unions, which themselves organised numerous leisure activities, including balls, picnics and excursions, as well as debating societies, libraries, lectures and newspapers, which encouraged a sometimes intense social and political debate. Unionism therefore fostered something similar to what Lawrence Goodwyn describes as the 'movement culture' of the Farmers' Alliances.

The values and institutions developed over the previous half-century were by 1914 the preserve of a minority of 'American' workers. By then 60 per cent of industrial workers were foreign-born, and many more were the descendants of immigrants. Immigrants tended to inhabit separate neighbourhoods, and their social needs were met by ethnic institutions, including taverns, fraternal lodges and benevolent societies, many of them centred upon the church. They lived their private lives very largely within ethnic communities. As John Bodnar has shown, East European immigrants brought with them a set of social values and beliefs very different to those of native workers. They had a very different attitude to the social order and their place within it. Having learned to see the world as a source of 'limited good', they tended to adopt a defensive posture in relation to industrial society, in order to protect themselves and their families.

Rather than one working-class community, therefore, a number of largely separate ethnic working-class subcommunities developed.

9. Montgomery, *The Fall of the House of Labor*, p. 174.

However, it has to be emphasised that these were in every case *working-class* communities. Even though they drew on different traditions, each represented an adjustment to industrial America. Though divided by culture and by history, all American workers shared the unifying experience of subjection to the exertions, the dangers, the indignities and the chaotic nature of industrial America.

Patterns of industrial conflict

Faced with such conditions, American workers, like workers elsewhere, responded by organising trade unions and by engaging in collective withdrawals of labour. But they did so at different rates from workers in comparable industrial nations. Trade union membership, which had slumped to 440,000 during the depression of the 1890s, rose to 2.1 million in 1904 but then remained stagnant until 1915, whereupon union numbers, nourished by the wartime boom, leaped to 5.1 million in 1920, only to sink back again during the 1920s. In 1914 no more than 10 per cent of the non-agricultural workforce was organised (in Britain the proportion was 23 per cent and in Germany 24 per cent). The majority of union members before the First World War were skilled workers, members of the craft unions affiliated to the American Federation of Labor or the highly conservative railroad brotherhoods, and employed in a very few sectors of the economy. The 407,000 union members in the building trades, the 298,000 in the railroad brotherhoods and the 261,000 unionised mine-workers together accounted for nearly half the organised workers in 1910. In contrast, unions were quite pathetically weak in mass-production industry. In steel, oil-refining, textiles, rubber, agricultural machinery, automobiles and meat-packing, that is in the most advanced, most rapidly-growing sectors of the economy, the open shop prevailed. The commanding heights of the economy, then, were largely union-free.

On the other hand, the incidence of strikes in the United States was, by international standards, remarkably high. Between 1886 (when the United States Bureau of Labor Statistics was founded) and 1905, 33,771 strikes were recorded. Between 1900 and 1905 the average number of strikes ran at 2,732 annually and the average number of strikers at 581,000, a figure proportionately higher than in any European country for which figures are available, except Italy. From 1915, when federal statistics were collected again, to

1922, the equivalent figures were 2,965 and 1,630,000. Not only were strikes frequent, they were fiercely contested, in terms of numbers engaged, duration and bellicosity. Industrial violence was almost endemic in the United States. Labour disputes were regularly scarred by beatings, shootings, bombings, arson attacks, riots and even pitched battles between strikers and strikebreakers, or strikers and police. At Homestead in 1892 sixteen were killed and hundreds injured; at Cripple Creek, Colorado in 1904 twenty-nine lives were lost; the Ludlow Massacre of 1914 took thirteen lives, in the course of a bitter struggle with the Colorado Coal and Iron Company in which sixty-six were killed. Hardly any major strike occurred without a substantial measure of associated mayhem. Graham Adams Jr. has described the years 1910–15 as 'the age of industrial violence', but the title is equally applicable to the whole period between the 1870s and the 1920s.

The level of industrial unrest proves that American workers were neither acquiescent nor inert. It provides evidence of a continuous undercurrent of dissatisfaction which regularly erupted into industrial conflict. The fact that most workers were not unionised did not mean that they were not militant. Strikes were common, for example, on the docks and in textile mills, which were not unionised. Indeed, it can be argued that the bitterness of industrial relations in this period was a direct consequence of the feebleness of trade unions. Stronger unions might have imposed a more orderly system of collective bargaining, but in the United States before the First World War, and indeed until the 1930s, trade unions were engaged in a constant struggle for survival. They were not accepted as a normal part of the industrial landscape nor recognised as legitimate social agents by employers, government or the middle-class public. So labour disputes commonly involved what may be called constitutional as well as substantive questions – not only terms of employment but also the union's very right to exist. It was for that reason that American labour struggles were so protracted and so violent.

The hostility of employers to trade unions is in no way surprising. They wished to maintain their freedom to bargain with individual workers on questions of wages and hours, and they insisted on their right to control their own factories without outside interference. At stake were not only matters of wages and hours but also control of work patterns and the imposition of industrial discipline. There-fore, labour agitators were turned out, strikers replaced wherever possible with 'scabs', union members placed on a blacklist, spies and detectives hired to root out 'conspiracy' and workers compelled to sign 'yellow-dog' contracts, which debarred them from joining a union as a condition of their employment. Any and all methods, it was believed, were warranted to eradicate trade unions and establish the 'open shop'. James Holt reckons that the exceptional obduracy of American, as compared with British, employers was one of the main obstacles to unionisation in that country. However, it is difficult to accept this as a key explanatory variable. That American employers behaved in a less accommodating fashion than their British counterparts was due less to any innate belligerence or intransigence of disposition than to the social, and above all the political, environment in which they operated.

The great American corporations were mostly successful in combating unions. After the defeat of the Amalgamated Association of Iron and Steel Workers at Homestead, the open shop was established in several of the plants operated by Carnegie Steel. At its formation in 1901, US Steel declared itself 'unalterably opposed to the extension of union labor' and, indeed, was committed to its ultimate extinction.[10] Following catastrophic defeats in 1901 and 1909, the union was left with no more than a fingerhold in one or two plants. Generally speaking, the open shop obtained throughout US Steel, and indeed throughout the industry. A company like US Steel possessed obvious advantages: it had the financial resources to starve out strikers; it could shift production from union to non-union plants; mechanisation left it less dependent on skill and enabled it to draw upon a wider pool of labour; its economic and political power bludgeoned local, and even state, governments to provide protection during strikes. There was to be no effective union in the steel industry until 1937, while other mass-production industries, like petroleum-refining, rubber, agricultural machinery and automobiles, were similarly inhospitable territory for organised labour.

Most of the successes enjoyed by organised labour came in its confrontations with smaller firms which, having fewer financial resources, operating in highly competitive markets, and relying in most cases on skilled labour, were in a much weaker bargaining position than powerful corporations like US Steel. It is easy to forget, in the face of the catastrophic failure of organised labour in almost all the major struggles, which take pride of place in the standard histories, that in many lesser contests, fought in most cases

10. Selig Perlman and Philip Taft, *History of Labor in the United States, 1896–1932. IV. Labor Movements* (New York, 1935), p. 108

at a local level, the unions prevailed. Some 60 per cent of strikes recorded in New Jersey during the 1880s were won by labour, and this may well have been typical for the period. In the construction industry, which was at the mercy of well-organised building crafts-men, in the engineering industry, in printing, in the garment trades, which were populated by thousands of marginal firms, and in many other such industries unions flourished. The small business sector provided most union membership before the New Deal. American industry was divided between a core of highly mechanised, technically advanced large firms operating in mono-polistic or oligopolistic markets and a periphery of smaller firms, less highly mechanised, less capitalised and operating under conditions much closer to a model of perfect competition. The core was virtually forbidden territory for organised labour; in the periphery, though still recognised by only a minority of employers, unions enjoyed intermittent success.

Even here, however, after the upsurge of union organisation around the turn of the century, small businessmen began to organise themselves in order more effectively to fight organised labour. After 1900 local employers' associations and 'citizens' alliances' appeared in cities like Dayton, Ohio and Los Angeles. Trade associations were formed, as in the metal trades, the cotton and woollen textile industries, printing and papermaking, for the same purpose: to exchange financial assistance, arrange for the provision of strikebreakers, compile blacklists, secure favourable notices in the press, and apply political pressure on government. From 1903 the National Association of Manufacturers, founded during the 1890s to promote foreign trade, devoted itself, under the zealous leadership of its new president David Parry, primarily to fighting unions. It lobbied effectively against labour legislation and kept up a flow of propaganda on behalf of the open shop, which was glorified as the 'American system'. Organised labour, claimed Parry, in its tyrannical claims to deny those who were not members the right to dispose of their labour as they saw fit, was infringing upon one of the most sacred and fundamental of American liberties. It was 'a mob power knowing no master except its own will'.[11]

Employers' propaganda played on a number of central themes in nineteenth-century American culture, such as the belief in self-reliance, the liberty of the individual and the ideal of a classless

11. Quoted in Larry J. Griffin, 'Capitalist resistance to the organization of labor before the New Deal' *American Sociological Review* 51 (1986), p. 149.

society. Unions had been linked with violence since the railroad riots of 1877. They were therefore perceived as a threat to the social order, to property and to business – that is any property, any business, including that of the petit bourgeois and perhaps the farm-owner as much as that of shareholders in US Steel or Standard Oil. In many respects the American middle class exhibited a higher degree of 'class consciousness' than did the American working class.

Certainly the composition of the American working class posed special problems for union organisers. The extraordinary geographical mobility of American workers hindered the development of stable working-class communities. The diversity of conditions and work experiences made it difficult to establish common ground and define common interests. Above all, immigration created a complex pattern of ethnic loyalties and antagonisms that cut across and sometimes obscured class divisions. Ethnic rivalries, which were often exploited to great effect by employers, regularly fractured the workers' unity in labour disputes, as in the steel strike of 1901 or in the textile strike at Lawrence, Massachusetts in 1912. But this, too, was by no means an insuperable obstacle to union organisation. Workers divided by culture and historical experience were also united by their workplace experience. 'Scientific management' and the homogenisation of working experience in the new factory system affected all workers. Under such conditions, strikes could spread like a contagion, from one group of workers to another, either in a particular factory like Homestead in 1892 or within a working-class neighbourhood like the packinghouse district of Chicago ('Back of the Yards'). Where, as in the anthracite fields of Eastern Pennsylvania during the 1890s and 1900s or at McKees Rock in 1909, determined efforts were made to organise immigrant workers, ethnic differences could be surmounted. It would be a mistake to regard ethnicity as a factor which categorically ruled out union formation. Its impact was refracted through local circumstances and the ways in which individuals and institutions responded to those circumstances.

The same might be said of most of the other factors adduced to explain the debility of American unionism. In most cases they simply explain too much. Trade unions did flourish in many localities and in many industries, and they did so for reasons which had as much to do with particular local histories as with any determining social or economic conditions. Where unions succeeded it was often because they had built up a record of successful organising and negotiation, brought material improvements in members' conditions of work and involved them in a collective enterprise. 'Class-consciousness', says Montgomery, 'was more than the unmediated product of daily experience. It was a project.'[12] Where unions failed it was often because of the absence of any tradition of union activity that might encourage men and women to place their faith in such an organisation, especially in view of the personal risks that membership entailed. But that was not usually because of any innate passivity among American workers, or any ideological or cultural incompatibility with the goals of unionism, but because of powerful external forces: one, as we have seen, was the power of big business; the other was the intervention of the state.

Organised labour and the state

Between the 1870s and the 1930s the efforts of organised labour were regularly confounded by the hostile intervention of the state. Since labour disputes often resulted in violent confrontations between strikers and strikebreakers, their resolution depended significantly on the actions of law-enforcement authorities. The laws governing trespass, obstruction and disorderly conduct were ambiguous enough to leave local magistrates and police authorities considerable scope for discretion. If they accepted that strikers had the right to demonstrate to protect their livelihood and treated the employment of scabs as a mischievous act, then the strike might come to a successful fruition; if, on the other hand, they regarded the presence of pickets as a threat to public order, they might take actions that would have the effect of breaking the strike. Thus it was the introduction of state militia at Homestead in 1892 and Cripple Creek in 1904, where company guards were simply deputised by the local sheriff, and federal troops in the Pullman boycott of 1894 that led directly to defeat of the union. The National Guard and the US Army were involved in over 500 strikes between 1877 and 1903.

The state often intervened in major industrial disputes in France, but it did so in most cases to persuade employers to make concessions. State intervention greatly increased the probability of a successful outcome for striking workers. In the United States, on the other hand, government intervention was almost invariably unfriendly and greatly reduced the probability of success. Whereas

12. Montgomery, *Fall of the House of Labor*, p. 2.

it was in the interest of French workers to raise the stakes by involving as many workers as possible, so as to precipitate government intervention, it was in the interest of American unions to avoid major confrontations and confine themselves to small-scale local engagements where their resources could be most profitably employed. Government suppression of mass strikes like those at Homestead and Coeur d'Alène during the 1890s influenced the expectations and behaviour of union leaders for a generation or more.

As a clutch of recent studies have shown, the law governing labour relations was inhospitable to successful industrial action. It must be noted that, in the absence of legislation on most aspects of the subject by the states or by Congress, labour law was primarily judge-made law. Even where state legislatures did attempt to modify the status of trade unions, by, for example, exempting them from conspiracy or antitrust prosecutions or forbidding 'yellow-dog' contracts, their handiwork was either ignored or overruled by the courts. American labour law was laid down on a case-by-case basis by the judiciary, and especially by the federal judiciary, which assumed jurisdiction over cases involving diversity of citizenship (that is where the contending parties resided in different states). As a federal circuit court judge explained in 1914, it administered 'the law as applicable to all the states', in a manner 'untrammelled by differing decisions of the state tribunals', according to 'the general principles of equity'.[13] Industrial relations law was defined by an application of English common law principles, which, ironically, had far more influence on industrial relations than in their homeland, where they were by 1900 largely displaced by statute law.

The courts at no point denied the right of workers voluntarily to form trade unions. Labour organisations were not in themselves unlawful conspiracies. However, they were merely associations of individuals with no corporate authority and no right to coerce or act oppressively towards individuals, whether members or non-members. Workers had a perfect right to quit their employment whenever they so desired, either individually or collectively, so long as the objects of the strike and the methods employed were accepted as lawful by the courts. Legitimate objects of industrial action included the improvement of wages and hours; they did not include the establishment of a closed shop, the reinstatement of discharged workers, interference with work rules or an expression

13. Quoted in Felix Frankfurter and Nathan Green, *The Labor Injunction* (New York, 1930), p. 17.

of sympathy with another group of workers. A strike was legal only when it did not force unwilling outsiders to participate. Industrial action would not pass judicial scrutiny if the court found that the methods employed involved the coercion of non-participants, by, for example, 'intimidatory' picketing or a 'secondary boycott'. Judges were liable to take a very broad view of what constituted 'intimidation', sometimes ruling the mere presence of groups of pickets as coercive. In one Pennsylvania case the attendance of a brass band was cited as 'intimidatory' behaviour. Indeed, some judges refused to acknowledge the possibility of 'peaceful picketing' any more than they would admit the possibility of a lawful lynching or a peaceful mob. A primary boycott, that is a boycott of an employer's products by the strikers themselves, was normally accepted, but a 'secondary boycott', that is a boycott of other businesses dealing with the targeted employer, was commonly condemned, as by 1908 was publication of an 'unfair list' inviting workers over a broader area to shun his products. Interestingly, although union members' right to boycott employers was circumscribed, the courts widely admitted employers' right to boycott union members, in the form of 'yellow-dog' contracts, and overturned state laws prohibiting the practice.

Thus trade unions had the right to exist and to call strikes, but most of the more effective methods that they would wish to employ were regarded as illegitimate and liable to prosecution by the courts. Under conditions where no effective barriers to entry obtained, some form of 'secondary activity', such as picketing of non-cooperating workers, or a boycott of non-cooperating businesses, was necessary to enforce the strikers' demands. Mass picketing was essential in contesting large-scale disputes, while the secondary boycott had emerged in the late nineteenth century as one of labour's most powerful weapons since it effectively marshalled the solidarity of working-class communities. Likewise, sympathy strikes, that is broadly-based class actions rooted in shared notions of moral economy, exploited the solidarity and neighbourhood bonds of working-class communities. Their prohibition greatly circumscribed the weapons available to organised labour. The law, in other words, ruled out aggressive tactics based on class solidarity and forced the unions to adopt the narrow, low-risk strategy of 'business unionism'.

As Herbert Hovenkamp has shown, judges proceeded in labour cases by applying the law of combinations. Trade unions and business combinations were treated by the same standard. Before

1890, combinations to raise prices or wages were regarded as legal, though unenforceable, as long as they did not involve the coercion of third parties. After the passage of the Sherman Antitrust Act it was uncertain whether combinations in interstate commerce were legal under any circumstances. Business combinations got round the difficulty by resorting to tight combinations, or mergers, and thereby becoming, in effect, single 'persons' who, after a lengthy period of uncertainty, were recognised as exempt from antitrust prosecution. Trade unions resisted the temptation to incorporate, fearing that it would increase their susceptibility to prosecutions and claims for damages, but this left them still open to antitrust suits. Therefore the Sherman Act was, in the early years, applied more often to labour than to capital. Uncertainty as to whether Congress intended that the law should apply to labour was removed when the Supreme Court affirmed in the *Danbury Hatters* case of 1908 that it should and that a boycott such as the Hatters' Union had imposed was a restraint of interstate trade under the terms of the act. As it stated in the parallel *Buck's Stove & Range* case, 'It covered any illegal means by which interstate commerce is restrained'.[14] In *Duplex Printing* (1921) the Court concluded that a perfectly peaceful strike violated the antitrust law if it had an adverse effect on interstate commerce.

After the turn of the century court injunctions were increasingly employed in labour disputes. The legal scholar Edwin Witte counted 1,845 injunctions between 1880 and 1930: 28 in the 1880s, 122 in the 1890s, 328 in the 1900s, 446 in the 1910s, and 921 in the 1920s. Rather than an extraordinary procedure designed to meet urgent and exceptional conditions, their use had become routine. Writs of injunction are court orders enjoining individuals to desist from certain actions which the court is persuaded would bring about 'imminent and irreparable damage' to the complainant's property for which ordinary legal remedies were inadequate. The courts came to accept a wide definition of 'property rights', including not only an employer's material assets but anything of 'pecuniary value', including his right to carry on a business, which greatly extended the range of actions in connection with labour disputes which might be considered enjoinable. Every action carried out by a trade union to enforce its demands would be liable to damage an employer's 'property' so defined, as well as causing a certain amount of injury to consumers or non-strikers. In

14. Quoted in Frankfurter and Green, *The Labor Injunction*, p. 9.

considering complaints, judges assumed the responsibility for deciding whether a strike was justified, in terms of its objectives, and whether the methods employed were legitimate. In effect, judges were assuming the responsibility to pass judgement on the most delicate areas of public policy and settle complex and highly problematic socio-economic issues as if they were questions of abstract law. Equity proceedings, said Witte, constituted 'a species of judicial legislation'.[15]

Equally objectionable were judicial procedures. A court would issue an *ex parte* restraining order without a hearing, on the basis of an affidavit from the complainant, usually without supporting evidence, if the judge was persuaded that 'irreparable damage' would result from further delay. A more permanent injunction would follow after a hearing, which might lead to a modification, or even a lifting, of the order. But all too often the preliminary injunction was in itself fatal. Contesting it would engage union leaders in tedious legal proceedings, exhaust union funds and, above all, dissipate the organisational momentum of the strike, which, once lost, would be difficult to recover. But refusal to obey the injunction would place the strike leaders, as well as rank-and-file participants, in contempt of court and therefore subject to trial, without benefit of jury, by the judge whose authority had been challenged. Thus labour was placed effectively in a 'Catch 22' situation: damned if it did and damned if it didn't. As far as organised labour was concerned, the employment of labour injunctions was a major grievance which absorbed their political energies for a quarter of a century or more.

The gravest problem facing the labour movement in the early twentieth century, therefore, was its ambiguous legal status. Whereas business corporations gained acceptance as equivalent to natural 'persons' under law, trade unions remained, in the eyes of the courts, no more than a collection of fractious individuals – the legal equivalent of a mob.

'Business unionism'

The unfavourable social and political conditions under which trade unions operated in early twentieth-century America appeared to give an evolutionary advantage to a particular kind of 'job-conscious' unionism which, rather than expressing common class

15. Edwin E. Witte, *The Government in Labor Disputes* (New York, 1932), p. 107.

interests, was founded upon the solidarity of small groups of workers who belonged to the same trade and focused upon a narrow range of workplace issues, such as work rules, wages, hours and job security. Accepting the reality of a corporate society, trade unions sought to find a place within it for themselves and their members. Limiting their objectives to what they considered 'realistic', they concentrated on protecting their members' jobs and working conditions and maintaining their own organisational integrity. Whereas early labour historians like Selig Perlman might see this rather limited brand of unionism as a necessary adaptation to an inhospitable environment, it can be argued that the strategies adopted by the craft unions associated with the American Federation of Labor contributed in no small measure to their marginal position in American industrial society.

The American Federation of Labor was organised by the national unions in 1886, largely as a coordinating agency in their struggle against the rival Knights of Labor. After the decline of the Knights, the AFL remained as the labour movement's most significant central voice. Although the Federation had limited authority over the affiliated unions, it played an important role in articulating the views of organised labour before the general public and lobbying before the national government. It stood, above all, as a symbol of a particular variety of unionism. AFL unionism defined itself very largely in the cause of its lengthy struggle with the Knights of Labor. In the first place, the affiliates were trade unions 'pure and simple', in contradistinction to the reform unionism of the Knights. Their leaders regarded political action as secondary to industrial organisation, believing that only through effective organisation on the shop-floor could men and women claim a voice in their conditions. Samuel Gompers, for nearly forty years the president and guiding light of the Federation, believed that the trade union movement was 'the one great agency of the toiling masses to secure for them a better and higher standard of life and work'.[16] Many early AFL leaders, including Gompers, were very much influenced by Marxist thinking about the role of the union movement and the primacy of economic over political action.

Two further principles of industrial organisation were funda-mental to the structure of the AFL. One was the principle of 'business unionism', which had developed over the years out of the experience of the early unions. This stressed the importance of

16. Foster R. Dulles and Melvyn Dubofsky, *Labor in America: A History* (5th edn, Arlington Heights, Ill.,1993), p. 149.

efficient organisation: the regular collection of dues, the accumulation of a strike fund, the establishment of benefit programmes to bind members to the union between strikes. The second guiding principle was that of 'craft autonomy', which, as a Teamsters leader later put it, was the 'rock' upon which 'the church of the labor movement' was built.[17] It followed from the original character of the member unions, which were craft unions, differentiated from one another according to their members' skill. Each union was, in theory, sovereign over a particular trade, thus hopefully avoiding squabbles over jurisdiction which would only redound to the benefit of the employers. These founding principles had significant implications for the way in which the labour movement developed over time.

In the first place, a progressive application of the tenets of 'business unionism' resulted in a growing bureaucratisation of the national unions. The management of benefit schemes and apprenticeship programmes, collective bargaining and the nego-tiation of trade agreements required skill and experience. Therefore full-time officials were hired who became, in effect, professional union administrators. To some extent, these career officials developed interests different from those of their members, preferring stability over risk-taking, and pursuing immediate bread-and-butter issues rather than broader objectives. They sought where possible to formalise relations with employers, which meant holding religiously to contracts and refraining from sympathy actions. Orderly patterns of collective bargaining were developed at the expense of traditional forms of class solidarity. 'The truth is', said Robert Hoxie, 'that the outlook and ideals of this dominant type of unionism are those very largely of a business type. Its successful leaders are essentially businessmen and its unions are organized to do business with employers'.[18]

Secondly, the AFL maintained an attitude of suspicion, and sometimes downright hostility, to industrial unionism, that is the organisation of workers on the basis of their employment in the same industry, rather than their possession of a common skill. It is true that a strict adherence to craft autonomy was progressively abandoned, as industrial departments were organised after 1907 and as some of the craft unions began to enrol workers without the

17. William E. Leuchtenburg, *Franklin D. Roosevelt and the New Deal* (New York, 1963), p. 110.
18. Quoted in Morton Keller, *Regulating a New Economy: Public Policy and Economic Change in America, 1900–1933* (Cambridge, Mass., 1990), p. 118.

appropriate skills, converting themselves into something half-way between craft and industrial unions. But a full commitment to industrial unionism was never made. A few industrial unions were affiliated to the AFL, like the United Mine Workers and the United Brewery Workers, but always with difficulty and under sufferance. Industrial unionism was obviously in conflict with the principle of craft autonomy, since an industrial union would necessarily include craftsmen who were also eligible for membership of the appropriate craft union. Industrial unionism impinged on the prerogatives of the existing craft unions. Yet how else were the great mass of factory workers to be organised, many of whom had no special skills? More significantly, the members of AFL unions, as skilled workers – the 'aristocracy of labour' – felt little inclination to unionise unskilled workers, who Gompers suspected were 'unorganizable', particularly as most of them were immigrants, believed to be ignorant of American standards and industrial ways. Immigrants sometimes met with strong prejudice from native workers. Still more did African-Americans, Chinese and women, who, native white workers believed, had no rightful place in the labour market. Thus the AFL made only halting efforts before the First World War to organise unskilled workers or to tackle mass-production industry.

Finally, the AFL became more cautious in its attitude to political action. In 1895 the AFL national convention passed a resolution, frequently reiterated, which stated that 'Party politics, whether they be Democratic, Republican, Socialistic, Populistic, Prohibition, or any other, shall have no place in the conventions of the American Federation of Labor'.[19] The AFL leaders' dealings with politicians during the formative years of the union movement had convinced them of the futility of political action. Gompers, as a syndicalist, believed in the primacy of industrial organisation and therefore, on good Marxist principles, refused to support a socialist or labour party. By 1900 Gompers and most other prominent figures in the AFL, whatever they had been earlier, were strongly anti-socialist, partly in response to repeated and vituperative attacks from Daniel DeLeon, the leader of the Socialist Labor Party. Gompers was highly sensitive to personal criticism, but he was also convinced that DeLeon and other socialists were committed to the destruction of the trade union movement. In any case, he feared identification of the movement with unpopular, 'un-American' doctrines. Gompers came increasingly to express the objectives of the labour movement

19. Quoted in Marc Karson, *American Labor Unions and Politics, 1900–1918* (Carbondale, Ill., 1958), p. 21.

in immediate terms, claiming that the AFL had no 'ultimate ends' but sought merely to attain the best possible conditions for the workers within the framework of the new industrial society.

Although local labour federations sometimes lobbied for wages and hours legislation, Gompers opposed almost any statutory regulation of working conditions, with the exception of the eight-hour law for government employees. 'It has been the constant struggle of the workers through the ages to get the tentacles of government from the throats of the workers', he claimed.[20] Workers should develop the industrial strength to compel employers to grant fair conditions of work, rather than relying on government to provide them by statute. Gompers was also discouraged by the unions' earlier experience with state legislation covering hours and conditions of labour, much of which fell victim to judicial review. Thus AFL unions felt drawn to a 'voluntarist' strategy by the peculiar structure of the American state. As legal historian William Forbath points out, the actions of the courts 'shaped labor's strategic calculus'.[21] Its attention was focused on securing repeal of unfavourable laws rather than seeking positive uses of state power. Forced into an essentially antistatist posture, it worked to decrease, rather than increase, the role of government in industrial relations. Thus the one major exception to the AFL's abjuration of political action was the ongoing campaign to eradicate labour injunctions and to secure exemption from the antitrust laws, which forms the subject of the following section.

Labour politics

Though pursuing a 'voluntarist' approach to the improvement of wages and working conditions, the AFL did have a political agenda and did engage in regular political lobbying to achieve its objectives. Indeed, one of the stated functions of the Federation from its foundation had been to lobby for legislation in the interests of working people, and Gompers and other union officials regularly appeared before congressional committees to press their case. In 1906, however, the AFL began to pursue its political objectives more vigorously than ever before.

20. Quoted in William M. Dick, *Labor and Socialism in America: The Gompers Era* (Port Washington, N.Y., 1972), p. 115.
21. William E. Forbath, *Law and the Shaping of the American Labor Movement* (Cambridge, Mass., 1991), p. 6.

An alarming conjunction of circumstances combined to induce a more urgent attitude to political action. The employers' counter-offensive had contributed to an abrupt cessation of the rapid expansion in union membership around the turn of the century and caused a disturbing loss of institutional momentum. Federal and state courts had delivered a series of judgements highly prejudicial to labour, culminating in the *Danbury Hatters* case, in which a federal circuit court had found against the Hatters' Union for conspiracy in violation of the Sherman Antitrust Act, and they had shown an increasing willingness to issue injunctions in labour disputes. For some years Congress had shown little inclination to enact labour legislation, while the Administration had shown little enthusiasm for enforcing those laws, like the federal eight-hours law, which were on the statute-book. The overall drift of federal policy was highly inimical to the interests of organised labour. An additional consideration was the need to pre-empt growing demands from within the Federation for an endorsement of the newly established Socialist Party of America. The 'nonpartisan strategy' initiated in 1906 and followed, on or off, for a decade or more played a critical part in Gompers's ongoing battle with the socialists for control of the labour movement. Some action had to be taken in response to the worsening political situation, and Gompers was anxious that it should be on terms which would not weaken his grip on the Federation.

In March 1906, therefore, an AFL delegation presented Congress with a 'Bill of Grievances' setting out the Federation's legislative demands. These included vigorous enforcement of the federal eight-hours law; legislation to protect labour from various forms of 'unfair' competition, from convicts, from Chinese workers and from 'induced and undesirable immigration'; the exemption of trade unions from the antitrust law; and, above all, the restriction of the power of the courts to issue injunctions in labour disputes.[22] Labour put its weight behind a measure which laid down that, while injunctions might be issued in order to prevent irreparable damage to property, 'no right to continue the relation of employer and employee ... or to carry on business of any particular kind' was to be considered as 'constituting a property right' (this was a procedure eventually followed in the Clayton Act).[23] Injunctions should not apply to actions that would be perfectly legal when performed outside the context of a labour dispute. The AFL's

22. *American Federationist* 13 (September 1906), pp. 689–90.
23. Frankfurter and Green, *Labor Injunction*, p. 155.

political platform was therefore very limited. It embraced the right of workers to organise and bargain collectively and their competitive position in the labour market; it did not include questions of hours and wages (other than for the federal government's own employees) or social insurance. Organised labour pursued a primarily antistatist solution to its problems. Its vision, its conception of natural rights, was narrowed by the actions of the courts to a demand merely to be 'let alone'.

The Republican Party, which dominated both houses of Congress during the first decade of the century, gave short shrift to labour's demands. Conservative Republicans, like Speaker of the House Joseph G. Cannon, refused to accept any diminution of the courts' authority. Most Republicans admitted that the prerogative had been abused but nevertheless defended the 'beneficent writ of injunction' as a necessary protection against violence and the destruction of property. Some, like President Theodore Roosevelt, were willing to see some procedural modification, for example by requiring notice and opportunity for a hearing before an injunction was issued, but insisted that any delay must not be such as to permit 'violation of the law or the jeopardizing of life or property'.[24] Since the case for an injunction was always based on the claim that irreparable damage would follow unless urgent remedial action was taken, such a requirement was more or less meaningless. Republicans clearly found it difficult to accept organised labour's demands for relief from judicial interference. Situations might arise, they believed, when legal action against trade unions was necessary to protect the rights of employers and the general public. Even those who accepted that the injunction power had been abused would not contemplate the removal of the courts' power to issue injunctions to prevent 'irreparable damage' to property. Certain kinds of action were rightly enjoinable. Roosevelt, for example, 'denounce[d] as wicked the proposition to secure a law which ... will legalize a blacklist or the secondary boycott, both of them the apt instruments of unmanly persecution'.[25] On this principle all but a few progressive Republicans agreed.

Democrats from all sections, on the other hand, agreed that the writ of injunction had been shamefully abused and that some effective legislation should be enacted to regulate its use. They

24. Theodore Roosevelt, Fifth Annual Message to Congress, in *The Works of Theodore Roosevelt*, (National Edition, 20 vols, New York, 1926), XV, pp. 284–5.
25. Roosevelt to Philander C. Knox, 21 October 1908, in Elting E. Morison *et al.*, eds, *Letters of Theodore Roosevelt* (8 vols, Cambridge, Mass., 1951–54), VI, p. 1312.

seemed ready to accept legislation such as the AFL proposed. The traditions of their party left Democrats readier than Republicans to acknowledge the existence of class divisions in society. It was also true that, as a minority party in the nation, but especially in the North, it needed to widen its voting base. That is why planter-statesmen of the New South so readily identified themselves with the cause of urban workers. Such a response on the part of the two parties left Gompers with little choice. While continuing to profess loyalty to 'independent nonpartisan action', the AFL leadership had in practice come very close to endorsing the Democratic ticket. But this was a shaky foundation for labour's new political strategy. The Democratic Party of William Jennings Bryan, and even that of Woodrow Wilson later, with its Jeffersonian tradition, its hetero-geneous competition, its domination by the South, and its highly instrumental reasons for encouraging the support of organised labour, was, as events would prove, a very uncertain ally.

It is not that the AFL endorsement did Democratic candidates much good. The Federation's political campaign lacked both funds and manpower. More importantly, it did not appear to swing many votes. The AFL failed to dislodge its main targets, like Cannon and Charles Littlefield of Maine. Across the board, Democratic gains in constituencies targeted by the AFL deviated little from the national swing. The labour campaign was wracked by divisions between national and local organisations and between Democratic, Republican and Socialist Party unionists. Often Democratic candidates were unattractive to labour voters, like Littlefield's opponent, who was persuaded only at the last moment to endorse the Bill of Grievances. It was not that American workers were unresponsive to appeals based on class interest but that they sometimes found it difficult to accept Democratic politicians as spokesmen for that interest.

Two years later, the AFL presented a similar list of demands to the national conventions of both parties. Again the Republicans responded coolly, while the Democratic platform incorporated most of labour's demands. Consequently, the AFL called upon its supporters to vote for the Democratic presidential nominee William Jennings Bryan, the first time that the Federation had endorsed a candidate for that office, as well as Democratic congressional candidates. Again, labour's electoral campaign, scanty and under-financed as it was, bore little fruit. Bryan was defeated by a decisive margin. In those congressional campaigns where labour was most active the Democrats made important gains, but these were too few to make more than a marginal difference to the complexion of Congress. After 1908 the AFL gave up its strategy of direct participation in election campaigns. Nevertheless, the Federation continued to endorse Democratic candidates for Congress and the presidency, including Woodrow Wilson in 1912 and 1916.

By 1908 the labour movement was becoming increasingly anxious about judicial interpretation of the Sherman Act in labour cases. The *Danbury Hatters* decision of 1908 suggested that any industrial action with an interstate dimension was liable to prosecution as a 'conspiracy in restraint of trade' in the federal courts. From that point modification of the Sherman Act became a paramount political concern of AFL leaders. Organised labour was only one of a number of groups calling for amendment of the Sherman Act. As we shall see in the following chapter, reform of the antitrust laws was one of the most controversial and difficult issues confronting national politics during the period between the National Civic Federation's abortive campaign in 1908 and the passage of the Clayton Act in 1914. It was generally accepted that some sort of exemption for labour organisations would be part of any solution to the problem, especially if that solution was to be devised by a Democratic Congress.

Woodrow Wilson and the Democratic Congress elected in 1912 proceeded to address the subject of antitrust legislation in 1914. The Clayton Act, which Gompers hyperbolically acclaimed as 'Labor's Magna Carta', grandly stated that 'The labor of a human being is not a commodity or article of commerce'; that trade unions were not illegal combinations under the terms of the antitrust law; and that the law should not be held to 'forbid or restrain the members of such organizations from lawfully carrying out the legitimate objects thereof'. Section 20 forbade the issue of injunctions in labour disputes 'unless necessary to prevent irreparable injury to property, or to a property right ... for which injury there is no adequate remedy at law'; and prevented the courts from restraining a list of labour practices, such as striking, picketing, boycotting or assembling, as long as they were carried out in a 'peaceful and lawful' manner.[26] The end-product left both Gompers and the president of the American Anti-Boycott Association (AABA) happy. As it turned out, the AABA president was more prescient in his assessment. The law's impact was undermined by the incorporation of phrases such as 'legitimate'

26. Henry S. Commager, ed., *Documents in American History* (2 vols, New York, 1949), II, pp. 279–81.

and 'lawful', which invited the courts to apply the same common law principles that they had always applied in adjudicating labour disputes. Section 20 prohibited injunctions 'unless necessary to prevent irreparable injury', but the danger of 'irreparable injury' was always cited as grounds for an injunction. The Supreme Court shortly affirmed that the courts' right to issue injunctions in labour disputes was in no important respects restrained by the Clayton Act, which it regarded as 'merely declaratory of the law as it stood before'.[27] If anything, the Clayton Act affirmed the injunctive powers of the federal courts. Indeed, the decade and a half following 1914 saw a greater use of injunctions than the twenty years preceding. Likewise, Section 6 did not declare that the antitrust law 'did not apply' to labour organisations, merely that their members were not prevented 'from lawfully carrying out the legitimate objects thereof'. Accordingly, the Supreme Court affirmed in 1921 that Section 6 did not exempt trade unions from 'accountability' under the Sherman Act where they departed from their 'normal and legitimate objects' and engaged in 'an actual combination or conspiracy in restraint of trade'.[28]

In the end Democrats, like Republicans, shied away from imposing radical restrictions on judicial authority. It was not that they were unaware of the significance of the language in which the law was cast; in leaving so much to the discretion of the courts, they must have known what the result would be. While possibly afraid of antagonising powerful business interests, most Democrats were moved, like Wilson, by a distaste for 'class legislation'. Wilson favoured an 'absolutely impartial enforcement of the law' and made it clear that he would not sign the bill if it contained a total exemption such as the AFL demanded.[29] Nor would he countenance an unequivocal authorisation of mass picketing or the secondary boycott. The legislation was designed to provide 'equal rights for all' but also to ensure that all were equally accountable for their actions. Democrats were no more prepared than Republicans to leave unions exempt from judicial scrutiny.

The fruits of labour's alliance with the Democratic Party were slender indeed. Congress established a Department of Labor in 1913, set up a National Conciliation Service, regulated the conditions of employment of seamen, imposed a statutory eight-

27. Herbert Hovenkamp, *Enterprise and American Law, 1836–1937* (Cambridge, Mass., 1991), p. 238.
28. Frankfurter and Green, *Labor Injunction*, p. 145.
29. Arthur S. Link, *Wilson: The New Freedom* (Princeton, N.J., 1956), p. 429.

hour day for railroad trainmen, and set in motion a vigorous, and mostly sympathetic, investigation of industrial relations, whose report, with its condemnation of management practice and its demands for legal protection of labour's right to organise and bargain collectively, was, in Montgomery's words, 'nothing less than a platform for an American labor party'.[30] But the essential legal position remained unchanged. Wilson had no special sympathy for the cause of organised labour. His party once in power had little need to propitiate labour and little to gain from chasing an evanescent 'labour vote'. At the same time, leading Democrats were anxious to demonstrate to business interests that they were safe and dependable. The party's leadership cadre was drawn from much the same social stratum as its Republican equivalents, small-town lawyers and businessmen, and was, at heart, as suspicious of the claims of organised labour. Big-city Democratic politicians were often connected to political machines with close ties to elements of the business community, only occasionally to organised labour. Though evidently in the process of change during the Wilson Era, the Democratic Party was still a long way away from the shape it was to adopt during the New Deal years.

Labour and the First World War

The outbreak of the First World War changed the industrial situation in ways which worked, at least in the short run, to labour's advantage. The wartime demand for labour increased workers' bargaining power and created an economic environment favourable to unionisation, while the imperatives of defence production forced the government to establish procedures for resolving labour disputes which, though temporary, prefigured in many ways the labour relations policy of the New Deal. Although postwar demobilisation, political reaction and employers' belligerency soon wiped out these gains, the wartime experience furnished useful precedents for the 1930s.

The immediate prewar years had already witnessed an epidemic of worker militancy, fuelled by resentment at the monotony, the dangers and the indignities of factory work. In textile mills, in clothing sweatshops, in electrical components factories, in metal-

30. Montgomery, *Fall of the House of Labor*, p. 361.

working shops and in coal-mines, as David Montgomery has shown, a 'new unionism' arose spontaneously out of shop-floor grievances, characterised by mass membership, militant, sometimes radical, leadership and a preference for industrial organisation. The outbreak of war in Europe both increased the demand for labour and, by placing inflationary pressure on living costs, fuelled wage demands. The incidence of strikes doubled between 1915 and 1916, which saw the highest number of disputes in any one year, a number which was nonetheless surpassed in 1917. Even after the United States had entered the war, several vital war industries were hit by strikes, including ship-building, coal-mining, copper-mining, munitions and meat-packing.

In order to deal with this unprecedented wave of strikes, and to remove other obstacles to industrial mobilisation, the government tightened its control over the nation's economy in the months after American intervention. A variety of agencies were established to manage the war economy. Certain key sectors, like railroads and coal-mines, were effectively brought under federal control; others were induced to accede to the government's wishes by the high profit-margins on war contracts and by its control, through the draft, of essential manpower. In the absence of an established administrative capacity to cope with such an emergency, the government was forced to rely on the managerial experience of businessmen, the so-called 'dollar-a-year men' who gave their services freely to the war effort but, in doing so, lent a heavily pro-business slant to the entire process. 'Loyal union leaders' also played a prominent part in the management of the war economy, especially in matters concerning labour relations. The AFL leadership seized the opportunity presented by the war to strengthen the political position of organised labour and cement its alliance with the Democratic Administration by dissuading workers from industrial action and by urging them to support the war. Gompers sat on the Advisory Committee of the Council for National Defense and the government-financed American Alliance for Labor and Democracy. Union representatives were appointed to many of the tripartite defence production committees, although they usually found themselves outvoted by the business and public representatives. They also found that several government departments and many of the key procurement agencies were indifferent or hostile to their claims for union recognition. Nevertheless, the continuing tide of labour unrest was menacing enough to force a more positive response from the federal government.

In order to prevent workers' grievances from obstructing war production, the government established a Mediation Commission and later, in 1918, a National War Labor Board (NWLB). Although the general policy was to ensure that neither side used the crisis to change existing standards, in so tight a job market government neutrality clearly tilted the balance in favour of labour. In fact, many of those responsible for managing the war effort, like Secretary of War Newton D. Baker and Secretary of Labor William B. Wilson, himself a former union official, were sympathetic to the goals of the 'responsible' labour movement; so were some of the public representatives on the bodies seeking to manage labour relations, like Felix Frankfurter and Frank P. Walsh. Under the benign leadership of Walsh, formerly chairman of the Commission on Industrial Relations, and (surprisingly) of former president William Howard Taft, the NWLB laid down a general labour relations policy. In return for a suspension of strikes, employers were urged to recognise trade unions, establish grievance procedures, an eight-hour day, union wage-scales and, in some cases, equal pay for women. The logic of its position – that labour relations should be regulated in the national interest, and that this required, in many cases, recognition of the right of workers to bargain collectively – anticipated New Deal labour policy. 'The NWLB ... instituted', says Melvyn Dubofsky, 'a mini-legal revolution.'[31] Although the Board had no statutory powers of enforcement, Wilson in effect made cooperation with its decisions mandatory. Recalcitrant employers came under intense pressure and were, at least in theory, liable to lose lucrative defence contracts and faced the possibility of government seizure of their plants and the drafting of their workers. Recalcitrant workers, including Socialists and radical unionists opposed to the war, were liable to government repression, with the more than tacit approval of the AFL leadership.

Trade union membership doubled between 1915 and 1920, reaching 5.1 million by the latter year. Unions flourished especially in sectors like railroads and coal-mining which were effectively under government control, and in those like clothing and munitions which profited especially from defence contracts. Where, as in clothing or mining, unions were already strong, enormous gains in terms of membership and employer recognition were possible. Organised labour even made inroads in what had formerly been forbidden territory, such as meat-packing and steel. Even non-union workers benefited from improved conditions, grievances procedures and the establishment of a shorter working day.

These gains proved ephemeral. The Armistice was followed by a precipitate demobilisation, resulting in widespread unemployment and economic dislocation. The following year, 1919, saw the greatest strike-wave in American history. Workers, freed from the inhibitions of wartime, sought to recover the ground lost to inflation, while animated also, Montgomery argues, by broader visions of postwar industrial democracy. At the same time, employers set out to break the unions and re-establish their work-place control. Sometimes abrogating agreements made during wartime, they refused to recognise unions or bargain collectively. They declined to cooperate further with wartime mediation procedures or engage in any tripartite planning of postwar reconstruction. Over 4 million workers took industrial action during 1919, including hundreds of thousands of miners, steel-workers and packinghouse employees, in a series of long and sometimes violent strikes. Without government support and under unfavourable economic conditions, unions fell prey to all their old enemies. Ethnic and racial divisions were ruthlessly exploited by employers, strikebreakers were shipped in, and police and National Guard units cleared the streets of strikers and pickets. Employer propaganda identified unions with the spectre of Bolshevik revolution that many of their more hysterical fellow-citizens saw stalking the land. The steel strike, for example, was described as 'an attempted revolution, not a strike'.[32] In the fevered atmosphere of postwar America, mass strikes alarmed the public.

Crucial, however, was the changing stance of government. The Democrats were fearful of identifying themselves too closely with organised labour, now the wartime emergency was over. They were nervous about the political impact of high prices and disruption and sensitive to public fears about law and order. The government's hopes for voluntary compromise were frustrated by workers' militancy and employers' intransigence. Wilson himself, though preoccupied with the peace settlement, warned against strike action and was sufficiently outraged by the coal strike to send federal troops into the coalfields and to the steel town of Gary, Indiana. An Administration once regarded as friendly to organised labour was now deploying federal troops to deal with domestic disturbances on

32. Robert K. Murray, *The Red Scare: A Study in National Hysteria, 1919–1920* (Minneapolis, 1955), p. 148.

a scale unprecedented since Reconstruction. The entire episode exposed the fragility of labour's political strategy, but it also demonstrated that, without the assistance of allies in govern- ment, organised labour was still too weak to take on the industrial and social power of the giant corporations.

Whatever happened to the American Left?

One of the striking features of American politics during most of this century has been the absence of a party of the Left. Unlike most other major industrial countries, the United States lacks a major social democratic or labour party. The absence of a substantial left-wing voice in American politics leaves a vast silence in American political discourse, excluding a whole spectrum of ideas from mainstream debate.

It was not always so. The golden age of the American Left was the early twentieth century. If ever it had a significant political presence it was then. The first two decades of this century were the heyday of the Socialist Party of America, a radical, class-conscious organisation which, at its peak in 1912, attracted nearly a million votes, 6 per cent of the electorate – easily comparable to the percentages polled by the British Labour Party before 1914. Indeed, among European socialist parties, only the German SPD enjoyed substantially greater support. And support for the Socialist Party had been growing steadily since 1900, with every expectation that its growth would continue. That it did not do so raises interesting questions about American politics and society and the relationship between them.

The Socialist Party of America, founded in 1900, was, unlike the doctrinaire and sectarian Socialist Labor Party, essentially a social democratic party committed to a parliamentary strategy for the attainment of power and a 'gradualist' approach to the achieve-ment of a socialist commonwealth. The party's national platform was definitely Marxist in its analysis of industrial society and its dedication to the ultimate goal of the socialist commonwealth, but it also incorporated a large number of 'immediate demands', designed to demonstrate the party's practical usefulness and to nourish its electoral base. Many of these were not strictly socialist. For example, the 1912 platform included an advanced social justice plank and a firm commitment to the conservation of natural resources, neither of which would have been out of place in a progressive manifesto. In this version, American socialism took on some of the character of a left-wing progressivism, especially at a local level, where municipal 'sewer socialism' attracted many voters who spurned the national ticket, enabling the party to elect mayors in cities from Lynn to Minneapolis. With its commitment to neighbourhood concerns as well as job conditions, the SPA in many localities 'resembled a labor party as much as a revolutionary organization – if not more so'.[33]

The SPA commanded the support of a substantial minority of trade unionists. Socialist candidates and resolutions regularly attracted between one-quarter and one-third of the votes at AFL conventions. Several national unions and local labour federations were under Socialist control. Socialism thrived in unions whose immigrant workforce had been weaned on socialist dialectics, like the German workers who constituted most of the membership of the United Brewery Workers or the East European Jews who formed the core of the garment trade unions. As J.H. Laslett has shown, where earlier traditions of labour radicalism were strong, measured, for example, by former association with the Knights of Labor, as among the shoemakers and many segments of the UMW, socialism also flourished. Industrial unions, which rejected the narrow, conservative focus of craft unionism, tended to be more hospitable to the Left. Finally, the Industrial Workers of the World (IWW), a radical anarcho-syndicalist organisation known inexplicably as the 'Wobblies', worked among groups of workers spurned by the AFL, like Western lumbermen, migrant farm-workers and Eastern factory hands. Apart from the IWW, the strategy of SPA unionists was to work within the AFL in the hope that, by a process of 'boring from within', the Federation might be converted to socialism.

For a while, during the decade or so before American intervention in the First World War, socialism enjoyed something of a fashionable *éclat* among writers and intellectuals. It presented what seemed like a certain path out of the intellectual difficulties of progressivism. A number of prominent writers and journalists joined the party, including Upton Sinclair, Jack London, Robert Hunter and William English Walling, while many others, like Lincoln Steffens, were attracted to socialist ideas without ever becoming converted.

Apart from the IWW, the most interesting and distinctive component of early twentieth-century American socialism was

33. Montgomery, *Fall of the House of Labor*, 286.

located in the lower Midwest and Southwest, in states like Kansas, Oklahoma, Texas and Arkansas where the SPA polled some of its largest percentages. Here the SPA appealed to railroad workers, lumbermen and miners, but also to migrant farm-workers and tenants, who responded to socialist proposals for a maximum legal rate of interest, state-owned grain elevators and assistance with the repayment of loans. Prairie socialism was, according to one assessment, 'an aggravated case of Populism'.[34] It focused on similar issues and retained some of the style of the earlier movement, with its camp meetings, its songs and its air of evangelical fervour. The leading socialist journal in terms of circulation, the *Appeal to Reason*, which at its peak sold as many as 760,000 copies, was published not in Chicago or New York but in Girard, Kansas. The *Appeal* offered a peculiarly American brand of socialism, mixing Marxist teachings with local traditions of radical protest and a strong admixture of evangelical religion. Thus socialism drew heavily on native American traditions – the Knights of Labor, Populism, evangelical Protestantism, Christian Socialism – as well as European Marxism. It was not an exotic plant, composed of alien doctrines and alien membership, but had at least some of its roots planted firmly in American soil. Its recurrent presidential candidate Eugene Debs, an ex-Populist, former leader of the American Railway Union and late convert to socialism, who, as his biographer shows, carried his faith with a strong infusion of Christianity and drew heavily on the traditions of American republicanism, 'helped evolve an indigenous democratic Socialism' which transcended ethnic, regional and occupational differences.[35]

Debs's 900,000 votes represented the SPA's best electoral performance. Why the party failed to convert a larger proportion of the electorate and why it failed to build upon its early successes is a question that has engaged historians for many decades. Many who have considered this question have used it as the occasion for a disquisition on the exceptional character of American society and culture. For example, Louis Hartz argued that the United States was 'born free', without a feudal past and without a tradition of class distinctions, and that almost all Americans subscribed to a liberal consensus. Socialists therefore were left out on a limb. Such explanations operate at too high a level of abstraction to carry conviction, and by their very nature they are untestable.

34. James Weinstein, *The Decline of Socialism in America* (New York, 1967), p. 16.
35. Nick Salvatore, *Eugene V. Debs: Citizen and Socialist* (Urbana, Ill., 1982), p. 225.

The German socialist Werner Sombart, in an early attempt at the problem, attributed the failure of American socialism to the success of American capitalism. The American working class benefited from an exceptional level of affluence. As Sombart appealingly put it, 'all socialistic utopias come to nothing on roast beef and apple pie'.[36] But roast beef and apple pie did not form a regular element in the diet of most American workers, especially unskilled labourers, who lived, as we have seen, close to the margin of subsistence. Sombart also pointed to the impact of social mobility, in the particular form of the Western frontier, on class consciousness. Social historians have highlighted what look like quite striking rates of occupational mobility and property ownership among American workers, although in each case only a minority was able to benefit. Here, too, it is dangerous to extrapolate from social circumstances to social and political ideas.

Another general explanation which is at the same time convincing and unsatisfying concerns the impact of mass immigration. Many socialists believed, like Engels, that the fatal hour of capitalism would not strike as long as the American working class was composed in the majority by foreign immigrants. Ethnic differences divided the working class, obscured class differences and hindered the development of a common class consciousness. As Ira Katznelson, among others, has argued, American workers suffered from a 'separation of consciousness': they thought of themselves as 'workers at work, ethnics . . . at home'.[37] Most immigrants to the United States around the turn of the century were from peasant backgrounds, ignorant of industrial society, accustomed to a hierarchical social order and bringing with them what Oscar Handlin calls 'the peasant's inherent distrust of radicalism'.[38] Most were also Catholics. Marc Karson sees the Roman Catholic Church as having played a particularly important role in turning American workers away from socialism. Since the 1891 papal encyclical *Rerum novarum* the Church had taken a vigorously anti-socialist line. The Church, on the other hand, supported workers' demands for a living wage and reasonable working conditions and accepted the need for trade union organisations to enforce them. That American trade unions met the Church's criteria for acceptability is evident in

36. Werner Sombart, *Why Is There No Socialism in America?* (trans. Patricia M. Hocking and C.T. Husbands, London, 1976), p. 106.

37. Ira Katznelson, *City Trenches: Urban Politics and the Patterning of Class in the United States* (New York, 1981), p. 18.

38. Quoted in J.H.M. Laslett, 'Reply', in Laslett and S.M. Lipset, eds, *Failure of a Dream: Essays on the History of American Socialism* (New York, 1974), p. 248.

its failure even to consider the creation of a separate Catholic union movement, as in many European countries. For the unions to have endorsed socialism would have been to drive many Catholics out of the labour movement. On the other hand, many immigrants, from Germany, from the Jewish Pale, later from Finland, had learned their socialism in Europe and brought their faith to America. The American working class consisted of numerous segments, some of which responded to socialism and some of which did not. What we cannot afford to do, as Aileen Kraditor does, is to substitute one form of essentialism for another by asserting that class identification did not determine the social and political behaviour of American workers but that ethnic identifications did. We do know that American workers were extraordinarily militant at the workplace, as measured in the incidence of strikes and other forms of industrial action, though less often in politics, and that is what needs to be explained.

As we have seen, the leadership of the AFL was, with few exceptions, hostile to socialism, clinging doggedly to a nonpartisan strategy which amounted to a *de facto* alliance with the Democratic Party. As William Dick points out, only in the United States did the union leadership stand so resolutely apart from the socialist movement. Although we cannot conclude that a different set of leaders could have briskly marched their followers into the Socialist camp, there is no doubt that union officials enjoyed substantial influence through the manipulation of union rules, through the distribution of patronage, and through their connections with the Catholic Church, which was, as we have seen, militantly anti-socialist, and the Democratic Party. The AFL leadership not only kept its distance from the Socialist Party but also turned aside various proposals to create a labour party which, while non-socialist, would, like its British and Canadian counterparts, represent the interests of industrial workers more effectively than either of the two major parties. The Federation was dominated by craft unions which were committed to narrowly defined particular-istic goals. Believing that they could more effectively protect their members' economic interests by shop-floor action, they felt that the limited political objectives that they did have could be achieved through the existing political parties. At the same time, the SPA leadership repeatedly resisted calls for a labour party, fearing that such an organisation, if it was controlled by Gompers and his cronies, would do little to advance the interests of socialism. Exceptionally among advanced industrial countries, the unions and the socialist movement had separate intellectual and organisational histories which had diverged greatly by the second decade of the century.

Gompers doubted, in any case, that there was any substantial unattached 'labour vote' waiting to be captured by a socialist or labour party. As one old miner sadly commented, 'Poor old Debs! . . . The people wouldn't vote for him the way they should have. He told people the truth, but they went on voting Democrat and Republican.'[39] Certainly in the nineteenth century the large numbers of votes polled suggest that most male workers were voting for Republican or Democratic candidates. But by the early twentieth century turnout was beginning to fall off dramatically. Working-class voters seem to have become detached from the electorate, or in the case of immigrants never to have become attached to the electorate, in larger proportions than their more affluent counterparts. There is no doubt that more demanding registration laws contributed to this outcome, but it is equally likely that working-class voters were alienated from the political process because they did not find that it spoke to them directly or catered for their immediate needs. The decreased working-class participation in elections in the twentieth century is equivalent, notes Walter Dean Burnham, to 'a gap in the active American electorate that was filled elsewhere by socialist parties'.[40]

It was not, claims Richard Oestreicher, that American workers were unresponsive to appeals based on class interests but that the American political system made it hard for them to mobilise politically. Most obviously, the central importance of the contest for the presidency militated against the organisation of a third party – any third party, whether Labour, Socialist, Prohibitionist, Populist or progressive. A vote for a third party-candidate, who, almost by definition, would have little chance of victory, appeared to be a wasted vote. It was tempting, therefore, except for the most dedicated of followers, to vote for the major party candidate who better reflected their views. In a system governed by simple majority voting it is difficult to build up support by a process of accretion. Third parties have no patronage to distribute, no 'loaves and fishes' with which to reward ambitious supporters. Even when they were able to attain local office, the power of elected Socialist officials was

39. Quoted in Salvatore, *Eugene V. Debs*, p. 268.
40. Walter Dean Burnham, 'The United States: the politics of heterogeneity', in Richard Rose, ed., *Electoral Behavior: A Comparative Handbook* (London, 1974), p. 679.

severely constrained by the federal system. It was therefore difficult for a socialist party in America to build up its strength gradually or to acquire leverage within a multi-party system. According to the socialist journalist William English Walling, 'The labor movement in this country has taken the shape of a business organization instead of a political machine, not because labor fears to go into politics, but because the game does not seem worth the candle'.[41]

Whatever potential existed for Socialist expansion was snuffed out by the First World War and its aftermath. The SPA (unlike European socialist parties) opposed the nation's intervention in the European conflict and continued to speak out against the war effort. This resulted in the defection of a substantial number of pro-war Socialists, including some of the more prominent figures in the party. The party's overt opposition to the war left it open to prosecution under wartime espionage and sedition laws. Debs and other leading Socialists were arrested, and the party's funds sucked into legal defence and bail payments, while the Socialist press was denied access to the mails and party meetings were frequently banned. Small-town locals were especially hard-hit by government repression. Nevertheless, the party survived the war largely intact. Indeed, it fed on widespread grass-roots dissatisfaction with a war the reason for which many ordinary Americans did not understand. Debs was able, while still serving time in Atlanta Penitentiary, to win as many votes as a Socialist candidate for the presidency in 1920 as he had gained in 1912 (though admittedly out of an electorate doubled by the enfranchisement of women). The IWW, on the other hand, found it hard to recover from the severe repression and vigilante violence that its militant anti-war stance left it open to.

Much of the vigour of the party was lost in 1919, when the newly established Communist International demanded that socialist parties throughout the world follow its direction. A segment of the Socialist Party of America seceded to form a Communist Party (and, indeed, for a while two communist parties), which was affiliated with the Third International. Most of the leadership of the SPA, realising that the Soviet experience could not readily be applied to American conditions, declined to follow its lead. However, many of the more vigorous and radical elements of the party were lost. In particular, the Foreign Language Federations, representing groups of recent immigrants, which had gained phenomenally in strength during the preceding decade, defected, weakening the links

41. Quoted in Keller, *Regulating a New Economy*, p. 133.

between the SPA and the immigrant communities. After 1919 the party remained a rump, unappealing to radicals and suspect to mainstream opinion.

The newly established Communist Party (CP) immediately fell foul of the Red Scare that flared up during the summer and autumn of 1919. The economic dislocations caused by over-rapid demobilisition, the unprecedented number of strikes that broke out in that year and the impact of a number of anarchist bomb attacks briefly aroused fears that a Bolshevik revolution was possible in America. Now revolutionary socialists were regarded as a serious menace, rather than an occasional irritant. The offices of the CP and the IWW were raided and their newspapers suppressed. Approximately 6,000 arrests were made, on a somewhat indiscriminate basis, and 249 radical aliens were deported to Russia. The SPA was largely unaffected by direct repression. But the political atmosphere of the 1920s, like that of the McCarthy Era, was inhospitable to the expression of radical views. Rather than maintaining personal and intellectual links with the political mainstream, the party was marginalised, with little influence on political discourse during succeeding decades.

Of course, to talk, as many have, of the 'failure' of American socialism assumes the possibility of its success. In retrospect, this was never likely. Yet what doomed the party to oblivion was not so much the intrinsic character of American society as, on the one hand, the structure of the American political system, which marginalised third parties of whatever complexion, and, on the other hand, the structure of American trade unions, which drove a wedge between the industrial and political organisations of the working class.

CHAPTER FOUR

Progressivism: The New Political Order

The riddle of progressivism

The early years of the twentieth century are commonly known as the 'Progressive Era', a period in which a group of reformers who called themselves 'progressives' addressed themselves to some of the problems of industrial society, problems such as poverty, political corruption and the concentration of economic power. And they proposed to do so by exercising the powers of government. The Progressive Era witnessed a dramatic growth in the power of the American state, though building, as we have seen, upon the regulatory experience of the previous generation; equally importantly, it saw a fundamental recasting of the institutions of government and with it, the creation of 'a new political order'.

To Benjamin P. De Witt, writing in 1915 what was probably the first comprehensive account of the 'progressive movement', its character and object were clear. Despite differences in emphasis, he insisted, the progressive factions within both political parties and the multifarious groups agitating on behalf of specific reforms constituted a coherent movement. It was 'a well-designed and well-intentioned attempt to prevent special interests from continuing to use the national government for their own selfish purposes', supported by virtually all sections of the community except for 'a minority of corrupt politicians and monopolists'.[1]

It is many years since historians have felt able to write with such confidence about the character and composition of the 'progressive movement'. In the 1950s and 1960s, particularly in the wake of the publication of Richard Hofstadter's influential *The Age of Reform* (1955), scholars began to examine in more detail the precise

1. Benjamin P. De Witt, *The Progressive Movement* (New York, 1915), pp. xix, 26.

identity of the progressives. Support for reform was variously attributed to Midwestern farmers, urban middle-class citizens suffering from 'an upheaval in status', corporate executives seeking to use the power of the state to consolidate their control over the economic order, working-class Americans preoccupied with immediate problems 'of the bread and butter type', and members of a technocratic elite impatient to create a more orderly and efficient society. Nor was there any greater consensus about objectives. Examination of the reformers' views on issues ranging from control of the trusts to prohibition revealed divisions of opinion which undermined still further the supposition that progressivism possessed the 'universal character' supposed by its earliest historians. In 1970, at a time when historical interpretations had reached new levels of luxuriant variety, Peter Filene suggested that what historians customarily described as the 'progressive movement' never really existed. If a social 'movement' comprises a number of individuals consciously and deliberately acting together to attain certain common goals, then the so-called 'progressive movement' was not a movement. Historians, as he points out, have signally failed to establish the existence of any 'unanimity of purpose either on a programmatic or on a philosophical level', and their attempt 'simply to generalize about the movement's membership has produced baffling inconsistencies'. They have experienced so much difficulty in defining 'progressive' policies and in identifying the 'progressives' that they would be better advised to abandon altogether the concept of a 'progressive movement'.[2]

Most historians have assimilated Filene's strictures into their interpretation of progressivism. The concept of a unitary 'progressive movement', which seemed so obvious to De Witt and his contemporaries, no longer commands the respect of the profession. Instead, historians like John D. Buenker accept that any meaningful interpretation must acknowledge the multiplicity of groups and interests, forming 'shifting coalitions around different issues', that contributed to progressive reform.[3] Progressivism, then, was not a 'movement', with a fixed membership, a common programme and an agreed set of leaders, not to mention an institutional framework. It embraced disparate elements in society,

2. Peter Filene, 'An obituary for the progressive movement' *American Quarterly* 22 (1970), pp. 27, 28, 32, 33.
3. Filene quoted in John D. Buenker, 'Essay', in John D. Buenker, John C. Burnham and Robert H. Crunden, *Progressivism* (Cambridge, Mass., 1977), p. 31.

including farmers, trade unions, business organisations, middle-class professionals and women's groups. Indeed, by the time the historiographical trawl was completed, barely any section of the community could be found which was not enrolled in some progressive cause or other. Each group, however, harboured a very different conception of what problems most needed to be addressed and what were the appropriate solutions. Their attention was directed to everything from banks to booze, railroads to racetrack gambling, embracing along the way conservation of natural resources, pure food and drugs, antitrust, education, child labour, housing reform, direct election of senators, women's suffrage, prohibition and much else besides. Their reform agendas were not necessarily consistent, nor even compatible, with one another.

Nevertheless, these miscellaneous endeavours shared certain common features which make it sensible, despite the diversity of their concerns, to continue to use the label 'progressive' to describe them. Progressivism was not so much a movement as a 'frame of mind', a set of moral attitudes and largely unspoken assumptions that guided men and women in their actions. Robert Crunden found, as have many scholars, a strongly religious impulse expressing itself in even the most secular activities of progressive reformers. Progressivism, he concludes, was 'a form of displaced Protestantism'.[4] For all their differences, argues John C. Burnham, reformers belonging to the 'progressive generation' shared a commitment to the ideal of a public interest, as against that of individuals, sections, or classes; they subscribed to an ethic of social responsibility and 'service'; they believed in the shaping influence of the social environment on human behaviour; and, though inspired by scientific ideals of efficiency and rational planning, they at the same time invested their actions with an intense moral fervour. This conjunction between a deeply felt moral purpose, what Frederic C. Howe described as an 'evangelistic psychology', and an equally profound commitment to the ideals of applied science perhaps denotes more clearly than anything else the special character of the 'progressive ethos'.

Progressivism was also a way of acting politically. It involved certain modes of investigation, publicity and pressure-group politics, certain modes of bureaucratic decision-making. Over a wide range of policy-making areas, reformers tended to create

4. Robert M. Crunden, 'Essay', in Buenker et al. *Progressivism*, p. 31, p. 76.

broadly similar institutional arrangements in order to realise their intentions, institutional arrangements which, in aggregate, constituted the basis for a new American state.

In the first volume of his history of *Our Times*, the journalist Mark Sullivan reflected on the disposition of what he called the 'forgotten man'. By 1900, he wrote, the average American had come to feel 'that he was being "put upon" by something he couldn't quite see or get his fingers on . . . that his freedom of action, his opportunity to do as he pleased, was being frustrated in ways mysterious in their origin and operation'. The 'purpose of the average man to make himself heard was part of a mood which determined much of the political and social history of this quarter-century; a mood in which the average American thought of himself as the under dog in a political and economic controversy, in which he was determined to fight for himself'.[5] While historians have, perhaps rightly, cast doubt on the notion of progressivism as a great popular movement, it is clear that a pronounced upsurge of public feeling was an important element in the politics of the period. No one can read far into the written records of the period without becoming aware of the 'very unhealthy condition of excitement and irritation in the popular mind' that troubled President Roosevelt in 1906, along with many of his fellow politicians.[6]

How can we account for this sense of 'vulnerability' felt by ordinary Americans at the beginning of the century? Certainly the 'crisis of the 1890s' engendered fears of social conflict and shook people's confidence in the future. A further precipitant was the rise of big business. As we have seen, a wave of mergers and combinations between 1897 and 1904 dramatically transformed the American industrial landscape. Now a relatively small number of giant companies dominated the scene. The fact that we now know how insecure the market situation of some of these conglomerates was, especially in view of their grossly overcapitalised asset structure, does not gainsay the impact of their appearance on public perceptions.

This process of consolidation had alarming implications. At the very least it would leave consumers open to exploitation through high monopoly prices, as well as the sale of inferior products. The contemporary inflation, though modest by recent standards,

5. Mark Sullivan, *Our Times* (6 vols, New York, 1926–35), I, pp. 70, 137.
6. Theodore Roosevelt to William Howard Taft, 15 March 1906, in Elting Morison *et al.*, eds, *Letters of Theodore Roosevelt* (8 vols, Cambridge, Mass., 1951–54), V, p. 183.

alarmed those familiarised, by the experience of a quarter-century, to falling prices and gave substance to such fears. Progressivism, as historians like David Thelen have pointed out, was at least in part a consumers' movement, concerned with issues like railroad rates, tariff duties and pure food. At the same time, industrial giants like Standard Oil, by their commanding presence, would close off entre-preneurial opportunity in vast areas of the American economy. This had more than economic implications; it entailed a fundamental reorientation of American society and culture. The economic order, to nineteenth-century Americans, did not merely produce material benefits; notionally at least, it offered individuals an opportunity to put themselves to the test, securing the rewards that their talents and endeavour warranted. The decline of opportunity, therefore, entailed a drastic redefinition of what America stood for. What was at stake, observed Judge Peter Grosscup in 1906, was 'the soul of republican America ... The loss that republican America now confronts is the loss of individual hope and prospect – the suppression of the instinct that ... has made us a nation of individually independent and prosperous people.'[7] Nobody stated this concern more eloquently than Woodrow Wilson in the presidential campaign of 1912. It was because of the peculiar cultural and moral values that were attached to the economic system in the United States that a process of industrial consolidation, which was common to all advanced economies, should there produce so dramatic and wide-ranging a political reaction.

The rise of big business had still graver implications. Might not democracy itself be in jeopardy? How could republican government survive in the face of such concentrations of economic power? Ever since the controversy over the Bank of the United States in the Jacksonian Era, Americans had entertained fears that moneyed corporations would seek to convert their wealth into political power. Again Woodrow Wilson stated the theme most persuasively. 'If America is not to have free enterprise', he warned, 'then she can have freedom of no sort whatever.' 'If monopoly persists, monopoly will always sit at the helm of government. ... If there are men in this country big enough to own the government of the United States, they are going to own it.'[8] Indeed, there appeared to be plenty of

7. Quoted in Richard Hofstadter, *The Age of Reform: From Bryan to F.D.R.* (New York, 1955), p. 221.
8. Quoted in Arthur S. Link, *Wilson: The Road to the White House* (Princeton, N.J., 1947), p. 514; Woodrow Wilson, *The New Freedom* (New York, 1913), p. 286.

evidence that the very outcome predicted by republican political theory was coming to pass.

The influence of 'muckraking' journalism was widely acknowledged by contemporary commentators, such as President Roosevelt, who conferred that title upon it. Senator Albert Beveridge maintained that 'the great volume of the cheaper magazines which are circulating among the people ... have wrought almost a mental and moral revolution among the people'.[9] What was significant was what they told people, and what they mostly told people about was corruption. The dominant theme to emerge was the corrupt linkage between business and government: what Richard L. McCormick calls 'the discovery that business corrupts politics'.[10] This discovery was precipitated not only by muckraking journalism, but also by a series of official investigations in almost every state of the Union during the early years of the century which produced alarming disclosures of corruption and business influence in government. In New York State the cathartic event was the revelation of the political activities of the life insurance companies; in the Midwestern states the political influence of the railroads aroused resentment. '[T]he people *know*', said Kansas editor William Allen White, 'that the attorneys of the railroads are prostituting local government.'[11] It is McCormick's contention that this 'discovery that business corrupts politics' acted as a catalyst, drawing together a number of political trends and providing a specific object for public anxieties to work upon. In that sense it was a key moment in the development of progressivism as a national phenomenon.

The paradox of antitrust

According to Thomas K. McCraw, 'the trust question dominated political discourse in America from the 1880s until the start of the First World War'.[12] The term 'trust', which actually referred to the specific legal form taken by some of the earliest industrial

9. Albert J. Beveridge to Joseph L. Bristow, 16 July 1910, Beveridge MSS, Library of Congress.

10. Richard L. McCormick, 'The discovery that business corrupts politics: a reappraisal of the origins of progressivism' *American Historical Review*, 86 (1981), pp. 247–74.

11. William Allen White to Theodore Roosevelt, 15 March 1907, Microfilm Edition of the Theodore Roosevelt Papers, Reel 72.

12. Thomas K. McCraw, *Prophets of Regulation* (Cambridge, Mass., 1984), p. 79.

consolidations, was applied to both loose combinations in restraint of trade, or cartels, and tight combinations formed by the merger of two or more formerly separate companies into a completely new one. It embraced both agreements between small firms that would make it possible for them to retain an independent existence in a harshly competitive world and mergers by which smaller firms lost their identity altogether. The legal and economic dimensions of the trust issue were fearfully complex, but they were complicated still further by the moral and political freight carried by such concepts as competition and monopoly.

As we have seen, Congress confronted the issue at an earlier date, at the time of the first wave of trust formation. Its efforts, not surprisingly, were hesitant and confused. In effect, the Sherman Act, which remained for decades the basis of American antitrust policy, did no more than write established common law principles into federal statute, so that offences could be prosecuted in the national courts. However, in doing so, it imported into federal law a fair degree of ambiguity. The common law was developed in a world of small business where restraint of trade was caused either by government favour or local collusion, rather than resulting from the scale of advanced industrial enterprise. The ancient doctrines of 'restraint of trade' and 'monopolising' were not easily applicable to the complex world of modern business. Nor was the traditional distinction between 'reasonable' and 'unreasonable' restraint of trade, which some assumed had been carried over into federal law.

Enforcement of the act was the responsibility of federal law officers, and in particular district attorneys, who were heavily burdened with other work. No extra resources were provided. Successive attorney-generals exhibited either indifference or hostility to the law, bringing only those cases which it was politically impossible to avoid, and then with little conviction. Only eighteen cases were prosecuted under the Sherman Act prior to 1901, most of them against loose combinations. The result was to discourage firms from entering into cartel agreements, whereas it appeared that tight combinations, or mergers, were exempt from prosecution. The decision of the Supreme Court in *US* v. *E.C. Knight Co.* (1896) – that, since the government had failed to demonstrate that an amalgamation of sugar refineries had any direct impact on interstate commerce, no offence against federal law had been proved – was widely taken as meaning that the Sherman Act did not apply to tight combinations. This encouraged companies enduring uncomfortable levels of competition to go down that road. When a second, and greater, wave of combinations came after 1897, most took the form of mergers or holding companies rather than the looser arrangements that had prevailed in the past. Thus the nature of the antitrust law, and the judicial construction placed upon it, greatly influenced the pattern of industrial consolidation in the United States, in comparison with countries like Britain and Germany where the law looked more kindly upon cartels.

The merger movement of 1897–1904 brought the trust issue very much into the public eye. Newspapers and magazine articles on the subject proliferated, while the issue was aired in a series of high-level conferences and government investigations. Some business leaders insisted that no harmful effects would follow from the growth of monopoly, regarding it as the natural outcome of a Darwinian process of natural selection. This was, however, a minority view. At the other extreme were those like William Jennings Bryan who, regarding monopoly as a menace to the economic and political welfare of the country, demanded that the trusts be broken up into their constituent parts, a stance which was as unrealistic economically as the first was politically. Most informed commentators gravitated to one of two positions. The first was predicated on the assumption that monopoly was unnatural and unstable and could not survive under normal conditions. Given full publicity and a fair field of combat, young and vigorous rivals would come forth to challenge Goliath. The second, held by many business leaders, especially those associated with the National Civic Federation (NCF), and economists such as Richard Ely, John B. Clark and Jeremiah Jenks, was that combination was, in its economic and social consequences, essentially beneficial. Indeed, in those industries characterised by substantial economies of scale and a high ratio of fixed to variable costs competition was at best unenforceable, at worst destructive. Although their behaviour should be subject to federal supervision, the antitrust law should be amended to permit 'reasonable' combinations in restraint of trade, replacing the present categorical ban with a more flexible statute, one which was more easily adjustable to real conditions in the business world. This was the view which would be taken by President Theodore Roosevelt.

Roosevelt, after his adventitious accession to the presidency following the assassination of William McKinley, confronted the trust question early in his term (1901–9). His first Message to Congress was regarded as moderate in tone and gainsaid his reputation as something of a political loose cannon. It therefore came as a shock when, in 1902, Roosevelt ordered his attorney-general to prosecute the Northern Securities Company. The Northern Securities Company was a combination of three railroads which created a virtual transportation monopoly in the northwestern quarter of the country. It was a holding company, but, unlike Olney in the sugar trust prosecution, Attorney-General Philander C. Knox stressed in his suit the impact of the combination on competition, arguing, as Olney had failed to do, that the purchase of stocks in itself had the effect of restraining trade and therefore contravened the Sherman Act – a view of the case which the Supreme Court eventually endorsed. The Northern Securities prosecution had a dramatic political impact. Judging by the press reaction, the president's action met with public approval. It appeared, superficially at least, that the trusts were at last being brought to heel. Roosevelt later claimed that this was one of the great achievements of his Administration because 'through it we emphasized in signal fashion, as in no other way could be emphasized, the fact that the most powerful men in the country were held to accountability before the law'. This, perhaps, was the principal point that he wished to establish. The actual economic effect of this, as of other such antitrust suits, on the structure of railroad rates was insubstantial. What did matter, as Roosevelt claimed, was that it 'definitely established the power of the Government to deal with all great corporations'.[13] He proceeded to build upon it with a series of further prosecutions, forty-three in all during his Administration, facilitated by the creation in 1903 of a Bureau of Corporations in the Department of Commerce and Labor and the provision, in the Expedition Act of the same year, of special funds earmarked for antitrust prosecutions.

The Supreme Court decisions in the *Northern Securities* (1904) and *Swift* (1906) cases appeared to affirm the Sherman Act's status, prefigured in earlier cases like *Addyston Pipe* (1899), as a categorical ban on any combination in restraint of trade. Rather than applying only to cases of 'unreasonable' restraint of trade, which by common law criteria meant those which sought to exclude third parties from the marketplace or which were judged detrimental to the public interest, for example by setting inordinately high prices, the law was now taken to cover all combinations in restraint of trade. The Sherman Act, as now interpreted, set down a standard of 'full and free competition' which both economists and business leaders

---

13. Roosevelt to George B. Cortelyou, 11 August 1904, in *Letters*, IV, p. 886; Theodore Roosevelt, *An Autobiography* (New York, 1913), p. 430.

considered unrealistic. As Justice Oliver Wendell Holmes Jr. commented with reference to the *Northern Securities* decision, the Court was engaged not so much in 'a regulation of commerce' as 'an attempt to reconstruct society'.[14]

Though angered by Holmes's dissent, Roosevelt shared his anxiety about the practical consequences of so absolute a construction of the Sherman law. A few months after the Northern Securities prosecution he told Congress, 'Our aim is not to do away with corporations; on the contrary, these big aggregations are an inevitable development of modern industrialization, and the effort to destroy them would be futile [or] work the utmost mischief to the entire body politic'. His aim, he explained in 1906, was to 'secure such rigorous and adequate control and supervision of the combinations as to prevent their injuring the public'. There must be some authority vested in the national government to monitor the actions of the trusts and prevent abuse of their power. Corporations that behaved themselves, however, would be exempt from prosecution. As he explained, 'We must draw the line against misconduct, not against wealth'.[15] Roosevelt wished to use the antitrust law, not to enforce competition, but to establish the rule of law in the marketplace.

In accordance with this philosophy, Roosevelt and his Commissioner of Corporations, James R. Garfield, carried out a policy of selective non-enforcement of the Sherman Act which constituted, in effect, a usurpation of judicial powers. 'Bad' trusts, like Standard Oil and the meatpackers, were punished by publishing the reports of federal investigations into their misdeeds and ultimately by antitrust suits. 'Good' trusts, and it seemed that US Steel, International Harvester and other companies connected with the Morgan interests came into this category, were more leniently treated: Bureau of Corporations reports on their activities were kept under wraps, and they were not prosecuted. What differentiated US Steel and other Morgan interests from 'bad' trusts like Standard Oil was far from apparent, unless it was simply their readiness to talk, with the appearance of frankness, to government officials.

This informal system of control was clearly unsatisfactory, de-

14. Quoted in Martin J. Sklar, *The Corporate Reconstruction of American Capitalism, 1890–1916: The Market, Law and Politics* (Cambridge, 1988), p. 141.
15. Theodore Roosevelt, Second Annual Message to Congress, in *The Works of Theodore Roosevelt*, (National Edition, 20 vols, New York, 1926), XV, pp. 141–2; Sixth Annual Message, in *Works*, XV, p. 366.

pendent as it was on a series of gentlemen's agreements between corporate managers and government officials. Moreover, as Roosevelt's Democratic opponents pointedly reminded him, it operated in blatant contravention of the antitrust law. It finessed, rather than resolved, the contradiction between law and economics created by the Sherman Act. Therefore Roosevelt asked Congress for 'a grant of supervisory power ... over these big corporations engaged in interstate commerce'.[16] Garfield's successor Herbert Knox Smith agreed: 'we must recognize concentration, supervise it, and regulate it. We must do this positively, through an active federal agency, and not merely by the negative prohibition of penal law.'[17] The Administration's plans coalesced with a movement to amend the Sherman Act that was masterminded by officials of the National Civic Federation. The corporate leaders associated with the NCF no longer challenged the right of the federal government to regulate their behaviour, but they objected to the disruptive force of a judicial interpretation which left any business contract or combination potentially liable to indictment. Negotiations between NCF officials like Seth Low and Ralph Easley and the Administration produced what went before Congress as the Hepburn bill. This proposed a radical modification of the antitrust law. Interstate corporations could register with the Bureau of Corporations, with which all charters and contracts would be filed. Such agreements, if approved by the Bureau, would be immune from later prosecution under the antitrust law. The proposal met with such intense hostility that it did not reach the floor of either house. Vigorous lobbying by the National Association of Manufacturers (NAM), an organisation representing mainly small firms which did not want to see big business exempt from prosecution under the Sherman Act and which objected still more to the proposal to grant immunity to trade unions, put great pressure on Congress. Congressmen were, in any case, well aware of the value which the public still attached to the ideal of free competition, and they were reluctant to grant such extensive authority to an executive agency in so crucial an area of public policy. The proposed measure not only conferred extraordinary powers of discretion in determining where the hammer of judicial prosecution should fall, but also created a system of detailed supervision of business contracts and arrangements including

16. Seventh Annual Message, *Works*, XV, p. 420.
17. Quoted in William Letwin, *Law and Economic Policy in America: The Evolution of the Sherman Antitrust Act* (New York, 1966), p. 247.

corporate structure, capitalisation, and even such matters as prices. The *New York Times* only exaggerated somewhat when it suggested that the bill would 'confer upon the President the power of control over the country's business'.[18] It was, says Martin Sklar, an astonishingly statist solution to the problem of government–business relations. The bill called for both a revolution in American social and economic ideas, namely the acceptance of a corporate society, and a revolutionary expansion in the powers of the state for which Americans were equally unprepared.

Just how unsatisfactory the legal situation was became evident during the term of Roosevelt's successor, William Howard Taft. Unwilling to play fast and loose with law enforcement like Roosevelt, he launched a series of antitrust suits, more in his four years than in Roosevelt's seven-and-a-half. The resulting uncertainty among the business community was only partly alleviated by the Supreme Court's decision in the *Standard Oil* case in 1911, which concluded that the Sherman Act should be read as applying to 'unreasonable' restraints of trade only, according to the standards of the common law. Otherwise, the Court would be left with the invidious choice of applying it to all contracts or none at all, since all contracts restricted trade to some extent or other. It was the duty of the courts to determine the 'standard of reason' that was to be applied. Standard Oil was judged to be guilty of 'unreasonable' restraint of trade because its actions showed a presumptive intent to exclude competitors from the marketplace. In fact, the 'rule of reason' was another version of the distinction between 'good' and 'bad' trusts made by Roosevelt and nearly everybody else who did not believe either that the trusts should be left to their own devices or that they should be destroyed by federal statute. The trouble with it was that its application by judicial process left businessmen in extreme uncertainty as to whether or not their actions would leave them liable to condign punishment at some future date. As Elbert Gary of US Steel told a congressional committee investigating the steel trust, 'I would be very glad if we knew exactly where we stand, if we could be freed from danger, trouble and criticism by the public, and if we had some place where we could go, to a responsible governmental authority, and say to them, "Here are our facts and figures ... now you tell us what we have the right to do and what prices we have the right to charge." '[19] Such uncertainty

18. Sklar, *Corporate Reconstruction of American Capitalism*, p. 247.
19. Quoted in Gabriel Kolko, *The Triumph of Conservation: An Interpretation of the Progressive Movement* (New York, 1963), p. 174.

strengthened the consensus within the corporate sector in favour of some form of federal regulation.

One such solution was offered by Roosevelt, in his campaign as a Progressive candidate in 1912, in the shape of a national industrial commission with complete power over the organisation and capitalisation of corporations engaged in interstate commerce. It has to be said, however, that many of Roosevelt's Progressive Republican supporters did not share his enthusiasm for an administrative solution and would have preferred a strengthening of the Sherman Act. The Democratic nominee, Woodrow Wilson, occupied similar ground. Following the advice of Louis Brandeis, a lawyer who had represented small business interests in a number of law suits, Wilson argued that the trusts were not an inevitable outcome of the operation of economic forces but, in most cases, the artificial product of restrictive practices, such as railroad rebates and price discrimination, which prevented the aspiring entrepreneur, the 'man on the make', from competing fairly in the market place. The answer, therefore, was not 'regulated monopoly', such as Roosevelt seemed to propose, but 'regulated competition'. By banning unfair practices, the government would once more open the channels of competition, forcing the trusts to meet prospective rivals on a fair battleground.

The differences between Wilson's so-called 'New Freedom' and Theodore Roosevelt's 'New Nationalism' became evident during the early years of the Wilson Administration. In 1913 Wilson pushed Congress to lower the barriers to trade posed by protective tariffs and, with more ambiguous results, to free credit for enterprise through reform of the banking system, in the shape of the Federal Reserve Act. The following year, the Clayton Act attempted to define more exactly the precise meaning of the antitrust law. There was, Wilson told Congress, sufficent experience of 'the actual process and methods of monopoly and of the many hurtful restraints of trade' for them to 'be explicitly and item by item forbidden in such terms as will practically eliminate uncertainty'.[20] What emerged was something much less rigorous and much less definite than many Southern and Western progressives had anticipated. Apart from offering an ambiguous and as it turned out, fruitless grant of immunity to labour and agricultural organisations, the eventual legislation limited itself to prohibiting various forms of business malpractice, such as price discrimination, exclusive dealing and interlocking directorates, but only where the result was 'to substantially lessen competition or tend to create monopoly'. Such language greatly detracted from the law's impact and left considerable scope for judicial review. According to Senator Joseph Reed of Missouri, the bill had degenerated from 'a raging lion with a mouth full of teeth' to 'a tabby cat with soft gums, a plaintive mew, and an anemic appearance'.[21]

The dilapidated final condition of the Clayton Act was partly a result of the fact that Wilson himself lost faith in it. He, like Roosevelt before him, was persuaded by business leaders, not only corporate representatives, but small businessmen who feared that strict antitrust laws would make illegal the trade associations to which they looked for protection and support, that a more flexible approach was needed. To rely on statutory law alone would place a 'strait-jacket' upon business. Therefore they urged the creation of a trade commission with the power to decide on particular cases. Wilson and Brandeis, who had at first proposed a 'weak' commission which would serve as 'an indispensable instrument for information and publicity', now came out in favour of a 'strong' commission.[22] The Federal Trade Commission Act of 1914 was different in tone from the Clayton Act. Rather than enumerating the proscribed practices in painstaking detail, it restricted itself to declaring 'unfair methods of competition' unlawful and allowing the commission created under the act to determine its application to particular cases. Herbert Croly, like many historians, regarded this as a 'radical reversal' of Wilson's original 'New Freedom' policies. However, it was a long way from Roosevelt's more comprehensive regulatory proposals, with their compulsory registration or licensing, their detailed scrutiny of contracts and agreements, their monitoring of prices and competitive practices. The vagueness of the phrase 'unfair methods of competition' and the inclusion of a section inviting judicial review of Federal Trade Commission (FTC) decisions effectively left the courts to determine the law's scope. All in all, the antitrust legislation of 1914 left the legal situation largely unchanged.

The operations of the FTC did little to disturb the business community. Lacking authority, strong leadership or a clear sense of purpose, the Commission failed to find a significant role. Unlike the equivalent Interstate Commerce Commission, it declined to lay

21. Quoted in Arthur S. Link, *Woodrow Wilson and the Progressive Movement, 1913–1916* (New York, 1954), pp. 72–3.
22. McCraw, *Prophets of Regulation*, p. 118.

down a body of administrative law or issue 'advance advice' that would have guided businessmen in their dealings. Instead, it became, in effect, an adjunct to the courts. The operation of the antitrust law continued to be determined by judicial, rather than administrative, procedures. The Wilson Administration, like its predecessors, carried on a vigorous campaign of antitrust prosecutions, which, as in the past, was more effective in breaking up loose, rather than tight, combinations. The latter benefited from the willingness of both the Administration, through so-called 'consent decrees', and the Supreme Court, most notably in the *US Steel* case (1920), to apply the 'rule of reason' in judging the market behaviour of large corporations.

The outcome of the progressive antitrust movement was ambiguous, to say the least. Two decades of popular agitation against the trusts had resulted in the political consolidation of a corporate economy. Despite the evidence that public opinion desired more drastic action against big business, despite the protracted campaign by small businessmen through organisations like the National Association of Manufacturers, despite the antitrust rhetoric indulged in by politicians, federal policy reflected the growing consensus among academic economists, spokesmen of big business like Gary and politicians like Roosevelt that big business was both necessary and desirable. The process of industrial consolidation was not reversed, even though it might have slowed down. According to business historian Alfred D. Chandler Jr., although it might have in some cases prevented outright monopoly and in others 'transform[ed] monopolistic industries into oligopolistic ones', federal action under the antitrust laws 'never transformed an oligopolistic industry back into a traditionally competitive one'.[23] Big business was now subject to government supervision, through the FTC and other agencies, although it is far from clear that that supervision imposed serious constraints upon its behaviour. 'Curiously', notes Louis Galambos, 'antitrust measures actually helped legitimize the role of the large corporation.'[24] Their enactment in 1914, in effect, ended the debate over the legitimacy of big business in American life.

23. Alfred D. Chandler Jr., *The Visible Hand: The Managerial Revolution in American Business* (Cambridge, Mass., 1977), p. 376.

24. Louis Galambos, *The Rise of the Corporate Commonwealth: United States Business and Public Policy in the Twentieth Century* (New York, 1988), p. 63.

Railroad regulation

'The federal regulation of the railroads', Gabriel Kolko suggests, was 'the first example of national Progressivism, and possibly its most important single illustration.'[25] For a generation state and federal governments had struggled with the economic and legal problems of railroad regulation. During the Progressive Era, in the shape of federal rate-making by an independent commission, a solution was found that was wholly characteristic of government–business relations in the early twentieth century. The political struggles that brought it into being exemplify the processes that created the new American state.

The movement for railroad regulation in the Progressive Era flowed from the deficiencies of earlier ventures in the field. As Justice John M. Harlan observed in 1897, the Interstate Commerce Commission had been left 'with power to make reports and to issue protests' but had 'been shorn, by judicial interpretation, of authority to do anything of an effective character'.[26] By 1900 its impotence was manifest. Yet many of the original problems remained, and new ones had appeared. Hence there developed a powerful movement to enlarge the Commission's powers, particularly by investing it with the power to set rates, which ultimately bore fruit in the shape of the Hepburn and Mann-Elkins Acts.

Although the structure of the railroad industry had changed quite substantially since 1887, with the consolidation of railroad systems and the establishment of 'communities of interest' between formerly competing lines, most demands for legislation still focused on essentially the same issue. Debate leading up to the passage of the Hepburn Act of 1906 concentrated primarily, not on the overall level of rates, but on discrimination between localities and shippers, which, if less extensive and more localised than a generation earlier, was irksome enough to those who suffered from it. The most striking instances of local discrimination were to be found in the West and South. Low through rates on transcontinental routes penalised intermediate points like Denver and Spokane or the cities of central Kansas, while the Southern 'basing-point' system gave rise to especially aggravated cases of local discrimination. It was quite

25. Gabriel Kolko, *Railroads and Regulation, 1877–1916* (Princeton, N.J., 1965), p. 6.
26. Stephen Skowronek, *Building a New American State: The Expansion of National Administrative Capacities, 1877–1920* (Cambridge, 1982), p. 157.

natural that those who suffered from the prevailing rate structure should prefer some other means of deciding a matter so crucial to their economic welfare. Of course, some shippers enjoyed favourable rates, as did some localities, and their natural inclination was to oppose any increase in the ICC's power to adjust rates. Therefore congressmen received numerous letters and telegrams from merchants and manufacturers objecting to, as well as supporting, the Hepburn bill.

Thus railroads were arrayed against shippers, and shippers against shippers. But an interpretation of the politics of railroad regulation in the Progressive Era which restricted itself to a classification of economic interest groups would be hopelessly wide of the mark. Public perception of the railroad question was determined by more than economic considerations. The wave of mergers, the exposure of communities of interest and the activities of infamous figures like E.P. Harriman and J.J. Hill combined to inflame popular apprehension of the monopoly power of the great railroad corporations. The railroads brought further contumely upon themselves by their own involvement in state politics, including the maintenance of permanent lobbies in state capitals, the cultivation of close relations with influential political leaders and the distribution of free passes to a still larger number of state officials, politicians and newspapermen. Public concern about the corrupting effect of business interests on the nation's political life naturally picked out the railroad corporations as a prime target. Thus anti-railroad feeling fed upon many of the sources that nourished progressivism as a whole.

The Interstate Commerce Commissioners themselves, ever since the adverse court decisions of the 1890s, had been pressing for an enhancement of their powers. Much of the impetus behind the movement for federal regulation came from their persistent efforts. At least from 1904, they enjoyed the support of President Roosevelt himself. Roosevelt in his approach to the issue was influenced by an acute sense of political priorities, combined with a strong, if not clearly articulated, moral conviction. Morality, to Roosevelt, meant offering a 'square deal' to all parties. It would be 'as gross a wrong', he insisted, for the government to fail 'to protect a railroad that was in the right' as to render 'an improper service to the railroad at the expense of the public'.[27] This led him to the conclusion that railroad regulation was essentially an administrative task. Only an

27. Quoted in Kolko, *Railroads and Regulation*, 112.

impartial administrative agency would possess the expertise to identify the solutions which best met the requirements of justice and harmonise the competing interests of railroads, shippers and the general public. The deliberations of impartial administrative experts were more likely to achieve these ends than the adversarial procedures of the courts or the particularistic concerns of legislators. Only a permanent commission could develop policy in an affirmative and systematic, rather than a reactive and intermittent, fashion. It became apparent that what mattered to Roosevelt was less the substantive provisions of the Hepburn bill than the administrative instruments which were to enforce it.

Roosevelt's Message to Congress in December 1905 addressed the subject of rate regulation in some detail:

> In my judgment the most important provision which such law should contain is that conferring upon some competent administrative body the power to decide, upon the case being brought before it, whether a given rate prescribed by a railroad is reasonable and just, and if it is found to be unreasonable and unjust ... to prescribe the limit of rate beyond which it shall not be lawful to go ... this decision to go into effect within a reasonable time and to obtain from thence onward, subject to review by the courts.

The power to establish a maximum rate was 'essential to any scheme of real reform in the matter of railroad regulation'.[28] Largely as a result of a deal struck between Roosevelt and congressional leaders trading inaction on tariff reform against action on railroad regulation, the House of Representatives passed a rate bill with remarkable dispatch.

The Republican leadership in the Senate, however, was less compliant. A powerful group of conservative senators led by Nelson Aldrich, John C. Spooner and former Attorney-General Knox believed the Hepburn bill to be objectionable in its failure to provide for judicial review. They devoted their energies to writing into the bill an amendment which would explicitly authorise the courts to review ICC decisions and to consider every question involved in the setting of rates. The defenders of narrow review, mainly Democrats and Midwestern Republicans, maintained, in contrast, that the Commission was the proper body to determine whether or not a rate was reasonable. As the Iowa Senator Jonathan P. Dolliver explained:

---

28. Roosevelt, Fifth Annual Message, *Works*, XV, pp. 275–8.

> The chief reason for creating a commission to determine these questions is because the questions require the skill of experts. They are not questions of law; they are questions of business policy which require in their settlement the experience and practical knowledge which is a small part of the education and habits of our courts. We know as well as we can learn anything from experience that the enforcement of law regulating commerce becomes ineffective if it is left in the hands of the courts.

Roosevelt and Dolliver acknowledged that the courts had authority to investigate whether the ICC had overstepped the limits of the power delegated to it by law and whether the rate imposed entailed in effect a 'confiscation' of railroad property, but they objected to any amendment which would, as Dolliver put it, 'enlarge the jurisdiction of the circuit court and make it practically an appellate Interstate Commerce Commission'.[29]

Following protracted and complex negotiations lasting most of the spring, when it became clear to Roosevelt and his supporters, and equally to Aldrich, that a majority could be assembled on neither a broad nor a narrow review amendment, the Republican factions came together behind a formula which, though wordy, said nothing meaningful about the scope of review, which was left to the courts themselves to determine. If the bill failed to limit the courts' jurisdiction, then neither did it offer the explicit invitation to a full review sought by Knox and Aldrich, who had been much more insistent on the need to clarify the position than had Roosevelt and his allies.

Some observers, like the muckraker David Graham Phillips, regarded the struggle over court review as a 'sham battle'. Although it is probably true that the lawyers in the Senate contrived to spin a more complex web out of the legal and constitutional issues involved than was strictly necessary, they were engaged in more than an exercise in legalistic hair-splitting. Railroad officials like William Truesdale of the Lackawanna were convinced that without broad review the bill would 'work great injury to the transportation interests of the country'.[30] Shippers, on the other hand, did not want crucial decisions transferred to the courts, from which past experience had taught them to expect little redress. Thus the issue of court review involved the question of whether the process of

29. Dolliver, 'Railroad rate legislation' *Independent* 60 (12 April 1906), p. 837; Thomas R. Ross, *Jonathan Prentiss Dolliver* (Iowa City, 1958), p. 209.

30. William H. Truesdale to John C. Spooner, 7 February 1906, Spooner MSS, Library of Congress.

regulation should be geared to protecting the interests of the carriers or the shippers.

More significantly still, the ICC was the first of a new species of government agency which, as the more timorous conservatives noted with foreboding, mingled legislative, executive and judicial powers in a manner which seemed quite contrary to the spirit of the American Constitution. It was to have the 'quasi-legislative power' of setting railroad rates, the executive power of investigation and enforcement, and the judicial power of hearing complaints and adjudicating disputes. To Aldrich and other Old Guard Republicans this entailed a dangerous consolidation of authority. They preferred to trust the wisdom of the courts, relying on traditional means of resolving economic conflicts. In contrast, Roosevelt insisted that the function of supervising railroad rates was 'unequivocally administrative'. The procedural form to be established was as significant as its contribution to the settlement of the specific problem of railroad regulation. What gave the question of court review such importance, then, in the eyes of Roosevelt and many of his supporters was the implications that its resolution would have for shaping the institutions that were to be entrusted with the regulation of the developing industrial society.

That the new law was only a partial solution to the railroad problem few denied. More radical proposals like Robert M. La Follette's proposal for a physical valuation of railroad assets as a basis for setting rates or Francis G. Newlands's plan for national incorporation of the railroads were voted down or ignored altogether. The fate of the La Follette and Newlands amendments points up the limitations of the Hepburn Act. As La Follette rightly observed, it was an act drawn up to protect the interests of shippers and, to some extent, railroads, rather than to promote the interests of the consuming public. More immediately, from the viewpoint of Administration and congressional leaders, it offered a solution to the conflicting political pressures that the shippers' campaign, together with the widespread public anxiety regarding the political power of railroads and other big corporations, had created. The 'railroad question' meant many different things to different people, but to government leaders it was essentially a political problem, one of mediating urgent and potentially explosive political demands, rather than undertaking a more systematic or rational examination of the problem. That so much time and energy should be spent on the issue of judicial review reflects the main priorities of those who wrestled with the problem. Like Roosevelt himself, they were preoccupied with procedural questions: of who was to hold power rather than how it was to be used; of institutional arrangements rather than economic policy. From a structural point of view the Hepburn Act had radical implications, prefiguring the growth of the regulatory machinery of twentieth-century American government. Its actual impact on the development of the railroad system was much less than its significance for the development of the American system of government.

Although the Hepburn Act greatly enlarged the regulatory powers of the Interstate Commerce Commission, it conspicuously failed to solve the 'railroad problem'. The Commission became much busier, achieving greater success in settling a larger number of complaints than had been possible under the old law. The Supreme Court did not insist on a broad review of ICC decisions, accepting in 1910 that the agency exercised essentially administrative functions and that the 'expediency or wisdom' of its actions should not be a matter for judicial scrutiny. The Commission's interventions went a long way to removing the more obvious abuses and anomalies in contemporary railroad practice. However, it is difficult to argue that, even in aggregate, they made a great deal of difference to the overall rate structure. Devoting itself almost exclusively to the adjudication of specific complaints, the Commission took as its starting-point the existing pattern of rates and confined itself to the examination of abuses as they were presented by individual shippers or railroads, rather than considering the structure as a whole. Thus many of the deeper structural imbalances and injustices remained. Continuing pressure for modification of the interstate commerce law demonstrated that the Hepburn Act had failed to meet the hopes vested in it. Shippers found particularly frustrating the inability of the Interstate Commerce Commission to intervene before the event to prevent the imposition of a higher rate, forcing them to undergo months of additional expense and inconvenience before they could secure relief. Meanwhile, the railroads sought adjustments in their own interests, particularly through the legalisation of traffic agreements.

To a considerable extent, however, the impetus for reform came from President Taft. As a jurist, Taft set great store by the constitutional principle of separation of powers, a principle which, in his eyes, was infringed by mingling in one agency what were essentially administrative and judicial powers. But for the judiciary to fulfil its responsibility for scrutinising the actions of executive agencies, at a time when the scale and complexity of government activity were expanding, specialised administrative courts, competent to adjudicate the technical issues increasingly confronting government, would have to be created. Hence Taft proposed to establish a Court of Commerce. His strategy was to incorporate in the bill creating the Court elements attractive to both railroads and shippers in order to construct a coalition powerful enough to secure its passage. The draft bill which Taft submitted to Congress in January 1910 provided for a Commerce Court which would have original jurisdiction over all cases under the interstate commerce laws; permitted railroads to make agreements covering rates; and empowered the Commission to suspend a new rate for sixty days pending an inquiry into its reasonableness and to consider the justness of rates and regulations on its own initiative. Even before its amendment by Congress, the president's bill constituted a very considerable increase in federal regulatory power.

The railroad bill was virtually rewritten by an alliance of insurgent Republicans and Democrats in Congress. The final Mann-Elkins Act was, like all legislation, a compromise, but it was one that the progressives could take more pleasure in than the president and his allies. The Court of Commerce remained, but its powers of injunction were carefully circumscribed. (After a history of confrontation with both the Commission and the Supreme Court, the ill-fated tribunal was legislated out of existence in 1913.) After a number of hostile amendments, the section legalising traffic agreements was quietly dropped. On the other hand, the authority of the ICC was extended over national telephone and telegraph systems. The Commission was authorised to investigate rates on its own initiative and, above all, to suspend rate increases for up to ten months. The economist William Z. Ripley, writing at the time, saw the suspension clause as 'a radical extension of the authority of the Commission'.[31] The burden of proof was placed upon the railroads to show that a rate increase was warranted, rather than on the shippers to show that it was not – a major alteration of the balance of power in the transportation marketplace.

The Mann-Elkins Act marked a significant shift in the politics of railroad regulation. The Commission began to concern itself more and more frequently with the overall level of rates, rather than with questions of discrimination. Responding to political pressures and reflecting public opinion, the ICC used its new powers to veto a series of joint rate increases proposed by the trunk railroads to

31. William Z. Ripley, *Railroads: Rates and Regulation* (New York, 1912), pp. 563–4.

compensate for the effects of inflation on wages and other costs. That the carriers had a stronger case than it was prepared to recognise was confirmed when the War Railway Board granted a 28 per cent rate increase on taking control of the system in 1918. The Transportation Act of 1920, which restored the railroads to private hands, conferred still more extensive regulatory powers on the ICC, including the authority to set minimum as well as maximum rates, to supervise railroad finances, and to provide financial assistance for weaker lines. It now had the authority needed 'to regulate railroad rates constructively' and to plan a consolidated railroad system, but the commissioners remained too preoccupied with the details of particular cases to take an overall view. Rather than checking abuses by ruthless and powerful railroad companies, they increasingly found themselves intervening to prop up ailing lines in the face of road and airline competition.

Progressive regulation is blamed by historians like Albro Martin for precipitating the economic decline of the railroads. Politicians blinded by the shibboleths of 'archaic Progressivism' and conscious of 'the unpopularity of higher railroad rates', failed to 'apply the principles of economics' to the railroad problem. This failure of comprehension, the argument goes on, led reformers of the Progressive Era to interfere with the mechanism in ways that were ultimately damaging to the railroads' future health and usefulness. A 'repressive policy of rate regulation' starved the industry of investment capital, leaving it unable to offer an efficient and competitive service and to meet the challenges of the new century.[32] 'The most damning line of criticism' of federal railroad regulation, argues Thomas McCraw, 'has rested on claims that the ICC has worked to impede economic efficiency' as a result of 'its concern for fairness', whether to shipper or carrier or both.[33]

Part of the problem was that the logic of railroad economics and the logic of American politics ran in opposite directions. The huge economies of scale involved in railroading and the high ratio between fixed and variable costs left scope for wide differentials in the rates charged, while creating intensely competitive conditions. Railroads responded by charging very low rates where competition operated and recouping their losses where it did not. This gave rise to a set of intensely felt but highly localised grievances of precisely the kind which the system of political representation was most

---

32. Albro Martin, *Enterprise Denied: Origins of the Decline of American Railroads, 1897–1917* (New York, 1971), pp. 355–6.
33. McCraw, *Prophets of Regulation*, pp. 63–4.

sensitive to. It must be remembered that the structure of rates and the flow of economic activity were themselves a cumulative product of the actions of the railroads over a period of decades, actions which had a shaping influence on the development of communities all over the United States. For such arbitrary power to lie in private hands was unacceptable. After all, as Roosevelt himself pointed out, the railroad was the primary 'highway of commerce . . . and we must do our best to see that it is kept open to all on equal terms'.[34] This, it was widely agreed, was a governmental responsibility that could not be wholly left in private hands. Failure to regulate had unacceptable consequences. In the last analysis, rate regulation was a necessary response to the economic and political pressures on government leaders. These political pressures, and the compromises and concessions that they necessitated, perhaps prevented the attainment of what might be regarded as an optimal pattern of regulation and control, with possibly deleterious consequences for the railroads. However, the particular regulatory solution adopted in the Progressive Era can hardly be blamed for the long-term decline of American railroads, which is matched in other developed countries, except where government subsidy or nationalisation has been applied.

Pure food and drugs

The federal Pure Food and Drug Act and the closely related meat inspection law emerged from the same congressional session as the Hepburn Act and were commonly regarded as part of the same general regulatory project. Each, believed Beveridge, recognised the principle that, 'when any business becomes so great that it affects the welfare of all the people, it must be regulated by the Government of all the people'.[35] Federal regulation of food and drugs offers another useful illustration of the development of the modern regulatory state.

The processed food industry expanded enormously during the late nineteenth century. The food products consumed by the American public were increasingly processed outside the home, distributed over great distances and preserved with the aid of a bewildering variety of chemicals. Food chemists used their skill not

34. Roosevelt, Fifth Annual Message, *Works*, XV, p. 281.
35. John A. Braeman, *Albert Beveridge: American Nationalist* (Chicago, 1971), p. 110.

only to preserve food beyond its natural life but sometimes, by ingenious feats of 'creative chemistry', to make quality products out of more ignoble ingredients. The South Dakota State Analyst reported, for example, how honey would be offered for sale which was composed largely of glucose and bugs, olive oil which was completely innocent of olives but made instead from cottonseed oil, and jars of potted chicken and potted turkey which were respectively devoid of chicken or turkey. Butter might contain carrot juice as a colourant and borax and formaldehyde as pre-servatives. The use of preservatives, in particular, was a technical question of some difficulty. Their application gave consumers access to a much wider range of foodstuffs than local soil, climate or seasons would normally allow. On the other hand, there was much uncertainty as to what quantities of such additives might safely be consumed. They also allowed materials to be marketed that were not really fit for sale and, more seriously, undermined public confidence in the industry by giving scope to wild but unsettling rumours of what went on to the public's dinner tables.

The Pure Food and Drug Act also embraced the patent medicine business. Numerous quack remedies competed for custom, exploiting contemporary fears about impotence, women's complaints, venereal disease, cancer and diabetes, with the promise of cures derived from Native American herbal lore or the miracles of modern science. Radol, for example, hinted at the curative properties of radium but contained, in the words of the muckraker Samuel Hopkins Adams, 'exactly as much radium as dishwater does' and was 'about as efficacious'. What impact patent medicines had was often derived from more mundane ingredients. Dr Church's Anti-Scrofulous Panacea, for example, did indeed 'permeate the system in a most delightful manner' for the very good reason that it contained one-third alcohol by volume, a property matched by many other popular nostrums.[36] By the beginning of the century journalists like Adams and Mark Sullivan, as well as committees of medical practitioners, had revealed how misleading, and sometimes dangerous, patent medicine advertising often was.

Such exposures did a great deal to arouse public anxiety regarding both patent medicines and processed foods. In particular, Upton Sinclair's novel *The Jungle* (1906), though dealing

36. Quoted in James Harvey Young, *The Toadstool Millionaires: A Social History of Patent Medicines in America Before Federal Regulation* (Princeton, N.J., 1961), p. 173; J.C. Furnas, *The Americans: A Social History of the United States, 1587–1914* (London, 1970), p. 907.

specifically with conditions in the meat-packing plants of Chicago, evoked a more general condition of queasy uncertainty. Reform groups like the General Federation of Women's Clubs, the Women's Christian Temperance Union and the National Consumers' League lobbied extensively for food and drug regulation. But they were joined by groups which harboured more particular motives.

Important elements within the food industry supported regulation. In some cases manufacturers who did not themselves make use of preservatives sought to gain an advantage over those who did, such as the Royal Baking Powder Company in its longstanding struggle with rival firms which added alum to their product; or companies which purveyed 'natural' products sought to penalise their competitors, like the producers of 'straight', as against 'blended' or 'rectified' whiskeys. Alternatively, they looked to regulation to allay public fears about their products. Thus, for example, the meat-packers welcomed federal inspection in order to restore confidence in export markets in the wake of the furore created by Sinclair's book. Finally, federal regulation would provide relief from the growing inconvenience of divergent state laws. Various professional groups developed an interest in regulation. Agricultural chemists played a major role in the pure food movement. The most prominent was Harvey Wiley, chief of the Bureau of Chemistry in the US Department of Agriculture, who, by accumulating evidence, testifying before legislative committees, organising publicity campaigns, and building coalitions of support, did as much as anyone to bring the movement for regulation to a successful conclusion. The medical and pharmaceutical professions were similarly active in the campaign against patent medicines. Their professional responsibility and special expertise seemed to impose an obligation to act in defence of the public interest. However, defence of the public interest also elevated the importance of that expertise and enhanced the status and prestige of the professionals themselves. Physicians and pharmacists, by controlling the patent medicine business, would restrict a dangerous set of rival practitioners in the business of prescribing for the public's ailments. Regulation therefore grew out of the activities of complex coalitions whose members held very different motives.

Such coalitions succeeded in placing a variety of pure food laws on the statute-books of many states. In 1906, following a campaign lasting over ten years, Congress passed the Pure Food and Drug Act. Earlier legislation had been shelved owing to the influence of the patent medicine and other lobbies and the hostility of influential senators like Henry Cabot Lodge, who spoke for the codfish of New England, preservation of which apparently required a liberal application of boracic acid; Nelson Aldrich, himself a wholesale grocer; and the Maine Senators William P. Frye and Eugene Hale, who represented the canners of 'imported French sardines' caught off the coast of Maine. By 1906, however, pressure from the American Medical Association and other groups forced the Senate leadership to relent. The resistance of Speaker Joseph G. Cannon in the House was similarly shaken by public reaction to the meat controversy. The object of the law, explained one of its sponsors, was to ensure 'that when we go into the market to buy an article of food or a drug to be used in the family, we shall get what we call for' and not 'some poisonous substance in lieu thereof'.[37] The law demanded truthful labelling of food and drugs, while prohibiting certain deleterious ingredients. Enforcement was entrusted to the Bureau of Chemistry, which was responsible for determining what ingredients were harmful. The meat inspection bill which was passed at the same time, as a result of public horror at the disclosures in *The Jungle* and intensive lobbying by President Roosevelt, provided for strict inspection of all meat entering interstate or foreign commerce 'from the hoof to the can'.

Pure food regulation illustrates the general character of early twentieth-century reform. In the first place, government regulation of private business was necessary to protect the consumer in modern industrial society. It could no longer safely be left to the market to ensure wholesome food products and beneficial drugs. Secondly, various pressure groups, ranging from food manufacturers to the medical profession, were instrumental in securing government action. Finally, by virtue of the highly technical nature of the issues involved in food and drug regulation, as in railroad regulation, professional expertise was necessary for their resolution. The public knew that it wanted effective pure food legislation but did not know precisely what it was or how to get it. For that it had to rely on the experts. The key decisions about particular substances and commodities would be made by federal officials in the Bureau of Chemistry, which quadrupled in size during the next two years, and its successor agency, the Food and Drug Administration. This was the pattern followed by much state and federal legislation during this period.

37. Porter McCumber in *Congressional Record*, 59th Congress, 1st Session, p. 1218.

The new political order

The regulatory reforms of the Progressive Era entailed, says Stephen Skowronek, a fundamental recasting of the institutions of government; 'it entailed building a qualitatively different kind of state'.[38] Not only the extent of government intervention, but the manner in which policy was formulated and executed changed beyond recognition. The main features were the appearance of regulatory agencies entrusted with wide discretionary power and a consequent diminution of the role of both legislatures and courts in the conduct of economic policy.

The development of a national economy, as we have seen, created numerous clashes of interest. Various groups of individuals organised to advance their common interests. 'We are living in an age of organization', declared the president of the National Association of Manufacturers in 1911, 'an age when but little can be accomplished except through organization.'[39] The most familiar were the business corporation and the trade union, but to these can be added farmers' cooperatives, trade associations and the many professional associations that sprang up around the turn of the century. Organisation provided greater bargaining power in the marketplace. It also provided greater political leverage. Organised interest groups lobbied government for measures that operated to their advantage, usually at the expense of some other group. Exploiting what might be called the 'strategic uses of public policy', they demanded government protection against their adversaries' 'unfair' practices.[40] Conflicts between interest groups, then, were transferred to the political arena. Thus trade unions asked for changes in the law governing labour injunctions, while the NAM did all it could to prevent it; shippers demanded regulation of railroad rates in order to improve their competitive position in relation to other shippers; and food manufacturers called for the prohibition of the methods and materials used by their rivals.

The regulatory legislation of the Progressive Era was shaped by the demands and pressures of organised interest groups, or shaped rather by the need to find ways of resolving them. Government officials were driven to find procedures for the settlement of

38. Skowronek, *Building a New American State*, p. 4.
39. Robert H. Wiebe, *Businessmen and Reform: A Study of the Progressive Movement* (Cambridge, Mass., 1962), p. 18.
40. Donna J. Wood, *The Strategic Uses of Public Policy: Business and Government in the Progressive Era* (Marshfield, Mass., 1986).

disputes which involved difficult, often highly technical questions of, for example, railroad rates or food standards. The nineteenth-century solution of referring such questions to the courts was no longer satisfactory, in view of the specialised knowledge required. Legislative bodies could not be expected to lay down regulations in sufficient detail to meet the wide range of circumstances that might arise. In any case, legislative politics was marked by particularism and parochialism, a tendency to make decisions by a process of 'log-rolling'. Instead reliance was increasingly placed on administrative agencies like the Interstate Commerce Commission, the Federal Reserve Board and the Federal Trade Commission, which were granted wide discretionary powers to decide cases on the basis of their technical expertise. They were expected to rise above partisan and sectional squabbles and arbitrate impartially between interests. The 'bureaucratic remedy' recommended itself as a means of resolving conflicts in society by entrusting their resolution to a body of experts who would decide on the basis of an impartial examination of the facts, applying professional or scientific standards and thereby, it was hoped, 'transforming ideological conflicts into matters of expertise and efficiency'.[41] Hence objective decisions would be arrived at, based on the public, not private, interest. As the rhetoric of progressive politicians often claimed, the creation of an appropriate administrative agency would take the issue 'out of politics'.

In practice, of course, this was an objective that could not be realised. To delegate important decision-making powers to a bureaucratic agency was merely to substitute one kind of politics for another. Indeed, it transferred the conflict to an arena in which organised interests were still more powerful, relative to the general public. The powerful business interests which regulatory agencies were set up to control were no less potent in the administrative arena.

The complex issues presenting themselves to modern government called upon various kinds of technical expertise for their resolution, introducing what James Willard Hurst calls 'a new disposition of calculation' into the policy-making process.[42] Perhaps the clearest illustration of this tendency, as Samuel P. Hays's study revealingly shows, is the conservation movement, in which the key role was played by members of professional and scientific elites,

41. Skowronek, *Building a New American State*, pp. 165–6.
42. James Willard Hurst, *Law and the Condition of Freedom in the Nineteenth-Century United States* (Madison, Wis., 1956), p. 73.

imbued with the spirit of rational planning, rather than by politicians, business groups or the general public. Those active in the movement sought to promote a system of decision-making more consistent with the demands of a rational management of resources on scientific principles than was possible in the haphazard arena of legislative politics. Skowronek ascribes a similar role to members of 'an emergent intelligentsia rooted in a revitalized professional sector and a burgeoning university sector' who worked to replace the traditional modes of governance with 'the discipline of cosmopolitan bureaucratic routines', in order to expand the capacity of the federal government to meet the demands of the new age and to institutionalise the influence of the new professionals in the affairs of state. 'The heart of progressivism', says Wiebe, 'was the ambition of the new middle class to fulfill its destiny through bureaucratic means.'[43]

Nineteenth-century Americans, as we have seen, inhabited a very different 'political universe' to that of today, one marked by extreme localism, a high level of popular participation in the rituals of democratic politics, and intense party loyalty. That universe was already undergoing important changes at the close of the last century; by the Progressive Era it was clearly in the throes of a fundamental transformation which would take it a long way towards the more disenchanted political world of the late twentieth century. Most obvious was a marked decline in the level of political participation. As early as 1904, turnout was well down on the levels of the 1890s, and the campaign was marked, in the eyes of experienced political observers, by a singular lack of popular excitement. Even the climactic confrontation of 1912 failed to draw the missing electors back to the polls. By the 1920s turnouts in presidential elections were averaging 52 per cent, which compared poorly with the 80 per cent of 1876–92. There were fewer election meetings, fewer parades and rallies, while those that were held attracted embarrassingly poor crowds.

Although this is a change of far-reaching significance, the reasons are far from clear. It was, in practical terms, less easy to vote than it had been in the nineteenth century. To prevent electoral fraud, and in part to weaken the hold of party machines, registration requirements were made more complex, thus increasing the opportunity costs of electoral participation in terms of time, energy and distraction. This had the effect, in particular, of

43. Skowronek, *Building a New American State*, p. 42; Robert H. Wiebe, *The Search for Order, 1877–1920* (New York, 1967), p. 166.

deterring less educated voters of lower socio-economic status, which in the South at least, with reference to African-Americans, was an intended consequence. Some scholars have traced the decline in turnout in particular states to the introduction of tighter election laws, but the correlation is far from consistent across the whole United States. Women received the vote in 1920, and in some states earlier. Not surprisingly, fewer women than men turned out to vote in the elections immediately following their enfranchisement. But voting levels had already begun to fall off before 1920. Had women been enfranchised in the more overtly political world of the past century, it is likely that they would have been attracted to vote in much greater numbers. The rate of female participation was less an independent variable than a symptom of a changing political culture. The early decades of the twentieth century offered many distractions that were not present a generation earlier, with the movies and spectator sport, later radio and television, competing for the attention of the citizen, while newspapers devoted much less space to politics than in the nineteenth century. The decline in political involvement is surely traceable, at least in part, to changing patterns of leisure and social interaction, although the inter-connections are obviously difficult to identify.

More fundamentally, perhaps, the decline in political participation followed from the nature of the new political order. Politics in the nineteenth century expressed people's involvement in communities and grew out of community concerns. In this century, however, as Hays pointed out in a famous essay, political power has become more centralised. Decisions once taken locally were transferred to city, state, or even federal level, seemingly remote from the influence of local communities. Decisions once taken by elected representatives were increasingly delegated to bureaucrats who had no direct relationship with the electorate. All of this tended to reduce the voter's sense of political efficacy, the sense that his or her vote would really make a difference to the policy-making process. Contemporary surveys have shown that feelings of political impotence are particularly prevalent among non-voters. It is possible that such perceptions were already influencing electoral behaviour at an earlier date and that the establishment of a bureaucratic state and the decline in turnout during the Progressive Era were more than merely coincidental.

Political participation in the nineteenth century was invariably carried out within the context of an intense partisanship, which was one of the salient political facts of the era. But during the course of the twentieth century American political parties, while still highly significant institutions, began to play a diminished role. What Walter Dean Burnham calls 'the onward march of party decomposition' was well under way by the first decade of this century, with sharp falls in electoral turnout and straight party voting, wide swings in the party vote from one election to another, and numerous manifestations of political independence and anti-party feeling.[44] The influence of personalities, particularly at a national level, became much more significant, and by the 1920s candidates were beginning to disassociate themselves from parties, preferring to build up their own campaign organisations and their own campaign strategies. However, while the popular appeal of a Theodore Roosevelt or a Ronald Reagan might attract people to vote in the short term, the long-term effect was to loosen the hold of parties and to weaken the habits of regular party voting that had drawn men and women to the polls in the past.

Above all, perhaps, the new modes of political action tended to bypass political parties. Like their Mugwump forebears, many progressive reformers considered the traditional practices of party politics antipathetic to rational decision-making. They hoped that reform would take key decisions 'out of politics'. The new pressure groups devised a range of lobbying techniques, involving the cultivation of close relations with relevant congressional committees and administrative agencies and propaganda campaigns appealing directly to public opinion. With experience, they developed a strong preference for bureaucratic procedures over the vagaries of legislative 'log-rolling', which was all too susceptible to constituency and partisan pressures. The growing importance of regulatory issues created in time a new kind of politics in which the force of localism and the influence of political parties were substantially diminished.

Progressivism, therefore, brought with it a 'new political order', one better designed to mediate conflicts between interest groups and cope with the problems of governance in the modern age. It was less well suited, however, to reflecting the aspirations of communities. It was less effective at creating a framework within which ordinary people, the unorganised, could participate and feel themselves to be purposefully engaged in the overall process of government. Ironically, as government came to exert a greater influence on people's lives and the stakes of political action increased enormously, individual citizens became less involved,

44. Walter Dean Burnham, *Critical Elections and the Mainsprings of American Politics* (New York, 1970), p. 91.

voting, as we have seen, in much smaller numbers. The lively, rumbustious spirit of nineteenth-century politics was also lost, and with it some of the innocence of that world.

CHAPTER FIVE

Patterns of Social Reform, 1890–1920

Introduction

In 1890 the journalist Jacob Riis shocked respectable New Yorkers with his graphic depiction of life in the tenement districts of Lower Manhattan in *How the Other Half Lives*. Both Riis's book and its reception reflected a mounting concern about the living and working conditions of the urban poor. They reflected also a changing attitude to the poor: one of compassion and under-standing rather than moral disapprobation, but also of fear rather than complacency, which provided the impetus for an extra-ordinary explosion of social reform activity during the generation following the publication of Riis's account.

The social reform movements of the Progressive Era drew on many sources. One was the revaluation of the nature and causes of poverty to which *How the Other Half Lives* made so signal a contribution. Another, reflected also in the urgent tone of Riis's account, was a growing middle-class fear of social disorder. Finally, the social reform movements of the period drew much of their force and much of their special character from the participation, on an unparalleled scale, of women. This participation, in turn, had important implications for women's broader political role. Likewise, social reform took many forms: an environmentalist project designed to produce social conditions conducive to responsible and productive citizenship; a 'child-saving' movement which addressed the particular problems of children growing up in urban society; campaigns to enact protective labour legislation for women and children; proposals to provide social insurance against some of the accidents of fate which forced working-class families into destitution; and an attempt to create a distinctively 'maternalist' welfare state. Though overlapping at many points, these movements, at least to some extent, require separate treatment.

During the period 1890–1920 the American states produced an extraordinary array of legislation designed to regulate living and working conditions which, taken in aggregate, constitute a major change in American social policy. Yet, impressive as they were, these innovations fall far short of equivalent advances in the countries of Western Europe and Australasia. In the enactment of minimum-wage laws, the provision of public housing and, above all, the introduction of elementary systems of social insurance, the corner-stone of a modern welfare state, most other industrial nations had advanced far beyond the United States. In this period, as Theda Skocpol remarks, 'the United States stands out for its lack of nationwide public protection for male workers and elderly people'.[1] For all their cumulative significance, the social reforms of the Progressive Era did not constitute even a rudimentary welfare state. That awaited a different era and very different circumstances.

Christian benevolence and 'scientific philanthropy'

Nineteenth-century American social policy grew out of the practice of philanthropy. It was preoccupied with problems of pauperism and dependency. Charities, public and private, assumed the task of classifying, evaluating and treating a succession of miscellaneous individuals who for one reason or another were in desperate need of assistance. The theory and practice of philanthropy were founded upon a number of simple, diagrammatic propositions about society in general and the causes of pauperism in particular. It followed from the principle of individual self-determination that each man was 'the architect of his fortunes' and that poverty was therefore a result of individual failings. 'Misery and suffering are the inevitable results of idleness, filth and vice', pronounced a charity organisation society handbook.[2]

There were, it was agreed, essentially only two causes of pauperism: 'misfortune', which included sickness, disability, widow-hood and orphanhood; and 'misconduct', which covered virtually

1. Theda Skocpol, *Protecting Soldiers and Mothers: The Political Origins of Social Policy in the United States* (Cambridge, Mass., 1992), p. 157.
2. Quoted in Paul Boyer, *Urban Masses and Moral Order in America, 1890–1920* (Cambridge, Mass., 1978), p. 146.

everything else. The 'deserving poor' were those whose plight was no fault of their own, principally widows, children and the elderly; the 'undeserving poor' were those who were held to have brought their condition upon themselves by their own defects of character, which included virtually all able-bodied males. The latter had no rightful claim on the community. Indeed, to extend relief might only confirm them in their habits of idleness and irresponsibility and encourage others to forsake the paths of honest toil. Many of those who administered charity, and many of those who funded it, believed that relief had a dangerously erosive effect on discipline in the labour market. This was particularly a danger with public welfare, whose indiscriminate and mechanical nature, according to Stephen H. Gurteen of the Buffalo Charity Organization Society, fostered 'habits of dependence, destroying manliness and self-respect'.[3] Yet nobody seriously suggested that paupers, even able-bodied paupers, should be turned away and allowed to starve, especially at moments of particular economic distress when the large number of unemployed males constituted a potential problem of public order as well as of philanthropy.

The solution to this dilemma lay in the application of the Poor Law principle of 'less eligibility'. The condition of those subsisting on relief must be made less desirable than that of the lowest-paid worker in private employment. As Josephine Shaw Lowell of the New York Charity Organization Society explained, 'the necessary relief should be surrounded by circumstances that shall not only repel everyone, not in extremity, from accepting it, but which shall also insure a distinct moral and physical improvement on the part of all those who are forced to have recourse to it – that is, discipline and education should be inseparably associated with any system of public relief'.[4] Dependency was regarded essentially as a moral condition which must be cured by strict deterrence combined with moral uplift. Rather than a passive response to physical need, charitable assistance should take the form of an active intervention in the lives of paupers, who had proved themselves defective in applying for relief, in order so to modify their behaviour and habits that they might lift themselves out of poverty. Charity workers like Lowell, no less than later progressive reformers, saw poverty as 'a wrong, an unnatural evil', which they 'should use every effort to

3. Quoted in Michael Katz, *In the Shadow of the Poorhouse: A Social History of Welfare in America* (New York, 1986), p. 73.
4. Quoted in Robert Bremner, *From the Depths: The Discovery of Poverty in the United States* (New York, 1956), p. 48.

eradicate'.[5] They believed, in Daniel Levine's words, 'that poverty was unnatural and unnecessary in prosperous America and could be eliminated' – a recurrent theme in American social policy from the late nineteenth century to the War on Poverty of the 1960s.[6]

Needless to say, the practice of relief in most American cities fell far short of this ideal. A bewildering array of private charities, denominational and non-denominational, specific and general in their terms of reference, and pursuing very different strategies, competed with public welfare agencies to produce a patchwork quilt of charitable provision that left both huge holes and substantial areas of duplication. An idiosyncratic mixture of bene-volence and miserliness militated against the application of any systematic policy. During the latter decades of the century charity organisation societies (COSs) were established in many cities to coordinate the efforts of the various agencies, in order to deploy their resources to the optimum effect and guard against the harmful effects of indiscriminate giving. In particular, they wished to expunge the corrupting influence of public outdoor relief.

The charity organisation movement worked towards the goal of a 'scientific philanthropy'. Comprehensive case records were kept to prevent duplicated or uninformed distribution of relief; professional agents were hired to assess clients' needs; and professional super-intendents coordinated the activities of the volunteer contributors and workers on whom the charities depended. Although the societies were managed by professional agents, the important task of home visiting was the responsibility of volunteer workers, mainly women. These so-called 'friendly visitors', acting not as almoners but as friends, were expected to develop a personal relationship with client families and guide them towards self-help and respectability, as much as anything by the example of their own behaviour and demeanour. They were supposed to impart their own virtues to the poor, offering inspiration and encouragement. As a mechanism for transferring middle-class values to the poor, whose principal need, it was believed, was not alms but moral guidance, 'friendly visiting' held a central place in COS strategy. Though suggesting a crass kind of paternalism, as well as being fundamentally unreal in its expectations, it represented a genuine attempt to restore the kind of contact between social classes that increasingly was denied by the segregated structure of the city.

5. Quoted in Katz, *In the Shadow of the Poorhouse*, p. 70.

6. Daniel Levine, *Poverty and Society: The Growth of the American Welfare State in International Comparison* (New Brunswick, N.J., 1988), p. 16.

Though heavy-handed, informed by a highly restrictive social theory, and often punitive in its practice, 'scientific philanthropy' was driven by a desire to combine benevolence with scientific principles and thereby to achieve real improvements in social conditions. By seeking to replace the indiscriminate philanthropic practices of the past with a more systematic and business-like approach, the charity organisation movement probed the limits of traditional thinking and pushed social policy into new areas. 'Scientific philanthropy' entailed a 'scientific' analysis of case records in order to discover the underlying trends. The information collected contributed to a more sophisticated awareness of the causes of poverty and laid the groundwork for the social reform movements of the twentieth century, while the growing profession-alisation of philanthropy led in due course to the development of social work.

As information and experience accumulated and the complexity of social problems became apparent, dealing with the poor became a full-time vocation. The management of charities increasingly fell into the hands of professional superintendents, and day-to-day contact with client families became the responsibility of paid workers. Thus 'scientific philanthropy' gradually evolved into professional social work. As knowledge and expertise accumulated, as decades of experience were codified and analysed, and as a professional method known as 'casework' took shape, training schools were established where practitioners could be initiated into the mysteries of their craft. Social work became institutionalised as a form of continuing contact with the poor and the disadvantaged. Though often preoccupied with individual adjustment to social conditions, to the exclusion of reform, and still bearing some of the intellectual inheritance of Victorian philanthropy, the social work profession has remained a source of information and ideas about, as well as commitment to, the treatment of poverty.

The 'discovery of poverty'

The individualistic interpretation of poverty that informed nineteenth-century philanthropy became less and less tenable as the new industrial society took shape. Evidence accumulated that poverty was a social problem, a product of social conditions. Most telling of all, perhaps, was the experience of mass unemployment in the depressions of the late nineteenth century, particularly that of the 1890s, when unemployment, by a cautious estimate, exceeded 3 million. The sheer number of men forced into involuntary idleness compelled recognition that their condition was, in Lowell's words, 'as much beyond their power to avert as if they had been natural calamities of fire, flood, or storm'.[7] At the same time, detailed investigation of the roots of pauperism revealed how frequently it was traceable to 'misfortune' (such as involuntary unemployment or industrial accidents), how relatively rarely to 'misconduct' (such as idleness or intemperance). Finally, writers like Riis drew attention to the sheer number of the poor. Robert Hunter in 1904, admittedly on the basis of very sketchy evidence, suggested that as many as 10 million Americans were living in poverty. Most, he insisted, were not reprobates but honest 'toilers' struggling to make a living under exceptionally difficult circumstances. Rather than a distinctive group with its own habits and mores, what in the later twentieth century would be labelled an 'underclass', the poor were just like everybody else in their values and aspirations.

It is evident that writers like Hunter and Riis were defining the problem in very different terms to their predecessors. What they sought to measure, describe and explain was not pauperism but poverty. Whereas pauperism presented itself as a problem every time an individual was forced to apply for charitable relief, thereby entering a state of dependency which was perceived in terms of moral as much as financial inadequacy, poverty was a more general condition of insufficiency. Poverty was defined by Hunter as a standard of living which fell below a level sufficient to maintain industrial efficiency (which exceeded the wages of most manual workers). To live in poverty was to live on a margin of subsistence, on the verge of dependency. Poverty was, in effect, a breeding-ground for pauperism, into which, by the accidents of life, a large proportion of the poor must inevitably fall. One of the objectives of social reformers was to prevent that from happening and, by alleviating poverty, to reduce the incidence of pauperism.

The findings of the numerous detailed investigations carried out during the Progressive Era, like the Pittsburgh Survey of 1911, led inexorably to the conclusion that poverty was a product of the social environment, due, in Hunter's words, 'to certain social evils which must be remedied and certain social wrongs which must be put right'. Thus the responsibility lay, not with the individual, but with society. 'Look at these pictures', said the socialist muckraker

7. Quoted in Walter I. Trattner, *From Poor Law to Welfare State: A History of Social Welfare in America* (5th edn, New York, 1994), p. 103.

Charles Edward Russell, commenting on a series of drawings of slum life, 'and reflect that for all these things not the ways of Providence are responsible, nor inevitable conditions ... but merely you and I.'[8] It followed that poverty, or at least most poverty, was unnecessary. If the social causes of poverty could be removed and the social environment sufficiently ameliorated, then the ancient curse of insufficiency could be driven from the land.

Many reformers were inspired by the belief that the eradication of poverty would bring about an improvement in moral conditions. Reversing earlier assumptions of cause and effect, they believed, in the words of Edward Devine, secretary of the New York COS, that vice and immorality were 'more largely the results of social environment than of defective character'. It was necessary therefore, in the words of the settlement worker Graham Taylor, to create an environment in which it was 'easier to live right and harder to go wrong', and this was one of the central objectives of social reform in the Progressive Era.[9] The child in particular was, in Riis's words, 'a creature of environment, of opportunity'. His or her development was all too easily 'nipped in the bud' by cramped tenements, child labour or unwholesome influences deriving from contact with street gangs, saloons or houses of prostitution. 'How is it possible to preserve purity amid such homes or to bring up children to be moral and decent?' asked a New York tenement reformer.[10] The child raised in the slum 'has no chance but to become wicked', said an article in the church magazine *Arena*. 'He is not free to choose good from evil ... any practical philanthropist ... will tell you how slight the chances are for children to be virtuous who grow up in that atmosphere.'[11] It was crucially important therefore to create a social and moral environment which was conducive to the raising of good citizens.

Such extreme environmentalism, with its overtones of determinism, did scant justice to the many working-class families who struggled to raise their children under difficult conditions, and it was, in its way, as unrealistically reductionist as the individualistic philosophy that had prevailed in an earlier generation. But it had the virtue of promoting social action. It conjured up millenialist

8. Robert Hunter, *Poverty* (New York, 1904), p. 98; Bremner, *From the Depths*, p. 137.

9. Quoted in Boyer, *Urban Masses and Moral Order*, pp. 224, 223.

10. Quoted in Roy Lubove, *The Progressives and the Slums: Tenement Reform in New York City, 1890–1917* (Pittsburgh, 1962), pp. 71, 45, 44.

11. Quoted in Boyer, *Urban Masses and Moral Order*, p. 179.

visions that, by wise social reform, poverty and a host of attendant evils might be substantially eliminated.

Such visions animated a wave of social reform movements whose object was no less than to eradicate poverty and, in doing so, to transform the face of urban America. The participants in these movements, like the members of the charity organisations of the late nineteenth century, were predominantly of upper-class or upper-middle-class origins, and they were relatively few in number. Organisations like the National Child Labor Committee and the Association for American Labor Legislation depended on the energies and financial support of small numbers of middle-class reformers and civic leaders, including clergymen and other professionals, and businessmen. Allen Davis's analysis of settlement house residents points to similar conclusions. They, too, were typically Anglo-Saxon Protestants, raised in comfortably affluent homes, college-educated at a time when such advantages were enjoyed by a tiny proportion of the population. They, too, like social reformers in general, were disproportionately female.

There were no doubt many personal reasons for involvement in social reform. Such activities offered opportunities for personal fulfilment and even career development, especially for women. As Robert Crunden has argued more generally, this generation of reformers was typically raised in deeply Christian homes – many were, indeed, the children of ministers – and instilled from childhood with a profound sense of religious obligation which, unlike in the preceding generation, was typically cast in secular terms. Some 90 per cent of settlement workers were active church members, and many male residents had seriously contemplated clerical vocations. Rather than joining the ministry or undertaking missionary work, they committed themselves to secular causes, investing them with much of the same sense of moral purpose. Thus, in this transitional generation, essentially religious drives worked themselves out through the medium of social reform.

Social reform was also a response to the challenge of urban America, which added a new urgency to more traditional philanthropic impulses. The sons and daughters of the middle class viewed the slums, sometimes with sympathy, but also with horror and a great deal of fear. The slums, they were convinced, offered a threat which, if left unchecked, would grow like a cancer and damage society as a whole. Most obviously, the slums were a breeding-ground for disease. Diseases like tuberculosis, the so-called 'White Plague', bred most vigorously in slum districts, where the death-rate was twice the city average, but could obviously spread from there to infect more affluent neighbourhoods. In a more general sense the metaphor of disease was used to express the menace that lurked within the slums. The slums, it was believed, bred immorality. The Social Gospel minister Josiah Strong saw tenement life as 'a commingled mass of venomous filth and seething sin, of lust and drunkenness, of pauperism and crime of every sort'.[12] Finally, the slums might breed social disorder. Crime, violence and riot, political discontent, anarchy and maybe even revolution might smoulder among what contemporaries sometimes called the 'dangerous classes'. What Strong called 'the volcanic fears of deep discontent' within the slums held an explosive potential. To Riis the slum population was a vast sea of people threatening to become a 'resistless flood ... sweeping all before it'.[13] Sympathy for the plight of the poor was mingled with a pronounced sense of moral disquiet and even fear. Therefore a desire for social justice went hand in hand with an impulse towards social control.

It has to be said, of course, that this environmentalist view of poverty, while influential among relatively small groups of social reformers and settlement workers, did not hold universal sway. Although certain categories of destitute individuals, like children and widowed mothers, attracted a broader measure of public sympathy, able-bodied paupers remained objects of suspicion. Traditional attitudes of contempt and hostility to the poor survived, while traditional Poor Law procedures still governed the administration of both public and private charities in most localities.

Dimensions of social reform

It must be emphasised at the outset that, according to the prevailing interpretation of the United States Constitution, social and labour legislation was wholly the province of the states. In 1895 the Supreme Court had affirmed that the protection of public health, morality and order was 'a power originally and always belonging to the States, not surrendered by them to the general government'.[14]

12. Quoted in Bremner, *From the Depths*, p. 6.
13. Quoted in Boyer, *Urban Masses and Moral Order*, pp. 130, 131.
14. Quoted in John Braeman, 'The Square Deal in action: a case study in the growth of the "national police power"', in John Braeman, Robert Bremner and David Brody, eds, *Change and Continuity in Modern America* (Columbus, Ohio, 1964), p. 39.

There were only one or two federal incursions in the field of social policy, significant more for what they portended than for their immediate impact. The reliance on state initiative gave some scope for experimentation, allowing individual commonwealths to act as 'laboratories of democracy', and some of the more advanced states evinced a willingness to draw fruitful lessons from the experience of others. A variety of national reform associations provided an element of coordination, offering both encouragement and advice to states considering legislation in their field of interest. For example, the National Housing Association gave advice to states on the drafting of housing codes, drawing largely upon the pioneering legislation of New York, while the National Child Labor Committee (NCLC) worked consistently to persuade the states to copy best prevailing practice in the field of child labour legislation. In that sense separate state action facilitated the progress of reform. On the other hand, interstate competition acted as a deterrent. Stricter regulation and higher taxes placed business interests in the more progressive commonwealths under a competitive disadvantage, which offered a telling argument against social reform. For example, the unwillingness of several, mostly Southern, states to give up the advantage, as they saw it, of child labour brought the movement for state regulation to an impasse and inspired the one major congressional intervention, the federal child labour laws of 1916 and 1918. Although neither in the end passed judicial scrutiny, this premature attempt at national regulation pointed up the apparent discrepancy between the federal system and the imperatives of an increasingly national economy.

Social reform in the Progressive Era followed many different directions. To those who adhered to an environmentalist interpretation of social problems, the physical refurbishment of the slums seemed paramount. 'The improvement of the homes of the people was the starting point for everything', claimed Lawrence Veiller, the secretary of the tenement house committee of the New York COS.[15] Veiller was convinced, and did much to demonstrate, that there was a clear correlation between bad housing and the incidence of disease, pauperism and crime. Theodore Roosevelt, then Governor of New York, agreed that tenement reform was 'an effort to cut at the root of the diseases which eat at the heart of the body social and the body politic'.[16] The tenement code adopted by

15. Quoted in Allen F. Davis, *Spearheads for Reform: The Social Settlements and the Progressive Movement, 1890–1914* (New York, 1967), p. 68.
16. Quoted in Lubove, *The Progressives and the Slums*, p. 125.

New York in 1901, and widely copied elsewhere, laid down a set of minimum standards for lot coverage, the provision of fire escapes and WCs, lighting and ventilation, and required that all new buildings conform with these regulations and that older ones should be brought so far as possible into conformity with them. There is no doubt that, over time, these regulations brought about substantial improvements in housing conditions and eliminated some of the worst features of past practice. However, they proved notoriously difficult to enforce, in the face of resistance from landlords, real estate interests and their political allies. More seriously, they failed to remedy the serious shortage of adequate low-cost housing in a city like New York. The negative solution of prohibiting bad housing practice was clearly insufficient. Yet, fearful of the political corruption and inefficiency that they assumed would be associated with it, Veiller and other housing reformers of the period shied away from the alternative, widely adopted in other countries, of constructing low-cost public housing at public expense. They could not believe that a political machine like Tammany Hall was capable of building and allocating public housing in an honest, efficient or equitable fashion. Here, as in many other ways, existing political structures and values constrained the possibilities for social reform.

Besides housing reform, progressive reformers sought to improve other aspects of the urban environment by working for cleaner streets, better policing and the provision of public parks, bath-houses and gymnasia. Some worked also to eliminate the saloons and brothels that clustered in working-class neighbourhoods. These efforts were linked by the hope that a comprehensive effort to improve the urban environment would lead substantially to the elimination of poverty.

'Child-saving' was a primary theme in early twentieth-century social policy. Indeed, a growing awareness of the special needs of children was one of the defining characteristics of social reform during the Progressive Era. From an environmentalist perspective, the child was plastic, his or her character as yet unformed, and reformers were anxious to provide the conditions most conducive to healthy development. That included most obviously the provision of better schools which would educate children for good citizenship; playgrounds which would afford the opportunity for constructive, rather than destructive, play; juvenile courts which would remove errant youngsters from the toils of the adult justice system and permit a more sensitive consideration of their special needs and problems; improvements in public health which would reduce the frightful levels of infant mortality; and, above all, the abolition of child labour. While the common objective was the protection of children, and the protection of children where possible within the security of the home, 'child-saving' did entail an unprecedented degree of intervention by the state in matters which were formerly a private preserve. For example, children were required to go to school and debarred from paid employment, sometimes against their parents' wishes. Government officials, like truant officers, social workers and, above all, juvenile court judges, who held quite extraordinary discretionary powers in determining the affairs of families whose offspring came under their jurisdiction, might intervene at several points. Such interventions, though nominally designed to preserve and strengthen the family unit, entailed a substantial weakening of its autonomy.

The most important component of the 'child-saving' movement was the campaign to regulate child labour. At least 2 million children under fourteen were employed in 1900 in a variety of occupations, ranging from street trades to factory work. Such early labour seemed unnatural to middle-class reformers, who naturally sympathised with the plight of the infants ('Such tiny-looking things, with bodies that looked as if they might be crushed between one's hands') discovered working in factories and mines.[17] Child labour brought not only present suffering but a denial of future opportunity. It stunted children's physical and intellectual development and denied them the education that would open wider opportunities in later life. As the New York Child Labor Committee explained, if children were denied 'an opportunity for elementary education and physical development sufficient for the demands of citizenship and the requirements of industrial efficiency', they would be unfitted for a useful and responsible adult life.[18] Society would pay the cost later in sickness, disability, pauperism and crime. Thus it was the prior claim of the community as a whole that was taken to warrant so radical an intervention in the affairs of the family.

By 1916 most Northern and Western states had passed legislation prohibiting the employment of children under fourteen and regulating the hours and conditions of children under sixteen, usually in association with compulsory school-attendance laws.

17. Quoted in Jeremy P. Felt, *Hostages of Fortune: Child Labor Reform in New York State* (Syracuse, N.Y., 1965), p. 68.
18. Quoted in ibid., p. 72.

Child labour laws, however, proved difficult to enforce. Not only employers, in industries like canning and textiles which employed large numbers of children, but many parents, dependent upon the wages of older children to supplement inadequate family budgets, had an incentive to break the law. Restrictions on child labour came into conflict with working-class family strategies, which required the pooling of all available resources, and failed to take adequate account of the economic context in which they operated. Reformers, of course, insisted that children's futures should not be sacrificed to short-term exigencies, but that did not gainsay the urgency of those needs. No state hired anything like a sufficient number of inspectors to police the thousands of factories and sweatshops where children might be employed. For example, in 1907 New York had fifty factory inspectors, when Florence Kelley believed that at least 500 were required. Child labour laws, therefore, worked intermittently, if at all, their influence coming more through a raising of standards and normative expectations than through the direct regulation of behaviour.

Many states, especially in the South, either failed to pass any child labour law or passed laws which, by virtue of their low age-limits, generous exemptions and lax enforcement procedures, were little better than no regulation at all. By 1914 only nine states had enacted legislation which met the standards laid down by the National Child Labor Committee. The alternative of prescribing national standards by federal statute appeared to be ruled out by the Constitution. In the *E.C. Knight* decision the Supreme Court, in making a distinction between commerce, which was potentially a national concern, and manufacturing, which was subject to local control, appeared to rule out the possibility of federal regulation of labour. Admittedly it had muddied the waters somewhat in *Champion* v. *Ames* (1903) by upholding a federal ban on the interstate shipment of lottery tickets as 'a reasonable and proper prohibition of immoral and unsafe trade through the channels of interstate commerce'.[19] This judgement opened the possibility that the interstate commerce clause of the Constitution might provide the basis for a 'federal police power' which would permit quite extensive incursions by the national government in the field of social policy. The passage of federal pure food and meat inspection laws in 1906 could be regarded as merely the first instalment in this nationalising trend. Senator Albert J. Beveridge was an early

19. Quoted in James E. Anderson, *The Development of the Modern Regulatory State* (Washington, D.C., 1962), p. 60.

advocate of a federal child labour bill based on the interstate commerce clause, arguing that 'the decision of the Supreme Court in the Lottery Cases absolutely settled its constitutionality'.[20] The failure of state legislation convinced a majority of the NCLC, and in due course President Wilson and a majority in Congress, of the necessity for federal action, and a law was passed in 1916 prohibiting the passage across state lines of goods whose manufacture involved the labour of children under fourteen. Two years later, however, the Supreme Court in *Hammer* v. *Dagenhart* concluded that regulation of child labour was not a proper application of the commerce power. Acceptance of Congress's right to prohibit the interstate movement of articles which were deleterious in themselves, like lottery tickets and adulterated food products, did not, it appeared, authorise use of the commerce power to regulate manufacturing, which was a matter for local regulation, when the goods produced were not intrinsically harmful. The same fate befell a subsequent attempt to tax child labour out of existence. The movement to regulate child labour appeared to have fallen into a chasm between the imperatives of a national economy, with intense interstate competition, and a restrictive interpretation of a Constitution drafted under very different conditions. Thus the reform movement came to something of an impasse.

Whereas the campaign against child labour, like the child-saving movement as a whole, attracted both male and female support, the campaign to regulate women's labour was predominately a female enterprise. Although state labour federations supported the regulation of the hours and wages of women workers, in the absence of any possibility of regulating those of men, the leading role was played by purely female organisations like the National Consumers' League (NCL), the Women's Trade Union League (WTUL) and local women's clubs. Both male unionists and female 'maternalist' reformers would have preferred to establish an adequate living wage for male breadwinners, in order that women should not be obliged to work outside the home. However, such legislation would be harder to achieve and almost certainly unconstitutional. Therefore, they were forced to direct their attention to protective legislation for women workers, for which an ideological and a legal case could more easily be constructed. It was much easier to evoke public sympathy for the welfare of 'helpless working women' than that of men, who were presumed able to look after

20. Albert J. Beveridge to Harriet Lake, 22 November 1907, Beveridge MSS, Library of Congress.

themselves. And women workers certainly needed protection, working long hours at wages from a half to a third below those of men. Their perceived vulnerability both inspired and validated government action.

According to current legal doctrine, which was crystallised in contemporary interpretation of the Fourteenth Amendment to the Constitution, the freedom of American citizens to make contracts should not be unduly restricted by state regulation. The developing interpretation of the Amendment had by 1906, with *Lochner* v. *New York*, effectively ruled out the possibility of regulating the wages and terms of service of adult male workers, who were expected, as free and equal citizens, to make their own contracts. Women, it was argued, needed special protection on two counts. One was their role in bearing and rearing children. Excessive and arduous physical labour would damage a woman's reproductive capacity, while long hours of work would deprive a child of maternal care and guidance. Secondly, women were perceived as more vulnerable than men, by virtue of their political disfranchisement and their gender role. Thus the case for regulation of women's hours of labour was founded on the premise that women were different from men, by virtue of their physiological structure as well as their social role, and this difference justified placing restrictions on their employment which would not be countenanced when applied to men. The famous 'sociological brief' presented by Louis Brandeis, but actually written by Josephine Goldmark of the NCL, in *Muller* v. *Oregon* (1908) dwelt overwhelmingly on the theme of difference. The force of such arguments was clearly reflected in the Supreme Court's decision:

> That woman's physical structure and the performance of maternal functions place her at a disadvantage in the struggle for subsistence is obvious. This is especially true when the burdens of motherhood are upon her. Even when they are not, by abundant testimony of the medical fraternity continuance for a long time on her feet at work, repeating this from day to day, tends to injurious effects on the body, and, as healthy mothers are essential to vigorous offspring, the physical well-being of woman becomes an object of public interest and care in order to preserve the strength and vigor of the race ... Differentiated by these matters from the other sex, she is properly placed in a class by herself, and legislation designed for her protection may be sustained, even when like legislation is not necessary for men, and could not be sustained.[21]

21. Henry S. Commager, *Documents in American History* (2 vols, New York, 1949), II, p. 224.

A similar case was made for minimum-wage laws, in this case supplemented by fears that low wages might impel women to resort to prostitution. Contemporary hysteria about 'white slavery' gave added impetus to the movement for minimum-wage laws for women. As a result of the effective lobbying activities of women's organisation, forty-one states had imposed limits on the hours of female workers by 1921, while fifteen states along with the District of Columbia also passed minimum-wage laws for women between 1914 and 1923, when the Supreme Court, in *Adkins* v. *Children's Hospital*, found this species of legislation unconstitutional.

Social insurance: 'the next step'

If children were to be kept out of the workplace and their mothers discouraged from working, financial provision had to be made for their support. If the children of widowed mothers were to be cared for within the home and their families kept together, then some form of public assistance was necessary. By 1919 thirty-nine states had provided for state pensions payable to widows responsible for the care of young children. Mothers' pensions were advocated by the same groups who favoured child labour laws, and they received active and effective support from women's organisations like the General Federation of Women's Clubs and the National Congress of Mothers, as well as leading women reformers. The rapid spread of such legislation, paralleled in only three other countries, is testament to the power of women's organisations in the Progressive Era.

These so-called mothers', or widows', pensions were not pensions in the modern sense, in that they entailed no presumptive right to assistance. They did not follow automatically from the status of widowhood and the possession of children; a measure of need had to be demonstrated. Pensions were discretionary, doled out by the authorities only in cases of proven distress. They were frequently administered by charitable agencies, even though such agencies had often opposed their implementation in the first place. The methods of philanthropic casework were commonly applied. Pensions were available only to 'worthy' recipients who could provide a 'fit' home for their children. In other words, moral and behavioural criteria were applied to assess eligibility, criteria which were defined so loosely as to leave enormous discretion to case-workers. Recipients were subject to continuing supervision to ensure that they met the required standards of housekeeping. Most state laws were permissive rather than mandatory, allowing counties to opt in or out of the scheme. A majority opted out. As a result, only a small proportion of needy widows with children were in receipt of mothers' pensions. The Children's Bureau estimated that about 45,800 families were covered in 1921 out of a total of between 1 million and ½ million female-headed families. And the sums received, though more generous than poor relief, were rarely adequate for women to support their families without additional financial resources. Over a half of the recipients worked to supplement their income, despite the fact that the initial objective had been to relieve widows of the need to seek outside employment.

Ann Orloff and Theda Skocpol argue that the inadequate provision of mothers' pensions reflected the subsequent under-funding of the programmes rather than their initial design. Programmes designed to 'honor motherhood' were undermined by the intrusive practices of local relief administration and the parsimoniousness of local communities. However, many of the flaws in mothers' pensions programmes were present from the start, including the insistence on an element of behavioural scrutiny, the fear of 'pauperising' women by conferring too easy an entitlement, and the local option clauses, which were added to forestall legislative opposition. As Linda Gordon suggests, it was principally because a modest version of mothers' pensions was presented that legislatures accepted it so readily. Rather than conferring an entitlement on widowed mothers for their services to the state, it defined them as especially worthy recipients of relief. Rather than a blanket programme, it allowed localities considerable discretion in how they administered the scheme and, indeed, whether they participated at all. The significance of widows' pensions lies not so much in its effectiveness as in its ancestral role in the development of the American welfare system, for the mothers' pensions of the Progressive Era became the Aid to Families of Dependent Children of today, which sadly inherited many of the defects of the earlier programme.

The nearest parallel to the social insurance programmes adopted during the early twentieth century in the nations of Western Europe and Australasia was what was called workingmen's compensation, that is insurance against industrial accidents. By the first decade of the century, both labour organisations and employers were growing dissatisfied with the arbitrary and unpredictable settlement of liability claims in the courts, which led many firms to take out private insurance. Though catastrophic in their impact upon individuals, industrial accidents were, from an actuarial point of view, predictable and could be insured against. Workingmen's compensation had the advantage from the worker's point of view of being virtually automatic. An injured employee was entitled to compensation, rather than having to prove his claim in the courts. From the employer's point of view, workingmen's compensation had the advantage of relieving him from unpredictable liabilities and eliminating a source of recurrent and acrimonious dispute with his employees. From the point of view of the reformers and social scientists who formed the membership of the American Association of Labor Legislation (AALL), it offered a preventive cure for a frequent cause of poverty, as well as a way of alleviating class conflict. Workingmen's compensation laws were passed therefore because they served a wide range of interests, including organised labour, big business, insurance companies and reformers. They won acceptance also because they represented a transfer of an existing legal problem from the courts to administrative tribunals, rather than the intrusion of government into a wholly new field.

By 1919 thirty-eight states had introduced a scheme of automatic compensation for injury, paid for out of a fund to which employers contributed regular amounts. Many of these laws were limited in coverage, sometimes only to 'hazardous occupations', administration was often entrusted to commercial insurance companies, rates of compensation were almost always low, and they rarely covered medical or hospital expenses. Only a skeletal bureaucracy was established to administer them. Sketchy and skimpy though workingmen's compensation was, however, it had a clear advantage over the contemporaneous mothers' aid programmes. Benefits were non-discretionary, following automatically upon certain ascertainable events, and administered according to a clear set of rules. Barbara Nelson argues that this discrepancy between the provision of income support for male workers and widowed mothers represented the beginning of what was to become a 'two-channel welfare state': one channel incorporating an element of entitlement, the other retaining important elements of the Poor Law tradition of discretionary grants and close moral supervision. 'These programs had different ideologies, clienteles, principles of entitlement, and administrative styles'.[22] Although Nelson is right to

22. Barbara Nelson, 'The origins of the two-channel welfare state: workingmen's compensation and mothers' aid', in Linda Gordon, ed., *Women, the State and Welfare* (Madison, Wis., 1990), p. 124.

point out the gendered nature of the difference between the two programmes, she overstates its immediate significance. The working-men's compensation laws of the Progressive Era provided neither a full and adequate programme of accident insurance nor a precedent for a comprehensive safety net of income support for manual workers and their families.

The success of workingmen's compensation seemed to point the way for other forms of social insurance. If workers could be insured against industrial accidents, a fertile cause of poverty, then why should they not be insured against other equally predictable causes of distress, such as sickness, unemployment and old age? The predominantly male reformers and academic professionals of the AALL believed that in a modern industrial economy the incomes of wage-earners were inevitably subject to intermittent interruptions against which even skilled workers lacked the resources to protect themselves, leading to deprivation, suffering and sometimes pauperism. Hence it made sense to spread the risk.

To social reformers, conscious of European ventures in the field of social insurance, this appeared to be the logical 'next step in social progress'. It was, however, a step that would not be taken for another twenty years. Social insurance faced powerful enemies, including private insurance companies fearful of losing business, corporations which were beginning to experiment with 'welfare capitalism', charities suspicious of indiscriminate giving, and special-interest groups like the American Medical Association (AMA). It was the AMA which in 1918–20 soundly defeated what had been regarded as the most promising social insurance programme, that for health insurance. Anxious to protect their own rather limited benefit schemes and generally suspicious of government interference, trade unions gave little support to social insurance, apart from a lukewarm interest in non-contributory old-age pensions, which, designed as they were for retired workers, did not compete directly with union activities. Thus organised labour, which might be regarded as the natural constituency for social insurance, was generally indifferent and sometimes down-right hostile. There was little public support for social insurance, which ran contrary to traditions of 'voluntarism' and 'self-help'. Both reformers and their critics shared doubts about the capacity of American government to administer complex insurance programmes with honesty and efficiency. John Graham Brooks, an early American advocate of social insurance, concluded that the American civil service 'would wreck any conceivable scheme of . . .

insurance in a year'.[23] The programmes that were established, mothers' pensions and workingmen's compensation, were relatively small in scale, were administered by the courts and skeletal bureaucracies with the assistance of private agencies like charities and insurance companies, and therefore imposed few administrative or financial burdens. On the other hand, the management of a contributory insurance scheme seemed quite beyond existing state capacities, while the management of a non-contributory scheme raised nightmare visions of incompetence, patronage and graft. Administration of the one comparable programme, the distribution of Civil War pensions, did not inspire confidence and, argues Skocpol, rather than providing a precedent for a comprehensive system of old-age and disability pensions, set back its introduction by a generation or more. The absence of a sufficient bureaucratic capacity, particularly at the state level, and fears of political corruption deterred American reformers from following European models of the welfare state.

Limitations of social reform

These reform endeavours were united by the hope that a comprehensive effort to improve the living and working conditions of the urban working class would lead substantially to the elimination of poverty and its attendant social problems. This, of course, did not happen. Uneven enforcement, opposition from affected business interests and their political allies, and the erosive impact of interstate competition militated against their success. Invariably, the states failed to create the administrative capacity necessary for adequate enforcement. More seriously, the negative approach adopted by the progressives limited the range of possibilities. Reformers devoted themselves to removing environmental obstacles to equal life-chances rather than providing an income safety net. 'It is significant', notes Daniel Levine, 'that it is called a quest for social *justice*, not a quest for social security.'[24]

Historians and social scientists interested in the comparative development of welfare states have offered a number of explanations for the relative backwardness of the United States. Interventionist social policies, it is argued, were inconsistent with the individualist strain in American social thought and the

23. Quoted in Levine, *Poverty and Society*, p. 169.
24. Ibid., p. 151.

commitment to *laissez-faire* in American government. This is far too blunt an instrument to apply to the history of policy-making. Individualist beliefs and *laissez-faire* policies, which in any case did not prevent a lavish expenditure on Civil War pensions during the late nineteenth century, were still less significant as principles for action in the Progressive Era. A second body of explanation points to the weakness of organised labour in pushing for welfare spending. It is true that the American labour movement was weak, divided in its attitude to protective labour legislation, suspicious of social insurance programmes and preoccupied with correcting perceived inequities in the laws governing trade union rights. Before the First World War, however, most European labour movements were not significantly stronger. They, too, played a secondary role in developing and promoting welfare programmes, which were much more likely to emerge from policy-making elites, which then sought to enlist the support of labour, than the other way round. As Theda Skocpol and her colleagues have shown, American reformers were less likely than their European equivalents to advocate large-scale social spending programmes because of their fears of administrative corruption and incompetence. The fact was that the American state lacked the administrative capacity to manage many of the tasks that European states were beginning to undertake in this period. The absence of a fully professional civil service, especially at a local level, deterred reformers from proposing elaborate social spending programmes, which they feared would be sucked into the maw of the patronage system. This applied both to social insurance and public housing programmes. Civil service reform was associated with a reaction against the kind of distributive politics typified by the Civil War pension system, rather than forming the basis for projected spending programmes.

America's peculiar constitutional framework had its influence on social policy. As we have seen, the constitutional rule confining social and labour legislation to the states distorted and constrained policy developments in a variety of ways. So did contemporary interpretations of substantive due process which ruled out the possibility of imposing legal limits, except in exceptional cases, on the hours and wages of adult male workers. This meant that American social reformers, unlike their European equivalents, could not, even at a local level, set a floor under wages or a ceiling under hours. Most reformers, including most women reformers, would have preferred to set an adequate family wage for male workers which would permit a decent standard of living, but this was ruled out on constitutional grounds. Only the wages and hours of workers who could be defined as especially vulnerable were subject to regulation, and this, among other things, predisposed reformers to concentrate on protective legislation for women and children, rather than adult men. 'If ... American states are ... behind progressive European countries in the field of social and labor legislation', observed the economist Henry R. Seager, 'it is chiefly because of the constitutional barrier.'[25] Here, as in other respects, American social policy was shaped by the need to work around prevailing legal doctrines and political structures.

For all their limitations, the social reforms of the Progressive Era left an important legacy. In the first place, an important body of legislation was laid down, especially in fields like housing regulation, public health and child welfare. Secondly, the Progressive Era bequeathed an institutional network, partly inside the walls of government agencies like the US Children's Bureau and the Wisconsin Industrial Commission, partly in university schools of social work, in private social work agencies and in reform associations like the NCL and AALL, within which future policy initiatives might be developed. Finally, and maybe most importantly, in probing the limits of a particular tradition of negative regulation, it pointed the way to more positive uses of government power during the New Deal.

The social settlements: a 'female dominion of reform'

An especially important role in social reform was played by the settlement houses, which were predominantly female in membership and in outlook. Not only did they promote a particularly female version of social reform, but they also enlarged opportunity, wherever possible, for women in public life.

The first social settlements were set up in the 1880s by young men and women, following the example of Toynbee Hall in London, who took up residence in the slum districts of American cities. They included Hull House in Chicago, established by Jane Addams and Ellen Gates Starr in 1889, the University and Henry Street Settlements in New York and many others. By 1910 as many

25. Quoted in Skocpol, *Protecting Soldiers and Mothers*, p. 261.

as 400 settlement houses were in existence. The initial aim of settlement house residents like Jane Addams was, by living among the poor, to do something to bridge the widening gap between social classes. Hull House was founded 'on the theory that the dependence of social classes on each other is reciprocal'.[26] The settlements offered a variety of social and cultural activities designed to integrate the poor into the mainstream of American life, including chamber music recitals, art exhibitions, libraries, pottery classes and, as Sinclair Lewis sarcastically put it, 'lectures delivered gratis by earnest advocates of the single-tax, troutfishing, exploring Tibet, pacifism, sea shell collecting, the eating of bran and the geography of Charlemagne's empire'.[27] These activities, though irrelevant to the needs and experience of most inhabitants of the neighbourhood, did much to open cultural opportunities to a small but significant number. Settlement houses provided facilities for the neighbourhood, such as day nurseries, kindergartens, playgrounds, employment exchanges, dispensaries and adult-education classes, many of which were later taken over and expanded by local and state governments. The settlement provided a much-needed focus for a neighbourhood constrained by poverty and social disadvantage and a much-needed sense of community in a population held apart by ethnic and religious differences. Most significantly, the residents themselves learned about the lives of the poor. Although a majority of settlements were little more than glorified religious missions or charitable agencies and confined themselves to immediate neighbourhood problems, some of the larger and more prominent houses served as centres of study, where reformers and researchers came to investigate social conditions, and played a leading part in movements for social reform. For a generation or more, they provided the most important interface between the urban community as a whole and its poorer neighbourhoods.

Settlement residents tended to be young university graduates, drawn, as we have seen, from relatively affluent households. And the majority, over 60 per cent, were female, with women constituting a still larger proportion of long-term residents. Several houses were founded and led by women like Jane Addams and Lillian Wald, and, as Robyn Muncy has shown, the settlements harboured a specifically female culture of reform. Although many women, like some men, spent a year or two in residence as a form

26. Quoted in Davis, *Spearheads for Reform*, p. 19.
27. Quoted in ibid., p. 41.

of postgraduate, premarital experience, most of the permanent residents were women, and it was they who set the tone for the life and work of the settlement. The Hull House community, and others like it, was made possible by the decision of a significant number of women, graduating from the expanding higher education system, not to marry. They evaded a fate of lonely and dependent spinsterhood by joining groups of like-minded women who gave one another the friendship, support, and often love, that others sought in marriage. The social atmosphere was that of a sorority house. In it women sought to recapture the fellowship and intellectual stimulation of their college years, while performing useful service. The settlements became therefore not only centres of reform but centres of feminist action, committed not only to protecting working-class women from the trials and tribulations of industrial society but also to extending the boundaries of possibility for women like themselves.

The social reform activities of women, like their con-temporaneous involvement in the prohibition and social purity movements, grew out of contemporary assumptions regarding women's place in society. Women were seen as occupying an essentially domestic role, responsible for housekeeping and the care of children. Women reformers justified their intervention in what was conventionally seen as the male world of politics by pointing to their obligation to protect other women and their children. Women should serve as 'housekeepers for the nation'. The suffragist Rheta Childe Dorr commented in 1910, 'Women's place is in the home. ... But Home is not contained within the four walls of an individual house. Home is the community. The city full of people is the Family. The public school is the real Nursery. And badly do the Home and the Family and the Nursery need their mother.'[28] This philosophy, reflecting both the class position and gender of its proponents, has been called by historians 'maternalism'. Maternalism incorporated a number of elements. One was an acceptance of the domestic role of women, an acquiescence in motherhood as the inevitable and rightful destiny of their sex, though not, of course, of the reformers themselves, who did not seem to regard it as anomalous that they, as women who had deliberately chosen to live their lives outside the holy bonds of wedlock, should prescribe that fate for others. The second was the assumption of a maternal role towards the poor, a role which

28. Quoted in William H. Chafe, *The Paradox of Change: American Women in the Twentieth Century* (New York, 1991), p. 15.

embodied both the authority conferred by their superior education and social position and the sympathy conferred by their gender. In this respect maternalism was to be distinguished from the more impersonal and domineering connotations of paternalism. Finally, it embodied the claim that the nurturing qualities associated with motherhood, whether actual or potential, fitted women to play a special role in the formation of social policy, particularly in matters relating to maternal and child welfare.

Numerous women's organisations grew up around the turn of the century, mobilising the energies of thousands of American women in a variety of reform causes, such as the regulation of female and child labour, the provision of playgrounds and juvenile courts, and the eradication of 'white slavery'. The National Consumers' League, established in 1899, with Florence Kelley as its executive secretary, was the principal organisation fighting for the regulation of female labour. Growing out of the activities of local consumers' leagues to improve working conditions for women in department stores and factories by persuading consumers, who were mostly women, to direct their purchases away from those firms which overworked and underpaid their female employees, the NCL worked to achieve protective legislation for women. It was, says Skocpol, 'a pure embodiment of gender politics', because it entailed a campaign by women reformers to engage the support of upper- and middle-class women in a campaign to improve the conditions of working-class women and their children.[29] Similarly, the Women's Trade Union League, founded in 1903, grew out of efforts by settlement workers to encourage the unionisation of women. Over time, as the extreme difficulty of organising women became apparent, the WTUL increasingly sought to attain the same objective, that of improving the wages, hours and conditions of female workers, by legislative means. Like the NCL, the WTUL operated as a gender-based and cross-class organisation which deployed the language of 'sisterhood' rather than the language of class.

These small groups of professional women reformers and settlement workers, themselves mostly unmarried, gained strength from their alliance with a larger body of married women of similar social status, who, sharing the same ideals of motherhood and 'municipal housekeeping', responded to their pleas for political and financial support. The largest body of organised women was to be found in the women's club movement. Women's clubs until the

29. Skocpol, *Protecting Soldiers and Mothers*, p. 353.

1890s were predominantly devoted to 'self-culture' and the study of literature, but around the turn of the century they began to discuss a range of social and political topics and to campaign for better schools and public health facilities and ultimately for social reform. In 1891 a General Federation of Women's Clubs (GFWC) was formed, which in 1911 claimed a membership of over a million spread across every state in the Union. Along with the similarly constituted National Congress of Mothers, the GFWC constituted a powerful lobby on behalf of reform in the interests of women and children.

The development of social policy in the United States during the Progressive Era was greatly influenced by this network of organised women. Despite their debarment from the suffrage and their exclusion from formal political power, middle-class women exerted extraordinary leverage, at least in the field of social policy. Large numbers of highly educated women, excluded from most professional careers, engaged in reform activities, either as full-time activists or through the medium of women's clubs. Denied access to the male world of patronage politics, women developed an alternative political style, based on campaigns of public education and moralistic appeals. Prominent women lobbied legislators and public officials, often exploiting the family and class connections that their social position afforded them. They organised letter-writing campaigns which, at appropriate moments, deluged legislators with impassioned pleas from female constituents who, though themselves non-voters, might influence the votes of unknown numbers of male relatives. Excluded from party politics, women could claim to pursue disinterested and nonpartisan goals. Their reform proposals were accepted largely because they impinged upon few important male prerogatives and challenged few important interests. Male politicians were often prepared, accepting the logic of maternalism, to defer to women on questions relating to motherhood and child welfare. It was largely because women contrived to exploit the space inside a male-dominated political culture that they were so successful in attaining their legislative objectives.

Towards a maternalist welfare state

A final layer in this female network of reform came in the form of women officials who, like Florence Kelley as factory inspector in Illinois during the mid-1890s, were responsible for enforcing social and labour legislation and also represented women's interests in government. In 1912, after a long campaign, women gained a permanent foothold in the federal government in the United States Children's Bureau, an agency which was established to collect and distribute information about child welfare but which also operated in effect as a women's bureau. Despite its small budget (initially $25,640) and staff (fifteen), it derived a disproportionate influence from its contact with women's organisations, whose members acted in effect as unpaid agents of the Bureau. The female reform network served therefore almost as an extension of the state. Both Julia Lathrop, the Bureau's first chief, and her successor Grace Abbott, were alumnae of Hull House; both retained their close links with the settlements. Indeed, the Bureau, says Molly Ladd-Taylor, 'functioned more like a social settlement than a government bureaucracy'.[30] Lathrop and Abbott worked conscientiously to find positions for like-minded women. Therefore the Bureau, being, according to Seth Koven and Sonya Michel, 'the only female-controlled state bureaucracy in the world', provided a rare focus of career opportunity for women in public service.[31] By shrewd cultivation of its organisational network and by placing its emphasis on less controversial issues such as infant mortality, the Bureau achieved a sixfold increase in resources by 1915 and a still greater role in enforcing the Sheppard-Towner Act and, more briefly, the federal child labour law. However, both federal child labour legislation and Sheppard-Towner were short-lived, and in the long term the Children's Bureau derived more significance as the focal point of a network of associational activities than as the administrator of substantive policy.

The Sheppard-Towner Act of 1921 was a final flourish of the progressive social reform ethos. It arose out of the Children's Bureau's interest in reducing the comparatively high US levels of infant mortality. Lathrop believed that the problem was largely caused by poor education in maternal and infant hygiene, so, by analogy with the Smith-Lever Act, which provided federal matching funds to support the work of the Agricultural Extension Service, she proposed that federal money be made available to supplement expenditures by the states on preventive health-care facilities, such

30. Molly Ladd-Taylor, 'Hull House goes to Washington: women and the Children's Bureau', in Noralee Frankel and Nancy S. Dye, eds, *Gender, Class, Race, and Reform in the Progressive Era* (Lexington, Ky., 1991), p. 112.

31. Seth Koven and Sonya Michel, 'Womanly duties' *American Historical Review* 95 (1990), p. 1095.

as outpatient clinics, public health nursing and education. Supported by a formidable array of women's organisations, marshalled by the newly established Women's Joint Congressional Coordinating Committee, and benefiting from congressmen's nervousness regarding the impact of the newly enfranchised female vote, the proposal passed with little overt opposition in 1921. This was a programme pregnant with possibilities. It initiated the growth of an administrative structure, both at federal and state levels, which was almost wholly peopled by female social workers and medical practitioners, and greatly expanded the potential uses of government power. In doing so it enlarged the role of the Children's Bureau as 'the central directorate of this possible maternalist welfare state'.[32] By imposing a novel emphasis on preventive, rather than *post facto*, health-care, it opened up a whole new area of medical practice. Finally, by pioneering the use of matching grants in social policy, it developed a fiscal mechanism by which the federal government could exert a compelling influence upon the states and promote the expansion of national welfare programmes. This system of federal/state financing, which fitted US social policy around the structures of the federal system, was to become a basis for American welfare programmes from the 1930s onwards. Sheppard-Towner was therefore an important first step in the development of the American welfare state. The infant and maternal care programmes themselves, sadly, fell foul of the mounting opposition of the medical fraternity, disturbed at the rise of a new and largely independent field of practice, and the growing conservative mood of the later 1920s, only later to re-emerge as Title V of the Social Security Act.

By the end of the 1920s, then, the maternalist programme was only partially achieved. In the space left by the absence of a strong working-class movement and a well-established civil bureaucracy, women's organisations had promoted their own vision of a 'maternalist welfare state', devoted to the protection of women and children, which gave American social policy in this period its distinctive character. In a way, as Kathryn Kish Sklar suggests, 'gender-specific legislation became a surrogate for class legislation'.[33] However, although women's hours were regulated in nearly every state in the Union, the movement for minimum-wage laws was stopped in its tracks by the *Adkins* decision. In the absence

32. Skocpol, *Protecting Soldiers and Mothers*, p. 523.

33. Kathryn Kish Sklar, *Florence Kelley and the Nation's Work: The Rise of Women's Political Culture, 1830–1900* (New Haven, Ct., 1995), p. 236.

of federal regulation, control of child labour depended on the uneven determination of the states to enforce their laws, and the decline in the number of children working that did occur after 1910 was due much more to changing parental expectations and changing industrial practices than to legal sanctions. Whether because of parsimonious and pernickety administration or, as is more likely, because of their initial formulation, mothers' pensions did not form the basis of an adequate or dependable income support for single parents. And the jewel in the crown of maternalist social welfare, Sheppard-Towner, met an early and discouraging demise. The maternalist programme, therefore, in which so much hope had been invested, while still constituting the brightest thread in social policy innovation in the Progressive Era, was largely abortive. When a true American welfare state was created during the 1930s it took on a very different character.

CHAPTER SIX

The 1920s

Prohibition

'After one year from the ratification of this article, the manufacture, sale, or transportation of intoxicating liquors within ... the United States ... for beverage purposes is hereby prohibited.' With these words, the Eighteenth Amendment to the Constitution, ratified in 1919, initiated the 'noble experiment' of prohibition. The enforcement and non-enforcement of prohibition provide us with some of our most vivid images of the 'Roaring Twenties': barrels of bootleg gin split open with an axe, spilling their contents into the gutter; dramatic raids on speakeasies; violent gun-battles fought on the streets of Chicago by rival contenders for the lucrative trade in bootleg liquor; champagne cocktails consumed with debonair grace by elegant men and women in fashionable attire. Indeed, the apparently futile attempt to control public drinking by federal law seems wholly at odds with the forces of social innovation and cultural modernism that gave the 'Jazz Age' its special flavour. Yet many intelligent men and women, like Herbert Hoover, regarded prohibition as 'a great social and economic experiment, noble in motive and far-reaching in purpose'.[1] It brought to its logical conclusion a series of campaigns to regulate the moral order and pushed to its limits a particular agenda of coercive reform. The Eighteenth Amendment was potentially the most significant amendment since Reconstruction. Like the Thirteenth Amendment, that abolished slavery, it condemned a substantial property interest and fundamentally altered social and economic relationships. It brought an unprecedented level of federal intervention into the lives of

1. Quoted in Norman H. Clark, *Deliver Us from Evil: An Interpretation of American Prohibition* (New York, 1976), p. 191.

American citizens and, as David E. Kyvig suggests, it sought to 'redraw for all time the boundary between the public and private spheres of American life'.[2] Prohibition was, among other things, a failed experiment in state-building.

National prohibition was the culmination of a crusade against the 'demon rum' that went back nearly a hundred years. For generations evangelical Protestant ministers had condemned liquor as 'a habit which estrange[d] the soul from the means of grace' and which led men and women into the reach of temptation.[3] Medical science had demonstrated that alcoholic beverages detracted from an individual's physical and mental efficiency, as well as producing cirrhosis of the liver, heart disease and even insanity. Owing to a generation of pressure from the Women's Christian Temperance Union, schoolbooks throughout the land taught that alcohol was 'a dangerous and seductive poison', that a little liquor created the appetite for more, and that degradation and crime were the inevitable results of intemperance.[4] Thus the generation that reached voting age in the early twentieth century had been fully indoctrinated regarding the evils associated with drink.

Above all, temperance had come to be identified with the middle-class ethic of Victorian America, with the bourgeois virtues of hard work, thrift and self-restraint. Temperance was a prerequisite for economic success, an 'emblem of respectability' that clearly distinguished decent hard-working folk from the dissolute, the degenerate and the indigent, who, it was believed, were poor and wretched precisely because they failed to practice the necessary prudential virtues. Therefore prohibition was largely a middle-class movement, drawing most of its support, as a number of local studies have demonstrated, from a rural middle class of commercial farmers and an urban middle class of small business people and white-collar workers. It was also a movement to protect the American home against the forces of social disruption and moral disorder, and it was for this reason that it won the support of so many women.

For most of the nineteenth century the temperance movement had relied on persuasion, on appeals to the conscience of Protestant America – to a shared set of moral values which, if not always practised, were generally acknowledged. But by the closing

2.   David E. Kyvig, 'Sober thoughts', in Kyvig, ed., *Law, Alcohol, and Order: Perspectives on National Prohibition* (Westport, Ct., 1985), p. 6.
3.   J.C. Furnas, *The Life and Times of the Late Demon Rum* (London, 1966), p. 203.
4.   Andrew Sinclair, *Prohibition: The Era of Excess* (London, 1962), p. 64.

decades of the century it had reached something of an impasse. Despite its efforts, large numbers of men and women, particularly in immigrant communities where the hegemonic values of Victorian middle-class culture did not hold sway, continued to imbibe. Despite its efforts, the liquor traffic, the commercial interests that profited from the corruption of men and the ruin of families – the 'drunkard-making business', as prohibitionists liked to call it – remained intact. Therefore, to achieve its goals, the temperance movement had to resort to legal prohibition. Furthermore, in view of the large and intractable pockets of resistance, in view of the power and scope of the liquor traffic, it ultimately had to resort to national prohibition.

As its title suggests, the leading prohibitionist organisation, the Anti-Saloon League (ASL), concentrated its fire upon the saloon, and particularly upon the urban saloon – not upon the drinker, who was more commonly characterised, in a manner consistent with the environmentalist assumptions of Progressive Era social reform, as a victim of the liquor traffic, rather than a sinner driven to ruin by his own personal demons. By the turn of the century the liquor problem was associated with the saloons that abounded in the slum districts of American cities, and therefore with the social and moral problems of the inner city. The liquor traffic was identified as a social evil, damaging not only to the individual but to society, and therefore warranting drastic punitive measures. It was perceived as a cause of poverty, crime and prostitution, of family breakdown, and of social disorder. Thus the prohibition movement touched upon many of the central concerns of progressive social reform. Many progressives saw the eradication of the liquor traffic as a necessary step in their progress towards a better and cleaner, as well as a more efficient, America. The liquor traffic was a social evil, equivalent to the other social evils, such as child labour, prostitution or monopoly, upon which the progressives turned their enormous capacity for moral indignation and against which they had no compunction about calling on the regulatory powers of government. Even if they did not necessarily regard it as a primary remedy, prohibition was endorsed by many progressives, including social reformers like Jane Addams and Robert Woods, social scientists like Edward Ross and Simon Patten, and congressional insurgents like William E. Borah and Albert B. Cummins. Many of the earnest, well-educated young men and women who supported reform causes came to view drinking in saloons as a barbaric and atavistic habit that had no place in modern civilisation. Without their support national prohibition could never have overcome the formidable obstacles that lay in its path.

The prohibition movement was well-organised and well-led. The Women's Christian Temperance Union, established in 1874, marshalled the forces of American women in the cause of temperance reform. With over 200,000 members by 1892 it was far and away the largest women's organisation in America. The Anti-Saloon League, formed in 1895, became one of the most powerful pressure groups in the country. Through its firm links with local Protestant churches, it marshalled the temperance vote with great skill, carefully exploiting the balance of power in each congressional or legislative district to maximise its political impact. 'I do it the way the bosses do it', explained its legislative super-intendent, 'with minorities.'[5] Candidates were judged solely on their promises to vote for legislation favoured by the ASL, and, if elected, their performance was carefully monitored by its legislative agents, with the threat of political annihilation hanging over those foolhardy enough to stray off line.

The effectiveness of the ASL raises the question of how much popular support prohibition really had at the time of the ratification of the Eighteenth Amendment. The requisite majorities were assembled in Congress and the state legislatures, in most of which urban populations were in any case scandalously under-represented, by the systematic application of balance-of-power politics. Only one state, Ohio, a state which came closer than any other to representing the nation in microcosm, held a referendum on the amendment, which produced a verdict against ratification by the narrowest possible margin: 479 out of a million votes. It is likely that a national referendum would have been similarly inconclusive. Taking into account all the referenda held on statewide prohibition before 1919, together with voting in Congress and the state legislatures, Kyvig concludes that prohibition might well have commanded the support of a slender majority of the national electorate, but that was still too fragile a basis on which to amend the Constitution and to attempt so drastic an intervention in the field of social behaviour.

It was no accident that the resolution transmitting the Eighteenth Amendment to the states was passed during wartime. The peculiar atmosphere of the First World War, with its repudiation of all things German, including brewers with German

---

5. Quoted in Blocker, *American Temperance Movements: Cycles of Reform* (Boston, 1989), pp. 96–7.

names, its calls for the conservation of food to feed the starving of Europe, its demands for level-headed sobriety in the name of military and industrial efficiency, its ready acquiescence in the exercise of federal power, and its appeals for personal sacrifice on behalf of the general good, was especially conducive to its attainment. Yet too much emphasis must not be placed on the psychology of wartime. The Congress that passed the resolution had been elected in 1916, as a result of a vigorous and successful campaign by the ASL, and half the population was already living under dry laws. The attainment of national prohibition, though greatly facilitated by the war, was already probable by 1917.

Our appreciation of the origins of national prohibition is made more difficult by the fact that it is necessarily refracted through the experience of the 1920s, when prohibition quite conspicuously failed to eliminate the illegal traffic in booze. According to our best estimates, by the late 1920s, consumption had recovered to about two-thirds of prewar levels. For those sufficiently intent on alcoholic refreshment, liquor could be obtained more or less freely, though at considerably greater cost, throughout the United States. Bootleg booze was derived from industrial, medical, and even sacramental alcohol, all of which were permitted under the Volstead Act. An estimated 15 million gallons of industrial alcohol went missing, while physicians blatantly abused their power, like the Detroit practitioner who issued a prescription for whiskey with the instruction to 'take three ounces every hour for stimulant until stimulated'.[6] Millions of gallons of booze seeped across the nation's extensive and lightly patrolled frontiers. Enough liquor crossed the border from Canada to feed rumours of a secret pipeline near Detroit, while liquor imports into the Bahamas increased by a factor of 386, with most of the increment no doubt finding its way across the narrow straits to Florida. Moonshine alcohol was created in thousands of stills all across America. As the Wickersham Commission, appointed by President Herbert Hoover to report on prohibition law enforcement at the end of the 1920s, admitted, 'few things are more easily made than alcohol'.[7] In Detroit alone, in the late 1920s, the turnover in illegal booze was estimated at $215 million a year, while the number employed, at around 50,000, was comparable to the number legally employed by the liquor industry before 1916. So large an illegal business provided rich pickings for

6. Larry Engelman, *Intemperance: The Lost War against Liquor* (New York, 1979), p. 33.
7. Quoted in Sinclair, *Prohibition*, p. 204.

criminal gangs, which controlled the traffic in most large cities. But they did so with the implicit connivance of local authorities. In many cities, especially those with large immigrant or Hispanic populations, the law was effectively nullified by non-enforcement. Galveston, for example, was described as being effectively 'outside the United States' as far as the prohibition laws were concerned.

In view of the enormity of the task of drying up the whole United States, it seems difficult to imagine how the prohibitionists ever expected to succeed, especially in view of obvious loopholes in the Volstead Act and, more importantly still, the failure, until the end of the 1920s, to appropriate sufficient resources to make its enforcement even remotely possible. For most of the decade the Prohibition Bureau had no more than 3,000 agents, nowhere near enough to patrol the thousands of miles of frontier and coastline that separated the United States from a drink-infested world, and the thousands of square miles of mountain and wilderness and the countless city blocks in which moonshine might be concocted. The prohibitionists depended upon local and state governments to provide what enforcement was required, without an intrusive federal presence. Yet many states passed enforcement legislation with the greatest reluctance and ignored it when passed, while some municipalities devoted few if any resources to the enforcement of laws of which a majority of their citizens did not approve. The prohibitionists made changes in law without creating the administrative machinery that was necessary to make them effective. They did not envisage a massive enforcement exercise equivalent to the creation of a police state. When, under the conscientious insistence of President Hoover, the Bureau's resources were expanded in a genuine effort to make prohibition effective and when tougher penalties were imposed for offences under the Volstead Act, the result was to antagonise the citizenry and increase support for its repeal.

Like other contemporary reformers, the prohibitionists believed, rather naïvely it must be said, that most citizens, or at least the majority of decent, law-abiding folk, would obey the law. While they never expected prohibition to be wholly effective, realising that unregenerate drunkards would always manage to find booze somewhere, they hoped that the worst temptations provided by the liquor traffic would be removed and, above all, that young people, the 'coming generation', would grow up in a world from which the baleful influence of the saloon had been purged. They did not appreciate how doggedly ethnic and religious minorities would resist a law imposed upon them against their will, and they did not anticipate that many of the 'better elements' on whose support they had relied would come to frequent speakeasies with such insouciant relish. Both men and women consumed cocktails in flagrant disregard for the prohibition laws and in open contempt for the moral and sexual taboos which had attached themselves for so long to drinking. Carrying liquor and serving cocktails now became a mark of distinction and, in view of its cost, an indication of the superior status of those able to afford it.

The problem was that many of the 'coming generation' were turning away from the moral standards of their parents, from the Victorian middle-class culture on which the whole ethos of temperance had been founded. The early decades of the century saw a 'deep change' in American society and culture, what Walter Lippman described as 'a vast dissolution of ancient habits', the end-product of which was twentieth-century American culture.[8] In an increasingly affluent society traditional inhibitions began to seem anachronistic, especially for urban middle-class families who were in a position to enjoy the fruits of prosperity without so much anxiety about the future. Contemporary advertising urged individuals to indulge themselves, suggesting that the road to personal fulfilment lay in the consumption of goods, while movies and magazines presented for emulation images of the good life in the shape of a flamboyant upper-class lifestyle. The early twentieth century saw what Frederick Lewis Allen, with no little exaggeration, called a 'revolution in manners and morals'. There appeared to be a new permissiveness abroad, particularly in the behaviour of young people and particularly in the behaviour of young women – symbolised most evidently in the 'Flapper' with her bobbed hair, bright lipstick, short skirts and rolled stockings, who smoked cigarettes in public and performed, to the sounds of the new and lascivious 'jazz' music, dances like the shimmy, the Charleston and the Black Bottom whose uninhibited and sensuous movements represented a drastic departure from the decorousness of the waltz. There were clear signs of changes in sexual attitudes, whether in the almost obsessive interest in the subject shown by newspapers, magazines and movies or the rising incidence of extramarital intercourse and premarital pregnancy. Young people, then, were in the course of fashioning a new lifestyle which valued individual gratification and self-fulfilment rather than restraint, impulse rather

8.   Quoted in William E. Leuchtenburg, *The Perils of Prosperity, 1914–1932* (Chicago, 1958), p. 176.

than conscience, and individual liberty rather than responsibility –
one which expressed a spirit of youthful rebellion, yet did so in a
manner that was wholly consistent with the needs of the new
'consumer society'. In such a world prohibition seemed hopelessly
out of place.

The blatant disregard for the law in many localities should not
blind us to the fact that over much of the country prohibition
enjoyed loyal support. Yet, even here, enforcement proved difficult.
The tortured history of prohibition law enforcement provides the
context for one of the most striking, but least understood, political
manifestations of the 1920s: the resurgence of the Invisible Empire
of the Ku Klux Klan. Reorganised by Colonel William Simmons in
1915 as a 'Christian, benevolent, fraternal organization', the Klan
began to grow rapidly after 1920 when its leaders made a deliberate
effort to tap the anxieties and prejudices of communities all over
America. Membership reached a peak of somewhere between 2
million and 5 million members in the mid-1920s. By virtue of its
identification with the spirit of 'hundred per cent Americanism',
the Klan offered a focus to those who were disturbed by alien
threats to Protestant Anglo-Saxon America. But it cannot be
comprehended simply as a movement of xenophobic reaction
against various Others: African-Americans, Hispanics, immigrants,
Catholics, Jews or Bolsheviks. Many decent, respectable men (and,
in its female auxiliaries, women) were attracted to the Klan
principally because it offered itself as an agency of moral and
political reform which promised to clean up political corruption,
prostitution, organised crime and, above all, bootlegging when local
governments conspicuously failed to do so. When most citizens in a
community were firmly committed to the goal of prohibition and
local authorities connived at blatant violation of the law, citizens
sometimes resorted to direct action, and the Klan was often the
agency through which they achieved their goals. 'We have scoured
Goshen and Bear Swamp for illicit distilleries and watched our
stores and streets for bootleg liquor for the past few years', claimed
the local klavern, 'until now Calypso is one of the cleanest little
towns in North Carolina.' 'The Ku Klux Klan', admitted the
superintendent of the Indiana ASL in 1924, in an unguarded
moment, '... is doing many things which we would have liked to
have done.'[9] Despite its sinister reputation, the Klan appealed to

9. Quoted in David M. Chalmers, *Hooded Americanism: The First Century of the Ku
Klux Klan* (Garden City, N.Y., 1965), p. 96; K. Austin Kerr, *Organized for Prohibition A
New History of the Anti-Saloon League* (New Haven, Ct., 1985), p. 230.

respectable citizens as a reforming organisation which carried on, rather than repudiated, the reforming idealism of the Progressive Era. In time, the Order turned out to be too corrupt, sometimes too violent, but everywhere too ineffective, to serve as the instrument of moral regeneration that many of its members were looking for.

Prohibition retained substantial support throughout the decade. Despite clear evidence that the law was not working well, its defenders, convinced that adequate enforcement would, over time, produce the desired results, refused to consent to modification, never mind repeal, of the Volstead Act. As late as the presidential election of 1928, when Hoover overcame the challenge of Al Smith, who as Governor of New York had allowed his state to repeal its prohibition enforcement act, it appeared that a majority of voters had opted for a continuation of the 'noble experiment'. Yet five years later national prohibition was dead. The Twenty-first Amendment repealed the Eighteenth. Many factors contributed to this extraordinary reversal. The proximate cause was obviously the Depression, which drastically undermined claims that prohibition would lead to prosperity and a betterment of social conditions. Instead, it was now argued that repeal would create jobs and restore, through excise taxes, a badly needed source of government revenue. The Anti-Saloon League, as K. Austin Kerr has shown, virtually imploded after 1919. Suffering from debilitating internal divisions, it failed to decide on an appropriate strategy for its new role in prohibition enforcement, and sources of funds virtually dried up. Its 'incredible powerlessness' left the dry cause without effective leadership.[10] On the other hand, the newly formed Association against the Prohibition Amendment launched an effective campaign, using sophisticated public relations methods which were as innovative as those of the ASL had been in their time.

Ultimately, however, prohibition failed because a critical number of Americans changed their minds about the acceptability of regulating personal behaviour in an age which increasingly valued personal freedom and the right to enjoy the fruits of a consumer society. The victory of prohibition occurred at the historical moment when the value system of Victorian America was in the process of disintegration. As the Wickersham Commission sadly remarked, the Eighteenth Amendment and the Volstead Act came at the best time for their adoption and the worst time for their enforcement. Indeed, the fate of prohibition, acclaimed by one

10. Kerr, *Organized for Prohibition*, p. 270.

generation and reviled by the next, reveals better than anything else the nature of the transformation in American culture that came to a head in the 1920s.

Prohibition failed, most obviously, because it did not enjoy the support of a sufficient proportion of the American people. It failed also because it was not adequately enforced. Yet adequate enforcement was impossible without creating an administrative machinery which would have fundamentally transformed the nature of the American state. It was largely because most Americans refused to contemplate such a transformation that prohibition was eventually allowed to wither on the vine.

The politics of 'normalcy'

The 1920s is remembered as an era of social and cultural experimentation, of Flappers and flivvers, of movies and jazz, of behaviourism and relativity, but the cultural and intellectual modernism of the decade sits oddly alongside its apparent conservatism in political matters. Its political life, complacent, backward-looking and reactionary, looks like a throwback to the 1890s. Consider our received images of the presidents: Warren Harding (1921–23), a small-town Ohio editor of admittedly limited intellectual ability, a genial politician of the old school whose chief diversions were poker, whiskey, golf and occasional philandering, whose chief talent lay in a kind of splendid but vacuous oratory that he described as 'bloviating', and whose cronies, trespassing on his kind and trusting disposition, threw themselves into an orgy of graft unsurpassed since the days of Grant; Calvin Coolidge (1923–29), who succeeded Harding on his premature death, an old-fashioned Vermont Yankee who made a virtue out of taciturnity, frugality and political inaction, a 'Puritan in Babylon', in William Allen White's telling phrase, whose exemplification of traditional virtues seemed so comfortingly to counterbalance the indulgences of the Jazz Age; and, finally, Herbert Hoover (1929–31), who sat fiddling while the economy nose-dived into depression, leaving it to Franklin Roosevelt to rescue the nation from collapse. The very word 'normalcy', which Harding coined in a moment of rhetorical excess and which has come to characterise the dominant political ethos of the decade, expresses a longing to retreat from the crusading idealism of the Progressive Era. However, such a reading of the politics of the 1920s as an inexplicable interregnum between the heroic reforming endeavours of progressivism and the New Deal not only raises serious problems of historical interpretation but does scant justice to the complexities of its history.

According to the journalist Herbert Croly, the election of 1920, in which an overwhelming majority of voters accepted Harding's pledge to return the nation to 'normalcy', represented 'the eclipse of liberalism or progressivism as an effective force in American politics'.[11] This judgement was, in retrospect, substantially, but not wholly, true. Certainly the conservatives who dominated the victorious Republican Party wished to liberate business from the restrictions and regulations imposed in the Progressive Era. 'We need vastly more freedom than we do regulation', said Harding. 'This is a business country', said Coolidge, 'and it wants a business government.'[12] And this Harding and Coolidge, and especially Coolidge, set out to provide. Whereas Harding was a more pliable politician, eager to mediate between the various Republican factions and willing to find space in his administration both for the traditional tax-cutting endeavours of Andrew Mellon and the more innovative projects of former progressives like Henry A. Wallace and Herbert Hoover, Coolidge was a doctrinaire believer in *laissez-faire* and limited government. 'Never before', said the *Wall Street Journal* in 1925, '... has a government been so completely fused with business.'[13]

With the encouragement of Andrew Mellon, the fabulously wealthy Pittsburgh banker who served as Secretary of the Treasury under all three presidents, Congress made deep cuts in federal taxation (which remained, however, well above prewar levels). The Revenue Acts of 1921, 1924 and 1926 cut surtax by two-thirds, the estate tax by half and repealed taxes on gifts and excess profits, saving in all $3.5 billion to the wealthiest taxpayers. At the same time the Fordney-McCumber Tariff of 1922 raised duties to levels which were virtually prohibitive as far as most imports were concerned. In this reversion to high protectionism, if in nothing else, the party recaptured the spirit of Gilded Age Republicanism.

The various agencies set up in the Progressive Era to regulate business corporations were transformed by a series of pro-business appointments, as well as severe budgetary constraints, leading the *Nation* to accuse the Administration of 'the deliberate breaking

---

11. Leuchtenburg, *Perils of Prosperity*, p. 124.
12. Quoted in Robert K. Murray, *The Harding Era* (Minneapolis, 1969), p. 171; Arthur M. Schlesinger Jr., *The Crisis of the Old Order, 1919–1933* (Cambridge, Mass., 1957), p. 61.
13. Quoted in ibid., p. 61.

down of the governmental safeguards against the evils of big business'.[14] The Federal Trade Commission, for instance, created in 1914 to enforce the antitrust laws, under the complaisant chairmanship of the conservative Republican William E. Humphrey, set out to serve as a 'help to business' instead of 'an instrument of oppression and disturbance and injury'.[15] Its scope for administrative discretion having been narrowly circumscribed by the Supreme Court during the early 1920s, the FTC restricted itself largely to policing fraudulent sales practices, such as 'false and misleading advertising in reference to hair-restorers, anti-fat remedies, etc.', rather than rooting out unfair methods of competition.[16] Rather than issuing 'cease and desist' orders, it preferred to negotiate private settlements, and rather than imposing codes of fair practice on business groups, it encouraged them to draw up their own. This, as we shall see, was wholly consistent with the 'associational' approach adopted by Hoover in the Department of Commerce. Unsurprisingly, in the wake of the *US Steel* decision, the Antitrust Division of the Justice Department did not seek to dissolve any large industrial combination, and it did nothing to check a new wave of mergers. While the Division turned a beady eye on the activities of trade associations early in the decade, from 1924 it too became more tolerant of private agreements regarding trade practices.

Likewise, the Federal Reserve Board, dominated by the banking interests that it was supposed to regulate, kept a loose rein over the money market, doing little or nothing to check the speculative bubble that was reaching dangerous proportions on Wall Street and elsewhere. However, it is doubtful that the Board possessed the statutory authority to supervise the currency reserves of banks or the availability of credit for stock-market speculation. The decentralised structure of the Federal Reserve System created in 1913 left much power in the hands of the regional reserve banks, especially the New York branch, which held a third of the system's assets. Under the aggressive leadership of Benjamin F. Strong, the New York Federal Reserve Bank largely set policy for the system as a whole, and that policy was conducive to low rediscount rates and easy money. Here, as in antitrust policy, the entropy of regulation during the 1920s was as much a consequence of defects in the original

---

14.   Quoted in G. Cullom Davis, 'The transformation of the Federal Trade Commission, 1914–1929' *Mississippi Valley Historical Review* 49 (Dec. 1962), p. 448.

15.   Quoted in ibid., p. 445.

16.   Morton Keller, *Regulating a New Economy: Public Policy and Economic Change in America, 1900–1933* (Cambridge, Mass., 1990), p. 40.

Progressive Era statutes as the product of some malign conspiracy to subvert regulation 'by a process of boring from within'.[17] It reflected the ambivalence that had characterised government–business relations during the Progressive Era.

The Republican administrations of the 1920s, while condoning quite extensive federal assistance to agriculture, for example through farm credits legislation, regulation of product exchanges and assistance to farm cooperatives, refused to endorse any effective support for farm prices. Operating in an increasingly protectionist international economy, American farmers were losing access to the overseas markets on which they relied to absorb about a quarter of what they produced. Their favoured solution, embodied in the McNary-Haugen bills of 1927 and 1928, was for the federal government to set an appropriate 'parity' price for staple crops, buy up the surplus that could not be sold at that rate and dump it overseas for whatever it would fetch. Such a system of farm subsidies Coolidge condemned as a violation of the spirit of American institutions, involving the appropriation of government resources for the benefit of one class of the population. It would incite farmers to produce more, not less, and the disposal of the surplus, if it could be managed at all, would provoke retaliation by America's trading partners, rendering an unstable international trading situation still more unstable. While the McNary-Haugen bill was a seriously flawed solution to the farm problem, the government failed to offer any effective alternative, allowing farm prices and farm incomes to slide still further, with damaging effects on the whole economy. Like the fall in the share of national income going to wages, which was exacerbated by government suppression of trade unions, the decline of farm incomes contributed to the collapse of mass purchasing power that brought the decade to its calamitous close.

More than three decades ago the historian Arthur S. Link posed the question 'What happened to the progressive movement in the 1920s?'. As he himself noted, and as others have confirmed, there never had been a unified 'progressive movement' in the first place. Progressivism was a broad church embracing miscellaneous reform movements, variously constituted and seeking diverse objectives. Many of these were very much alive during the 1920s, including the surviving segments of organised labour, the farm bloc, social reformers, and the champions of public power.

17.   John D. Hicks, *Republican Ascendancy, 1921–1932* (New York, 1960), p. 66.

Republican insurgents, particularly from the Midwest, resisted the conservative, pro-business alignment of the party's Eastern wing. Men like Robert M. La Follette, Hiram Johnson and George Norris continued to fight for more vigorous prosecution of the antitrust laws and against private exploitation of hydro-electric sites like Muscle Shoals in Alabama. They continued to promote the interests of their predominately farming constituents. The insurgents were numerous enough at times, in alliance with Democrats representing rural constituencies, to hold Congress to ransom and extract concessions for agriculture, such as farm credits legislation, aid to farm cooperatives and the McNary-Haugen bill, which twice passed Congress only to be vetoed by Coolidge. The so-called 'farm bloc' was, in fact, as greedy, aggressive and ruthless in pursuit of its constituents' economic advantage as any other interest group during the 1920s. Nevertheless, in pursuit of their objectives the insurgents were drawn to support quite positive, and sometimes radical, uses of state power, for example in the shape of farm price supports and public control of water-power sites.

Although there were sizeable contingents of progressive Republicans, throughout the Progressive Era the Democratic Party at a national level proved more consistent in its support for reform. But the Democratic Party suffered badly from the widespread public disenchantment with the First World War. During the 1920s it was also seriously divided between its two main wings: on the one hand European immigrants and their descendants, mainly Roman Catholic in religion, living in the larger cities of the North and Midwest; on the other hand, the agrarian population of the South and West, of older American stock and Protestant faith. It was something of a historical accident that these two groups should share the same political home; they had little in common except their hatred of Republicans. They were naturally at loggerheads over a range of ethnocultural issues that were especially salient during the 1920s. Internecine warfare raged over questions like immigration restriction, the Ku Klux Klan and, above all, prohibition throughout the decade, culminating in the angry conflict over the presidential candidacy of Al Smith, a devout Catholic of Irish ancestry. Disagreement over such issues greatly detracted from the effectiveness of the Democratic Party as a national force. According to Frank Freidel, 'much of the failure of progressivism in the 1920s can be explained by this elementary fact'.[18]

18. Arthur S. Link, 'What happened to the progressive movement in the 1920s?' *American Historical Review* 64 (1959), p. 840.

Although the social reform movements of the Progressive Era largely dried up in terms of legislative progress, various groups were still at work during the 1920s, as Clarke Chambers has shown. The membership of organisations like the National Consumers' League and the National Women's Trade Union League declined after 1920, but many reform groups, especially women's organisations like the League of Women Voters and the Women's Joint Congressional Committee, retained their vigour. A coalition of women's groups secured passage of the Sheppard-Towner Act of 1921 and, after the Supreme Court twice overturned federal child labour laws, a resolution submitting a constitutional amendment prohibiting child labour to the states. However, the implications of Court decisions invalidating the federal child labour law and a District of Columbia minimum-wage law for women had a demoralising effect on social reformers for the rest of the decade. 'Truly we are like a semi-paralyzed centipede', commented Florence Kelley.[19] Although a number of states passed rudimentary and ineffective non-contributory old-age pension laws during the 1920s, social insurance made little headway in the face of powerful business lobbies and the indifference of most politicians, but this was the decade in which reformers, by working through various options for unemployment and old-age insurance, laid the ground-work for the Social Security Act. Without the reform activities of the 1920s the creation of the welfare state during the 1930s would have been much less feasible.

There was no shortage of concern about social deprivation, no lack of organised activity to improve social conditions, as the expansion of social work, the growth of Community Chests (agencies which collected funds from the general public for philanthropic purposes), and the work of the Young Men's Christian Association and other such organisations testify. What held social reform back in the 1920s was not so much indifference to social problems as a reluctance to resort to statist solutions. Like other progressive reform movements, it fell foul of what Frank J. Bruno of the Minneapolis Associated Charities described as 'the terrible reaction against all attempts to say by law what people shall do or shall not do'. As Lynn Dumenil observes, 'Antistatist rhetoric permeated the decade; newspapers, journals and congressional debates reverberated with the evils of federal expansion'. This Bruno attributed, among other things, to the postwar 'let-down

19.   Quoted in Clarke A. Chambers, *Seedtime of Reform: American Social Service and Social Action, 1918–1933* (Minneapolis, 1963), p. 73.

from idealism and from the sacrifices stimulated by war psychology'.[20] In America as in Europe, the apocalyptic destruction of the First World War left a residue of disillusionment and dismay that discredited the kind of reforming idealism in whose name the war had been fought. At the same time, the hyperpatriotism of wartime vitalised a spirit of hyperbolic 'hundred per cent Americanism' that was antipathetic to reasoned dissent. Social insurance, for example, was variously branded as 'made in Prussia' and 'Bolshevik-inspired'. As William L. Chenery explained, the detailed regulations imposed during wartime 'left many people cold to any extension of national control'.[21] The wartime mobilisation, with its conscription, wage and price controls, and suppression of dissent, had brought the federal government for the first time into the lives of many men and women who had before enjoyed only a tangential relationship with it, and in an especially oppressive and aggravating form. The popular reaction to the 'regimentation' of wartime explains much of the public hostility to government control during the decade. This was reinforced by the impact of prohibition, which, as Dumenil puts it, 'brought federal law into the lives of millions'. Its unpopularity with large sections of the population fuelled suspicion of government power and, by implication, discredited other forms of interventionist social policy. Although this suspicion attached itself particularly to federal regulation, drawing on established fears of what Senator William Borah called 'the remorseless urge of centralization, the insatiable maw of bureaucracy', many of the objections applied equally to state legislation.[22] Thus the reforming impulses of the Prosperity Decade tended to be channelled into non-statist forms.

Herbert Hoover's New Era

This is especially true of one of the most interesting reform projects of the era, namely the work of Herbert Hoover in the Department of Commerce. Although Hoover, because of his mistaken identification with 'rugged individualism', his tragic failure to cope with the Depression and his repudiation of the New Deal, later came to

20. Quoted in Chambers, *Seedtime of Reform*, p. 90; Lynn Dumenil, '"The insatiable maw of bureaucracy": antistatism and education reform in the 1920s' *Journal of American History* 74 (Sept. 1990), p. 518.
21. Chambers, *Seedtime of Reform*, p. 42.
22. Quoted in Dumenil, 'Insatiable maw of bureaucracy', pp. 522, 518.

be seen as the spokesman for an outmoded conservatism, he was regarded in 1920, Carl Degler reminds us, as 'the darling of the progressives'.[23] A mining engineer by profession, he acquired a reputation, through his organisation of food relief and his management of the Food Administration during the war, for successfully combining organisational efficiency and humanitarian concern. As Secretary of Commerce under Harding and Coolidge 'and assistant secretary of everything else', with a finger in almost everybody else's pie, he worked towards a progressive solution to the problem of government–business relations.

Hoover regularly proclaimed the virtues of the 'American system'. American society, he believed, was founded on the virtues of local initiative and individual self-reliance, as against the alien doctrines of 'despotism' and 'socialism', which stifled initiative and enterprise under a blanket of bureaucracy. But the individualism that Hoover valued was not 'rugged individualism', not a system of cut-throat competition, red in tooth and claw, or, as he called it, 'individualism run riot', but a spirit of voluntary cooperation which he described as a 'higher individualism'. 'My concept of America', he said, betraying his Quaker origins, 'is a land where men and women may walk in ordered freedom.'[24] Modern conditions demanded that groups of individuals sharing common goals should cooperate to coordinate their activities. 'We are passing', he said in 1924, 'from a period of extreme individualistic action into a period of associational activities.'[25] Examples of fruitful cooperation included professional associations, trade unions, trade associations and farm cooperatives. The government could assist this process by collecting and disseminating information, by offering advice and guidance, and by providing initiative and persuasion – by acting in other words as a kind of facilitator. Hoover organised hundreds of conferences and commissions to foster associational activities. But the government should at no point exert compulsion or seek to do things for people. This network of voluntary organisations was a substitute for, not a servant of, government bureaucracy. This, then, was a middle way which Hoover saw as the American way, 'a new economic system based neither on the capitalism of Adam Smith

23. Carl Degler, 'The ordeal of Herbert Hoover', in Barton J. Bernstein and Allen Matusow, eds, *Twentieth-Century America: Recent Interpretations* (2nd edn, New York, 1972), p. 199.

24. Quoted in Joan Hoff Wilson, *Herbert Hoover: Forgotten Progressive* (Boston, 1975), p. 7; Martin L. Fausold, *The Presidency of Herbert C. Hoover* (Lawrence, Kan., 1985), p. 4.

25. Quoted in Wilson, *Herbert Hoover*, p. 68.

nor upon the socialism of Karl Marx', which would, by avoiding the extremes of unregulated individualism and government regimentation, preserve the American spirit of independence in an era of bureaucratic collectivism.[26]

Even though, like many progressives, he welcomed its productive efficiency, Hoover was well aware of the waste and inefficiency present in the existing organisation of American business. The eradication of waste (of which Hoover enumerated thirteen varieties) would expand output and make more wealth available to all. The elimination of cyclical fluctuations in output and employment by the coordination of inventories and investment would increase production over the long term and remove a fertile source of human misery and social discord. The institution of higher competitive practices would raise the overall standard of business conduct. And a more humane and socially responsible pattern of labour relations, practised in the most progressive companies in the guise of welfare capitalism, would make for a more harmonious and efficient society. Government control, however, was not the way to achieve these ends It was 'not the function of government to manage business', a task for which it was signally unsuited, but to investigate problems, distribute information and promote cooperative action.[27]

Businessmen were encouraged to form trade associations through which they could pool information, promote research, standardise products, and establish codes of fair practice in such matters as advertising and labour relations. The experience of wartime mobilisation had hinted at the economies that might be made through such cooperative ventures. Hoover's programme represented an attempt to institutionalise aspects of the wartime economy in a form appropriate to peacetime conditions. By such means a more orderly and rational business system might be created. 'Associationalism', or 'industrial self-government', according to Hoover's vision, offered a means of combining efficient planning and orderly development with the spirit of individualism. It would avoid both the wasteful and destructive aspects of free competition and the bureaucracy, red tape and rigidity of government supervision. Hoover's project, then, was by no means an attempt to return to the spirit of untempered *laissez-faire* but rather to negotiate a new relationship between government and business appropriate to the new century. His was a thoroughly progressive vision.

26. Quoted in Wilson, *Herbert Hoover*, p. 42.
27. Quoted in Hicks, *Republican Ascendancy*, p. 67.

The basis of Hoover's 'new era' was to be an alliance between the federal government and the great corporations and trade associations. This did not, as critics suggested, represent a capitulation by government to monopoly capitalism. Hoover was animated by a technocratic ideal in which government would point out the rational answers to social and economic problems and, by its educational activities, persuade others to follow them. He believed, said David Burner, 'that a rational intellect, shown the rational thing to do, will do it without coercion'.[28] Hoover recognised the need, on occasions, to resort to government regulation to prevent abuses of private power, but ultimately he trusted in the social responsibility of enlightened business leaders. Yet they were much less willing than he was to see the virtues of labour organisation, much slower to seize the advantages of standardisation, and uncomfortably eager to use trade associations for the purpose of price-fixing. Without government sanctions, associationalism turned all too easily into a vehicle for pressure group competition in which political and economic leverage weighed heavier than rational considerations of the public interest. Although the contradictions implicit in his vision did not become fully apparent during the 1920s, they soon did when Hoover, as president, confronted the challenge of the Depression.

Boom and bust

Nothing seems clearer in retrospect than the contrast between the 1920s and the 1930s in America. The Wall Street Crash of October 1929 marks a clear boundary between prosperity and depression, optimism and despair. However, the economic collapse must be set against the background of affluence and optimism that seemed to characterise the preceding decade. 'I have no fears for the future of our country', said Herbert Hoover in his inaugural address in March 1929. 'It is bright with hope.'[29] It was not just the newly elected president who failed to read the writing on the wall; almost every leading figure in the worlds of politics, business and the academy was equally sanguine. The 'economic condition of the world seems on the verge of a great forward movement', declared

28.   David Burner, 'Before the Crash', in Martin L. Fausold and George T. Mazuzan, eds, *The Hoover Presidency: A Reappraisal* (Albany, N.Y., 1974), p. 51.
29.   Quoted in Schlesinger, *Crisis of the Old Order*, p. 155.

the respected financier Bernard Baruch in June 1929.[30] Therefore the Crash came as an enormous shock to almost everyone, shattering confidence and expectations as categorically as it shattered economic institutions. In fact the seeds of the Depression of the 1930s were sown in the heady boom years of the 1920s: in the developing structure of industry, in the frenetic speculation, in the mal-distribution of wealth, and also, it must be said, in the careless and complacent economic policies of the federal government in the Harding–Coolidge era.

After a severe but short-lived postwar recession, the American economy resumed the pattern of growth that it had followed for a generation or more. In fact, the aggregate rate of growth during the 1920s was little faster than it had been in the first two decades of the century, but it took spectacular new forms, particularly in the development of a full-blown consumer society. Industrial prod-uction rose by 52 per cent over the course of the decade, as a result of the further application of mass-production techniques, the growing use of electric power and the development of scientific management. 'The old business of putting science into industry has been followed more intensively than ever before', explained a government report at the end of the decade. It went on to draw attention to the striking range of new products that gave visible form to this new abundance: 'Among consumers' goods, the conspicuous instances are automobiles, radios and rayon. But the list also includes . . . household electrical appliances in great variety, automobile accessories, antifreezing mixtures, cigarette lighters, propelling pencils, wrist watches, airplanes, and what not.'[31]

The automobile was the most spectacular example. Access to private automobiles, of course, had an almost revolutionary impact on the lives of those fortunate enough to own them. In view of the fact that there were over 26 million automobiles on the road by 1929, that one for every five Americans, that included a majority of families. The automobile also had a major impact on the American economy. The industry pioneered in the development of mass-production techniques. It was in the manufacture of Ford's popular Model T saloon that the first true assembly line was intro-duced, enabling a tenfold increase in throughput and a threefold reduction in costs. It was the Model T that brought car ownership

30.   Quoted in J.K. Galbraith, *The Great Crash 1929* (revised edn, Harmondsworth, Middx., 1975), p. 95.

31.   *Recent Economic Changes in the United States*, in Oscar Handlin, ed., *Readings in American History* (2 vols, New York, 1970), II, p. 199.

within the reach of families on modest incomes. The automobile industry pioneered in the cultivation of a mass market. This followed logically from the development of mass-production: auto- mobile manufacturers had to dispose of huge volumes of output in order to cover their fixed costs. Therefore companies like Ford pioneered in the development of instalment selling, in order that so expensive a purchase should be brought within the reach of ordinary families. Roughly three-quarters of all sales in the 1920s were carried out on a hire-purchase basis. Consumer credit was a significant departure from traditional ideals of thrifty inde- pendence, but it was absolutely crucial to the continuing health of the economy. Auto companies spent enormous sums on advertising, stressing in doing so the status, glamour and prestige associated with ownership of their products rather than their locomotive convenience. They produced increasingly elaborate and stylish models, designed to appeal to women as much as men, like the new Model A Ford ceremoniously unveiled in 1927 or, even more, the new models introduced annually by General Motors, which had already begun to build a measure of 'planned obsolescence' into its production schedules.

The automobile industry was central to the American economy in the 1920s. Not only was it a gigantic industry in itself, directly employing hundreds of thousands of workers, but it stimulated the production of rubber, glass, electrical components and petroleum products. Still more important was the influence of automobile traffic on highway construction. Local and state governments spent $16 billion during the 1920s on building 400,000 miles of roads, an investment comparable in its economic impact to the construction of the railroad network in the nineteenth century. Furthermore, the availability of private cars stimulated the suburban development which formed a major component of the real estate boom of the 1920s. In other words, a substantial portion of the American economy during the 1920s was directly or indirectly linked to the health of the automobile industry.

Other industries were linked to the automobile business in that they experienced the same problems. These were recently developed high-technology industries selling goods like radios, refrigerators and other electrical appliances which, like auto- mobiles, were both expensive and non-essential. They, too, were heavily dependent on advertising and consumer credit to stimulate and maintain demand. They, too, were engaged in what J.K. Galbraith later called the 'synthesis of desire'. According to William

E. Leuchtenburg, the United States was for the first time in the 1920s 'confronted with the need to fashion instruments and attitudes appropriate to an economy of abundance'.[32] A mass-production economy must also be a mass-consumption economy if it is to thrive. The collapse of the economy at the end of the decade signifies that the United States in the 1920s had not successfully negotiated that balance.

In the late 1920s optimism about the future prospects of the American economy was largely founded on the buoyant condition of the stock market. As share prices joyously spiralled upwards, money poured into the exchanges and the nation indulged itself in a frantic orgy of speculation. Rising share prices were widely read as an index of the economic health of the nation. But much of the increase in stock-market prices in the later 1920s was speculative in character, produced by the willingness of men, women and institutions to buy shares in the expectation that their price would rise, an expectation that would be met as long as everybody behaved like that. Speculative purchases were typically made 'on margin', with the purchaser paying only a fraction of the price, ranging from 10 to 50 per cent, and borrowing the remainder on the security of the stock. This enabled a given quantity of speculative money to do a great deal more work – the phenomenon known as 'leverage'. The high rates of interest on brokers' loans attracted capital from all over the world. As long as everybody kept buying and prices continued to rise, the speculative bubble continued to grow and money continued to flow into the market.

However (and, as Galbraith points out, it was bound to happen some time), eventually the bubble burst. There came a moment in October 1929 when, for various reasons (and it is immaterial precisely which, for, to quote Galbraith again, 'it is in the nature of a speculative boom that almost anything can collapse it'), a sufficient number of dealers unloaded shares to set in motion a wave of selling.[33] Some were forced to meet short-term liquidity requirements; others chose that moment to take their profits. Since so large a proportion of the money invested in the market was looking for short-term speculative gains, any downward movement of prices could spark off a wave of panic selling. Once that happened, those who had bought stock on margin were forced to sell rapidly before its value sank to a level which would not cover their loans. Leverage worked equally powerfully in reverse. On 24

32. Leuchtenburg, *Perils of Prosperity*, p. 11.
33. Galbraith, *Great Crash*, p. 113.

October, 'Black Thursday', panic set in. After a brief lull, still more frenetic selling took place on 29 October, 'Black Tuesday', when 16.4 million shares changed hands. For a while shares were unloaded faster than the Exchange could handle them, a state of affairs which created still greater uncertainty among investors. The wave of panic selling continued, wiping out half the value of shares on the New York Exchange within a month. Despite a few periods of remission, the stock market continued to plunge until, in July 1932, the average value of shares had fallen to roughly one-sixth of its September 1929 level. That, as Galbraith points out, was what was really unusual about the Great Crash. The events of October 1929 were no more dramatic than those of October 1987, for example, but after 1929 the market continued to plummet, with the result that almost nobody escaped unscathed.

The impact of the stock-market crash was catastrophic. It wiped out the assets of millions, not only those who had speculated in the market themselves, who numbered no more than a million or so, but also those whose savings had been held by banks, investment trusts and insurance companies which had been unable to resist the high rates of interest on brokers' loans. Therefore a large part of the financial system collapsed like a house of cards when the stock market went down. This not only intensified the sufferings of a great many individuals whose retirement plans had been abruptly ruined but also made recovery a great deal more difficult. Not until American financial institutions had been substantially reconstituted could they once more inspire confidence as the facilitators of investment and exchange. Equally serious was the searing impact of the Crash on business confidence, which was all the more traumatic by virtue of the extravagant hopes that had been invested in the stock market. Investors, having been severely burned, remained cautious, reluctant to invest or take risks throughout the 1930s, and this, perhaps more than anything else, delayed recovery. As Hoover's Secretary of Labor foresaw, the Crash produced 'an epidemic of fear and extreme caution, causing a retrenchment and curtailment of buying' which resulted ultimately in lower incomes and mounting unemployment.[34]

In fact, the financial system was riddled with structural defects that turned a short-term panic into a major crisis. The banking system was, in Ellis Hawley's words, 'rigged to collapse when

34. Quoted in Fausold, *Presidency of Herbert C. Hoover*, p. 75.

subjected to pressure for monetary liquidity'.[35] The thousands of small independent banks with too little capital to come under the shelter of the Federal Reserve System – many of them tied to the fate of a single industry, in most cases agriculture – were extremely vulnerable to economic adversity. Indeed, hundreds of rural banks went under every year during the Prosperity Decade. The shock waves emanating from Wall Street, combined with the fall in farm incomes and the crushing burden of farm debt, brought many more to ruin – 8,986 in all between 1930 and 1933. This contributed to a contraction of the nation's money stock, which fell by a third between 1929 and 1933. It is not probable, as monetarists like Milton Friedman and Anna Schwartz would argue, that the decline in the money supply itself precipitated the Depression that followed. The sequence of events is not consistent with a monetarist explanation. In particular, short-term interest rates, which would be expected to rise as a result of monetary constriction, remained low during the early years of the Depression. A shortage of credit was less important than a lack of demand. Nevertheless, the banking crisis caused a great deal of local inconvenience, reduced the liquidity of many individuals and firms and added to the general uncertainty that inhibited economic activity during the early 1930s.

The speculative boom of the late 1920s had hidden fundamental weaknesses in the American economy that would have made a recession highly probable even without the Crash, although it need not have been so calamitous in its effects. The market for automobiles and other consumer goods was already beginning to show signs of saturation. By then two in three households had at least one car. New demand could only come therefore from purchase of a second car, which obviously few families could afford; replacement of a still roadworthy vehicle with a new one, which, again, few families could afford and most families could defer; or purchase of an automobile by the (presumably) low-income households that did not already possess one. This would be impossible given the existing structure of consumer preference and the existing distribution of income. Maintenance, never mind expansion, of the market required either a lowering of prices or a redistribution of incomes which would place additional spending power in the hands of lower-income households which harboured more unfulfilled desires than their more affluent counterparts.

This did not happen during the 1920s. The prices set by large

35. Ellis Hawley, *The Great War and the Search for a Modern Order* (New York, 1979), p. 183.

corporations, operating in oligopolistic markets, were too inflexible to maintain demand over the long term. The distribution of income, if anything, became more, not less, unequal over the course of the decade. A study by the Brookings Institution estimated that the top 1 per cent of the population received 12 per cent of the national income in 1920 and 19 per cent in 1929, an outcome produced very largely by the reduction of federal taxes on high incomes. On the other hand, they discovered that in the latter year 42 per cent of households were below the poverty line and another 36 per cent living in 'minimal comfort'. Less than a quarter of the population therefore had sufficient disposable income to participate freely in the much-vaunted consumer culture of the 1920s.

Substantial sections of the workforce did not share in the decade's prosperity. While the richest 1 per cent enjoyed a 63 per cent rise in disposable income between 1923 and 1929, the bottom 93 per cent, that is nearly everybody else, saw their disposable income drop by 4 per cent. Although real wages rose by about 13 per cent between 1922 and 1929, that was by much less than the 62 per cent increase in corporate profits and the 65 per cent increase in dividends over the same period. Farmers, faced by depressed international markets, saw their incomes fall by as much as 40 per cent between 1919 and 1921 and then recover very slowly over the rest of the decade. Average farm incomes in 1929 were a quarter of average non-farm incomes. Too much of the national income went to profits and salaries, too little to wages and farm incomes. As the banker Frank Vanderlip put it, 'Capital kept too much and labor did not have enough to buy its share of things'.[36] The result was underconsumption, or, to put it another way, overproduction. There was, in the words of George Soule, 'a fatal lack of balance between industrial production and popular purchasing power'.[37] Corporate America had signally failed to solve the problem of maintaining demand in a mass-production economy.

In addition to America's domestic difficulties, the world economy was largely stagnant in the 1920s, seriously limiting export markets for American goods, and particularly American farm goods. The problem was, however, exacerbated by the policy of economic isolationism pursued by the United States. The almost prohibitive tariffs imposed in 1922 and again in 1930 made it nearly impossible

36. Quoted in Hicks, *Republican Ascendancy*, p. 230.
37. Quoted in Alan Dawley, *Struggles for Justice: Social Responsibility and the Liberal State* (Cambridge. Mass., 1991), p. 337.

for foreigners to earn the dollars that would enable them to buy American goods, while the inflexible attitude of the United States government towards repayment of the massive war debts owed by European nations ensured that a large part of the dollars that they did earn would be devoted to that end. The international system had come to depend heavily on flows of American capital, and was therefore highly vulnerable to a reduction of capital flows after October 1929. The result was a disastrous sequence of financial crises in Europe beginning in the summer of 1931, shock-waves from which set off renewed deflationary pressures within the United States.

Whereas the Depression clearly resulted from fundamental structural imbalances in the American and world economies, there is nevertheless a case for arguing that government policies during the 1920s contributed significantly to the outcome. Federal regulation of financial institutions failed to prevent a variety of lax and sometimes improper practices that contributed to the speculative excesses of the late 1920s. The Federal Reserve Board, and more importantly the powerful Federal Reserve Bank in New York, made no attempt to prevent or control the speculative boom on Wall Street. Indeed, its easy money policy fuelled the speculative boom. Given that the bubble was bound to burst sooner or later, the further it was allowed to expand the more damaging the eventual explosion would be. Regressive tax policies exacerbated the maldistribution of incomes. The failure to act decisively to maintain farm prices ensured that a large section of the population would be restricted in its purchases of goods and services. The anti-union policies of federal and state governments helped depress wage levels and therefore the purchasing power of industrial workers. Finally, the tariff and war debt policies raised further barriers to international trade. Even though it is far from clear that the Depression could have been prevented, or even what actually caused it, it is likely that wiser government policies might have allowed some mitigation.

Depression America

Just how far the Depression of the 1930s bit into the fabric of American life can be judged from the simple figures. The national income declined by 30 per cent in real terms. By 1932 industrial production had fallen to 57 per cent of 1929 levels, with some industries producing investment or consumer durable goods, like steel or automobiles, experiencing falls of up to three-quarters. New investment virtually ceased. By the summer of 1932 unemployment was at least 13 million, 25 per cent of the working population. Farm prices which had fallen by 40 per cent since 1919 fell by another 63 per cent during the next three years, driving many farm-owners into tenancy and many more off the land altogether.

Town and country alike presented scenes of the starkest poverty. Beggars appeared on street corners, clerks and teachers resorted to selling apples on street corners, men, women and children scavenged on rubbish tips, and bread-lines stretched for several blocks wherever food was distributed. Not surprisingly, numerous cases of malnutrition and even deaths from hunger were reported. In Harlan County, Kentucky, in the heart of the depressed soft-coal region, 231 children died of diseases caused by malnutrition between 1929 and 1931. Hundreds of thousands rode the rails and hitched rides in search of opportunity, or perhaps merely to escape the dismal wreckage of their lives, making temporary homes in freightcars, under bridges, in caves, or in the shanty towns which grew up on waste ground in or around every American city and which were derisively dubbed 'Hoovervilles', where they kept themselves warm with their 'Hoover blankets' (sheets of old newspapers) and flourished their 'Hoover flags' (empty pockets turned inside out). Settlement house nurses on the New York's Lower East Side reported scenes that 'might have come out of the tales of old Russia'.[38] Like the group of West Africans who, in an interesting reversal of the expected patterns of international aid, sent the sum of $3.73 to feed the starving in New York, they emphasised just how far beyond normal American experience the Depression had taken them.

Millions were out of work for years, discouraged by repeated rejections, increasingly dispirited and demoralised as their family relationships, their social networks, their very sense of their own identity and status were disrupted and degraded by enforced idleness, destitution and the humiliation of accepting public relief. 'Being on relief just breaks you all up', commented one recipient. Although relatively few allowed their despair to carry them to such lengths, a federal relief investigator in 1934 reported that 'almost every one of her clients' had 'talked of suicide at one time or

---

38.   Quoted in William E. Leuchtenburg, *Franklin D. Roosevelt and the New Deal, 1932–1940* (New York, 1963), p. 2.

another'.[39] However, not only the unemployed and the impoverished were affected by the catastrophe. Insecurity was still more pervasive than material distress. It was no longer possible to believe that jobs were part of the general order of things, nor to assume that if the job one had was lost another could easily be obtained. The result was that fear became the predominant emotion in Depression America: fear of being made redundant and of being eventually reduced to destitution and want. Many were untouched by hunger and deprivation; few in the 1930s were untouched by fear, and that profound sense of insecurity was to have a decisive effect on the reorientation of American government and politics in the New Deal.

The normally mild AFL president William Green warned that 'Revolutions grow out of the depths of hunger', while a farm leader assured a congressional committee that 'there are more actual reds among the farmers in Wisconsin than you could dream about'.[40] Despite many such warnings and many expressions of bourgeois panic, the Depression years provided little evidence of revolutionary sentiment among the unemployed. Relative to the enormity of the crisis and their own expectations, neither the Socialist nor the Communist Party substantially expanded its support. There were, it is true, many manifestations of discontent, many more in all probability than local newspapers liked to report. Widespread hunger marches, Unemployed Councils which demonstrated against relief cuts or evictions, veterans marching on Washington to demand early payment of bonuses for wartime service, groups of farmers who took forcible action to prevent the sale by auction of the property of bankrupt neighbours all revealed strong undercurrents of resentment. But most unemployed workers, most migrant farm-workers, most destitute farmers did not join in organised protest actions. Most responded passively, bewildered by their fate. Workers on relief were described as 'terrifyingly patient'. Investigators repeatedly commented on their 'apathy', 'their bleak downcast eyes, their broken spirit'.[41] Some turned their anger in upon themselves, perceiving theirs as individual problems brought on by personal failings. The novelist Sherwood Anderson picked up hitch-hikers 'who apologised for being down and out. They

39. Quoted in Robert S. McElvaine, *The Great Depression: America, 1929–1941* (New York, 1984), pp. 178, 175.

40. Quoted in Schlesinger, *Crisis of the Old Order*, pp. 185, 176.

41. Quoted in McElvaine, *Great Depression*, p. 177; John A. Garraty, *Unemployment in History: Economic Thought and Public Policy* (New York, 1979), p. 180.

accepted the whole responsibility themselves.'[42] But most unemployed workers, especially those who were accustomed to periods of unemployment, as most industrial workers were, even during the boom years of the 1920s, took a more realistic view, recognising that social and economic forces beyond their control were responsible for their plight but believing equally that there was little that they could do to improve their situation. Therefore they concentrated their efforts on keeping themselves and their families alive. As numerous contemporary studies showed, unemployment resulted in a withdrawal from community life, a breaking down of social networks and a decline in organisational activities, including religion, recreation and politics. It is no surprise, therefore, that the unemployed were not for the most part politically militant. If anything, organised protest increased after 1933 in response to the interventionist policies of the New Deal, which brought the unemployed together, gave them hope, and engendered a feeling of entitlement and a sense of political leverage that was absent during the darkest days of the Depression.

The ordeal of Herbert Hoover

The Depression, which, unfortunately for Hoover, began six months after his accession to the presidency, severely tested the viability of his approach to government–business relations. Contrary to the reputation that he later unjustly acquired, Hoover did not believe, like many bankers, businessmen and orthodox economists of the day, that the government should allow the trade cycle to take its course in order, as Mellon put it, to 'purge the rottenness from the system'.[43] Not only did he believe wholeheartedly in the responsibility of government to act dynamically against the deepening Depression, but he mobilised its powers in ways unimaginable to almost any of his predecessors in the office.

The central drift of Hoover's anti-depression strategy, building on the associational activities of the previous decade, was to encourage cooperative efforts to break the deflationary cycle. Business leaders were persuaded at a series of White House conferences to reach agreements not to lay men off or cut wages,

42. Irving Bernstein, *The Lean Years: A History of the American Worker, 1920–1933* (Boston, 1960), pp. 435–6.
43. Quoted in Michael E. Parrish, *Anxious Decades: America in Prosperity and Depression, 1920–1941* (New York, 1992), p. 421.

actions which, apart from their damaging social repercussions, would merely deepen the Depression. Remarkably, some of the larger companies did attempt for several months to hold the line. Eventually, however, the fall in consumer demand forced them to make cuts, and there was nothing, of course, that the president could do to stop them. Bankers were induced to set up a National Credit Corporation through which strong banks could extend assistance to their more vulnerable rivals. Not surprisingly, large conservatively run banks showed slight inclination to bail out smaller and less prudent institutions, and the terms for borrowing set by the Corporation were so stringent that only $10 million had been lent by December 1931. The President's Emergency Committee on Employment, and later the President's Organization on Unemployment Relief, worked to stimulate and coordinate local relief activities. Hoover looked to a massive voluntary effort to care for those in need. He also urged state and local governments to expand their public works programmes, but their desperate fiscal condition, in fact, forced them to make severe cuts in their construction programmes, from $3.3 billion in 1929 to $1.3 billion in 1933. The fate of Hoover's cooperative endeavours demonstrates all too clearly the limits of voluntarism in the face of such an emergency.

Farmers, too, were urged to cooperate. The Federal Farm Board, established in 1929 just before the Crash, made loans to farm cooperatives and crop stabilisation corporations, which sought to maintain prices by buying above the market price. This was an attempt to bring agricultural marketing into line with corporate practice in the hope of attaining the same kind of price stability, but to do so, in accordance with Hoover's regulatory philosophy, through cooperative associations that would regulate behaviour without resort to government controls. Such exercises were in the circumstances almost totally futile. The Cotton Stabilization Corporation poured around $250 million in the market, with little discernible effect on prices, while the Wheat Stabilization Corporation was by 1930 buying up one-quarter of the nation's crop to no greater effect. It had, said one observer, found 'a first-class way of throwing good money into a bottomless pit'. As one farm bloc senator wryly observed, the Farm Board, in order to achieve results, would 'pretty near have to kill off 20 per cent of the farmers'.[44] Such an expedient went far beyond the parameters of Hoover's voluntarist philosophy.

44. Quoted in Hicks, *Republican Ascendancy*, pp. 219, 264.

At the same time, Hoover struggled to restore confidence in the economy. As Roosevelt was to do more successfully, he tried to persuade Americans that their fears were unreasonable. Many of his waking hours were spent in devising and delivering reassuring statements. In the wake of the stock-market crash, he assured the country that the 'fundamental business of the country' was 'on a sound and prosperous basis', while in March 1930 he promised that the recession would be over in sixty days.[45] Admirably intentioned though such pronouncements were, they did nothing for Hoover's public image. It sometimes seemed as though every time the president opened his mouth to issue an upbeat statement about business conditions the market took another fall. Though an able administrator and a perceptive and sensitive man, he was quite inept at public relations. Taciturn, ill-at-ease in front of crowds, and cursed with an opaque and uninspiring prose style, Hoover, as his press secretary admitted, 'experienced the greatest difficulty in interpreting himself and his acts to the public'.[46] Uplifting pronouncements, which in FDR's voice were brilliantly successful, in Hoover's appeared either lugubrious or jejune.

In time, his anxiety to support business confidence drove Hoover to accept the need for direct government aid, but this was sparingly given and carefully directed. The Reconstruction Finance Corporation (RFC), established in January 1932, was allocated $2 billion to lend to banks and other financial institutions in order to rescue them from insolvency. By restoring confidence in financial institutions, he hoped to free their assets for investment. But RFC funds were expended with the greatest caution (almost all were repaid) and in quite inadequate quantities. Loans were only granted to companies that were adjudged 'sound', which in the context of the Depression meant very few. While they increased the reserves of borrowing institutions, they did not necessarily cause those funds to be released for investment. Nevertheless, the creation of the RFC constituted a recognition of the need for direct federal intervention. William E. Parrish rightly describes it as 'the boldest antidepression measure ever undertaken by the federal government'.[47] The programme was criticised for providing relief to the nation's bankers but not to the unemployed, and during the summer of 1932 Congress directed the RFC to loan up to $300 million to the states for direct relief, although they had to take a

45. Quoted in Schlesinger, *Crisis of the Old Order*, p. 158.
46. Quoted in Degler, 'Ordeal of Herbert Hoover', p. 208.
47. Parrish, *Anxious Decades*, pp. 253–4.

veritable 'pauper's oath' to qualify, and $1.5 billion to finance self-liquidating public works projects, although here, too, the application was restricted by stringent eligibility rules. This was the first time since Reconstruction that federal funds had been made available for purposes of relief on such a scale. The failure of voluntarism, therefore, drove the Administration to progressively more radical strategies which, though too belated and too parsimonious to turn the tide of depression, nevertheless set important precedents for the future.

More significant, perhaps, than what Hoover was willing to do was what he would not contemplate. Some economists, like John Maynard Keynes in Britain and William Trufant Foster in America, recommended public works programmes, if necessary funded by government deficits, as a way of reducing unemployment and stimulating purchasing power. So did many congressmen, attracted by the prospect of jobs for their constituents, although few as yet were ready to countenance systematic deficit financing. Hoover, too, welcomed the use of public works spending as a countercyclical device and had initiated projects worth up to $800 million by July 1930, but he was unwilling to endorse any projects that could not be paid for out of current revenues. He became obsessed with the need to balance the federal budget, which he believed to be 'the most essential factor to economic recovery'.[48] Therefore he vetoed a series of public works bills. Since tax revenues fell along with the level of economic activity, the relatively small increase in federal construction was in no way sufficient to compensate for the vertiginous decline in investment by private companies and by state and local governments.

Direct relief funded by the federal government, insisted Hoover, would sap the resolve of the American people and leave them dependent on a federal 'dole' (the derogatory use of the English word suggesting the alien and un-American connotations of government welfare). 'The thing you are proposing to do, to give a gratuity to an individual, is divesting men and women of their spirit, their self-reliance', said his Secretary of War. 'It is striking at the very foundations of the system on which this Nation is builded.' It would, added Hoover, 'destroy local responsibility, and introduce graft, politics, waste, and mismanagement'. It was up to 'local communities, through their voluntary agencies', to provide relief.[49]

48. Quoted in ibid., p. 257.
49. Quoted in McElvaine, *Great Depression*, p. 80; Hicks, *Republican Ascendancy*, p. 236.

This might come from private charities or local government, but the important thing was that it should come from within the community, rather than being imposed from outside. The fact that local resources were hopelessly inadequate to cope with a problem of need that, in the words of the American Association of Social Workers, went 'beyond local control and local experience' did not bend Hoover from his course of principled opposition.[50]

Hoover was equally reluctant to resort to government compulsion. This ruled out compulsory crop reduction, so-called 'domestic allotment' schemes; it ruled out proposals to place government sanctions behind plans for industrial self-regulation, as suggested by Gerald Swope and Henry Harriman, two prominent business leaders whose ideas would be partially realised in the shape of the National Recovery Administration (NRA). 'You cannot extend the mastery of government over the daily life of a people without somewhere making it master of people's souls and thought', declared Hoover.[51] Once men and women were forced to submit to government control they would lose their independence of spirit, their self-reliance. Central to Hoover's philosophy of government was an insistence on the need to preserve the American character and American institutions, which must not be abandoned for reasons of expediency or temporary advantage. His duty as president was, above all else, to maintain the 'American system' intact. The current crisis did not absolve him of this responsibility. Indeed, it was precisely because of the intensity of the crisis that he should stand firm against temptation and false counsel. Rather than regarding, as increasing numbers of his fellow-citizens were coming to regard, the Depression as an unprecedented crisis requiring unprecedented solutions, Hoover, as William Allen White perceived, was constrained throughout by 'his passionate, almost bigoted, belief in America'.[52]

Many scholars now see a greater degree of continuity between the politics of the New Era and the New Deal than an earlier generation was willing to admit. So-called 'revisionist' historians, following an early essay by Carl Degler, see Hoover as an immediate precursor of the New Deal: when 'seen against the backdrop of previous administrations', said Degler, 'the gulf between them shrinks appreciably'.[53] Both Hoover and Roosevelt drew heavily on

50.   Quoted in Hicks, *Republican Ascendancy*, p. 270.
51.   Quoted in Albert S. Romasco, 'Herbert Hoover's policies for dealing with the Great Depression', in Fausold and Mazuzan, eds, *The Hoover Presidency*, p. 71.
52.   Quoted in Fausold, *Presidency of Herbert C. Hoover*, p. 111.
53.   Degler, 'Ordeal of Herbert Hoover', p. 212.

their wartime experience. Both considered government–business cooperation essential to economic recovery. Both accepted that the structures of the state must be adjusted to cope with the emerging problems of the twentieth century. Both were ready to engage in a series of imaginative experiments to find a way out of the Depression. Hoover's efforts, in Stephen Skowronek's phrase, provided 'a rich seedbed for further experimentation' during the New Deal.[54] More specifically, the RFC was to play a major role in Roosevelt's reordering of the nation's financial system and in funding a whole variety of New Deal enterprises; the very first legislative action of the Roosevelt presidency, the Emergency Banking Act of March 1933, was mainly drafted by Hoover's officials and built on initiatives suggested by his predecessor; and NRA, the centrepiece of the First New Deal, represented in part a codification of the associational activities of the 1920s. 'We didn't admit it at the time', said Rexford Tugwell, one of Roosevelt's advisers, 'but practically the whole New Deal was extrapolated from programs that Hoover started.'[55]

Nevertheless, while recognising the strong threads of continuity between the Hoover and Roosevelt presidencies and the deep vein of conservatism at the heart of the New Deal (which is, incidentally, the real point of the 'revisionist' interpretation), it is important not to lose sight of the critical differences between them. As one of Hoover's biographers explains, by 1932 'his socioeconomic views had been stretched to their limits'.[56] In two respects especially his policies fell well short of FDR's. One was his reluctance to resort to legal compulsion, his preference for voluntary cooperation, which, while of limited efficacy in the boom years of the 1920s, was doomed to fail under conditions of severe depression. Although most New Deal programmes also relied where possible on persuasion and voluntary cooperation, there was a greater willingness to resort to compulsion where necessary. Still more critical was his reluctance to countenance government spending as a tool of economic and social progress. He was hostile to the very idea of what later became the welfare state. Hoover's preferred solutions to the problems of twentieth-century America were essentially non-statist in character. They did not envisage, indeed deplored, the prospect of a developing structure of federal regulation, a

54. Stephen Skowronek, *The Politics Presidents Make: Leadership from John Adams to George Bush* (Cambridge, Mass., 1993), p. 282.
55. Quoted in Wilson, *Herbert Hoover*, p. 158.
56. Ibid., p. 159.

systematic use of federal spending power, the creation of a welfare state, and the formation of an extensive federal bureaucracy. Hoover's failure represented the end of the New Era project of negotiating a system of managed capitalism without building the apparatus of a modern state. It cleared the way for the application of new ideas, for new uses of state power. This, then, was the irredeemable difference between the New Era and the New Deal and the reason why the 'revisionists', for all their helpful insights, are essentially wrong. A fundamental change did occur in 1933, when Franklin Roosevelt entered the White House.

CHAPTER SEVEN

The New Deal and the Political Economy of Twentieth-Century America

Introduction

Sixty years after its inception, the meaning of the New Deal is still not wholly clear. At its simplest, the New Deal represented a political response to the Great Depression, which compelled the federal government to react with unaccustomed vigour (except, of course, in wartime) to the problems that it both created and exposed. On one hand, the economic crisis generated a clutch of economic and social problems of the greatest urgency. When Franklin D. Roosevelt took office in March 1933 at least 13 million men and women were unemployed, industrial production had fallen by 43 per cent from its 1929 level, farm prices had virtually hit the floor, and the banking system was on the verge of total collapse. On the other hand, the Depression exposed longstanding social injustices and economic imbalances which had been obscured by the prosperity of the 'Roaring Twenties'. The New Deal was more than a set of short-term responses to an economic emergency; many of its reforms had a significance which extended far beyond the end of the Depression and did much to shape the social and political world of the late twentieth century.

It must be remembered that, with the inauguration of Franklin D. Roosevelt, the progressives were back in power. Roosevelt, his wife Eleanor (who was, in fact, Theodore Roosevelt's cousin) and leading members of his Administration like Harold Ickes, Frances Perkins and Donald Richberg had participated in the reform movements of the Progressive Era. There was a considerable degree of continuity, both in personnel and purpose, between the earlier reform endeavours and those of the New Deal. One of the most important political consequences of the Depression was that, by discrediting the standpat Republicanism that had dominated the 1920s, it both created the conditions for a Democratic hegemony that was to last for at least a generation and provided a window of opportunity for liberals and progressives to carry out some of the projects that had been incubated during the Harding–Coolidge years.

Following the failure of the Hoover Administration to cope constructively with the emergency, Roosevelt entered the White House having pledged himself in his acceptance speech to 'a new deal for the American people'. What he meant by that phrase was by no means clear. It is not much clearer in retrospect. The legislative and executive initiatives that are grouped under the heading of the New Deal exhibit an immense variety of objectives and methods. Roosevelt was above all else a pragmatist, which is perhaps another way of saying that he was a liberal. This was partly a measure of his extraordinary political skill, his great flexibility and adaptability to circumstances, but it seemed also to reflect an absence of fixed ideas. 'My philosophy?' he responded to a journalist's query, 'I am a Christian and a Democrat – that's all.'[1] That was about as disingenuous as most of Roosevelt's political remarks. In fact, as we shall see, on a number of issues Roosevelt held very firm and unshakeable ideas which, subtly rather than blatantly, shaped the development of the New Deal.

TABLE 7.1   *New Deal agencies and legislation, 1933–38*

Emergency Banking Act (March 1933): prevented collapse of banking system by reorganising banks and offered financial assistance to sound institutions.

Civilian Conservation Corps (CCC, est. 1933): employed young men on reforestation and other conservation programmes.

Federal Emergency Relief Administration (FERA, 1933–35): distributed federal grants to states for relief purposes.

Banking Act (June 1933): separated commercial from investment banking and provided federal insurance for bank deposits.

Securities Act (1933): required accurate disclosure of information about stock issues.

Home Owner's Loan Corporation (HOLC, est. 1933): refinanced loans for house purchase.

Farm Credit Administration (FCA, est. 1933): refinanced farm mortgages.

(*cont.*)

---

1. Quoted in Frances Perkins, *The Roosevelt I Knew* (New York, 1946.), p. 267.

TABLE 7.1   *New Deal agencies and legislation, 1933–38 (cont.)*

Tennessee Valley Authority (TVA, est. 1933): used federally operated hydroelectric power projects as basis for wider economic development of a depressed region of the South.

Agricultural Adjustment Act (1933): crop reduction programmes, funded by a tax on food-processing industries and administered by Agricultural Adjustment Administration (AAA).

National Industrial Recovery Act (1933): created National Recovery Administration (NRA) to administer 'codes of fair competition' in industry; Public Works Administration (PWA) spent $3.3 billion on large-scale public works programmes.

Civil Works Administration (CWA, 1933–34): temporary employment programme.

Securities and Exchange Commission (SEC, est. 1934): responsible for regulation of stock exchange.

Federal Housing Administration (FHA, est. 1934): insured loans made by private institutions for house purchase, in order to stimulate construction.

Works Progress Administration (WPA, 1935–43): large-scale work relief programme, including Federal Art Project, Federal Writers' Project, Federal Theater Project and National Youth Administration (NYA).

Resettlement Administration (RA, 1935–37): to assist displaced tenant farmers and migrant farm workers and resettle them on new farms.

National Labor Relations Act (Wagner Act, 1935): obliged an employer to recognise and bargain in good faith with a trade union if a majority of workers wished to be represented by it.

Revenue Act (1935): raised taxes on high incomes and large corporations.

Public Utilities Holding Companies Act (1935): legislated against monopolies in electric power industry.

Social Security Act (1935): established a national system of old age insurance; national/state system of unemployment insurance; federal aid to state schemes for 'categorical assistance' to the indigent elderly, the blind and dependent children.

Banking Act (1935): increased government control over Federal Reserve System and over monetary policy.

Farm Security Administration (FSA, est. 1937): carried on work of RA.

US Housing Administration (est. 1937): to provide funds for public housing projects.

Soil Conservation and Domestic Allotment Act (1936): following Supreme Court's ruling against AAA, to achieve crop reductions in name of soil conservation.

Agricultural Adjustment Act (1938): established new acreage allotments paid for by subsidies from Treasury, rather than processors' tax.

Fair Labor Standards Act (1938): set minimum wages and maximum hours for most workers.

Table 7.1 lists the principal measures of the New Deal. It will be seen that most of them were enacted in the early months of Roosevelt's term, in what was known as the 'Hundred Days', and in a second burst of legislation during the summer of 1935, not surprisingly referred to as the 'Second Hundred Days'. These periods of intense legislative activity are sometimes perceived as exhibiting two distinct approaches. The Second New Deal that began in 1935 was in some ways markedly different to the First New Deal of 1933–34. Whereas the First New Deal consisted largely of relief and recovery programmes designed to reverse the economic decline and alleviate its immediate social effects, the Second New Deal incorporated important measures of structural reform, like the National Labor Relations Act and the Social Security Act, which constitute the most important legacies of the Roosevelt years. There were, it is true, significant changes in emphasis, but there were also, as we shall see, substantial elements of continuity.

The social and labour policy of the New Deal will be examined in separate chapters. The focus of this chapter will be New Deal economic policy, particularly the programmes relating to agriculture and industry, before turning to look at the broader impact of the New Deal on American politics and the development of the American state.

The New Deal on the land

The crisis on the land engaged Roosevelt's sympathies, as well as his attention. Secretary of Labor Frances Perkins observed that Roosevelt identified more readily with the problems of farmers, with whom, as a gentleman farmer himself, he claimed a certain oneness, than with those of urban workers. He and his advisers regarded the imbalance in rewards to agriculture and industry during the 1920s as a principal cause of the wider economic distress. The inability of farmers to buy their fair share of the goods so plentifully produced by American industry had precipitated the crisis of demand that lay at the root of the Depression. Roosevelt also retained an almost Jeffersonian conviction that rural existence was in some way morally superior and that the social, as well as the economic, health of the nation would be somehow in jeopardy were farming as a way of life to decline. In that sense he was something of an 'agricultural fundamentalist'.

At first sight the 'farm problem' appeared simple. Owing to the decline of their export markets, farmers produced a surplus which, even in the prosperous years of the 1920s, seriously depressed prices. Even though exports amounted to only about one-sixth of overall output, that unsold fraction, in view of the inelasticity of demand for farm products, lay like a lead weight on agricultural markets. The collapse of incomes after 1929 merely accentuated the problem. Farm prices fell by 63 per cent between 1929 and 1932, having already fallen by over 40 per cent during the previous decade, bringing normally prosperous farm-owners to the brink of bankruptcy, and in many cases beyond. The solution seemed equally clear: eliminate the surplus, and thereby raise farm prices to a 'normal' level, increase farm incomes and restore the purchasing power that would enable the farming population once more to purchase its share of the world's goods. Thus a solution to the farm problem would advance the wider goals of economic recovery.

There were other aspects to the farm problem, however, or rather other farm problems. One was the long-forgotten world of rural poverty. Half the farm population received no more than 10 per cent of agricultural income. In the South in particular, ever since the Civil War, sharecropping, the burden of indebtedness and an unequal access to political power had trapped a majority of black, and many white, farmers in a condition of seemingly perpetual penury. Little seemed to shake this almost hidden world of deprivation until the New Deal brought the problem to the fore, as much by inadvertance as by intent. If most Americans in the 1930s lived in blissful oblivion of the plight of the sharecroppers, they could hardly avoid noticing the impact of the Dust Bowl, detritus from which coloured the evening sky in cities across the land. The Dust Bowl resulted from the intensive farming of semi-arid land on the southern Plains. A succession of years of low rainfall in the early and mid-1930s left the worn top-soil at the mercy of the prairie winds, blowing away with it the livelihood of those who cultivated it. The Dust Bowl was only an extreme case of a broader pattern of erosion caused by indiscriminate use of the land, without regard for its natural capacity. This was evidently a problem of a very different order to the surplus, involving insufficient, rather than excessive, production, but it had a common root cause in the unplanned and reckless exploitation of the soil over several decades.

Legislation to deal with the farm problem was made necessary not only by the gravity of the situation but also by pressure from the farm bloc in Congress and manifestations of growing agrarian unrest, especially in the Midwest, where members of the Farmers' Holiday Association withheld supplies of milk and other produce and forcibly prevented the auctioning of foreclosed farm property. Edward O'Neal, president of the American Farm Bureau Federation (AFBF), warned in January 1933, 'Unless something is done for the farmers, we will have revolution in the countryside within less than twelve months'.[2] Apocalyptic though such warnings were, the threat of mounting disruption, more visible in countryside than city, impelled Congress to act.

Although, in order to propitiate the vocal proponents of McNary–Haugenism and the equally vocal and still more numerous proponents of monetary inflation, Congress incorporated alternative remedies in the Agricultural Adjustment Act passed in May 1933, the heart of the new law lay in its crop-reduction programme. Roosevelt and his advisers never seriously considered inflation and regarded McNary–Haugenism as an open invitation to farmers to fill their granaries to the roof-joists at guaranteed prices, creating an open-ended drain on the Treasury which still might not get rid of the surplus. Their preference was for the 'domestic allotment' plan designed by the farm economist M.L. Wilson. Rather than buying up the surplus in order to restore 'parity', Wilson proposed to eliminate it by the (theoretically) simple expedient of persuading farmers not to grow so much. The failure of Hoover's exhortations to produce less made it evident that material inducements would have to be offered. These would be paid for by a tax levied on the processors of agricultural commodities, like millers and textile manufacturers, and ultimately therefore on the consumer. Just as industrial corporations controlled production to maintain price levels, so should farmers, acting collectively under government guidance. The benefits that urban businessmen derived from corporate organisation farmers would gain through government-sponsored production controls.

The new law defined as its object the attainment of 'parity' between agricultural and industrial prices. Parity was defined as a level of farm prices that would give agricultural commodities a purchasing power in relation to the articles that farmers bought equivalent to the purchasing power of agricultural commodities in a base period, which for most major commodities was 1909–14, a period of relative prosperity for agriculture. It provided a number

2. Quoted in Theodore Saloutos, *The American Farmers and the New Deal* (Ames, Iowa, 1982), p. 43.

of methods for achieving parity prices, including agreements with producers voluntarily to reduce acreage, in return for rental or benefit payments, marketing agreements, export subsidies and, at the insistence of Western and Southern congressmen, silver inflation. The costs would be met by a processing tax. Extraordinary discretion in enforcing the law was vested in the Secretary of Agriculture. Roosevelt's choice for this post was Henry A. Wallace, the editor of a well-known farm journal, who, with his rumpled appearance and boyish manner, had, in the words of a friend, 'corn country' written all over him. Though sometimes given to strange enthusiasms and odd bouts of mysticism – he once gave an official radio address on the subject of 'The strength and quietness of grass' – he was a knowledgeable and hard-headed farm leader, well aware of the urgency of taking steps to restore farm incomes and therefore of acting quickly to dispose of the mounting surplus.

By the time the crop-reduction programme was under way the 1933 crop was already in the ground. Therefore crop-reduction meant crop-destruction. In order to prevent an embarrassing glut of cotton, 10.5 million acres of cotton were ploughed under, destroying roughly a quarter of the crop, in return for $162 million in compensation payments. In order to forestall a similar glut of pork products, 6 million piglets were slaughtered amidst scenes of gruesome carnage which aroused public dismay. Wallace treated popular tenderness on the subject with sarcasm. 'To hear them talk', he said, 'you would have thought that pigs were raised for pets' and should be allowed to live out their full span of years in old pigs' homes.[3] Roosevelt's contribution to this debate was to ask whether birth control might not be a more effective solution, and this is what New Deal farm policy ordinarily entailed.

The programme normally proceeded on a more orderly basis. Rather than ploughing under crops, the acreage sown was reduced in advance. The crop divisions of the Agricultural Adjustment Administration (AAA), set up to enforce the Act, decided on the appropriate output, and acreage allocations were worked out in detail by local committees of farmers. By such means in 1934 an area equal in size to the state of Illinois was taken out of production. To prevent farmers from defeating the objects of acreage reduction by pouring fertiliser and labour into the remaining acres, particularly in the Southern staples of cotton and tobacco,

3. Quoted in Arthur M. Schlesinger Jr., *The Coming of the New Deal* (Boston, 1958), p. 63.

supplementary legislation in 1934 provided for production controls in those crops. In addition, the Commodity Credit Corporation offered loans which were secured by crops in storage at a rate above the market price. If the price rose above the set rate, farmers could sell their crops and repay the loans; otherwise they had an incentive to keep them off the market. This became an increasingly important price-support mechanism. 'Triple-A' enjoyed substantial success in reducing output and boosting farm incomes. The output of cotton and corn was substantially reduced, as, with the help of the Dust Bowl, was that of wheat. Corn, which in Iowa had been selling for 10 cents a bushel in the darkest days of the Depression, had reached the respectable heights of 70 cents a bushel by 1935. Overall, between 1932 and 1936 farm prices rose by two-thirds and, in consequence, farm incomes by a half.

Over the years the Department of Agriculture, with its responsibility for the promotion of agricultural research and the dissemination of information, had developed through the Extension Service a network of county agents who worked together with committees of local farmers. These so-called farm bureaux, which consisted mainly of the wealthier and more influential producers in each locality, combined to form the American Farm Bureau Federation. Hence AAA, to a much greater extent than most other New Deal programmes, especially NRA, could capitalise on an existing administrative structure that reached into every county and a parallel system of grass-roots organisation. This accounts in part for the relative success and durability of New Deal farm policy. The AAA crop-reduction schemes depended on the voluntary cooperation of farmers, to both administer and legitimise the policies. They operated avowedly in the spirit of 'grass-roots democracy'. Acreage allotments were decided at a local level by committees of farmers, usually organised and selected by the county agents, in which the larger producers played a dominating role. In the short run the government had little option but to make use of the agricultural establishment. Its cooperation was a prerequisite for the execution of any effective farm policy. Yet the outcome of such an arrangement was to solidify the *status quo* in American agriculture, to reinforce the economic position of the larger producers and the political power of farm organisations like the AFBF, which gained a new voice during the New Deal years as a spokesman for the largest, most influential farmers and, after its members had attained their own desires, as an increasingly conservative force in American politics. Ironically, as Richard S.

Kirkendall points out, 'The New Deal for agriculture had, in a sense, created its own strong opponent'.[4]

Wallace, the AAA chief George N. Peek and his successor Chester Davis, like most of the architects of AAA, were Midwesterners, familiar with the problems of Midwestern farming. Most of the thinking about the farm crisis – in land-grant colleges, in the Extension Service and in the Department of Agriculture itself – concentrated on the plight of the typical Midwestern farm, owner-operated, highly mechanised, and applying advanced methods to unusually fertile land. Such a farm would expect to make a comfortable working profit under normal market conditions. AAA was designed to provide just such conditions for just such farms.

Triple-A had a more ambiguous impact on the welfare of Southern tenants and sharecroppers, who constituted three-quarters of all farmers in the cotton South. Nearly 8.5 million people lived and worked on tenant farms, 3 million of them black and 5.5 million white. Effectively tied to the land by a combination of poverty, ignorance and indebtedness, tenant farmers experienced conditions of extreme deprivation. A government survey found that Arkansas tenant families earned on average $300 per annum. They inhabited squalid and dilapidated shacks, suffered from chronic malnutrition and a variety of infectious and deficiency diseases, including malaria, pellagra and hookworm, and displayed exceptionally high rates of illiteracy. To the journalist Frazier Hunt they 'seemed to belong to another land than the America I knew and loved'.[5] During the 1930s Americans began suddenly to notice the sharecroppers, who were the subject of a clutch of official investigations, social surveys, observer-participation studies such as James Agee and Walker Evans's *Let Us Now Praise Famous Men*, novels like Erskine Caldwell's *Tobacco Road*, and a great deal of documentary photography.

The plight of the sharecropper was an ancient problem which Americans had contrived to ignore for half a century. What brought it to public notice was the impact of New Deal policies. Compensation for crop-reduction was paid in the first instance to landlords, in recognition of the peculiar relationship of dependency that existed between tenant and landlord in the plantation South. Landlords were supposed to pass on to their

---

4. Richard S. Kirkendall, 'The New Deal and agriculture', in John Braeman, Robert Bremner and David Brody, eds, *The New Deal* (2 vols, Columbus, Ohio, 1975), I, p. 105.

5. Quoted in Schlesinger, *Coming of the New Deal*, p. 374.

tenants and sharecroppers a proportion of the benefits equivalent to the share of the crop that they were normally entitled to, but it is evident from the complaints voiced by tenants all over the South, corroborated by the results of an investigation by the Department of Agriculture economist Mordecai Ezekiel, that frequently they did not. The local committees responsible for local administration were generally unsympathetic to their pleas for redress. Tenants and sharecroppers were unrepresented on county committees. As a county agent revealingly exclaimed when asked why this was so, 'Hell, you wouldn't put a chicken on a poultry board, would you?'.[6] It was especially difficult for black tenants to appeal successfully to a committee of white planters. At the same time, a reduction of acreage meant that fewer tenants and labourers were needed to work the land. The standard AAA cotton contract, which required landlords to retain the same number of tenants, but only 'insofar as possible' and as long as they were not 'a nuisance or a menace to the welfare of the producer', offered little protection.[7] Many thousands were therefore evicted and left to struggle 'along the highways and byways of Dixie . . . lonely figures, without money, without homes and without hope'.[8] Thousands more, like the Okies of Steinbeck's *The Grapes of Wrath*, travelled west in search of opportunity.

Although the victims were mostly silent and unheard, in a few localities resistance was more vigorous. In the Arkansas Delta in 1934 a Southern Tenant Farmers' Union (STFU) was established to fight evictions. Its activities were forcibly suppressed by the landlords, with the connivance of the local authorities, in what was described as a 'reign of terror'. The members of the STFU were spurned by AAA officials as 'reds', but their protest attracted considerable publicity, to the Administration's considerable embarrassment. For a while the issue was the subject of a bitter internal dispute in AAA. Liberals like Jerome Frank and Alger Hiss in the General Counsel's Office, some with Communist connections, most from non-farming backgrounds and woefully ignorant of the mechanics of farming, took up the cause, demanding that landlords be compelled to retain their tenants, and were in consequence 'purged' from the Department in 1935. Not only did the representatives of the planter class who staffed AAA's Cotton

6. David E. Conrad, *Forgotten Farmers: The Story of Sharecroppers and the New Deal* (Urbana, Ill., 1965), p. 81.

7. Paul E. Mertz, *New Deal Policy and Southern Rural Poverty* (Baton Rouge, La., 1978), pp. 25–6.

8. Conrad, *Forgotten Farmers*, p. 167.

Division harbour typical Southern attitudes regarding shiftless sharecroppers and feckless African-Americans, while disdaining criticism from the 'social planners' and 'fellow-travellers' in the Legal Division, but men like Chester Davis and, to a lesser extent, Wallace also considered their reformist ideals to be misplaced. To intervene in disputes between landlords and tenants, they believed, would be quite fatal to the success of the cotton programme. The political repercussions might blow AAA out of the water altogether. AAA should concern itself with the general problem of agricultural recovery, that is with raising farm prices, rather than taking on the task of reforming the social structure of the plantation South, not to mention challenging the political power of Southern planters, which was so amply represented in Congress.

In 1935 Roosevelt used part of an emergency relief appropriation to set up the Resettlement Administration (RA) to tackle the problem of rural poverty. Apart from establishing camps for migrant farmers, its principal functions were to establish marginal farmers on better land and to provide others with operating loans. During its lifetime it managed to resettle no more than 4,141 families, although 536,300 were in receipt of small loans or grants, too meagre to do much more than relieve immediate suffering. Its successor agency, the Farm Security Administration (FSA), created by the Bankhead-Jones Farm Tenancy Act of 1937, operated on a more extensive scale but faced the same difficulties. Financial stringencies and the opposition of powerful farm leaders prevented it from doing more than scratch the surface of the problem. Over a ten-year period no more than $294 million was provided to enable 47,104 tenants to purchase their farms, while 399,000 received smaller rehabilitation loans.

The truth was that the rehabilitation of poor farmers ran contrary to the general orientation of federal farm policy, that is raising farm prices. Obviously, if poor tenant farmers could be elevated to the status of independent, commercially viable farmers they would produce more, exacerbating the overall problem, as it appeared to AAA. The two policies ran counter to one another in their economic effects. In this case, as elsewhere in the New Deal, economic recovery took precedence over social (not to mention racial) justice. Moreover, AAA depended for its success upon the cooperation of the more powerful farmers, which in the South meant the planters, who objected to the way in which FSA, with its aid to tenant farmers and labourers, undermined traditional relations of dependence. Department of Agriculture officials exhibited, according to Pete Daniel, 'an eagerness to please larger farmers' and 'an ill-disguised contempt for small-scale farmers'.[9] In any case, they believed, as Theodore Saloutos explains, that too many poor farmers were attempting to scratch a meagre living from the soil who would be better advised to seek employment elsewhere: 'the nation suffered from a surplus of farmers as well as from a surplus of crops'.[10] Therefore the resources devoted to rehabilitation were a fraction of those devoted to maintaining prices and hardly more than a token effort designed to salve liberal consciences. In any case, as Theodore Saloutos points out, 'It was expecting far too much of the New Deal to undo within a few years a system of tenancy and sharecropping that had been years in the making.'[11]

In 1936 the Supreme Court declared the processing tax to be an illegitimate application of the tax power involving 'the expropriation of money from one group for the benefit of another'.[12] Justice Owen Roberts, speaking for the majority in *US* v. *Butler et al.*, pronounced, with astonishing disregard for economic realities, that agriculture was a purely local activity properly subject only to state regulation. Unwilling to return farming to the maelstrom of the free market, Congress responded with a Soil Conservation and Domestic Allotment Act which paid farmers to grow crops which restored the fertility of the soil. Since the soil-conserving crops, such as grasses and legumes, were not in surplus, while those which depleted the soil, like wheat and cotton, were, this had the not unintended effect of reducing surpluses and achieving indirectly the goals of the original AAA. When the act failed to achieve the former aim under the excellent growing conditions that prevailed during 1937, it was replaced in 1938 by a second Agricultural Adjustment Act, which made voluntary acreage control under the soil conservation programme permanent; allowed for the imposition of compulsory quotas if two-thirds of producers voted for it in a referendum, in which case excess sales would be penalised by prohibitive taxes; and authorised price-support loans on crops in storage, which became perhaps the principal price stabilisation mechanism in succeeding decades.

9. Pete Daniel, *Breaking the Land: The Transformation of the Cotton, Tobacco and Rice Cultures since 1880* (Urbana, Ill., 1985), p. 3.

10. Theodore Saloutos, 'New Deal agricultural policy: an evaluation' *Journal of American History* 61 (Sept, 1974), p. 405.

11. Ibid., p. 410.

12. *US* v. *Butler*, in Henry S. Commager, ed., *Documents in American History* (2 vols, New York, 1949), II, p. 428.

New Deal farm policy was highly ambivalent in its effects. On the one hand, it involved a degree of government intervention in agricultural markets that could not have been anticipated a generation earlier. The government intervened systematically to maintain farm prices, and it involved itself in the individual marketing and land-use decisions of every farmer. The system of farm subsidies established in the New Deal, though greatly modified after the Second World War and curtailed in the Reagan years, remains substantially in force. No more than any of its competitors could the United States contemplate returning agriculture to the vagaries of the open market, the social as well as the economic consequences of which were too uncertain to contemplate. Yet this radical intervention in the market was carried out essentially for conservative purposes. The objective was to induce farmers to act collectively in their common interest – to behave like a business corporation, tailoring supply to meet demand. It fostered therefore the commercialisation of American agriculture.

New Deal farm policy was less successful in addressing problems which could not be solved merely by raising commodity prices. A number of agricultural scientists during the 1930s, working under the shadow of the Dust Bowl, examined the problem of soil conservation and offered a number of proposals to deal with it, but at the end of the decade conservation plans had been developed for only a small fraction of the land that the Soil Conservation Service considered liable to erosion. The Soil Conservation Act was designed to regulate production rather than to conserve the soil. Conservation generally took second place to the primary aim of price stabilisation. The planners' attempts to replace the traditional individualism of the American farmers, and its destructive and exploitative tendencies, with a spirit of cooperation and prudent land-use went against the commercial imperatives that dominated the Department's agenda.

Federal farm policy, finally, did little to alleviate rural poverty. Whereas billions of dollars were expended on price supports for commercial farmers, RA, FSA and their successors were kept on slender rations. Furthermore, as Daniel has shown, the acreage-control and soil conservation policies that began with the New Deal had the effect of driving many small farmers from the land, especially in the South. Along with the mechanisation of cotton-picking during and after the Second World War and the growing use of herbicides rather than human labour to control weeds, such policies converted the South from a land of impoverished tenant farms to one of large mechanised plantations. Since a large proportion of those who were uprooted were black, an unanticipated consequence of federal farm policy was the 'Great Migration' of African–Americans from the rural South to the urban North.

NRA and the economics of scarcity

Washington in March 1933, said the journalist Arthur Krock, felt like 'a beleaguered capital in war time'.[13] Confronted with an economy seemingly on the verge of collapse, Roosevelt and his 'brains trust' found it natural to turn for guidance to the last great crisis that the nation had faced, namely the First World War. Many, like Roosevelt himself as Assistant Secretary of the Navy, had played an important part in the wartime mobilisation of 1917–18 and sought to apply those lessons to the present emergency, drawing upon the experience of managing the war economy, and particularly the work of the War Industries Board, in developing their programme for industrial recovery. As in wartime, they believed, private enterprise must be made to serve public ends; the nation's resources must be mobilised through a mixture of industrial self-government and administrative guidance; and planning and cooperation must replace wasteful competition. Similar insights had inspired Hoover's 'associationalism' during the 1920s, and this provided another stream of ideas and experience that fed into the making of New Deal industrial policy.

According to Hugh Johnson, who was entrusted with the administration of the industrial recovery programme, 'The very heart of the New Deal is the principle of concerted action in industry and agriculture under government supervision looking to a balanced economy as opposed to the murderous doctrine of savage and wolfish individualism, looking to dog-eat-dog and devil take the hindmost'.[14] The guiding assumption behind what became NRA was that the fundamental economic problem was one of excessive competition. Under these conditions producers were forced into a cycle of repeated price-cutting and cost-cutting – reducing wages, laying off workers, and employing women and children in place of

13. Quoted in William E. Leuchtenburg, 'The New Deal and the analogue of war', in John Braeman, Robert Bremner and David Brody, eds, *Change and Continuity in Modern America* (Columbus, Ohio, 1964), p. 104.

14. Quoted in Schlesinger, *Coming of the New Deal*, p. 88.

adult males. Although such actions might appear to be in the short-term interest of any one firm, their aggregate effect was disastrous. In purely economic terms wage-cuts and lay-offs reduced consumer demand, lowered profits, and initiated a further deflationary cycle of wage-cuts and job losses – as Johnson put it, 'a downward spiral into an economic hell'.[15] At the same time, unemployment and poverty left a trail of human suffering, family breakdown and social disorganisation. By a kind of commercial Gresham's Law, the far-sighted and socially responsible businessman was continually under-cut by short-sighted and irresponsible competitors. Attempts, as during the Hoover presidency, to induce firms to combine to hold prices and wages steady were always in the end defeated by individual producers who refused to sign the agreements or, having signed, to abide by them. Whereas it was in the collective interest of producers to combine to maintain prices, it was in the interest of any one firm to break ranks to increase its market share. Hence voluntary efforts invariably failed. Businessmen were by 1933 increasingly willing to accept an element of government com-pulsion to enforce their agreements.

Business organisations hoped to use federal authority to give force to their own associational activities, enabling 'enlightened' businessmen to engage in cooperative planning while the govern-ment stamped on the 'chiselers' who undermined their efforts. They envisaged a programme designed by them and enforced by government. Such views were reflected in the Administration by Raymond Moley and Hugh Johnson. Rexford Tugwell, on the other hand, envisaged a stronger measure of central direction, enabling rational industrial planning in the interest of society as a whole, rather than the narrow and particularistic interests of businessmen. Such a programme was both politically and administratively impracticable in the context of 1933. Finally, organised labour and its congressional allies hoped by federal wages-and-hours legislation to raise purchasing power and spread employment. It was the imminent prospect of the passage of a bill introduced by Senator Hugo Black of Alabama which would have imposed a maximum thirty-hour week in the production of goods entering interstate commerce which, as much as anything, propelled the Administration towards an early decision on its industrial recovery programme.

The resulting National Industrial Recovery Act, which became law in June 1933, was the product of many hands. Reflecting in its

15. Quoted in Ellis Hawley, *The New Deal and the Problem of Monopoly* (Princeton, N.J., 1966), p. 81.

make-up a variety of intellectual approaches and economic interests, it was essentially an enabling act capable of supporting a number of different versions of industrial policy. This failure to decide between competing strategies and to lay down clear principles of action bedevilled New Deal industrial policy from the start, confusing the process of administration and allowing private interests more leeway than was necessary. Each industry was encouraged to draw up a 'code of fair competition' which, once approved by the president, would have the force of law. It would also be exempt from prosecution under the antitrust law. Industrial associations were given wide freedom of action, what amounted to virtually a blank cheque, in drawing up codes. Among the few positive stipulations, included to keep organised labour onside, was the requirement that the codes set standards for wages and hours and grant workers the right to bargain collectively through unions of their choice (Section 7a). It was generally anticipated that the codes would regulate prices and production as well as wages and hours, although, despite heated exchanges in the Senate, this was neither explicitly authorised nor debarred. The objective was, by preventing cut-throat competition, to stabilise wages and prices. As the president told the United States Chamber of Commerce in April 1933, the intention was 'to prevent over-production, to prevent unfair wages, to eliminate improper working conditions', or, as Johnson more colourfully put it, to 'eliminate eye-gouging and knee-groining and ear-chewing in business'.[16]

Hugh Johnson, the man chosen to run the National Recovery Administration which was set up to administer the act, was a pugnacious ex-cavalry officer and War Industries Board veteran. 'You're familiar with the only comparable thing that's ever been done – the work of the War Industries Board', Moley told him.[17] Despite this experience, Johnson was not a wise choice. Impetuous, emotional, vain, thin-skinned and truculent, prone to periodic bouts of alcoholic excess, he lacked the discretion or *sang froid* to control so massive an undertaking, although his headlong enthusiasm equipped him magnificently for the preliminary task of mobilisation. With evangelical fervour, Johnson sallied forth to enlist support for NRA by means of a massive publicity campaign, modelled on the campaign to sell Liberty Bonds during the First World War. Those who participated were entitled to carry on their

16. Quoted in Schlesinger, *Coming of the New Deal,* p. 98; William E. Leuchtenburg, *Franklin D. Roosevelt and the New Deal* (New York, 1963), p. 65.

17. Quoted in Leuchtenburg, 'The New Deal and the analogue of war', p. 118.

letterheads and on their products the symbol of the Blue Eagle, which bore the legend 'We Do Our Part'. In parades and rallies and through personal exhortation, businessmen were urged to put the public interest before their private concerns, do their patriotic duty and enlist in the recovery campaign, which Johnson visualised as a great army mobilising under the standard of the Blue Eagle with himself at its head. By September nearly every major firm in the country had signed a basic agreement on wages and hours. Eventually 2 million firms signed over 500 NRA codes. Even the dog food manufacturers, the shoulder-pad manufacturers and the burlesque theatre industry were included. In the headlong rush to sign up everyone and everything, however, Johnson hopelessly overstretched the administrative resources available to him – did the government really want to get involved in the question of how many stripteases should be performed in a burlesque show? – and ensured that NRA would be perpetually entangled in a thicket of minor disputes. He was, more seriously, compelled to make damaging concessions and turn a blind eye to blatant contradictions and inequities in order to recruit reluctant industries. His refusal to lay down general rules generated a chaotic array of variations, anomalies and exceptions.

Whatever potential there was for comprehensive industrial planning was squandered under Johnson's administration of NRA. Industry leaders were left to design and administer their own codes. The codes, indeed, were often virtually identical to those drawn up by trade associations during the 1920s; the code authorities themselves were virtually the trade associations under another guise. A programme of 'industrial self-government' left little scope for national coordination, for planning in the national interest, rather than that of particular groups of businessmen. However, there was probably no choice but to organise the recovery programme along these lines. The United States lacked the administrative capacity to plan and execute a comprehensive economic programme; it lacked both a sufficient number of civil servants and the trained expertise to carry out the task. It especially lacked a body of commercial information, equivalent to that possessed by the Department of Agriculture on farm prices and production, to make informed decisions. Ezekiel estimated that it would take at least ten years to develop the capacity to do the job properly. Yet NRA only had a statutory life of two years, by the end of which period its political credit was all but played out. In the emergency, the government necessarily had to rely on businessmen to staff NRA, latter-day equivalents of the 'dollar-a-year' men who, sixteen years earlier, had organised the economy for war. Business domination of NRA was more a result of a lack of administrative capacity than a deliberate sell-out of the public interest by pro-business officials.

NRA codes, it transpired, were a good deal easier to draft than to enforce. Johnson depended ultimately on exhortation rather than compulsion, that is on the same public spirit that had united the nation in 1917–18. NRA, he believed, should operate on the principle of 'industrial self-government'. The ultimate sanction available to him on such terms was to expel an offender from the programme: to withdraw the Blue Eagle, 'his badge of public faith and business honor'. 'The threat of it', he declared, 'transcends any puny provision in this law.'[18] However, so terminal a sanction was virtually unusable because every company banished weakened the effectiveness of a programme which depended on total coverage. Therefore he was repeatedly forced to compromise rather than punish. He was still more reluctant to employ the licensing powers available to him under the act, by means of which offenders might be debarred from interstate commerce, because of doubts about their constitutionality. Fearful of putting his powers to the test, he resorted to bluster and ultimately to compromise. As evidence mounted of widespread, even systematic, violations, especially by small businesses which felt unfairly victimised by the codes, the compliance procedures became clogged up and ultimately ineffective. Business lost faith in its capacity to achieve the goals through NRA. An inability to enforce compliance, observes Colin Gordon, was the 'fundamental defect of the NRA'.[19]

NRA, like AAA, was based on a spirit of cooperation and partnership between government and enterprise. It assumed a spirit of unity in the face of a common foe, namely the Depression. The nation, reacting as if 'invaded by a foreign foe', would 'wage a war against the emergency' and move 'as a trained army willing to sacrifice for the good of a common discipline'.[20] This was the language of Roosevelt's inaugural address and the language which he and other New Dealers persistently resorted to in explaining their programmes during the first two years of the New Deal. However, as William Leuchtenburg points out, these were

18. Quoted in Leuchtenburg, *Franklin D. Roosevelt and the New Deal*, p. 67.
19 Colin Gordon, *New Deals: Business, Labor and Politics in America, 1920–1935* (Cambridge, 1994), p. 186.
20. Franklin D. Roosevelt, First Inaugural Address, in Commager, ed., *Documents*, II, p. 421.

dangerous and misleading assumptions; the analogy of war was by no means wholly appropriate. Most seriously, it overlooked the ways in which economic policies necessarily affect different groups in different ways and call for different degrees of sacrifice. It ignored the conflicts of interest intrinsic to any society, as for example between capital and labour or between big and small business, conflicts which could not, in peacetime, be resolved by calls for national unity. NRA was therefore founded upon a false assumption of consensus and communality of interest which was inevitably confounded by events, yet NRA itself provided no mechanisms for the effective resolution of such conflicts. Any meaningful enforcement of competitive rules must necessarily impose costs on somebody, something which Johnson was always reluctant to acknowledge. Its short career, therefore, was marred by disputes which became over time increasingly numerous and increasingly rancorous.

The unanimity and esprit of the early Blue Eagle campaign was soon dissipated in mounting conflict and criticism. In the first place, there were complaints that in many industries the programme gave undue influence to the larger companies. A Review Board headed by the veteran liberal lawyer Clarence Darrow found the administration of codes largely dominated by the larger producers. 'In Industry after Industry', it reported, 'the larger units ... have for their own advantage written the codes and then ... assumed the administration of the codes they have formed.'[21] Though written from a highly critical point of view and to some degree biased against big business, the report more or less accurately reflected the state of affairs in many industries and certainly reflected the attitude of grievance shared by many small businessmen. The labour provisions of the codes gave rise to even greater dissension. There were numerous disputes over wages and hours, and employers were reluctant to recognise labour organisations, other than company unions that they themselves controlled. Anxious not to jeopardise the success of the enterprise by alienating powerful employers, NRA officials were reluctant to exact penalties for unfair labour practices. The labour problem, as it turned out, could not be resolved within the terms of reference of NRA. NRA was also criticised by consumer groups for forcing up prices. Consumers' interests were formally represented in NRA,

21. Quoted in Eric F. Goldman, *Rendezvous with Destiny: A History of Modern American Reform* (New York, 1952), p. 270.

though rarely on the code authorities, and, like labour representatives, they had little influence.

Price was, indeed, as Gordon puts it, 'the focal point of NRA'.[22] To most businessmen its main function was the stabilisation of prices and production. A majority of codes contained some form of price regulation, mainly through the prohibition of selling below 'cost', however defined, and the requirement that prices be filed in advance with the code authorities. Though not always effectively enforced, such restrictions did have the effect of raising prices by a substantial margin in many industries. A 12 per cent rise in non-agricultural prices during the second half of 1933 can be at least in part attributed to their impact. NRA officials were quite acquiescent in the early stages, but, under mounting pressure from labour and consumer groups, they were driven in 1934 to issue guidelines discouraging anti-competitive practices. These proved largely unenforceable in face of the outraged opposition of businessmen and the established complexion of the code structure. The effect was not so much to overturn the existing price controls as to weaken their administration and antagonise businessmen who were already becoming disenchanted with the 'bureaucracy' and 'regimentation' associated with NRA and, above all, with its labour provisions. Existing practices largely continued, but under conditions of increasing friction and disaffection.

A programme of price-fixing and production control, while allowing businessmen the chance to make profits for the first time in years and preventing further perpetuation of the destructive cycle of falling wages, prices and employment, offered little prospect of bringing about a full economic recovery. Empty factories, silent machines and idle men and women could only be restored to productive activity if aggregate demand were increased. It is true that NRA was supposed to be accompanied by a massive programme of public works. Title II of the National Industrial Recovery Act appropriated $3.3 billion to be expended by a Public Works Administration, which, however, under the curmudgeonly management of Harold Ickes, proceeded too slowly to provide any immediate economic stimulus or any dramatic rise in employment. In the absence of expansionary spending, the NRA codes could only have increased aggregate purchasing power by redistributing incomes, that is by allowing wages to rise while holding price rises to a minimum. Instead it operated much more successfully to raise prices than wages.

22. Gordon, *New Deals*, p. 181.

The achievements of NRA were substantial. It certainly contributed to the stabilisation of prices, stemmed what Johnson called 'the saturnalia of destruction', and provided a psychological boost at a time of national despair. NRA codes improved wages and working conditions in many sectors of the economy, eliminating many sweatshops and reducing the incidence of child labour. But, as a comprehensive Brookings Institution report concluded in 1935, they generated little or no increase in the purchasing power of workers, since prices rose at least as fast as wages, and, in so far as they contributed to the creation of 2 million jobs, this was achieved by spreading the existing work through shorter hours rather than by creating new employment opportunities. At best NRA was, in the words of Arthur M. Schlesinger Jr., 'a holding action, not a positive stimulus'.[23] These were not insignificant gains. But they came at the cost of increasing dissension and frustration which led Roosevelt to comment, at the time of its destruction by the Supreme Court, that it had become 'an awful headache'.[24] As long as the basic contradictions at the heart of NRA – between the competing objectives of promoting the cartelisation of business and boosting mass purchasing power, between 'self-regulation' and effective enforcement – were unresolved, no other outcome was likely. The court judgement in *US* v. *A.L.A. Schechter Poultry Corpn.*, with its perhaps justifiable criticism of the uncontrolled delegation of power under NRA and its unjustifiably restrictive reading of the interstate commerce clause, terminated an experiment in cooperative industrial planning that was proving increasingly difficult to sustain.

After Schechter

The *Schechter* decision and the end of NRA reopened the debate about New Deal economic policy. Although the Supreme Court judgement had intervened like something of a *deus ex machina* to slay the troubled agency, its existence was becoming increasingly problematic, and although Roosevelt and some of his advisers, like Tugwell and Richberg, retained a fond regard for NRA, little enthusiasm could be aroused in the business community, outside a few troubled industries, for its reconstitution. Whereas government and farm leaders rushed to replace AAA after *Butler*, NRA

23. Schlesinger, *Coming of the New Deal*, 174.
24. Quoted in Arthur M. Schlesinger Jr., *The Politics of Upheaval* (Boston, 1960), p. 289.

commanded much less loyalty. On the other hand, no alternative to the NRA model attracted sufficient support to take its place on centre-stage. The result was that economic policy after 1935 lacked a coherent vision or a clear sense of direction. Instead, a number of alternative strategies ran alongside one another in a state of uneasy coexistence.

The demise of NRA compelled the enactment of new measures, if only to fill the more obvious holes left by its absence. NRA was a kind of blanket programme intended to fulfil a number of economic and social objectives. Its disappearance, for one thing, encouraged Roosevelt to give his support to Wagner's labour relations bill which was designed to reinforce, and would now replace, Section 7a of the National Industrial Recovery Act. It also made necessary the enactment of global wages-and-hours legislation to afford the protection that NRA codes had once fitfully provided, which eventually came in 1938 with passage of the Fair Labor Standards Act. In a more immediate sense, fragments of NRA were reconstituted in the shape of special legislation promoting cartelisation in particular industries which could make a claim for special treatment by virtue of the severity of their problems, their relationship to the conservation of natural resources or public health, their status as public utilities or the political power of industry pressure groups. These included bituminous coal, petroleum, food and drugs, retailing, trucking and civil aviation. The Guffey–Snyder Act of 1935, for example, virtually re-enacted the old bituminous coal code, while small retailers secured the protection of resale price maintenance in the Miller–Tydings Act of 1937. This post-*Schechter* planning was disjointed and haphazard in character, responding to particular problems and political pressures, rather than embodying an all-embracing plan for the economy, but it formed an important thread in the economic policy of the Second New Deal.

The most trenchant critique of NRA from the start had come from diehard supporters of antitrust, like Senators William E. Borah and Robert M. La Follette Jr., and from those who, because of their intellectual affiliation to the aged Justice Louis Brandeis and his chief disciple Felix Frankfurter, have been described as Brandeisians. From his vantage-point at the Harvard Law School, Frankfurter, who acted virtually as a one-man 'employment agency' for the New Deal, dispatched a stream of able and enthusiastic young disciples, known for self-evident reasons as the 'happy hot dogs', to staff the many jobs opening up in the expanding federal agencies, including men like Benjamin V. Cohen, Thomas G. Corcoran and James M. Landis who became increasingly influential in the later New Deal, while Brandeis, from his eyrie in the Supreme Court, issued a stream of lapidary pronouncements on the evils of 'bigness'. Brandeis and Frankfurter were convinced that the Depression was caused, not by too much competition, but by too little – by the rigidities and anomalies created by monopolistic concentrations of power. Under monopolistic conditions prices, rather than being set by the market, were 'administered' by corporate managers, who, when confronted by falling demand, cut production rather than prices, resulting in men being laid off and investment postponed. The 'disappearance of price competition', agreed Roosevelt in 1938, was 'one of the primary causes of our present difficulties'.[25] The answer was the restoration of competition, not its constriction by NRA codes. 'Market restoration', then, was one of the principal directions taken by post-NRA policy.

Certainly Brandeisian influences can be seen in the Second New Deal. This is most obvious in the Public Utilities Holding Companies Act of 1935, which broke up some of the labyrinthine structures of consolidated ownership in the electric power industry into 'geographically and economically integrated' units. Though modified in response to intensive lobbying by the utility companies, it nevertheless imposed a 'death sentence' on combinations that could not be justified in terms of economic efficiency or geographical proximity, producing a rationalisation of ownership and control which was ultimately beneficial to both customers and shareholders. Hardly less significant were the powers given to the Securities and Exchange Commission (SEC) to regulate the companies' financial dealings and to the Federal Power Commission to regulate their rates and services.

The so-called 'Soak-the-Rich' tax law of the same year was more than a gesture towards populist demands for drastic redistributive taxation from men like Senator Huey Long of Louisiana; it was also an attempt to break up concentrations of capital. Brandeis, disenchanted with the results of a generation or more of antitrust prosecutions, had concluded that progressive taxation was the most effective way of breaking up the trusts: 'By taxation bigness can be destroyed'.[26] Partly for that reason the tax bill not only increased top rates of income tax and imposed inheritance and gifts taxes, but

25. Hawley, *New Deal*, p. 412.
26. Ibid., p. 344.

also penalised large corporations by graduated rates of corporation tax, as well as a new tax on undistributed profits. Greatly weakened during its passage through Congress, the Revenue Act, while slightly increasing the contribution of higher-income groups to tax revenues, had no measurable effect on the distribution of wealth and still less on the structure of corporate ownership.

In the wake of the recession of 1937–38, under the leadership of Thurman Arnold, a trenchant critic of past antitrust policy, the Antitrust Division of the Justice Department acted with renewed vigour. In the next few years antitrust suits were prosecuted at a quite unprecedented rate and with unprecedented effectiveness. However, Arnold was more concerned with removing 'roadblocks' from the highways of commerce than with root-and-branch restructuring of American industry, employing antitrust prosecution to penalise antisocial behaviour, such as extortionate pricing policies, rather than to restore the lost world of small business. Operating on a pragmatic, case-by-case basis, and acting continuously to keep open the flow of commerce – like a traffic policeman at a busy intersection maintaining the flow of traffic, to use Arnold's own analogy – the work of the Antitrust Division expanded enormously in size, necessitating a fivefold increase in its staff. Thus the old trustbusting procedures were adapted to create new mechanisms for industrial control. From an ideal, said Hofstadter, antitrust had become a technique.

Brandeisian dreams of decentralisation and the liberation of small business enterprise were only modestly fulfilled during the later years of the New Deal; the 'market restorers' only partially got their way. The government was too heavily dependent on business, and particularly big business, to invest, to purchase and to employ in order to attain the primary goal of economic recovery to contemplate disruptive actions. Only a few especially vulnerable and unpopular targets, like the Power Trust, met the full force of the antitrust crusade. At the end of the day, antitrust was a policy that had many enemies but few natural supporters.

The New Deal saw a thickening of the regulatory strings that bound business enterprise. Following the Emergency Banking Act of March 1933, the Glass-Steagall Act in June of that year installed more permanent safeguards against the kind of banking collapse that had occurred during the previous winter by separating commercial from investment banking, in order to secure customers' deposits against speculative use by bank officials, and creating a system of federal deposit insurance, in order to protect depositors against loss in the event of bankruptcy, thereby increasing public confidence in banking institutions. The Banking Act of 1935, by increasing government control of the Federal Reserve System, whose Board of Governors was now to consist of presidential appointees, made possible a more effective federal control of monetary policy. Regulation of Wall Street began in 1933 with the Securities Act, which required a full disclosure of information relating to the value of securities, making dealers and issuers of stocks liable for its accuracy, and continued in 1934 with the Securities and Exchange Act, which provided for federal regulation of stock-exchange practices and created a commission, the SEC, to carry it out. Although the securities legislation is sometimes seen as exemplifying the Brandeis approach – 'Sharply at variance with the NRA philosophy of government-business co-operation in the interest of national planning', according to Leuchtenburg – it was, in fact, fully compatible with either.[27] Like banking reform, it followed naturally and inevitably from the nature of the financial crisis and from the revelations of malpractice and institutional inadequacy that followed. The restoration of confidence in America's financial institutions required effective federal regulation of both banks and stock markets.

New regulatory agencies proliferated during the 1930s, like the Securities and Exchange Commission, the National Labor Relations Board, the Federal Communications Commission and the Civil Aeronautics Authority, while older agencies, like the Federal Power Commission, the Federal Trade Commission and the Interstate Commerce Commission, received important new powers. New Deal regulation built on the principle laid down in the Progressive Era 'that economic regulation by expert commissions would bring just results'.[28] Such agencies were believed to be better equipped than either legislatures or courts to deal with complex economic questions. They were able not only to settle disputes but also to offer direction and guidance, setting policy through a series of carefully calibrated interventions tailored to particular situations as they arose. The New Deal, said Cohen, in what could stand as a classical statement of the principles of modern regulatory policy, involved 'a penetrating understanding of the complicated character and functioning of modern economic life, a delicate sense of balance, and alert sensitivity to constant change'. It was 'deliberately flexible and unlogical in its approach to conditions rather than

27. Leuchtenburg, *Franklin D. Roosevelt and the New Deal*, p. 59.
28. Thomas K. McCraw, *Prophets of Regulation* (Cambridge, Mass., 1984), p. 212.

theories', recognising 'that necessity of dealing with multitudinous concrete instances which is the essence of government'.[29] Hence, like the Antitrust Division, the regulatory agencies grew in size. The SEC, for instance, had by 1941 a staff of 1,678 and a budget of $5.3 million. The New Deal therefore greatly enlarged the dominion of the regulatory state.

Finally, a number of economists like Alvin Hansen, William T. Foster and Lauchlin Currie advocated a policy of large-scale public works to pull the nation out of depression. Although their ideas did not receive a complete theoretical validation until the publication of Keynes's *General Theory* in 1936, proto-Keynesian ideas were widely broadcast across the community of academic economists, while the pork-barrel potential of public spending programmes was not lost on members of Congress. Their desires were partially met by the public works component of the National Industrial Recovery Act, despite its ponderous progress, and more immediately by the profusion of New Deal relief measures. However, Roosevelt himself, while convinced of the virtues of public works, did not accept the fundamental tenet of Keynesianism, that is the desirability, indeed necessity, of deficit spending during periods of recession. His Director of the Budget Lewis Douglas, who considered Hoover's spending policies wildly extravagant, believed that the 'immediate fate of Western civilization' depended on the achievement of a balanced budget, and Roosevelt by and large agreed with him. As Mark Leff has shown, Roosevelt was a deep-died fiscal conservative, saved only from a flinty dogmatism by a concern for human suffering and a sensitivity to political pressures. The New Deal spent billions of dollars on relief throughout the decade, and it is probable that much of what economic recovery occurred resulted from that spending – yet it did so reluctantly and half-heartedly. Half-measures took the nation only half-way towards recovery.

This became clearer after 1937, when Roosevelt, eager to make some firm gestures to balance the federal budget, cut back heavily on public works spending, with catastrophic results. It was time, he agreed, in the words of Secretary of the Treasury Henry Morgenthau, to 'strip of the bandages, throw away the crutches' and see if the patient 'could stand on its own two feet'.[30] Evidently it could not. The economy went sharply into a nose-dive from which it was only pulled out a few months later by the restoration of the

29. Schlesinger, *Politics of Upheaval*, pp. 226–7.
30. Alan Brinkley, *The End of Reform: New Deal Liberalism in Recession and War* (New York, 1995), p. 27.

cuts. With that, however, went a recognition that government spending was a crucial agent in economic recovery and an acceptance, to some extent at least, of the principles and practice of Keynesianism. Roosevelt acknowledged in April 1938 that 'We suffer primarily from a lack of buying power'. Government spending could be used 'to put idle money and idle men to work, to increase our public wealth . . . and to help our system of private enterprise to function'.[31] Tax revenues could not be raised sufficiently to balance the budget without increasing the national income. This was underlined by the impact of the Second World War, which began after 1939 finally to pull the nation out of depression. With its enormous public spending on armaments, with its conscription of millions of men into the armed forces, making the works projects of the New Deal seem puny in comparison, the war effort could be seen, in macroeconomic terms, as a massive public works programme, gladly financed by deficit spending on a gargantuan scale. The federal deficit rose from $3.9 million in 1939 to $57 billion at the height of the war, while 17 million new jobs were created. The war experience did as much as anything to convince policy-makers, as well as many business leaders, of the validity of Keynesian methods of demand management. For a generation after the war they became accepted as the principal tools of economic policy. In place of grand schemes of economic planning, drastic programmes of market restoration or redistribution of income, fiscal policy came to be regarded by liberals almost as an economic panacea, attractive for the very reason that it did not require them to address the more fundamental contradictions and imbalances in the American economic order or encroach drastically on the freedom of private business.

The New Deal did not change the basic structure of American industry. It left the degree of economic concentration unaltered. Although banking and the stock market were now subject to much tighter regulation, as were specific industries, like food and drugs, private business remained responsible for the primary decisions regarding investment, production and pricing. It is true that it now was subject to higher rates of taxation, and it now had to deal with organised labour, newly empowered and militant in defence of its rights. This, above all, businessmen resented. This, above all, led them to condemn the New Deal as a radical interference with their liberties. But really it was no such thing. When the dust settled, it became evident that the political economy bequeathed by the New

31. Ibid., p. 104.

Deal was an extension of the developing system of regulated capitalism that had its roots in the Progressive Era, leavened with a measure of Keynesian demand management and welfare state liberalism.

The New Deal and American politics

The legislation of 1935 established the lasting character of the New Deal, forging a new relationship between government and people. The presidential election of the following year emphatically demonstrated just how popular Franklin D. Roosevelt and the New Deal were. Roosevelt was re-elected by an overwhelming majority, conceding only two states to his hapless Republican opponent. He appeared to have been granted an unequivocal mandate to carry still further the reforms of the New Deal, and there was evidently – with 'one-third of a nation ill-housed, ill-clad, ill-nourished' – a great deal still to do.[32] Yet, despite the swollen Democratic majorities in both houses of Congress, the legislative returns of Roosevelt's second term were relatively meagre. The second Agricultural Adjustment Act, the Fair Labor Standards Act, the Wagner-Steagall housing law and the Bankhead–Jones Farm Tenancy Act were far from insubstantial measures, but they fell far short of both the needs of the situation and the demands of the Administration. On the other hand, Roosevelt's attempts to reorganise the structures of government, in order to protect and consolidate his New Deal reforms, did bear some fruit. Roosevelt, says Barry Karl, planned in his second term a dramatic reconstruction of presidential administration, amounting to a 'Third New Deal', which, though only partially successful, went a long way to reconstitute the practices and possibilities of American politics. Therefore, says Sidney Milkis, 'the New Deal is properly viewed as the defining moment in setting the tone of twentieth-century politics in the United States'.[33]

Roosevelt in 1936 asked voters, quite simply, to compare 'four years ago and now'. Few Americans did not feel some benefits from the various policies of the New Deal, and many of them returned the favour by voting for Roosevelt. Industrial workers were grateful to the Democrats for the support given to trade unions, farmers for

---

32. Leuchtenburg, *Franklin D. Roosevelt and the New Deal*, p. 231.
33. Sidney M. Milkis, *The President and the Parties: The Transformation of the American Party System since the New Deal* (New York, 1993), p. vii.

price supports and rehabilitation loans, millions of middle-class citizens for help in refinancing the mortgages on their homes, the unemployed for places on public works projects, and millions more for the federal relief cheques that brought them from the brink of starvation. Most strikingly, African–Americans, who for many years had loyally voted on the principle that 'The Republican Party is the ship and all else is the sea', deserted what was once the party of Lincoln but was now the party of Hoover. Though discriminated against by nearly every New Deal agency, especially in the South, they were almost never excluded from assistance altogether. Even in the South New Deal agencies forced local administrators to treat their claims seriously, listen to their grievances, allow them to vote in crop control elections and, in short, to acknowledge, however begrudgingly and however incompletely, their humanity. Although Roosevelt himself, anxious not to antagonise powerful Southern congressional leaders, declined to intervene actively in the cause of civil rights, many figures close to him, most notably Eleanor Roosevelt, conspicuously took up the cause. More important than that, however, was the simple fact that the New Deal provided African–Americans with immediate economic assistance that stood between them and complete destitution. By 1940 black voters were as loyal to the party of Roosevelt as they had once been to the party of Lincoln.

Each of these groups had reasons to be grateful to Roosevelt and the New Deal, which had extended assistance to them and their families, assistance of a personal and concrete kind that could be seen and felt. 'I would be without a roof over my head if it hadn't been for the government loan', said one farmer. 'God bless Mr. Roosevelt and the Democratic party who saved thousands of poor people all over this country from starvation.'[34] Although not all of those who voted for Roosevelt in 1936 maintained their allegiance, that feeling of gratitude for the New Deal remained a factor in American politics for a generation or more.

The policy innovations of the New Deal were accompanied by an electoral realignment – what Samuel Lubell called the 'Roosevelt Revolution' – which left Roosevelt's Democratic coalition in a dominant position in national politics not just in 1936 but for several decades. Not only did the Democratic vote nearly double between 1928 and 1936, but its composition changed dramatically. To the Democratic strongholds in the Solid South and the

34 Leuchtenburg, *Franklin D. Roosevelt and the New Deal*, p. 193.

bailiwicks of traditional urban machines the New Deal coalition added a wider working-class support which built up regular Democratic majorities in the larger cities and industrial areas of the North. Polling data, as well as the distribution of the vote across election districts, suggest overwhelming support for Roosevelt from blue-collar workers and lower-income groups, as well as from voters of European immigrant or African-American background. Many of the supporters of Midwestern progressives like Floyd Olson in Minnesota and the La Follettes in Wisconsin who voted for Roosevelt in 1936 also ended up in the Democratic Party after the retirement of their nominally Republican leaders. States which had once sent progressive Republicans to Congress were, after the Second World War, regularly represented by liberal Democrats like Frank Church, Hubert Humphrey, George McGovern and Walter Mondale. Like all landslides, that of 1936 gave off misleading signals. Roosevelt's popular appeal did not always rub off on his party's state and congressional candidates. The Republican Party retained considerable grass-roots strength in the rural North and West. Within a few years it was close to compiling a majority in Congress and confidently anticipated electing a Republican president once Roosevelt had departed from the scene. Although across the country the Democrats had a majority of registered voters, the two parties were competitive in most states outside the South. Indeed, it was still the Solid South that tipped the electoral balance. The New Deal realignment, while greatly enlarging the Democratic Party, reinforced its schizoid character, with a predominantly liberal urban Northern wing coexisting uneasily with a predominantly conservative Southern wing. It soon became clear just how unsatisfactory an instrument for liberal reform, for all its numerical strength, the new Democratic Party was.

After 1937 the New Deal was placed increasingly on the defensive. The turning-point, it is generally acknowledged, was Roosevelt's confrontation with the Supreme Court. A majority of the justices were constitutional conservatives, appointed in the 1920s by Harding and Coolidge, who held a narrow view of the Constitution and of the scope of federal powers. Although it took some time for cases to work their way up through the lower courts, from 1935 the Court struck down a series of New Deal programmes, including particularly NRA and AAA, in most cases on the basis of a narrow construction of the interstate commerce clause (which was the basis for almost all federal regulation of the economy). With a fine disregard for logical consistency, the Court also disallowed a number of state laws under a tortured interpretation of the Fourteenth Amendment. The constitutional theories evidently entertained by a majority of the justices would, as Roosevelt complained, leave the government with 'no control over national economic problems' and create a 'no-man's land' where neither federal nor state authority ran. It seemed that no important New Deal programme could withstand their fundamentalist rigour. Roosevelt declined to blame the Constitution for his difficulties. The blame, he claimed, lay with elderly and conservative judges who held on to a 'horse-and-buggy definition of interstate commerce' which was more appropriate to the 1830s than the 1930s and persisted in reading their own prejudices into the Constitution.[35]

For that reason Roosevelt set out to reform the Court, rather than seeking to amend the Constitution, an uncertain process which, even if successful, would have taken years to complete. Seizing on the expedient used by Herbert Asquith during his confrontation with the House of Lords in 1911, he proposed to pack the Court with additional judges. Roosevelt was taken aback by the intensity of the opposition to his court-packing proposal. Even many of the leaders of his own party would not go so far. 'Boys, here's where I cash in my chips', commented the chairman of the House Judiciary Committee on learning of the plan.[36] Enough of his congressional supporters deserted the president to ensure the bill's defeat. The Senate Judiciary Committee, on whose approval the president depended to get the bill through the upper house, declared that an independent judiciary was 'the only certain shield of individual rights'.[37] The Constitution was sacred, the main testament to the principle that this was a government of laws not men. It was no surprise that conservatives, anxious to protect the rights of property and, in the case of Southerners, the rights of the states, should rush to the defence of the Court, but many liberals, who in other respects applauded the New Deal, fretted over the implications of court reform. In view of events across the sea, the late 1930s was not a time to contemplate the undermining of American constitutional liberties. 'The greater the insecurity of the times', notes Leuchtenburg, 'the more people clung to the few institutions which seemed timeless.'[38] Both opinion polls and the

35. William E. Leuchtenburg, *The Supreme Court Reborn: The Constitutional Revolution in the Age of Roosevelt* (New York, 1995), p. 90.

36. Leuchtenburg, *Franklin D. Roosevelt and the New Deal*, p. 234.

37. William E. Leuchtenburg, *The New Deal: A Documentary History* (New York, 1968), p. 214.

38. Leuchtenburg, *Franklin D. Roosevelt and the New Deal*, pp. 235–6.

content of congressional mailbags clearly indicated that a majority of voters did not want to see the powers of the Court interfered with. Roosevelt was, for once, guilty of hubris. Emboldened by his unprecedented election victory, he had moved too rapidly to challenge the Court, assuming that his own reading of the situation was shared by his supporters in Congress and the country, and neglecting to consult his political allies or take the necessary soundings of public opinion which would have saved him from disaster.

It is difficult to evaluate the impact of the Supreme Court fight. Roosevelt claimed that he had lost the battle but won the war. That is because within a few months of the introduction of the bill one of the less dogmatically conservative justices, in the famous 'switch in time that saved nine', had joined a new majority which found the Wagner Act and the Social Security Act constitutional, as well as a Washington State minimum-wage law, and, in doing so, effectively delivered a death-blow to the court-packing scheme. Within a few years a majority of the Court, many of whom had resisted retirement and even, it seemed, deliberately stayed alive to frustrate the president, had either stepped down or expired, allowing Roosevelt to select new judges more amenable to his views. Having been unable to appoint a single judge during his first four years, Roosevelt had by 1943 named nine. His appointments transformed the nature of the Court. From now on it consistently declined to intervene in the economic sphere, accepting once and for all a federal right and responsibility to legislate on such matters. In effect, the states' rights argument that had bedevilled economic policy-making for half a century was settled. On the other hand, the Roosevelt Court became, as we shall see, decidedly interventionist in cases involving civil rights, the protection of civil liberties and due process, to such an extent that later generations of conservatives would denounce the Court no less vehemently than had Roosevelt in the 1930s. Thus the New Deal produced a judicial realignment in many ways as significant in its effect on American politics as the electoral realignment.

On the other hand, the immediate consequences of the struggle were highly damaging. The controversy built up political resistance to the Administration, providing a focus for those who opposed it for other reasons. Defence of the Constitution was a convenient rallying cry for enemies of the New Deal. The defeat demonstrated that a president whose popularity and success had for years intimidated potential enemies might after all be vulnerable to attack. Many of those who broke with FDR over court reform never again showed the same loyalty. Although there were many reasons for the growing opposition to the New Deal in the late 1930s, there is no doubt that the Supreme Court battle dramatically changed the political atmosphere.

While Congress was deliberating on the Supreme Court bill, Roosevelt also presented plans for administrative reform which in his eyes were hardly less significant. The New Deal had thrown off a large progeny of miscellaneous agencies, hastily organised and staffed, with overlapping and sometimes conflicting authority. The executive reorganisation bill presented to Congress in 1937 gave the president wide-ranging authority to rationalise the government by transferring and consolidating agencies, extended the merit system, reorganised fiscal management, provided the president with administrative assistants, and created a National Resources Planning Board with responsibility for central planning and coordination of government programmes. The objectives were to consolidate New Deal agencies by giving them a permanent home; to consolidate the position of the New Dealers by bringing as many as possible under civil service rules; to create an administrative apparatus appropriate to the enlarged responsibilities of a welfare state; and to equip the president for the task of national leadership.

The proposals antagonised a host of interest groups which maintained a fruitful association with one executive bureau or another and did not wish to see it disturbed, while no interest group could see any positive benefit arising from it. Unlike most other New Deal reforms, executive reorganisation lacked a constituency. Congressmen, too, disliked any disruption of the cosy relationships that they had built up in the various departments. More generally, this appeared to be yet another plan for the aggrandisement of presidential power. The reorganisation bill, declared Senator Josiah Bailey of North Carolina with characteristic hyperbole, would give Roosevelt 'all the powers of a dictator'.[39] Nevertheless, recognising the need for greater managerial efficiency, Congress consented to a modified measure, passed in 1939, which allowed the president to draw up plans for the reallocation of agencies, subject to congressional approval, and to appoint six assistants. Roosevelt used this authority to negotiate some rationalisation of administrative functions and, more significantly, to create the Executive Office of the President, including the

39. Richard Polenberg, *Reorganizing Roosevelt's Government, 1936–1939* (Cambridge, Mass., 1966), p. 125.

Bureau of the Budget and the National Resources Planning Board, which gave his successors a much greater capacity to plan and coordinate policy. To a considerable degree, the institution of the modern presidency, at least in domestic affairs, is a product of this reorganisation.

From 1937 a conservative coalition in Congress, consisting of Republicans and mostly Southern Democrats, obstructed New Deal legislation. It was rooted, first of all, in conservative opposition to what were seen as increasingly radical policies. By 1935 organs of business opinion were becoming openly critical of Roosevelt and his works. In that year both the NAM and the US Chamber of Commerce passed resolutions explicitly condemning the New Deal. Conservative fears were intensified by alarm at the growing power of organised labour, and in particular at the apparent lawlessness of the 'sit-down strikes' of 1937, which provoked fears of Communist infiltration. In conjunction with the attack on the Supreme Court, the sit-down strikes appeared to denote a dangerous assault on law and property rights. Conservative congressmen, in Bailey's words, claimed to stand for 'Constitutional Representative Government as opposed to mass Democracy'.[40] The conservative coalition, secondly, reflected rural opposition to policies favouring the cities. Unlike the earlier New Deal, its later manifestations seemed disproportionately to benefit the urban working class by the promotion of trade unions, wages and hours laws, and public housing programmes. Rural congressmen, while pragmatically supporting New Deal policies in support of agriculture, saw little merit in such policies.

Most importantly, perhaps, congressional opposition to the New Deal reflected Southern fears regarding race relations. Southern congressmen resented the way in which New Deal programmes disturbed the status of Southern blacks. The possibility of relief payments, unemployment insurance and social security, the minimum wage and the rehabilitation programmes of the FSA threatened the social control which white landlords exerted over their black workforce. They noted the growing influence of the black vote and the growing sympathy of urban liberals for civil rights. When New Deal liberals like Robert Wagner gave their support to anti-lynching bills, even though Roosevelt himself steered well clear of endorsing them, they presciently noted that the prospect of federal civil rights legislation was not too far away. 'To any discerning person',

40. Leuchtenburg, *Franklin D. Roosevelt and the New Deal*, p. 252.

remarked the conservative Senator Carter Glass of Virginia, 'it is perfectly obvious that the so-called Democratic party at the North is now the negro party, advocating social equality for the races.'[41] Southern congressmen also objected to measures which, as they saw it, wrongfully deprived their section of the competitive advantage of cheap labour. The Fair Labor Standards Act they condemned, in Roger Biles's words, as 'a sectional bill disguised as a humanitarian reform'.[42] By the end of the decade half the South's senators and a similar proportion of its representatives were consistently voting against the New Deal.

As the New Deal after 1935, and more decisively after 1937, began to take a social democratic turn, the conservative opposition gathered strength. A coalition of Republicans and conservative Southern Democrats, though loosely organised and shifting in membership, stood in the path of progressive legislation. After the dramatic successes of Roosevelt's first term, the New Deal seemed to be treading water, fighting to maintain rather than to extend its programmes. The result was a political deadlock which extended beyond Roosevelt's presidency far into the postwar era. The frustrations of the second term illustrate the difficulties of political change in America, the barriers to reform inherent in the American political system.

An evaluation

Two generations of left-wing critics have pointed out the limitations of New Deal reform. It brought only partial recovery, with 8 million still unemployed at the end of the decade, real incomes barely creeping back to the levels of 1929 and private investment still sluggish. It failed to cure poverty and social injustice. The plight of blacks, slum-dwellers, tenant farmers and other specially disadvantaged groups was little altered. The New Deal welfare state, as we shall see, did little to redistribute income or reduce inequality, and, rather than showering its benefits equally, devoted its principal efforts to securing the livelihood of middle-income groups. New Deal farm policy acted principally to encourage the rehabilitation of commercial agriculture and did little to challenge, indeed often exacerbated, inequality and exploitation on the land. The distribution of wealth and power was hardly changed, the degree of

41. Frank Freidel, *F.D.R. and the South* (Baton Rouge, La., 1965), pp. 91–2.
42. Roger Biles, *The South and the New Deal* (Lexington, Ky., 1994), p. 139.

business concentration unaltered, and private enterprise retained primary responsibility for running the economy. Even the most evidently radical aspect of the New Deal, its labour policy, while strengthening the union movement and enhancing the bargaining power of at least some industrial workers, did little more than create another interest group, one representing no more than a quarter to a third of all workers, which was soon coopted into the economic and political order.

Above all else, the New Deal catered to the craving of many elements of society, but especially perhaps of middle-income groups, for a degree of economic security at a time of great uncertainty – through farm price supports, in some cases through government-sponsored cartelisation, through insurance of bank deposits, through social insurance, through mortgage relief, through support for trade unions and in many other ways. 'Underlying all the wants and needs of people today is an overwhelming desire for security', noted Undersecretary of Agriculture M.L. Wilson.[43] And this the New Deal recognised. In his State of the Union message in 1944, Roosevelt made this commitment explicit: 'We have come to a clear realization that true individual freedom cannot exist without economic security and independence.' It entailed a new understanding of the rights of the citizen which went beyond individual liberties to incorporate an 'economic declaration of rights'.[44] These included the rights to employment, to adequate food, clothing and shelter, to adequate medical care, to protection against the fear of old age, sickness or disability, and to education – rights that were, in theory at least, elevated from aspirations to entitlements, which the government was obliged to redeem.

That these commitments were not fully met is evident. The New Deal welfare state fell far short of what the Administration, or at least liberals in the Administration, had desired. So did tax reform, aid to poor farmers and slum clearance. In almost every part of the New Deal damaging concessions and compromises were made which greatly hampered its effectiveness. To some extent these failings can be put down to an intellectual confusion over ends and means that lay at the very heart of the New Deal. The Administration was divided in mind and spirit, as different factions

43. Donald Worster, *The Dust Bowl: The Southern Plains in the 1930s* (New York, 1979), p. 154.
44. Alan Dawley, *Struggles for Justice: Social Responsibility and the Liberal State* (Cambridge, Mass., 1991), p. 386; Commonwealth Club Address, in Richard Hofstadter, ed., *Great Issues in American History: From Reconstruction to the Present, 1865–1969* (New York, 1969), p. 349.

contended for control, with sometimes one, then another, establishing a fragile hegemony. Roosevelt himself both reflected and encouraged this eclecticism, often with creative, but sometimes with confusing, results. And then, while receptive to miscellaneous ideas and broad in human sympathies, Roosevelt possessed at the core of his being a profound conservatism, expressed, for example, in his continuing quest for a balanced budget and in his suspicion of organised labour.

Even if the Administration had been wholeheartedly committed to liberal policies, external barriers to reform would still have limited the possibilities for their attainment. It confronted a Congress ruled by the principle of seniority in which the leading positions fell to men (almost always men) who were old, conservative, rural and Southern. It confronted a Supreme Court which stood obdurately in the path of a radical extension of national authority, giving way only after a debilitating struggle. It confronted state governments which were, with a few noted exceptions, more conservative than the New Deal and which consistently hampered the local implementation of federal programmes. Yet the federal government was heavily reliant on local officials to implement its programmes for the very reason that it lacked the administrative capacity to carry them out itself. Although the New Deal saw an enormous expansion in the size of the federal bureaucracy, its operations were continuously inhibited by the lack of an existing civil service with the expertise and manpower to plan and enforce its policies.

Although Roosevelt's personal popularity and the prevailing sense of national emergency gave him exceptional leverage, enough to make the New Deal possible in the first place, the enactment and administration of New Deal programmes were shaped by organised interests. In the furtherance of 'grass-roots democracy', the New Deal fostered the development of a 'broker state' in which organised interest groups competed for attention. It was inevitable that organised would exert more influence than unorganised groups, like the poor or the unemployed, and that among organised pressure groups some would turn out to be more powerful than others. According to George Peek, the first head of AAA, 'The truth is that no democratic government can be very different from the country it governs. If some groups are dominant in the country, they will be dominant in any plan the government undertakes.'[45]

45. Goldman, *Rendezvous with Destiny*, p. 272.

Finally, the New Deal was pulling against the underlying conservatism of the American people (or at least of those portions which were politically vocal), their belief in limited government, in the free market, in limited taxation, in self-help, their attitude to the poor as morally deficient and their constitutional conservatism. This was especially true in business circles where conservative views proved remarkably resistant to economic circumstances. Returning to the small town in Indiana which had been the subject of their classic sociological study *Middletown*, Robert and Helen Lynd observed that, had a latter-day Rip Van Winkle fallen asleep at a Rotary Club dinner at the time of their first visit in 1925 and woken up ten years later, he could not have discerned, from the tone and content of the speeches, any evidence of changing economic circumstances. By the late 1930s opinion polls showed declining support for new legislation in almost all sections of the population. Sizeable majorities of those polled expressed the hope that the Administration would pursue a more conservative course; sizeable majorities plumped for a balanced budget, even at the expense of cuts in relief spending. By the late 1930s the New Deal was clearly to the left of public opinion. Richard Polenberg concludes that 'The New Deal declined after 1937 because most Americans did not want to extend it much further'.[46] Indeed, more remarkable than the failures of the New Deal were its successes, in view of the obstacles to reform built into the American political system. As James Patterson reminds us, such moments of dramatic, non-incremental political change are rare in American history. In the twentieth century only the early years of the first Wilson Administration (1913–14) and the mid-1960s, between the death of John F. Kennedy and the sucking of the United States into the ground war in Vietnam, can match the reforming intensity of the New Deal.

Yet, if the structures of American politics held back New Deal reform, the New Deal itself did a great deal to change those structures. It created a Democratic Party whose majority status was founded upon a 'New Deal coalition', many of whose components were committed to the maintenance and extension of the New Deal. Though held back by the congressional power of its Southern wing, party leaders recognised that it could only win national elections by appealing to its urban blue-collar constituency. The New Deal forced a realignment of the Supreme Court, which played a very different role in the next half-century to that which it had

46. Richard Polenberg, 'The decline of the New Deal', in Braeman *et al.*, eds, *New Deal*, I, p. 255.

played in preceding decades. It fuelled the growth of the 'administrative state', of a partly independent bureaucracy invested with wide discretionary powers in administering existing federal programmes and designing new ones. Along with that, while building on the achievements of his progressive predecessors, Roosevelt was chiefly responsible for the creation of the modern presidency. Both by virtue of his own peculiar leadership skills – his facility in interpersonal relationships, his mastery of the media, his extraordinary charisma, his ability to inspire subordinates and his exceptional political touch – and, more importantly, by his creation, in the Office of the President, of an institutional basis for presidential leadership, he not only set an example for future chief executives but also provided the template for a generation of academic study of the presidency. Above all, perhaps, the New Deal provided a model of committed and disinterested reform, of enlightened leadership and imaginative problem-solving, of dedication to the interests of the 'forgotten man' which, however idealised, however partially fulfilled, set the standards of expectation for liberal reform in the future.

CHAPTER EIGHT

The Rise and Fall of Organised Labour

Introduction

In an earlier chapter we explored the weakness of organised labour in early twentieth-century America. It is true, as we have seen, that the unions' membership surged during the period of the First World War, but they were unable to maintain their strength after the Armistice. An employers' counter-offensive, conducted in the atmosphere of the postwar Red Scare, proved too powerful for a labour movement itself seriously divided along lines of ethnicity and race. The climate of the 1920s was inhospitable to organised labour. Membership fell from a peak of 5.1 million in 1920 to 3.6 million in 1929 – a mere 11.7 per cent of the non-agricultural workforce.

Yet, despite the crushing impact of the Depression, maybe because of the impact of the Depression, the labour movement entered upon a period of explosive growth during the 1930s, which continued during the Second World War. By 1945, 14.8 million men and women held union cards, 35.8 per cent of the non-agricultural workforce – a fourfold increase in numerical terms, and a threefold increase in proportional terms, over the space of little more than a decade. Now large and powerful industrial unions bargained collectively on behalf of their members, significantly adjusting where they did so the balance of power in the workplace. Now organised labour gained recognition as an important interest group in modern American society. Now the unions held an important place within the congress of interests that Roosevelt had attached to his New Deal coalition. As the president of the United States Chamber of Commerce acknowledged in 1944, 'Measured in numbers, political influence, economic weight, or by any other yardstick, labor is a power in our land'.[1] Although, as we shall see, this reordering of industrial relations was limited in its extent, conservative in its implications, and, as it turned out, insecure in its foundations, it marked a striking departure from the industrial world of the 1920s. The weakening of organised labour in recent decades has had correspondingly significant implications, both for the workplace experience and the broader political influence of American workers.

The lean years

In order better to understand the transformation that was to follow, it would be helpful to look at the status of organised labour in the 1920s – at the weakness which later became strength. The reasons for the enfeebled condition of American trade unions were, in fact, broadly similar to those which had militated against their success in earlier decades. Employers remained resolute in their opposition to unionism, combining traditional anti-union tactics, such as the blacklist and the 'yellow-dog' contract, with the newer strategy of 'welfare capitalism'. This entailed in some cases improvements in wages and working conditions, more often the establishment of pension and stock-ownership schemes for loyal workers, as well as medical facilities, cafeterias, sports teams and other miscellaneous welfare programmes. Such programmes were introduced, explained Elbert Gary of US Steel, 'because it is the way men ought to be treated, and secondly, because it pays to treat men in that way'.[2] It paid in so far as improvements in morale could be translated into higher levels of productivity and an abatement of the staggering levels of turnover that troubled contemporary industrial relations specialists. It paid also in that, if employees could be persuaded that the benefits for which trade unions strove – higher wages, better working conditions, economic security – could be obtained without the assistance of trade unions, then trade unions would come to seem unnecessary. Instead, employees were encouraged to join company unions, which offered a safer, more easily controlled form of employee representation. By 1929 approximately 1½ million

1. Quoted in David Brody, *Workers in Industrial America: Essays on the Twentieth Century Struggle* (New York, 1980), p. 174.

2. Quoted in David Brody, 'The rise and decline of welfare capitalism', in John Braeman, Robert Bremner and David Brody, eds, *Change and Continuity in Twentieth-Century America: The 1920s* (Columbus, Ohio, 1968), pp. 154–5.

workers had joined 'employee representation plans', nearly half as many as were enrolled in independent unions.

It is difficult to gauge the impact of welfare capitalism. It was confined to a relatively small number of large enterprises, and even there the pension and stock-ownership schemes brought benefits only to the minority of workers with stable employment records. There can be no doubt that most employees treated such gestures of benevolence with appropriate scepticism. Nor did employee representation schemes do more than cast a transparent film over the naked realities of managerial power. Yet, as Lizabeth Cohen has most revealingly shown, the rhetoric, as much as the application, of welfare capitalism presented workers with a vision of 'moral capitalism' that conferred upon them certain intrinsic rights – rights to representation and equity of treatment – which formed part of the set of ideas and expectations that they carried into the 1930s. Moreover, company unions accustomed workers to participation in industrial organisations and later, ironically, pro-vided a profitable recruiting ground for the new industrial unions.

The Republican administrations of the 1920s used the power of government to repress strike activity in a manner reminiscent of the late nineteenth century. Although Herbert Hoover repeatedly sought to mediate between warring interests, urging employers and unions to cooperate with one another to improve productivity and stabilise employment, other federal officials, like Harding's ill-starred Attorney-General Harry L. Daugherty, were more forcefully anti-union. The court injunction that Daugherty sought, and obtained, to quell the railroad shopmen's strike of 1922 matched in its scope and draconian terms that delivered against the Pullman boycott in 1894. The federal courts continued to issue injunctions with mounting frequency, restrained not at all by the anti-injunction provisions of the Clayton Act. With few exceptions, state power continued to be exercised in a fashion highly prejudicial to the prospects of organised labour.

The ethnic and racial divisions that hampered union organisation before the First World War remained very much alive. Industrial workers identified themselves with ethnic sub-com-munities, despite the pervasive influence of mass culture – of radio, the movies, phonograph records, the tabloid press, advertising and chain-store shopping – which, as Cohen has demonstrated, was mediated by the family and neighbourhood contexts in which it was consumed. Ethnic communities provided the social networks and cultural resources that made up the fabric of everyday life. More importantly, they furnished most workers with the systems of support, formal and informal, that offered security against the many uncertainties of industrial society. These ranged from family connections to the mutual benefit associations to which working-class housewives regularly contributed small premiums. It was to such networks of support that most workers looked in times of financial difficulty.

The 1930s brought massive changes in the parameters of working-class life. Most obviously, the Great Depression sowed the seeds of union growth. Whilst the early 1930s saw a decline in membership, as mass unemployment bit into the labour force, the decline – from 3.6 million in 1929 to 2.7 million in 1933 – was much less crippling than in past depressions, and, indeed, as a proportion of those in work was hardly noticeable at all. More importantly, the Depression brought about significant changes in the attitudes of American workers towards trade unions and the role of the state. With the failure of their own institutions to cope with the problems of mass unemployment and deprivation, as family funds dried up and ethnic-group associations were swamped by the sheer volume of need, workers turned to the government and to trade unions to provide the security that could no longer be provided from within. According to David Brody, their 'accommodation to the industrial system had broken down under the long stretch of the Depression'.[3] All the expedients, all the mechanisms that went to make industrial existence tolerable were now in jeopardy.

Whatever confidence workers might have had in the protective shield of welfare capitalism was shattered by the response of employers to the crisis. After some major companies had held the line for several months, wages were cut and men laid off. The much-vaunted welfare programmes were among the first casualties. So much, it seemed, for welfare capitalism, so much for the spirit of 'trusteeship'. According to *Nation's Business* in 1929, modern business was based on the 'the sincere belief that the interests of the employer and the employee are mutual and at bottom identical'.[4] This turned out not to be the case. Business had promoted a set of expectations and then, at a moment of crisis, failed to live up to them. The result for those workers who had believed in the

3. David Brody, 'The emergence of mass-production unionism', in John Braeman, Robert Bremner and David Brody, eds., *Change and Continuity in Modern America* (Columbus, Ohio, 1964), p. 247.
4. Quoted in Brody, 'Welfare capitalism', p. 150.

protestations of corporate spokesmen was a profound sense of betrayal. Both Brody and Cohen see this as a significant contributor to the working-class militancy which was so pronounced a feature of industrial relations during the 1930s. If so, it fed a more general stream of resentment. The experience of many workers had long been one of maltreatment, discrimination and abuse at the hands of foremen and company officials, and subjection to a host of petty grievances. These were longstanding grievances, but they were more intensely felt during the Depression. Under the fiercely competitive conditions of the Depression years, workers were subjected to speed-ups, increasingly dangerous working conditions, deskilling and, above all, a profound sense of insecurity. Company hiring policies seemed all the more arbitrary and discriminatory. Workers demanded a system of hiring and firing that recognised the claims of seniority, a measure of control over the speed of the production line, some organised procedures for the expression of grievances, and an end to what Mike Davis calls 'the petty despotism of the workplace'.[5]

Such conditions led to an explosion of militancy. 'It is like a force of nature[,] irresistible as a tide', declared the journalist Mary Heaton Vorse.[6] In many industries the thrust for organisation came from rank-and-file workers, acting in response to low wages, long hours, dangerous conditions, an intolerable pace of work, the exactions of tyrannical foremen and the sheer irrationality and injustice of the system under which they worked. But, although radical historians like Staughton Lynd and social historians like Lizabeth Cohen are correct in asserting its fundamental importance in shaping the development of the labour movement, the limitations of grass-roots militancy must also be recognised, especially after the dousing of the early enthusiasm of 1933–34. In some industries, like the electrical manufacturing companies studied by Ronald Schatz, the militants were relatively small numbers of skilled workers, many with backgrounds in political radicalism, whose privileged position in the factory gave them freedom to express their grievances. Many of the critical actions of the heroic age of the CIO, like the Goodyear strike at Akron and the Flint 'sit-down strike', involved minorities of workers, while the rest held back and waited to see which way the wind blew. Deeply felt though the grievances were, in industries like automobiles and steel, with long

5. Mike Davis, 'The barren marriage of American labor and the Democratic Party' *New Left Review* 124 (1980), p. 46.

6. Robert Zieger, *The CIO, 1935–1955* (Chapel Hill, N.C., 1995), p. 43.

histories of persecution of union activists, any display of overt militancy carried a risk. Workers had to be convinced that the organisation would be permanent, that it would bring material benefits and, above all, that membership would not bear an intolerable risk of dismissal. This makes evaluation of the extent of rank-and-file militancy extraordinarily difficult. While it is probable that most workers harboured a sense of frustration and a desire for change, the overt expression of such feelings under existing conditions was extremely perilous. What the more sensitive historical accounts of workers' behaviour during the 1930s reveal is a complex interplay between feelings of anger and fear, radicalism and conservatism, militancy and submissiveness.

In any case, the grass-roots impulse was not sufficient in itself to transform the fortunes of American unions. At several moments in the past, such as the 'Great Upheaval' of the 1880s or the 'new unionism' of the 1910s, working men and women had joined labour unions, participated in industrial action and pursued their collective goals with renewed enthusiasm, only to retreat in the face of repeated setbacks and overwhelming obstacles. Grass-roots militancy was a necessary but not a sufficient condition for trade union growth. Needed also was a new and more vigorous form of labour organisation, better adapted to the demands of modern industry. Needed still more urgently were changes in law and in the exercise of government power, and these came in the shape of the labour legislation of the New Deal.

New Deal labour policy

The accession of Franklin D. Roosevelt to the presidency brought labour's friends back into power. However, there was nothing unambiguous about the Democratic Administration's commitment to organised labour. For all their professed, and probably genuine, sympathy for labour, Roosevelt and his Secretary of Labor Frances E. Perkins shared a fundamentally progressive approach to industrial relations, seeking to balance and reconcile the competing interests of capital and labour, rather than aligning themselves with the union movement. Roosevelt was not especially interested in labour issues. His posture was one of benign neglect punctuated by occasional irritated interventions at moments of crisis. In fact, the industrial relations policy of the New Deal was not for the most part formulated by the president and his closest advisers. Its architects were a group of labour lawyers, economists and industrial relations specialists who staffed the National Labor Board and its successor the National Labor Relations Board and a number of sympathetic congressmen, notably Senator Robert Wagner of New York. Wagner, above all, provided the leadership, the political skill and the continuity of commitment that made possible the passage of the legislation that bears his name. In doing so, he and his allies were able to exploit, as Howell Harris puts it, 'the extraordinary openness and confusion of the policy-making and administrative process in the mid-1930s'.[7]

For all their natural sympathy with the plight of labour, for all their sensitivity to the working-class electorate, Wagner and other liberal Democrats were primarily concerned with the ways in which stronger trade unions might serve the principal objective of economic recovery. In the first place, they feared that the rising tide of labour militancy, expressed in a wave of strikes during 1933 and 1934, might jeopardise the fragile recovery that followed early New Deal measures. The best way to contain grass-roots militancy, they believed, was to channel it into responsible labour organisations. The best way to moderate the damaging level of industrial conflict was to empower workers to bargain on terms of equality with management. Secondly, they attributed the Depression to deficient consumer demand. Effective unions, by strengthening the bargaining power of industrial workers, would raise wages, increase purchasing power and boost the level of aggregate demand. Greater protection for workers' incomes would mitigate the catastrophic fall in living standards and consumer demand that had occurred since 1929 and prevent its recurrence in the future. This analysis of the relationship between union power, wages and consumer spending was regularly reiterated by the advocates of trade union reform. As the preamble to an early version of the Wagner bill put it, the objective was 'to ensure a wise distribution of wealth between management and labor, to maintain a full flow of purchasing power, and to prevent recurrent depressions'.[8]

As we have seen, the National Industrial Recovery Act, the flagship of the First New Deal, contained a Section, 7(a), which guaranteed workers the right to bargain collectively through a

7. Howell Harris, 'The snares of liberalism? politicians, bureaucrats and the shaping of federal labour relations policy in the United States, ca. 1915–1947', in Steven Tolliday and Jonathan Zeitlin, eds, *Shop Floor Bargaining and the State: Historical and Comparative Perspectives* (Cambridge, 1985), p. 167.

8. Quoted in Christopher L. Tomlins, *The State and the Unions: Law and the Organized Labor Movement in America, 1880–1960* (Cambridge, 1985), p. 119.

union of their choice. This constituted the first unequivocal recognition of such a right in federal law. However, it was included mainly for tactical reasons: to head off Black's thirty-hours bill. While Wagner believed that the reconstitution of industrial relations was fundamental to solving the nation's economic problems, most of the architects of NRA regarded it as a way of facilitating cooperation between employers, rather than between employers and unions. That Section 7(a) was essentially peripheral to the thinking that lay behind NRA was made clear by the manner of its enforcement.

Section 7(a) stimulated workers to organise, in the conviction that their actions enjoyed federal approval. In the words of Frances Piven and and Richard Cloward, 'It was as if incipient struggles had now been crowned with an aura of ... "natural justice". Felt grievances became public grievances, for the federal government itself had proclaimed the workers' cause to be just.'[9] The twelve months after the passage of NIRA witnessed the revival of formerly strong unions, like the United Mine Workers (UMW) and the Amalgamated Clothing Workers (ACW), and an upsurge of organising activity in industries, like textiles and steel, that had not seen effective unions for decades. But employers refused to recognise unions unless they were already strong, except in industries like coal-mining and garment-manufacturing where their participation helped stabilise intolerable competitive conditions. In some cases company-dominated 'employee representation plans' were smuggled in as bargaining agents under the terms of the act. Disputes over wages and hours, as well as union recognition, were endemic. Therefore a wave of strikes broke out like summer lightning across the country, many of them protracted and bitterly fought, as in copper-mining and textiles. In arbitrating such disputes NRA officials, themselves mostly drawn from the ranks of business, proved unsympathetic to labour. They regarded Section 7(a) as an encumbrance, believing that workers were best protected by the wages and hours provisions of the codes themselves rather than by collective bargaining, and they were conscious of the need above all to retain the allegiance of the business community in order to make NRA work. It was only when the NRA experiment foundered that the way was cleared for a fresh approach to the labour problem.

The agencies set up to mediate industrial disputes, the National

9. Frances F. Piven and Richard A. Cloward, *Poor People's Movements: Why They Succeed, How They Fail* (New York, 1977), p. 113.

Labor Board (NLB) and later the National Labor Relations Board (NLRB), lacked authority to act effectively within the parameters of NRA, but they did offer a forum in which government officials could give sympathetic consideration to the issue. In dealing with labour disputes they began to work, however tentatively at first, towards the articulation of a body of case law which could be applied to their resolution. First enunciated in August 1933 in connection with a strike of hosiery workers in Reading, Pennsylvania, the 'common law' of labour relations consisted of three elements. The first and most significant, indeed momentous in its implications for federal policy, was the principle of majority rule: workers should be represented for purposes of collective bargaining by the agent chosen by the majority in a secret election organised by the Board. The second was the understanding, driven home by experience, that a fair and free expression of employees' views could only be obtained if employers were restrained from acting in an intimidatory fashion towards union activists. Thus the Board developed a doctrine of 'unfair labour practices' which became central to later legislation. A third principle was that company unions could never provide a full and free representation of workers' interests. In the absence of independent powers of enforcement, the Board was only occasionally able to put these principles into effect. Employers refused to abide by the result of representation elections, emboldened by the opposition of Johnson and the ambivalence of Roosevelt, who approved a formula for the automobile industry which allowed proportional representation of minority bargaining agents, including company unions. Nor, crucially, could the NLB and NLRB protect union activists from dismissal or punish other violations of workers' rights. Experience of the deficiencies of this first systematic federal venture into the field of labour relations provided the basis for what was to become the Wagner Act, which was largely drafted by NLRB officials, in consultation with Wagner and members of his congressional staff.

The National Labor Relations Act, which became law on 5 July 1935, reaffirmed the right of workers to bargain collectively. If a majority of the workers in any plant decided, in a federally administered election, that they wished to be represented by a trade union, the employer was legally obliged to recognise the union and to bargain with it in good faith. The act prohibited certain 'unfair labour practices', including forcing workers to sign 'yellow-dog' contracts, the dismissal of union members, and recognition of company unions. Indeed, it was defined as an 'unfair labour practice' to restrain employees' 'right of self-organisation'. This was, on the face of it, an extraordinarily one-sided piece of legislation. It conferred certain rights on labour, while restraining certain actions on the part of management; the balance of benefits and penalties was all one way. Furthermore, unlike its predecessor, the Wagner Act was vigorously enforced by a National Labor Relations Board with greatly enhanced powers. The NLRB determined bargaining units, conducted elections, certified unions and in other respects exercised considerable administrative discretion, subject only to limited review by the higher courts. Thus the arbitration of labour relations was substantially removed from the courts, where they had been determined for a century or more, to an independent administrative agency – a transfer of authority in which the Supreme Court surprisingly acquiesced.

Thus the federal government decisively entered the field of labour relations, which, it was now believed, could no longer safely be left to private negotiation. The public interest was too heavily involved in the resolution of industrial conflict and the stabilisation of wages. The way to achieve these goals was to be through public support of independent trade unions. Thus the Wagner Act drew labour relations, in the words of Christopher Tomlins, into 'the regulatory ambit of the fast-growing administrative state'.[10] In accepting government support, the unions were transformed into public agencies, responsible for their behaviour, and that of their members, to the community as a whole. They became tied up in a web of restrictions and obligations. This new status carried with it a public responsibility and a loss of some of their traditional autonomy, which Tomlins regards as a Faustian bargain. But such strictures are ungrounded. The benefits of union autonomy were, in fact, illusory. Only through a fundamental transformation of their legal status could unions hope to strengthen their position in the industrial arena and gain the bargaining power which would enable them effectively to protect their actual and potential members. Such a transformation was only possible through the mediation of government officials who, however sympathetic, sought to empower unions, not primarily for their own benefit, but in pursuit of broader public objectives. Thus power and responsibility were necessarily conjoined. As David Montgomery concludes, New Deal labour reforms were 'simultaneously liberating and cooptive for the workers'.[11]

10. Tomlins, *The State and the Unions*, p. 101.
11. David Montgomery, *Workers Control in America* (Cambridge, 1979), p. 165.

Explaining the passage of the Wagner Act has provided the material for a minor academic industry in recent years. As with its companion measure, the Social Security Act, interpretations fall into three broad schools. One, which may loosely be termed 'corporate liberal', attributes the labour policy of the New Deal to the machinations of influential and highly sophisticated fragments of the capitalist class. Stanley Vittoz and Colin Gordon believe that businessmen saw trade union bargaining as a way of alleviating the cut-throat competition that had proved so damaging in many industries and which earlier efforts, like Hoover's 'associationalism' and NRA, had failed to alleviate. By stabilising wages and equalising competitive conditions, union bargaining would serve the needs of industry as well as labour. Other proponents of the 'corporate liberal' thesis regard legal support for trade unions as a way of incorporating and managing what could have become a dangerous working-class movement and preventing the spread of radical ideas among the disadvantaged. Plausible though they sometimes are, such interpretations find it hard to overcome the clear evidence that industrialists, almost without exception, regardless of industry, region, scale of operation or level of economic and political sophistication, opposed the Wagner Act to the bitter end. Nor is there much clear evidence that the officials and legislators who drafted the law were acting to serve business interests, except in the very broadest sense that, as with all New Deal programmes, they wished to conserve the institutions of capitalist America by reforming them, rather than to create a radically different social and economic system. Only in that trivial sense can the 'corporate liberal' thesis be applied to the Wagner Act.

An opposing explanation, though with a similar ideological grounding, sees the Wagner Act as a reaction forced upon government officials by labour militancy. So strong and vigorous was the popular uprising expressed in the organising drive of 1933–34, so disruptive were mass strikes to the prospects of economic recovery and social stability, that they were virtually compelled to make concessions. 'The most reasonable hypothesis to account for the passage of the NLRA', argues Michael Goldfield, 'is that labor militancy, catapulted into prominence by the 1934 strikes and the political response to this movement, paved the way for the passage of the act.' Awareness of the dangers consequent upon a failure to contain an increasingly militant labour movement, notes Goldfield, 'runs like a bright yellow thread through the hearings and floor

debates of both Houses' on the Wagner bill.[12] Yet, as Theda
Skocpol and Kenneth Finegold point out, the nature of the crisis
did not determine the precise nature of the response. That was
shaped, they argue, by the character of the American state, the
structure of political institutions and the presuppositions of
prominent policy-makers like Wagner himself. What made the
Wagner Act possible, they argue, was, on the one hand, the failure
of NRA, which for a short time at least 'left industrial capitalists
unusually impotent to influence New Deal policy-making' and left
the Administration scurrying around in search of alternative
solutions to the economic crisis; and, on the other hand, the impact
of the congressional elections of 1934, which strengthened the
forces of urban liberalism within the ruling Democratic Party.[13]
These conditions created a conjuncture unusually propitious to
radical labour legislation, one which allowed substantial freedom of
action to Wagner and his allies. Obviously, to array a state-centred
approach against one which gives priority to social forces is to set up
a false dichotomy. Writers like Skocpol are correct to draw attention
to the importance of political structures in the policy-making
process and to remind us of the freedom of manoeuvre that
policy-makers sometimes enjoy, but policy is not created in a
vacuum. Legislators are aware of the social situation in which they
operate, the state of public opinion, or at least of especially salient
segments of it, and the power of important organised interest
groups. Whilst the interplay of competing pressures may create
space for substantial legislative discretion, such discretion is in the
last analysis constrained by social and economic forces.

The rise of the CIO

The organising momentum of 1933–34 was dissipated as effectively
by the response of the established union leadership as by
unsympathetic enforcement of the labour provisions of the National
Industrial Recovery Act. The American Federation of Labor was
dominated by long-established craft unions which were jealous of

12. Michael Goldfield, 'Worker insurgency, radical organization and New Deal
labor legislation' *American Political Science Review* 83 (Dec. 1989), pp. 1273, 1274–5
13. Kenneth Finegold and Theda Skocpol, 'State, party and industry: from
business recovery to the Wagner Act in America's New Deal', in Charles Bright and
Susan Harding, eds, *Statemaking and Social Movements: Essays in History and Theory*
(Ann Arbor, Mich., 1984), p. 177.

their prerogatives and highly defensive in their attitudes. Their leaders, many grown decidedly long in the tooth, confronted the new opportunities with decided suspicion. They were reluctant to consent to the formation of industrial unions. Craft unions dominated the Federation, which existed largely to defend and perpetuate their privileges. Each affiliated union was recognised as holding an exclusive jurisdiction, which amounted in the extraordinarily legalistic thinking of the AFL to a proprietorial right, over a particular group of workers. The new accessions were predominately unskilled or semi-skilled workers. It was difficult to fit them into the formal structure of the AFL without impinging on the jurisdiction of one or other of the craft unions and to absorb them without seriously altering the character of the union movement itself. Unskilled or semi-skilled workers, mostly African-American or of New Immigrant stock and including many women, the newcomers differed markedly in character from the unions' existing membership. Union officials commented, not too privately, on the 'rubbish', the 'riff raff', the 'good-for-nothings', who had recently joined their ranks. At worst such comments exhibited simple prejudice – prejudice of race, prejudice of ethnicity, prejudice of gender; at best they expressed genuine doubts about the constancy of workers who lacked a record of consistent involvement in the labour movement. As Dan Tobin of the Teamsters put it, 'We are not going to desert the fundamental principles on which these organizations have lived and are living to help you organize men who have never been organized'. To Brody these deep-rooted suspicions were more significant than the constitutional issues. The formal structure could always have been adjusted, as it had been in the past and would be again in the future. At the bottom lay a 'crisis of will'.[14]

AFL leaders appeared to be embarrassed by the influx and alarmed at the enthusiasm and militancy of their new recruits, whose importunate demands for action conflicted with the cautious stance that battle-hardened veterans had learned to adopt. The Federation devoted few resources to the organising drive. Indeed, its business agents appeared to be more concerned with discouraging militancy than with maximising recruitment. All too often the newcomers were ignored, thwarted, shunted off into temporary 'federal unions' pending their allocation to more suitable homes or, perhaps it was hoped, their disappearance altogether. Approximately 100,000 auto-workers were enrolled

14. Brody, 'Emergence of mass-production unionism', pp. 233, 235.

during 1934, a remarkable number given the industry's record of blacklisting and repression; by 1935 only about 10,000 remained. In the steel industry a similar number of recruits was whittled down to a few thousand, as the Amalgamated president Michael ('Grandmother') Tighe almost proudly informed the AFL convention. Joining a union was a brave and perilous step for men and women who had little personal experience of collective action, especially in view of the brutal anti-union tactics openly pursued by employers like Ford. Those who took such a step expected support and leadership from the established unions; they expected some kind of positive action rather than passivity and delay. That they began to feel dispirited was not surprising.

For that reason a small number of more combative union leaders, dissatisfied with the passivity of the Federation, seceded from the AFL. They were led by John L. Lewis, the outspoken and massively egotistical president of the United Mine Workers, who, after leading his union to virtual destruction in the 1920s, had vigorously exploited the opportunities created by NRA; and Sidney Hillman of the Amalgamated Clothing Workers, a long-time advocate of industrial democracy. Both, significantly, were among the leaders of the small number of industrial unions within the AFL. Lewis and Hillman were convinced of the need for urgent action. The new political situation, the new rank-and-file militancy had created a moment of opportunity that might never recur. Organisational problems were secondary to positive and immediate action. They also believed, in the words of Charles Howard of the Typographical Union, that 'in the great mass-production industries industrial organization is the only solution'.[15] Industrial unionism, founded on the principle of solidarity in the workplace, made more sense to production-line workers than the AFL's demand that they be separated according to their craft, real or supposed. Thirdly, Lewis, Hillman and their fellow dissidents held to a more inclusive conception of unionism than was common within the ranks of the AFL. CIO unions like the Auto Workers made genuine overtures to African-American workers, who played such a prominent role in the industry and whose exclusion, they realised, would seriously weaken their organisation. This drew them into a defence of civil rights. They were also willing to admit women workers, although this did not lead to a more radical assault on gender roles in the workplace. Although they enrolled and defended women workers, they

15. Quoted in ibid., p. 224.

subscribed to the principle of the family wage and hoped that, under the more favourable conditions towards which they strove, women would no longer be required to enter the masculine world of industrial labour. As Robert Zieger points out, the founders of the CIO represented 'American labor's heritage of dissent', but at the same time they 'operated well within the traditional boundaries of the labor movement'.[16] Although it harboured left-wing elements, at least in the early years, responded more positively to rank-and-file opinion, supported a broad range of social and economic reforms, and pursued a more active political role than the AFL, the CIO grew out of the previous experience of the labour movement and promoted traditional union goals of higher wages, job security and limited forms of workers' control. Its militancy was devoted to the attainment of a measure of dignity and job security for industrial workers. As Zieger notes, 'the CIO simultaneously exhibited both the pageantry and idealism of a great liberation movement and the determination to foster responsible, contractual unionism in the mass-production sector'.[17]

Finally, the founders of the CIO attached greater importance to political action than did leaders steeped in the 'voluntarist' tradition of the AFL. The political environment was critical to the organisation of mass-production workers, who needed at least the acquiescence of government authorities to engage in successful picketing. A political strategy was fundamental to their campaign. Men like Lewis and Hillman hoped to utilise their influence with New Deal Democrats to secure political conditions favourable to the unionisation of industrial workers; they hoped in turn to mobilise the electoral strength of their mass membership behind sympathetic political figures. Their campaign to transform labour relations entailed a campaign to transform the political life of industrial communities. The CIO, mainly out of UMW funds, made massive contributions to Roosevelt's re-election campaign in 1936, while union officials and members were active in canvassing votes in areas of CIO strength. In industrial communities the Roosevelt campaign took on a strongly labourite, even social democratic stance. The CIO identified the Democratic campaign with its own struggle for industrial unionism and interpreted Democratic victory as a vindication of its cause.

Following angry exchanges at the AFL convention in November 1935, which culminated in an exchange of blows between Lewis and

16. Zieger, *CIO*, pp. 28, 29.
17. Ibid., p. 22.

William Hutcheson of the Carpenters, the dissidents bolted from the Federation to form a Committee on Industrial Organization, which three years later was reconstituted as an independent Congress of Industrial Organizations. At once the CIO undertook a vigorous campaign to organise mass-production industry. Apart from some early successes in the rubber plants of Akron, the most spectacular gains came in the automobile industry, since its foundation a stronghold of the open shop. The National Labor Relations Act had created mechanisms for holding elections to decide issues of union recognition. But at the end of 1936, when CIO organisers approached the massive automobile plants around Detroit, it was far from clear that these mechanisms could usefully be exploited. In the first place, most industrialists and most of their attorneys were convinced that the Wagner Act was unconstitutional and that it would not be sustained by the Supreme Court. Indeed, the record of the Supreme Court to that date gave few grounds for any supposition to the contrary. Therefore, few industrialists and few public officials gave serious credence to the new legislation. Secondly, it was far from certain that the CIO could command the loyalty of a majority of auto-workers. The union could only overcome their fears by conducting a successful strike, which would be virtually impossible without majority support. It was unlikely that the union could have carried an NLRB representation election. For that reason it resorted to the dramatic tactic of the 'sit-down strike', most spectacularly employed at the Fisher body plant of General Motors. Rather than leading a walk-out from the factory, union supporters occupied it and kept the management and its agents at bay for a period of weeks. The sit-down strike was as much an organising device as a form of industrial action, a dramatic gesture designed to generate mass support. And it worked effectively on both counts. Once the company realised that neither the state government under the Democratic Governor Frank Murphy nor the federal government under Roosevelt was going to take action to eject the strikers, who were strictly speaking, of course, engaged in acts of simple trespass, it came to terms with the union. By the end of 1937 all the major automobile producers except for Ford had surrendered, and the recently formed United Automobile Workers (UAW) laid claim to a membership of 400,000.

Three weeks later, United States Steel gave in without a fight. Like the automobile companies it faced the prospect of making substantial profits in 1937, for the first time since 1929, and was unwilling to pick a fight with a militant labour organisation. By the end of 1937 the Steel Workers Organizing Committee had 325,000 members. Large firms in the rubber industry, in meat-packing and in the electrical goods industry followed suit, especially after the Supreme Court ratified the Wagner Act in April 1937. Within a few months, therefore, the newly formed CIO unions had stormed many of the bastions of the open shop. Firms that had staunchly resisted unionism for years were now substantially organised.

It is difficult to evaluate the degree to which these advances were dependent on government support. In view of the fact that some of the most spectacular victories of the CIO preceded the Supreme Court decision in *NLRB* v *Jones & Laughlin*, it might be thought that they resulted primarily from the successful marshalling of shop-floor militancy by new and vigorous industrial unions. Yet this would be misleading. In the first place, the sit-down strikes themselves could hardly have lasted a day without the benevolent neutrality of the state and federal governments. It was the refusal of either Governor Murphy or President Roosevelt to provide the military resources with which to eject the trespassers from company property, or even to allow the company to use its own resources to the same end, which made their success possible. Secondly, a Senate Committee chaired by the Progressive Republican Robert M. La Follette Jr., set up in 1936 to investigate employers' violations of workers' rights, attracted public attention to the tactics, such as espionage and intimidation, which were employed to quell unionism. Thirdly, from April 1937 employers had little option but to deal with the NLRB, whose pro-labour judgements were, with one or two exceptions, endorsed by the Supreme Court. After the summer of 1937, at a time when the CIO was meeting increased employer resistance, labour benefited greatly from the protection of federal law. During a period of mounting reaction the NLRB offered the surest defence of workers' rights. It also furnished the surest route to recognition and bargaining rights for workers in mass-production industry. The extra-legal expedient of the sit-down strike, which even the CIO unions eventually had to renounce, could not form a regular part of their armoury, and, as the violent repulse of more conventional mass strikes against Republic Steel and Ford made clear, the barriers to the unionisation of mass-production industry were still forbidding. Above all, the NLRB acted vigorously to protect union members against retribution at the hands of management, permitting, for a time at least, a more open expression of shop-floor opinion.

It is difficult to overestimate how radical the impact of the NLRB was at this juncture. In Melvyn Dubofsky's words, its members 'acted almost as missionaries for worker rights and industrial unionism'.[18] The NLRB naturally drew the fire of employer groups. It also antagonised the AFL, which complained that NLRB decisions discriminated in favour of industrial unions, by its preference for the largest possible bargaining units and its indifference to the historical claims of craft unions. As early as the second half of 1937 it was becoming increasingly vulnerable to attack. Both the NAM and the AFL had powerful friends in Congress who targeted the NLRB for investigation and censure. Condemnation of the illegality of the sit-down strikes and charges that CIO unions had been infiltrated by Communists (it is true that Communist activists played a prominent, sometimes an indispensable, role in the organising efforts of many CIO unions) provided substance for the attack. Southern Democrats, who had generally favoured labour reform in the Wilson Era, were becoming increasingly nervous about the linkages between CIO unions and the civil rights movement and anxious to protect from outside interference the South's distinctive combination of low wages and racial discrimination. The weakening of the Administration's political position after the Supreme Court fight, and especially after the onset of the 'Roosevelt recession' of 1937–38, left the NLRB increasingly exposed. Proposals for reform, which anticipated features of the later Taft-Hartley Act, passed the House but were buried by sympathetic hands in the Senate Labor Committee. Such friendly offices could not prevent the House from launching a hostile investigation of the NLRB under the chairmanship of Congressman Howard Smith of Virginia or save the agency from the attentions of Martin Dies's Committee on Un-American Activities. Inevitably, changes in the political climate and in the membership of the Board towards the end of the 1930s caused it to moderate its pro-labour policy by accommodating to a greater degree the interests of employers and AFL unions.

Nevertheless, despite the backwash against the decidedly pro-labour turn in federal policy during the 1930s, the decade left organised labour in a radically improved position. Whilst the CIO unions found it hard to build on their spectacular achievements of 1936–37, AFL unions began to recruit members with unprecedented vigour. By 1939 the AFL and CIO together claimed some 8.9 million members, 28.9 per cent of the non-agricultural

18. Melvyn Dubofsky, *The State and Labor in Modern America* (Chapel Hill, N.C., 1994), p. 150.

workforce.[19] Although the bitter internecine conflict between the rival union organisations was highly damaging in political terms, it had an invigorating effect on their organising activities. Above all, the legal position of organised labour was fundamentally transformed. The right to bargain collectively was affirmed in law, many of the traditional anti-union practices were now prohibited, and in the NLRB organised labour had a government agency which, even in its modified form, was directly committed to fostering the growth of unions as a prime objective of public policy.

Labour and the Second World War

Even before December 1941, the growing entanglement of the United States in the European war changed once more the shape of the American labour market. Under the favourable conditions of wartime the CIO and the resurgent AFL made further inroads into open-shop territory. On the other hand, the involvement of labour in the wartime economy tightened still further the web of restrictions confining trade unions and bound them still further to the demands and expectations of the state.

The heightened level of demand caused first of all by the requirements of the Allies and then by the mobilisation of the American military machine greatly improved the bargaining position of organised labour. The rapid disappearance of the pool of unemployed workers, shortages of skilled labour and industry's natural craving to capture the commercial opportunities of wartime enabled the unions to win a series of important strikes during 1940 and 1941. Even the doggedly anti-union citadel of the Ford Motor Company, anxious to convert to wartime production, came to terms with the UAW, while companies like Bethlehem and Republic Steel which had staunchly resisted unionisation in 1937 capitulated in 1941 in the face of industrial actions which, in their intensity and rank-and-file support, recaptured some of the spirit of the CIO's glory days. General Electric, Westinghouse, Allis-Chalmers, and International Harvester were among other large firms to make

19. Figures for CIO membership are highly unreliable for the early years. CIO unions claimed a membership of 4 million at the end of 1938, including 'workers under contract' (i.e. covered by a union contract) and 'exonerated' (i.e. unemployed) members, but collected dues from only a third of that number. Nevertheless, in the fluid conditions of the late 1930s, the union was right to count many of those who were not formally enrolled as potential (and, as it turned out, eventual) members.

terms with CIO unions. The contracts that were negotiated under these especially favourable conditions enabled large numbers of industrial workers to engage in proper collective bargaining for the first time, embracing not only substantial improvements in wages but also agreements covering work-rules, grievance procedures and seniority.

After Pearl Harbor, the unions pledged themselves to refrain from strikes for the duration of the war. In return for this gesture of self-abnegation, the National War Labor Board, established on the First World War model, imposed 'maintenance of membership' contracts on employers. Such agreements required union members in plants covered by union contracts to maintain their membership for the duration of the contract. This was regarded as a necessary compensation for the distortion of industrial relations in wartime. If unions were to be deprived of their central weapon, they must be protected from hostile action by employers, while workers who could see no obvious benefits from union membership must be required to pay their dues. Maintenance of membership, or union security, clauses greatly solidified union membership. On the other hand, the wage settlements imposed by the NWLB, acting in effect as an anti-inflation agency, tied wage increases to the cost of living, which roughly protected workers against wartime inflation but did not allow them to claim a share of the enormous profits that firms derived from defence contracts or compensate them for their contribution to increased production targets.

In return for union recognition and NWLB-imposed contracts, unions were expected to refrain from industrial action and to prevent, so far as they could, the wildcat strikes which began to break out with increasing frequency as the war progressed. Long hours, stagnant real wages, increased pressure of work and the continuing recalcitrance of some employers engendered high levels of shop-floor discontent which, as the war went on, increasingly erupted into sporadic industrial action. There were 2,970 strikes in 1942, 3,700 in 1944, over 5,000 in 1944. The typical union, observed Philip Murray, was forced to act like 'a fire department.'[20] Union officials were placed in the invidious position of having to discipline their membership, appearing as they did so in the guise of agents of management. John L. Lewis in 1943 repeatedly led the mine-workers out on strike to contest the failure of employers to live up to their agreements, but the risk of being seen to engage in disloyal

20. Zieger, *CIO*, p. 178.

or treasonous actions deterred other union leaders from following his example.

The war brought ambiguous results. Yet in the last analysis it reinforced organised labour's position in American society, building on the work of the New Deal. The unions numbered nearly 15 million members at the end of the war, three times their strength in 1919. Furthermore, their new institutional strength and, above all, their new legal position enabled them to survive an employers' counter-offensive, a Red Scare and a conservative reaction with their numbers hardly dented and their position largely intact. The twelve months after V-J Day saw more days lost in strikes than any similar period, as management and labour tested their strength in a series of large-scale confrontations, especially in automobiles, steel and coal-mining, which never, however, matched the levels of violence of 1919–20. The outcome was a stand-off, rather than a crushing defeat for the unions. The conduct of the postwar strikes, for all their rumbustious character, exemplified the more orderly pattern of industrial relations that had emerged from the experience of the New Deal and the Second World War.

Unions in postwar America

Among the newer buildings that adorn downtown Washington is the AFL–CIO Building, an imposing edifice designed to express the power and importance of organised labour in postwar America. The reunion of the AFL and CIO in 1955 signified not only the end of two decades of debilitating internecine conflict but also the growing institutionalisation of the new industrial unions. Although in 1947 Walter Reuther, newly installed as UAW president, might declare the labour movement to be 'the vanguard in America . . . the architect of the future', the movement was already beginning to lose whatever radical character it had once possessed and settle into a prosperous and respectable middle age.[21]

The merger, according to James B. Carey, Secretary-Treasurer of the CIO, followed 'two almost incredible decades, unmatched and unparalleled in the entire history of the American labor movement'.[22] Unions were accepted as bargaining agents by most major companies. A survey conducted by *Fortune* in 1952 discovered that in 82 out of 102 large manufacturing companies over 50 per

---

21. Quoted in Brody, *Workers in Industrial America*, p. 139.
22. Zieger, *CIO*, p. 355.

cent of the workforce was organised (with most of the remainder holding white-collar jobs). In railroads, coal-mining, steel, automobiles, rubber, and several other basic industries, union density was in excess of 85 per cent. In consequence wage rates for production workers rose by 45 per cent between 1945 and 1950, by 56 per cent in the 1950s and by 46 per cent in the 1960s. In addition, union contracts were beginning to include holidays, pensions, insurance, health-care and other secondary benefits, as well as wages and hours. By the late 1950s roughly half the employees in union plants had pension plans, nearly three-quarters some form of health coverage. Such privately negotiated schemes provided some compensation for the deficiencies of the American welfare state, though admittedly limited in scope and restricted in coverage to the minority of blue-collar workers enrolled in unions.

Union contracts also covered personnel issues, including promotions, lay-offs, transfers, rehiring and the exercise of seniority rights, recognition of which met one of the prime grievances of workers during the 1920s and 1930s. The institution of grievance procedures was a major achievement for the unions. It offered workers some protection against arbitrary treatment at the hands of managers and foremen and contributed to the establishment of what Brody calls a 'workplace rule of law'.[23] Although such restraints existed within the context of firmly-maintained managerial prerogatives, they nevertheless eliminated what workers had long regarded as the greatest evil, their total submission to foreman and boss. Indeed, the very existence of a union contract, in place of the arbitrariness and apparent unfairness of management personnel policies in the 1930s, marked more than anything else the change in industrial relations that had come about. Union contracts became more and more voluminous, covering an ever-increasing range of subjects. Each item to some degree eroded the independent power of management; each item also detracted from the autonomy of grass-roots workers who, instead of expressing their grievances through immediate shop-floor action, were expected to channel them through the formal mechanisms laid down by contract. The right to strike was severely curtailed, sometimes denied altogether during the period of a contract. What Brody calls 'workplace contractualism' seriously inhibited the freedom of action of employers, workers and unions; all were subject to the 'workplace rule of law'.

23. Brody, *Workers in Industrial America*, p. 206.

Through the medium of its Political Action Committees (PACs), organised labour now wielded considerable political influence. Although several leaders of AFL craft unions retained an affiliation to the Republican Party and although several CIO unions, at least up to the late 1940s, contained Communist cadres, the CIO as an organisation developed strong connections with the Democratic Party, connections which it considered indispensable to the protection of labour's political interests. The CIO–PAC, along with many of the constituent unions, provided funds for Democratic candidates, and so from 1952 did the AFL. For example, the AFL–CIO Committee for Political Education mobilised 191,000 activists in the week before the 1968 election and provided a quarter of the party's national campaign funds. In an industrial state like Michigan the proportion was closer to two-thirds. In many industrial areas, in many states, the unions were, for nearly half a century, the party's most dependable source of support. Furthermore, labour played an important part in determining the character of postwar liberalism. Organised labour was the one major economic interest group which consistently supported liberal programmes like full employment, a more equitable tax system, civil rights, the enlargement of social security, health insurance and public housing, the one interest group which endorsed substantial government intervention over a wide range of issues. The CIO, and later the AFL–CIO, consistently endorsed a broad programme of liberal reform and contributed greatly to its partial attainment in the 1960s. Ironically, however, the unions were much less successful in winning support for their own particular agenda of labour reform, which after 1947 consisted above all of the repeal of the Taft-Hartley Act. Even when, as in the mid-1960s, the Democrats enjoyed overwhelming majorities in Congress and when a nominally friendly figure occupied the White House, even partial repeal could not be forced through. It often seemed as if the commitment of organised labour to the Democratic Party was a great deal stronger than that of the party to labour.

Like the Democratic Party to which they were affiliated, the CIO unions became more conservative over the years. The Communist activists who had played so fruitful a role in the heroic age of industrial unionism were expelled at the urging of the CIO leadership under Philip Murray. In 1946 twelve out of thirty-five CIO affiliates had Communist or pro-Soviet leadership, while the Left held significant influence in another six. Many non-CP members supported its goals of US–Soviet cooperation and progressive change in America, believing that 'Communists are only liberals who mean it'.[24] The broad Left could claim the support of about a third of the delegates at the 1946 CIO convention. However, mounting disagreements over foreign policy and the decision by the CP and its allies to back the independent candidacy of Henry Wallace in 1948 undermined the Left's political position. Largely in order to forestall proto-McCarthyite criticism and to reinforce their links with the Truman Administration, many CIO unions, like the UAW under Reuther, set out to purge their ranks of Communists and 'fellow-travellers', while the CIO expelled unions like the United Electrical, Radio and Machine Workers which failed to do so. During 1949 and 1950, eleven unions were expelled from the CIO, leaving their members subject to raids by rival unions, especially as under the Taft-Hartley Act unions whose officials refused to sign an anti-Communist affidavit were denied access to the services of the NLRB. Severing its links with the CP and those who were suspected of being associated with it, like the Wallace Progressives, meant severing its links with some of the sources of reforming energy that had inspired and supported the labour movement during an earlier era. It destroyed what remained of the distinctive political culture of the early CIO – that combination of organising zeal and grass-roots enthusiasm, that willingness to take political risks and challenge established social and political authority. Like the national Red Scare, labour's own witch-hunt turned its face to the right.

After the 1940s the union movement became in many respects a conservative force in American society, interested in maintaining the *status quo* in the face of new kinds of radical activism – from the student Left, from feminism, from Black Nationalism. Galbraith described the AFL–CIO leadership as 'aged, contented and deeply somnambulent'. Union leaders devoted themselves to the day-to-day interests of their members. 'Our goals as trade unionists are modest', declared AFL–CIO president George Meany, 'for we do not seek to recast American society . . . we seek a rising standard of living.'[25] So limited a conception of the unions' role might have troubled Samuel Gompers. Negotiating and monitoring elaborate union contracts and managing complex grievance procedures, union officials became more and more immersed in the details of union management. With their impressive office buildings, lavish

---

24. Robert Zieger, *American Workers, American Unions, 1920–1985* (Baltimore, 1986), p. 127.

25. Brody, *Workers in Industrial America*, p. 236.

salaries and expense accounts, they grew more and more like businessmen in lifestyle, and to some extent in aspirations, and in consequence became increasingly remote from the shop-floor. The growth of 'business unionism' greatly strengthened the capacity of the unions to serve the interests, though narrowly defined, of their members, but it inevitably weakened the linkages between union leadership and grass-roots feeling, while the narrowing of focus diminished their capacity to forge alliances with other social movements.

The decline of organised labour

In the post-New Deal concert of interests Big Labour was accepted alongside Big Business and Big Government as a focus of economic and political power. Yet in important respects labour's new-found strength was illusory. Its position was undermined by many of the old problems that bedevilled its career in the past and by some new ones. After the Second World War the rapid expansion of the labour movement ceased. Membership rose from 14.8 million in 1945 to 18.0 million in 1954, remaining around 35 per cent in percentage terms. By 1974 enrolment had reached 21.6 million, but that represented a fall to 28.0 per cent in relative terms. From that date membership commenced a decline in absolute terms as well, until by 1993 16.6 million men and women paid union dues, 15.8 per cent of the workforce – a proportion far below the levels of union density that obtain in most Western European countries. At the same time labour's success-rate in NLRB certification elections declined from around 75 per cent in the late 1940s to under 45 per cent in the early 1980s. By the 1980s the process of 'pattern bargaining' established in the late 1940s and early 1950s and maintained for a generation or more was beginning to break up, as unions found it increasingly difficult to defend their members against cuts in real wages and erosion of the fringe benefits that they had long enjoyed.

After scaling the commanding heights of the corporate economy in the 1930s and early 1940s, the labour movement was less successful in unionising an equivalent proportion of smaller firms, which were relatively costly to organise, in which industrial relations were less distant and less confrontational than those which obtained in larger units of production, and which were often located in small-town and rural communities without established traditions of union organisation. Union density was usually lower in service industries, where the workforce comprised a mixture of low-paid, unskilled workers, many of them women, who were difficult to organise, not least because of their shifting and marginal relationship with the labour market, and white-collar workers, whose outlook, social background, work experience, remuneration and career prospects were very different from those of the traditional working class. The one major exception was in public employment. After the longstanding rules debarring government workers from union membership were relaxed in the early 1960s, large numbers of public employees, including clerks, postal-workers and schoolteachers, were organised. Indeed, public sector unionism is one of the few growth areas of recent decades.

The South posed a special problem for the labour movement. Apart from occasional pockets like the New Orleans waterfront, the region lacked a strong tradition of unionism. For decades Southern industry had depended on low labour costs to compete with more technologically advanced Northern firms. The regulation of local labour markets was inextricably linked with the definition of race relations, one critical component of which was a well-defined and carefully monitored demarcation between the occupational opportunities, status and wages of black and white workers. All of these considerations made Southern communities extraordinarily sensitive to outside interference in their labour relations. Union organisers were condemned, as by a Mississippi minister in 1947, as 'foreign-born, communisitic Yankees'.[26] Thus a CIO campaign to organise Southern textiles in 1937–38 failed, as did a more comprehensive unionisation drive after 1946. Both campaigns met bitter resistance, including frequent recourse to violence by local law-enforcement authorities and vigilante groups. Workers, still close to their agrarian roots, steeped in the culture of pentecostal religion and isolated in paternalistically organised mill villages, were unusually resistant to the message of unionism. Both campaigns were vitiated by serious strategic errors. Resources of money and manpower were small in relation to the magnitude of the task. In order to allay local suspicions, CIO organisers minimised the involvement of radicals and African-Americans. Instead of building on areas of past success, such as lumber, tobacco-manufacturing and food-processing, all of which employed large numbers of black

26. Quoted in Harry A. Millis and Emily C. Brown, *From the Wagner Act to Taft-Hartley* (Chicago, 1950), p. 169.

workers, they concentrated on the traditionally lilywhite textile industry, where unions had never flourished. Unwillingness to tackle the race issue head on meant that any gains could only be slight and probably inconsequential. To state this, though, is to indicate how difficult, maybe impossible, the task was. In any case, the defeat of the CIO in the South was a critical setback. The region remained a virtual desert for organised labour, while Southern society and politics were still more tightly locked into a defensive, reactionary mode.

The relative decline in union strength since the 1950s follows from the above trends. Since the Second World War American industry has tended to shift from older 'rustbelt' sites to locations in the 'Sun Belt', that is from areas of relative union strength like Pennsylvania and Illinois to areas like North Carolina and Texas where unions had never been strong. Indeed, the avoidance of union restrictions was one of the principal reasons for migrating. Technological advances have greatly reduced the need for human muscle-power and for many kinds of traditional skill. Skilled manual workers are therefore replaced by technicians, who are rarely unionised. Already by 1960, in firms like Exxon, Westinghouse and Du Pont blue-collar workers constituted less than half the total workforce. In a more general sense, industrial employment as a fraction of total employment has declined. Sectors of the economy, like the service industries, where unionism is relatively weak have grown at the expense of sectors, like mining and manufacturing, where unionism is relatively strong. By the mid-1980s the number of fast-food workers and private security guards exceeded the number of steel and automobile workers.

The general economic environment over the last two decades has not been favourable. Since the 1970s average real wages have tended to decline, after increasing by 41 per cent between 1945 and 1970, and unemployment has remained at levels consistently higher than those of the immediate postwar period. As American manufacturers have become increasingly uncompetitive with producers in Europe and the Far East, the commanding giants of the American economy, firms like General Motors and US Steel, have been forced to close plants and reduce their workforce. This is obviously one of the factors driving 'runaway' plants to the low-wage, non-union havens of the South or 'cornfield sites' in the Midwest. Repeatedly, 'economic necessity' has been urged upon unions as a reason for concessionary bargaining, and there is no doubt that the secular recession that began with the oil crisis of

1974 has made union organising more difficult than in the 'golden age' of the 1950s and 1960s. But the relative, if not the absolute, decline in union membership began in the 1950s, as much as two decades before the economic downturn. Moreover, while the late 1970s and early 1980s saw a copious haemorrhaging of support, the mid-1980s boom brought no corresponding reversal in fortunes, as the tide of membership loss and concessionary bargaining continued almost unabated.

As Michael Goldfield has argued, it is unwise to accept too deterministic an explanation of the decline of unions in postwar America. It is true that the structure and location of industry and the character and composition of the workforce have changed considerably since mid-century. Such transformations are the common currency of economic and social change, no greater in scope than those which attended the 'second industrial revolution' of the late nineteenth century. Although the decline in industrial employment has been detrimental to the union movement, the fall in membership has been nearly as pronounced in the manufacturing sector as elsewhere in the economy. Although there have been numerous changes in the workforce since 1945 – the large-scale participation of women, the entry of large numbers of African-Americans, the growth of white-collar employment, the industrialisation of the South – the new workers, contrary to expectations, are no less sympathetic to unionism than the old. Attitudinal surveys have found non-unionised women workers, African-American workers and even white Southerners no less willing than other groups of workers to join a trade union if the opportunity were to present itself. It is therefore elsewhere that we must look for the sources of decline.

Left-wing critics like Michael Goldfield, Mike Davis and Kim Moody place much of the blame at the door of the union movement itself. Since the 1950s the sums spent on organising new workers have fallen. Instead of the AFL–CIO merger providing the impetus for a major organising drive, as Reuther had urged, the search for increased membership was left to the affiliated unions, which often found it more profitable to poach from each other than to enter new territory. Apart from the expansion of public sector unionism, the labour movement has signally failed to compete in the growing areas of the economy or to enrol new workers. By its own estimates the AFL–CIO recruited only 2 million out of the 35 million who entered the workforce between 1960 and 1980. Little sustained effort was made therefore to replace, by organising new groups of workers, the losses due to inevitable changes in the economy.

Employers, as Howell Harris has shown, while bowing to *force majeure* and accepting the necessity to bargain collectively, with a few exceptions, never inwardly reconciled themselves to the desirability of unions. The irreducible fact, admitted *Business Week* in 1978, 'is that American business has by and large never really accepted unionism'.[27] When obliged to do so they fought unions step by step in the negotiating chamber or in grievance proceedings; when opportunity arose they struggled to free themselves of unions altogether. The number of complaints against unfair labour practices, principally the discharge of workers for union activity, increased sixfold between 1950 and 1980. Even if employers were sometimes ordered to reinstate and compensate the victimised workers, retribution rarely came soon enough or certainly enough to mitigate the deterrent effect of such actions upon other workers. Increasingly employers exploited the potential for delay implicit in NLRB procedures, holding up representation elections, refusing to bargain and engaging in protracted litigation.

Above all, we must look once more to the role of the state. Business lobbies had long agitated for changes in the admittedly one-sided terms of the Wagner Act, and Republican victories in the congressional elections of 1946, which reduced the number of liberal Northern, rather than conservative Southern, Democrats, provided an opportunity for the enactment of the anti-labour legislation which enemies of the CIO had been advocating since 1939.

The resulting Taft-Hartley Act was in many ways a companion measure to, some would say a logical extension of, the Wagner Act. It was a reaction against the unequivocal pro-labour bias of the NLRA, protecting the rights of individual workers against 'power-drunk labor bosses' and employers against unions.[28] The NLRB was to be transformed, in the words of Congressman Fred Hartley, from 'an advocate of organized labor ... to an impartial referee'.[29] It was a complex measure which, among other things, limited the right to strike by allowing the president to suspend for a 'cooling-off' period of up to sixty days strikes which he believed created a state of 'national emergency'. It defined certain union activities as illegal (just as the Wagner Act had proscribed certain

27. Quoted in Brody, *Workers in Industrial America*, p. 248.
28. Dubofsky, *State and Labor*, p. 202.
29. Quoted in Zieger, *American Workers, American Unions*, p. 110.

unfair practices on the part of management), including secondary boycotts, sit-down strikes and jurisdictional disputes between unions, and made them subject to damage suits and court injunctions, thereby resurrecting one of the labour movement's oldest and most feared enemies. The act gave employers the right to initiate decertification proceedings and to communicate their views to their employees prior to an NLRB representation election. The closed shop was prohibited, while individual states were permitted to pass so-called 'right-to-work' laws which outlawed union security agreements. By 1965 nineteen states had availed themselves of this opportunity.

Hartley proclaimed that the Taft-Hartley Act had shifted the whole emphasis of labour relations policy, while union leaders condemned it categorically as a 'slave-labour law'. Clearly they protested too much. The new law left the institutional structure erected in 1935 largely intact. Yet it made a number of subtle modifications which, in aggregate, made a substantial difference to the direction of policy and left the legal environment significantly less favourable to trade unions. Most obviously, it resurrected the possibility of labour injunctions and, by laying down a definition of 'unfair labour practices' by trade unions, created extensive opportunities for employers to tie up unions in the courts. The 'cooling-off' provision, in the hands of a hostile president like Reagan, or even a nominally friendly one like Truman, was a dangerous weapon. The condemnation of secondary boycotts and mass picketing deprived the unions of weapons which had proved valuable during the organising drives of the late 1930s and early 1940s. Employers now had the power to mount vigorous campaigns during representation elections, which, various studies found, had a significant influence on the results. State right-to-work laws have also had a detrimental effect on union organising and encouraged the promotion of anti-union campaigns at a state level. Like the Taft-Hartley Act itself, they 'sent a clear antiunion signal'.[30] A recent statistical analysis of the influence of legal changes on union membership finds that the Taft-Hartley Act had an impact equivalent to the Wagner Act, though obviously in the opposite direction. A number of scholars have drawn a contrast with Canada, where branches of the same labour organisations face many of the same corporations under broadly similar social and economic conditions but where, rather than declining after the 1950s, union

30. Zieger, *CIO*, p. 247.

membership continued to grow, now standing at twice the proportion in the United States, largely because Canadian labour law, itself modelled on the NLRA, continued to expedite representation elections, curtail employers' involvement in the process and penalise employers' violations of workers' rights. In other words, while hardly constituting a reversion to the legal situation before 1932, the Taft-Hartley Act, along with the Landrum-Griffin Act of 1959, which tightened further the restrictions on secondary boycotts and proscribed certain forms of picketing, substantially eroded the privileges accorded organised labour under the Wagner Act and left it more vulnerable to prosecution and hostile action by employers.

The contemporary influence of organised labour can be gauged by the fact that for the first time, in 1980, a former union leader was elected President of the United States. The fact that that president was Ronald Reagan, a former president of the Screen Actors' Guild but now converted to forthright opposition to unionism, nicely illustrated by his insistence on non-union entertainers at his 1985 inauguration ball, is also an indication of the extent to which that influence has been in decline. Ronald Reagan wore his anti-union proclivities quite openly on his sleeve. 'The union busters are in hog heaven now', commented an AFL–CIO official in 1985.[31] His ruthless suppression of the air-controllers' strike in 1981, which sent a clear signal to anti-union employers, his appointment of anti-labour representatives to the NLRB, and the accumulation of conservative appointees on the Supreme Court bench, all testify to the hostile political world in which the unions now operate. Yet their ability to fight back through their friends in the Democratic Party has been diminished by the unwillingness of leading Democratic contenders for the presidency to associate themselves too closely with labour in the public eye. As Thomas Edsall noted in 1984, 'key Democratic elected officials treated the leadership of the AFL–CIO with disdain'.[32] This underlines the point that the weakness of American labour is, in the last analysis, essentially a political weakness.

---

31. Quoted in Michael Goldfield, *The Decline of Organized Labor in the United States* (Chicago, 1987), p. 6.

32. Quoted in Zieger, *American Workers, American Unions,* p. 194.

CHAPTER NINE

The Making of the Welfare State

Introduction

In its broadest sense the term 'welfare state' is tautological in that the *raison d'être* of any state is to promote the welfare of its citizens. However, the term came to be used in Britain during the Second World War to express an intention to integrate all forms of income support, including public assistance and social insurance programmes, into a complete system of social protection for all citizens. In that sense the United States does not have a comprehensive welfare state. In the first place, the components of public assistance ('welfare') and social insurance ('social security') are not integrated but quite firmly separated – in terms of their institutional arrangements, political support, intellectual validation and rhetorical description. This makes for wide variations in the treatment of different categories of the population. Secondly, the federal system, which encourages substantial devolution of welfare functions to the states, produces a patchwork quilt of varying provision and practice. Finally, many of the features which might be seen as characteristic of a modern welfare state are either absent or under-developed. These include family allowances, medical insurance, a system of state-funded health-care, and the construction or subsidising of low-cost housing at public expense.

The peculiar composition of the American welfare state follows from the way in which it was designed and constructed during the 1930s. The legislation of the New Deal, and in particular the Social Security Act of 1935, constitutes the basis of modern American welfare provision. It has been compared to a 'big bang', a critical moment when the configuration of future social policy was substantially determined. The welfare state created in the 1930s is, in its essentials, the welfare state that Americans rely upon today; though modified and expanded, its basic structure is unchanged. It is like an old mansion to which a variety of extensions – large or small, of greater or lesser prominence, more or less consistent with the original design – have been added, but whose central fabric remains intact and still constrains the possibilities for future development of the site.

The problem of relief

If a welfare state in the modern sense is a product of the New Deal, welfare is as old as Anglo-America itself. Ever since colonial times Americans have accepted the responsibility for relieving poverty and distress. The task of caring for the homeless, the indigent and the aged fell to local communities, which carried out their responsibilities in a variety of ways, involving varying mixtures of public and private funding and administration. Although state governments from the late nineteenth century began to impose a much closer scrutiny, the provision of relief, whether public or private, remained very much a local responsibility.

The Great Depression placed intolerable pressures upon existing structures. However strict the administration of relief, however rigorous the rules governing eligibility, they proved unable to cope with the tremendous number of applicants, in excess of 20 million, who urgently and desperately called out for assistance. Local provision effectively broke down under the strain. The result was a crisis of relief which was the starting-point for the New Deal revolution in social policy. The Depression demonstrated, first of all, the incapacity of private relief to handle a crisis of such magnitude. Private funds rapidly dried up, no matter how close to the bone assistance was pared. To attempt to meet the emergency out of private resources was, as one relief worker put it, 'about as useless as trying to put out a forest fire with a garden hose'.[1] After 1933 public welfare would remain dominant. Secondly, the Depression showed the inadequacy of local resources. Neither local nor state governments, constrained by a limited tax base, limited borrowing capacity and in some cases constitutional restrictions on their indebtedness, possessed the financial capacity to cope with need on so calamitous a scale. It therefore became a federal

1. Quoted in Walter I. Trattner, *From Poor Law to Welfare State: A History of Social Welfare in America* (5th edn, New York, 1994), p. 274.

responsibility, in the words of Roosevelt's welfare adviser Harry Hopkins, 'to feed the hungry and Goddamn fast'.[2]

This, then, was a pivotal moment in the expansion of federal power during the twentieth century. It entailed a substantial renegotiation of the distribution of powers within the federal system, involving the federal government once and for all in the business of welfare and in the formulation of social policy, matters which in the past had only peripherally engaged the attention of national policy-makers. This was an assumption of responsibility that was not so much undertaken voluntarily or with relish – far from it – as virtually enforced by the sheer enormity of the crisis. Only through a stony indifference to human suffering or a ruthless devotion to strict ideological or constitutional principles could government officials fail to comprehend this, and these were failings from which Roosevelt, for all his limitations, did not suffer. It is true that the federal government retracted to some extent from the commitments undertaken in 1933 and that state and local authorities retained an important influence on the shaping of welfare provision, but the broad contours of American social policy from that date were to be defined in Washington rather than in Albany or Des Moines.

Within a few weeks of the commencement of his Administration, in May 1933, Roosevelt persuaded Congress to appropriate $500 million for emergency relief, half of which was to be distributed in the form of matching grants, with the United States providing one dollar for every three expended by the states, and half in the form of direct grants to localities where the need was greatest. The Federal Emergency Relief Administration (FERA), which was modelled on a programme set up during Roosevelt's governership of New York, was headed by a former social worker, Harry Hopkins, who, according to one contemporary, 'had the purity of St. Francis of Assisi combined with the sharp shrewdness of a race-track tout'.[3] Hopkins moved with extraordinary dispatch to get resources to those in distress, authorising the allocation of $5 million before he had even moved into his office. By the winter of 1934 FERA was contributing to the support of 4.5 million households, while monthly relief payments were raised from an average of $15.15 per family in May 1933, when FERA commenced operation, to $29.33 in

2. Quoted in Eric F. Goldman, *Rendezvous with Destiny: A History of Modern American Reform* (New York, 1952), p. 256.
3. William R. Brock, *Welfare, Democracy, and the New Deal* (Cambridge, 1988), p. 181.

May 1935. By the time the agency closed its doors, in June 1936, it had spent just under $3 billion and was contributing nearly three-quarters of the total relief expenditure. These figures testify to the immensity of the reallocation of responsibility in the provision of welfare.

The transformation in social policy, however, fell far short of the establishment of a comprehensive federal relief system. As Hopkins admitted, 'We have never given adequate relief'.[4] The $25 a month allotted to the average relief family in 1934, though a great deal higher then local relief, was no more than a quarter of what contemporary social workers regarded as an adequate family budget. The matching-grant requirement resulted in wide variations between states according to their capacity, or willingness, to contribute. For example, a family in Kentucky received on average only $6.78 a month, whereas a family in New York received $45.12. The allocation of relief, in the absence of a federal welfare bureaucracy, was still dependent on local relief administrators, varying widely in competence, who continued to apply traditional poor law procedures, imposing rigorous and sometimes humiliating means tests to establish eligibility, distributing food and rent orders rather than cash grants, and discriminating against women and minority groups. In Southern states black clients were regularly paid half as much as whites, sometimes even less, while in plantation districts relief was customarily withdrawn altogether at times when labour was required in the fields. Hopkins fought a running battle against local administrators to ensure that applicants were treated fairly and equitably, and against local politicians to ensure that FERA was not turned into an adjunct of the patronage system, a battle in which he attained no more than partial success.

Roosevelt, in any case, was anxious to get the federal government out of the business of relief, which he feared would become a 'habit' with the country. FERA was never regarded as other than a temporary expedient. Therefore, shortly after the passage of the Social Security Act, the agency's activities were terminated, and relief, or 'general assistance', was returned to the states. Federal money continued to account for the overwhelming bulk of social spending, and federal regulations continued to govern many aspects of its distribution, but the administration of hard-core relief once more became a local responsibility. Rather than moving towards a uniform system of national assistance, the United States

4. Quoted in James T. Patterson, *America's Strugggle against Poverty, 1900–1985* (Cambridge, Mass., 1986), pp. 58–9.

retreated part-way to localised provision. With the demise of FERA an opportunity was lost to create a national standard of basic subsistence, to lay down a basic entitlement to a minimum standard of living for the people of the United States. The 'end of the FERA', the social reformer Edith Abbott believed, 'has been one of the tragedies of the Administration's program'.[5]

Roosevelt, hardly less than Hoover, was uncomfortable with the 'dole', which he regarded as 'a narcotic, a subtle destroyer of the human spirit'. The need to work, he believed, was a basic human instinct, essential to individual self-esteem. 'Give a man a dole', observed Hopkins, 'and you save his body and destroy his spirit. Give him a job and pay him an assured wage and you save both the body and the spirit.'[6] Therefore work relief was strongly preferred by the New Dealers as a way of maintaining work habits and skills among the unemployed and of restoring morale. There were, it is true, some public figures like William T. Foster and Robert Wagner who saw public works expenditure as a way of stimulating demand and promoting economic recovery, but it does not appear that these proto- Keynesian arguments greatly influenced Roosevelt, who retained, as we have seen, distinctly orthodox fiscal views. It was not macro-economic considerations, which he did not fully comprehend, that drew Roosevelt to support public works so much as social and moral assumptions regarding the preferability of work over direct relief.

Even before the emergency relief appropriation, Congress had created the Civilian Conservation Corps, which provided work for unemployed youths, principally in reforestation projects, while Title II of the National Industrial Recovery Act established a Public Works Administration, which was responsible for large-scale construction projects. FERA also provided work relief for, at various times, between 1.4 and 2.4 million individuals. In addition, during the autumn of 1933, Roosevelt created a Civil Works Administration (CWA), under the direction of Harry Hopkins, to tide the country over what promised to be a difficult winter. At its peak CWA employed over 4 million men and women, at hourly wage-rates equivalent to those in private employment, on a variety of hastily devised schemes: completing unfinished roads, schools and hospitals, laying out parks and playgrounds, digging ditches for sewers and water mains, refurbishing public buildings, teaching adult literacy classes, surveying coasts and harbours, and establishing symphony

5. Quoted in ibid., p. 62.
6. Quoted in ibid., p. 59.

orchestras. 'Above all', in Schlesinger's words, 'it supplied work to four million Americans who would otherwise have festered in humiliation and idleness.'[7] When the private sector failed to mop up the unemployed workers discharged when CWA was wound up in April 1934, the government was compelled to appropriate further sums for emergency relief, out of which was financed the most famous New Deal work relief agency, the Works Progress Administration (WPA).

The WPA, which ran from 1935 to 1943, at its peak employed over 3 million workers, about a third of the total number of unemployed. Under its aegis a number of arts and cultural programmes were established, including the Federal Art Project, the Federal Theater Project and the Federal Writers Project, which produced a great deal of exciting and imaginative work: murals by Diego Rivera, performances of plays by Clifford Odets, a series of local guidebooks, and invaluable collections of oral history and folklore. One interesting by-product of the federal relief programmes therefore was an unprecedented level of government patronage of culture, involving a genuine attempt to make the arts more democratic and more accessible to the public. However, the spectacular nature of these projects must not distract attention from the fact that most WPA work consisted of repetitive, sometimes pointless and demoralising, manual labour. Most female workers were employed in sewing rooms, most male workers on construction projects. As a result of the lack of money for equipment and materials and a shortage of trained supervisors and skilled labour, in view of the requirement that workers should be taken from the relief rolls and that WPA projects should not compete with private enterprise, administrators had difficulty devising a sufficient number of worthwhile projects for so large a workforce. Unlike CWA, WPA paid a 'security wage' which was substantially below the rate prevailing in the private sector and ensured, along with the ban on the enrolment of more than one member of any family, that WPA workers and their families would live well below a recognised subsistence level.

For most workers, therefore, WPA offered tedious work at low wages under conditions that prevented work relief from enjoying the same legitimacy as private employment. The low pay, the anti-nepotism rules, the drawing of workers from the relief rolls, and the nature of the work emphasised that WPA was a work relief

---

7. Arthur M. Schlesinger Jr., *The Coming of the New Deal* (Boston, 1958), p. 270.

rather than a public works programme. Nevertheless, in participants' eyes, WPA employment was far better than the dole, offering not only the wages but also the dignity of work. The letters sent to Roosevelt and other federal officials and the observations of federal investigators make it clear that most workers were almost pathetically grateful for the opportunity. In view of the obstacles that it faced – business opposition, the budgetary conservatism of president and Congress, the lack of administrative capacity, and the conflicting goals that followed from the merging of public works with relief – it is remarkable how much WPA achieved.

Social insurance

Roosevelt never regarded relief as an adequate long-term solution to the problem of need. Instead he favoured a system of social insurance 'from the cradle to the grave' which would offer protection 'against the hazards and vicissitudes of life', such as unemployment and old-age.[8] Roosevelt, who as Governor of New York had advocated unemployment insurance and old-age pension legislation, was committed to social insurance from the start, and his support as president was crucial to its enactment. In the last analysis, Social Security came to pass because Roosevelt placed his influence behind it.

Social insurance offered numerous advantages. In the first place, it afforded protection against many of the causes of poverty. As social reformers had discovered a generation earlier, destitution commonly resulted from one of a number of eventualities – old-age, widowhood, sickness, industrial injury or unemployment – which affected large numbers of lives in an actuarially predictable fashion and against which individuals and their families could be insured. Secondly, in place of charitable relief for those in distress, social insurance offered the promise of payment as an 'earned right', as an entitlement in equity founded upon previous contributions. Rather than negotiating with parsimonious relief administrators or charity officials, rather than submitting to a means test or some such invidious procedure, individuals could claim benefits on the basis of some observable criterion, such as reaching sixty-five, falling sick or becoming unemployed. Thirdly, it would lay down for many

8. Quoted in Blanche D. Coll, *Safety Net: Welfare and Social Security, 1929–1979* (New Brunswick, N.J., 1995), pp. 34–5.

Americans a minimum standard of living below which they could not fall. It would thus act as an economic stabiliser, preventing incomes from sinking to catastrophic levels in some future slump while taking in more funds than were disbursed during years when the economy was buoyant.

The social insurance proposals of the Progressive Era, elaborated further during the 1920s, brought few practical results, beyond the workingmen's compensation and widows' pension schemes instituted in many states during the second decade of the century. Before 1932 no state had established even a rudimentary old-age or unemployment insurance programme. Seventeen states had begun to pay old-age pensions, but these were non-contributory, poorly funded, restricted to the needy, and therefore, strictly speaking, a form of poor relief. Twenty states also provided pensions for the blind. More comprehensive proposals ran contrary to the prevailing ethos of 'voluntarism' which stressed an individual's responsibility to secure his and his family's future by prudent investment in private insurance or other savings plans. They also antagonised powerful interest groups, including life insurance companies and industrial corporations which had set up their own employee pension schemes.

The Depression seriously undermined the voluntarist principle. Many families had always found it impossible to save as a result of low wages and irregular employment; for large numbers of Americans old age had always been a problem. Now middle-income families were sucked into the maelstrom of uncertainty. Many of those more fortunate families who had set aside what they believed to be adequate funds against their retirement saw their savings dwindle to almost nothing in the aftermath of the Great Crash, as banks, insurance companies and trust funds went bankrupt. These were, of course, respectable middle-class citizens who identified themselves with traditional American values. They saw themselves as respectable, hard-working men and women who had played the game according to the rules that they had been taught, and suddenly, when there was no chance for them to make a fresh start, they had been let down. Not surprisingly, they felt betrayed.

Much of their resentment was channelled into a movement for lavish federal pensions led by Francis Townsend, a retired physician from California. Townsend's proposal, attractive in its simplicity, was that the government should furnish every citizen over sixty with a pension of $200 a month – a generous sum, which was over four times the average amount later paid out under federal old-age assistance. The one undemanding requirement was that they should spend every dollar within that period, so that the rest of the population might benefit from the trickle-down effect of senior citizens' spending power. This largesse would be paid for out of the proceeds of a 2 per cent tax on business transactions. The Townsend Plan, not surprisingly, struck a chord among the over-sixties. To his followers, mostly middle-class Americans of conservative views, the plan was not in the least radical; it seemed like simple justice to old folks. For all its extreme fiscal irresponsibility (the proposed levy would barely cover a fraction of the cost, which would, in fact, consume all federal, state and local taxes twice over) and its extraordinary generosity (it would mean handing over half the national income to 8 per cent of the population), a considerable political steam built up behind the Townsend Plan. There were by now nearly twice as many old people as there had been a generation earlier, and their profound sense of indignation and insecurity was a potent political force. Edwin E. Witte, one of the authors of the Social Security Act, regarded the Townsend movement as a 'terrible menace'. Without pressure from the elderly, he doubted 'whether anything … would have gone through at all'. Frances Perkins agreed: 'without the Townsend Plan it is possible that the Old Age Insurance system would not have received the attention which it did at the hands of Congress'.[9] Pressure from the aged was therefore one of the major forces behind what became the Social Security Act.

The Townsend movement formed only part of a wave of protest which swept across the country during the early New Deal years. Labour unrest, the Farm Holiday movement, the activities of demagogues such as Huey Long, the Unemployed Councils and other groups of militant unemployed workers and relief recipients, which are heavily documented in the writings of Frances Piven and Richard Cloward, combined to engender a sense of political crisis among Administration officials and Democratic party leaders. Pressure for welfare reform also came from the social work profession, which had been both enlarged and radicalised during the New Deal years, and elements of a labour movement which was beginning to abandon its earlier commitment to 'voluntarism'. The support of organised labour was, Linda Gordon suggests, 'a

9. Quoted in Michael Katz, *In the Shadow of the Poorhouse: A Social History of Welfare in America* (New York, 1986), p. 235; Ann Orloff, 'The political origins of America's belated welfare state', in Margaret Weir, Ann Orloff and Theda Skocpol, eds, *The Politics of Social Policy in the United States* (Princeton, N.J., 1988), p. 67.

necessary condition for the Social Security Act'.[10] New Deal social policy, however, was only partially determined by public opinion or by popular movements like Townsend's. Popular protest made the Social Security Act possible, but it by no means determined what shape it would take. Indeed, there was very little popular demand for a social insurance programme such as that which was enacted in 1935. What Townsend wanted, and what most people seemed to expect of Congress, was not a system of contributory old-age insurance but a system of old-age pensions financed directly from the Treasury.

The Social Security Act, even more than the Wagner Act, has become an important test-case for the 'corporate liberal' thesis. Writers like Colin Gordon, Jill Quadagno, J. Craig Jenkins and Barbara G. Bents argue that 'strategic business leadership groups' played a guiding role in the creation of federal social insurance.[11] While they point to business leaders' desire to appease social unrest, forestall more radical legislation, and stabilise the economy, the main line of argument traces the continuity between 1920s welfare capitalism and New Deal social policy. For various reasons – to reduce labour turnover, to encourage shop-floor morale, to discourage union membership, and perhaps as an expression of their commitment to 'social service' – a number of firms introduced pension plans. Limited in coverage though they were, such programmes proved very costly to maintain, particularly after 1929, and left their initiators at a distinct disadvantage against less conscientious rivals. The alternatives were to abandon them altogether or to impose similar costs on their competitors, either directly or through the tax system. State insurance legislation would evidently not solve, indeed would exacerbate, the inequality of burdens. With several states establishing old-age pension prog-rammes during the early 1930s and many giving close consideration to unemployment insurance, businessmen operating in interstate markets viewed the situation with trepidation. They faced the prospect of bewilderingly inconsistent legislation with a 'maddening diversity of benefits'.[12] Only federal legislation would restore a level playing-field on which welfare costs would be equalised. Therefore federal social insurance enjoyed the support of enlightened

10. Linda Gordon, *Pitied But Not Entitled: Single Mothers and the History of Welfare* (New York, 1994), p. 216.

11. J. Craig Jenkins and Barbara G. Bents, 'Capitalists and Social Security: what did they really want?' *American Sociological Review* 55 (1991), p. 129.

12. Colin Gordon, *New Deals: Business, Labor and Politics in America, 1920–1935* (Cambridge, 1994), p. 262.

business executives like Gerald Swope of General Electric and Marion Folsom of Kodak. Liberal capitalists both endowed and played an important part in reform organisations like the American Association for Labor Legislation and the Rockefeller-funded Industrial Relations Council where many of the ideas that later became embodied in the Social Security Act were worked out. Their influence was expressed, not directly or overtly, but through a continuous involvement in policy formulation.

Critics of the 'corporate liberal' thesis, like Theda Skocpol and Edwin Amenta, point out that, according to survey evidence and the views expressed by organisations like the NAM and the US Chamber of Commerce, an overwhelming majority of businessmen opposed Social Security. The few businessmen who had a voice in designing the legislation were a very unrepresentative sample of the American business community, having been selected by the Administration itself on the basis of their liberal views on social policy. The fact that they shared the same objectives as reformers and policy-makers does not mean that they had a controlling influence. Indeed, in one important respect, namely the institution of national standards for unemployment insurance, they were unsuccessful in attaining their desires. It is true that those involved in designing Social Security, both in government agencies and in the ranks of 'policy intellectuals', were mostly sensitive to the needs and wishes of business. As in the Progressive Era, liberal reformers and liberal capitalists formed part of a broader reform community. This matrix can only be called 'corporate liberal' in the sense that those involved did not challenge the corporate system and, indeed, had its long-term survival at heart.

According to Skocpol, 'the policy process through which Social Security was planned and drafted in the mid-1930s was strikingly closed'. Its authors, rather than bending to popular pressures, 'saw themselves as bulwarks against social groups and political forces attempting to open up the federal treasury'.[13] The social security proposals of the New Deal were drafted by a Committee on Economic Security (CES) set up by Roosevelt in 1934, partly to head off congressional proposals for unemployment compensation and non-contributory old-age pensions. The committee was composed of academics and social policy experts, many of whom, including Witte, the executive director of the CES, and Arthur J. Altmeyer, who headed its Technical Board, were drawn from Wisconsin, the

13. Theda Skocpol, *Social Policy in the United States* (Princeton, N.J., 1995), pp. 153, 155–6.

state which had developed the most advanced state programmes and in which, since the Progressive Era, the worlds of academic research and policy-making had been most closely intertwined. Those associated with more radical, non-contributory approaches were excluded from its deliberations.

Following Roosevelt's instructions as well as their own inclinations, the members of CES approached their tasks with certain principles in mind. Firstly, they grounded their proposals in principles of 'sound finance', ruling out the possibility of uncontrolled claims on public revenues. Fiscal conservatism, as Mark Leff has shown, was very much part of Roosevelt's nature. Though ready to incur extraordinary deficits to provide emergency relief, he was insistent that permanent programmes should be paid for out of current revenues. Secondly, they wished to separate the social insurance components of the legislation from relief programmes, which were to be separately administered and separately funded. Individuals would establish a right to social insurance benefits by the contributions that they had paid. The government, Roosevelt explained, using a metaphor which obviously took his fancy, would merely act as a piggy bank where individuals placed money in readiness for the time when they needed it. People would, in effect, do their own saving. Apart from the element of compulsion, the government was doing no more than replicate the private insurance schemes to which more prosperous Americans entrusted their savings. Roosevelt was anxious to stress how conservative his proposals were, both in principle and in actuarial practice. His was, indeed, in the context of the Depression, a distinctly conservative conception of social insurance in that payments were based entirely on contributions, that is on an individual's employment record. So rigorous an application of equity principles had not always formed part of social insurance proposals before the New Deal, which in America and in Europe had usually involved some contribution from government revenues and therefore some measure of redistribution. Nor was it necessary to sell the measure to Congress, which appeared ready to support more generous provisions. In practice, the American social security system always contained an element of cross-subsidy, and increasingly so over time. Roosevelt's disarming metaphor of the piggy bank was, in fact, misleading, but also dangerous, because it entailed a simplistic and confining model of social insurance. Its attractions were more political than economic. The equitable claim that would be created by the accumulation of individual contributions would, Roosevelt believed, make the programme virtually immune to political attack. 'With those taxes in', he later proclaimed, 'no damn politician can ever scrap my social security program.'[14]

Thirdly, the committee accepted the necessity under the federal system of relying where possible on the states. Edwin Witte and Frances Perkins were convinced that neither Southern conservatives in Congress nor a majority of the Supreme Court would accept a fully national unemployment insurance scheme, and therefore they pushed the committee towards the most federal of the proposals before it. At the same time, some members of the committee, including Witte, wished to protect the state unemployment insurance programmes that were already in operation in Wisconsin and close to enactment in several other states. These varied according to whether payroll taxes were kept in separate 'employer reserves', as in Wisconsin, or pooled, as in Ohio; and the extent to which taxes on individual employers were graduated according to the number of lay-offs for which they were responsible, a system known as 'merit rating'. The 'tax-offset' plan which was finally adopted by the committee allowed almost complete freedom to the states in shaping their own programmes. It therefore relieved the committee of the difficult responsibility of arbitrating between competing plans.

The character of existing state provision influenced the development of federal social policy. No state had seriously considered old-age insurance, so federal legislation in this area would not trespass on their activities, whereas a number were close to creating unemployment insurance programmes. By 1935, twenty-eight states had begun to pay old-age assistance, and forty-five provided widows' pensions, although nearly all the programmes were seriously underfunded and reached only a small proportion of the target populations. The so-called 'categorical assistance' features of the Social Security Act were explicitly designed to supplement, not supersede, existing state programmes. Thus the allocation of powers between federal and state governments depended upon how far the states had already entered a particular field. According to Andrew Achenbaum, 'the original social security bill sought to improve existing systems, taking new initiatives only when absolutely necessary'.[15] Discussion centred on ways in which the imperfections of past policies might be remedied, rather than

14. Quoted in W. Andrew Achenbaum, *Social Security: Visions and Revisions* (New York, 1986), pp. 22–3.
15. Ibid., p. 19.

the most appropriate way to respond to prevailing social conditions, a process continuously repeated in the history of American social policy in the twentieth century.

Congress spent little time on the technical details of the legislation and accepted most of the committee's proposals without demur. Its members were more concerned with immediate problems of welfare than with long-term programmes of insurance, which they only vaguely understood. They voted for old-age insurance because it was part of a package which contained things that they wanted more, particularly old-age assistance. The most significant resistance came from Southerners, anxious to retain control over their plantation labour force, who compelled the removal of farm labourers from the social insurance sections and the erosion of national standards for 'categorical assistance'. Southern congressmen were as eager as anyone to take advantage of federal grants, but they did not wish, in doing so, to overturn local social arrangements. Here as elsewhere in the New Deal, the peculiar interests of the South, and its extraordinary congressional leverage, had an oddly distorting effect on policy.

The Social Security Act

The law enacted in August 1935 initiated a suite of programmes which, taken together, form the basis of the American welfare state. The Social Security Act created a federal system of old-age insurance financed by contributions from employers and employees. Both contributions and benefits would be roughly proportionate to income. Unlike old-age insurance, which in recognition of the mobility of American workers was a purely federal programme, unemployment insurance was to be administered by the states, but the funds in effect came from a federal payroll tax, from which states with suitable unemployment insurance programmes could claim a 90 per cent rebate. The states were permitted a wide degree of discretion in determining what form their programme would take, although nearly every state in time adopted pooled funds, rather than separate 'employer reserves', and some form of 'experience rating'. They were also allowed to set their own standards of eligibility and payment levels.

Federal money was made available to the states, on a matching-funds basis, for various kinds of 'categorical assistance', that is assistance for specific categories of needy individuals who roughly corresponded to what used to be called the 'deserving poor', including in particular the indigent aged and dependent children. The former programme was designed to cater to the needs of men and women too old to contribute to Old Age Insurance (OAI) but desperately in need of assistance. It both reinforced and extended the existing state pensions. For many years Old Age Assistance (OAA), as it was called, supported more people than received benefits as a result of OAI, for which only 20 per cent of the over-65s had qualified by 1940. Not until the 1950s did the number of individuals receiving social security exceed the number receiving OAA, which gradually withered away as more and more elderly persons were covered by OAI.

Aid to Dependent Children (ADC), now virtually synonymous with 'welfare', had a relatively minor place in the formulation of the Social Security Act. In effect, it offered federal support for the widows' pensions schemes originating in the Progressive Era. The intention was the same: to enable single, presumably widowed, mothers to support their children without having to seek paid employment. Although dependent children were, in Theda Skocpol's words, 'the quintessential deserving poor', those who administered ADC were still anxious to ensure that the women who were, of course, the actual recipients should be worthy of the trust placed in them. Following the practice of earlier administration of widows' pensions, they sought to restrict assistance to women who could provide a 'suitable home' for their children, a criterion which was largely interpreted in moral terms, and deny it to those who cohabited with men. Such tests, of course, provided scope for excessively prurient and censorious administration. They were also anxious to prevent able-bodied young women from living off the state and frequently denied assistance to 'employable mothers' of school-age children. The hybrid character of this legislation, which, rather than defining economic assistance as a 'legitimate, constructive end in itself', combined it with 'casework goals aimed at family rehabilitation', Roy Lubove argues, stored up problems for the future: 'A major source of conflict and tension in the subsequent evolution of the American public assistance system has been this tendency for behavioral considerations to compete with problems of objective economic need.'[16] The result was a combination of continuing harassment and inadequate assistance which served the interests of neither client nor society.

16. Roy Lubove, *The Struggle for Social Security, 1900–1935* (Cambridge, Mass., 1968), p. 111.

'In many ways', concludes Leuchtenburg, 'the law was an astonishingly inept and conservative piece of legislation.'[17] It denied protection to many of those who were most in need. Domestic servants and agricultural labourers were excluded from both insurance programmes, partly for administrative convenience but also for political reasons. Their omission was, in fact, a concession to Southern congressmen, who feared that federal insurance would increase the independence and raise the expectations of agricultural workers, many of whom, of course, were African-Americans. It is significant that the two major excluded categories contained disproportionate numbers of blacks and women. Also excluded from social insurance were, of course, the unemployed, since participation was based on an individual's employment record. In 1939, therefore, only 43.6 per cent of the workforce paid contributions to social security, and a similar proportion was covered by unemployment insurance.

Dependence on the states, though dictated by both political and constitutional considerations, also had deleterious consequences. Unemployment insurance programmes varied widely in the scale of benefits. The same applied to OAA and ADC, where the size of benefits depended upon local resources and inclinations. For example, the average monthly ADC payment ranged from $8.10 to a family in Arkansas to $61.07 in Massachusetts. To propitiate Southern congressmen and secure the passage of the bill, it was necessary, in Witte's words, 'to tone down all clauses relating to supervising control by the federal government'. That included the removal of a clause requiring states to furnish assistance at a level that would provide 'a reasonable subsistence compatible with decency and health', which, it was feared, would make blacks independent enough to refuse plantation labour.[18] A clause explicitly prohibiting discrimination on the grounds of race was also removed. The states were allowed virtually a free hand in setting eligibility criteria. It is possible therefore that, whatever its authors' intentions, the Social Security Act had the effect of actually widening regional differences in welfare expenditure.

OAI was wholly self-financing, with no contribution from public funds. There were powerful political reasons for this: it made the programme easier to defend against cost-conscious congressmen

17. William E. Leuchtenburg, *Franklin D. Roosevelt and the New Deal* (New York, 1963), p. 132.
18. Edwin E. Witte, *The Development of the Social Security Act* (Madison, Wis., 1963), pp. 143–4.

and Treasury officials and left it virtually immune to a later conservative backlash, because the accumulated social security fund represented both a powerful right in equity and a potent interest group of past contributors and future claimants. Politically expedient though such a course of action was, the absence of a federal contribution ruled out the possibility of more than an incidental redistribution of income. Indeed, the graduation of contributions and benefits according to income meant that class differences would substantially continue into old-age. Wealthy and middle-class claimants would receive a larger income than their less affluent contemporaries, with benefits ranging at first from $10 to $85 per month. Thus social security was designed not to redistribute income but to protect a family's relative standard of living after retirement.

The most obvious omission was some form of health insurance, according to Walter I. Trattner 'the oldest form of compulsory social insurance in the world'.[19] Although Roosevelt had believed that any complete system of social insurance 'from the cradle to the grave' must include some form of protection against medical costs, although the CES had included it in its early deliberations, and although there was, according to contemporary opinion polls, wide-spread popular support for medical insurance, the influence of the American Medical Association was sufficient to block any such proposals, as it had blocked all such legislation since 1918. Roosevelt dropped the issue at an early stage for fear that its inclusion would jeopardise the whole bill. This turned out to be a critical reverse. The influence of the AMA and its conservative congressional allies, in the atmosphere of the Cold War years, was sufficient to stall any further plans for 'socialised medicine'. Even in the more favourable political atmosphere of the 1960s all that could be achieved were specific programmes catering to the needy and the aged. In the meantime the vacuum was partially filled by private health insurance, which became a standard feature of the employment contracts negotiated by trade unions and granted to most white-collar workers.

Contrary to the expectations of the Committee on Economic Security, the various income-maintenance programmes incorporated in the Social Security Act were not associated with plans to guarantee full employment. As the committee's title suggests, its brief included the consideration of means to assure 'economic

19. Trattner, *From Poor Law to Welfare State*, p. 293.

security'. The first objective, it was assumed, must be to provide as many jobs as possible, where necessary through public works programmes. But the 'economic assurance' proposals incorporated in the initial draft of the Social Security Act were eliminated. Those indigent individuals who were eligible for neither social insurance nor categorical assistance and who could not secure work relief were, after the cessation of FERA, once more the responsibility of the states. The Committee on Economic Security had anticipated that, with the inauguration of social security, 'the residual relief problem will have diminished to a point where it will be possible to return primary responsibility for the care of people who cannot work to the state and local governments'.[20] Social insurance, in combination with public works, it hoped, would minimise the number seeking relief. Roosevelt anticipated a residue of only 1.5 million individuals. In fact, owing to the failure to establish a comprehensive public works programme, the number receiving public assistance stood at 4.7 million in 1937 and remained high throughout the 1930s. The temporary public works agencies that did exist, like WPA, were wound up during the Second World War and not replaced thereafter. Instead, after the Second World a strategy of Keynesian demand management was intermittently applied, which did little to alleviate pockets of high unemployment. Therefore the system of public assistance continued to bear an unanticipated burden.

'The most obvious characteristic of the new order', observes James T. Patterson, 'was its primary reliance on contributory social insurance and its concomitant distaste for welfare.'[21] The former was central to the new system of income support, politically acceptable and morally immaculate; the latter was regarded as distasteful and morally suspect. Social security appeared analogous to private insurance. Benefits were distributed ungrudgingly to those with satisfactory records of contribution; the beneficiaries were treated as upright, honest, hard-working citizens who thoroughly deserved to enjoy the fruits of their own labour. The programme was, in Skocpol's words, 'administratively sovereign, politically privileged, and fiscally insulated'.[22] On the other hand, the various public assistance programmes carried all the shabby, misbegotten aura of the old poor law. Welfare was handed out begrudgingly after a series of humiliating tests, claimants were treated almost *ipso*

20. Quoted in Patterson, *America's Struggle against Poverty*, p. 60.
21. Ibid., p. 76.
22. Skocpol, *Social Policy in the United States*, p. 165.

facto as if they were seeking to defraud the state, and their moral probity was continuously called into question. The distinction was exploited ruthlessly by Arthur Altmeyer and the newly-established Social Security Board to promote their pet programme and to discredit its rivals. 'As salesmanship, their strategy was brilliant', notes Michael Katz. 'For by dissociating social insurance from relief, they won public allegiance to welfare for the middle classes.'[23] For all its revolutionary features, New Deal social policy perpetuated, indeed gave new life to the traditional distinction between the 'deserving' and the 'undeserving poor', which in its new form became the central feature of the American welfare state.

For all its faults, many of which were entailed by the structure of the American political system, the Social Security Act set important precedents. Ironically, although the original aim of New Deal social policy had been to provide emergency relief, its major legacy was a system of social security. As Roosevelt told Congress in June 1934, 'the security of the home, the security of livelihood, and the security of social insurance' constituted 'the minimum of the promise that we can offer to the American people.'[24] The Social Security Act also provided for a continuing federal contribution to, and therefore influence over, a variety of programmes caring for dependent groups. The states were persuaded, or rather bribed, to pro-fessionalise their relief administration, introduce a variety of new programmes, and greatly increase their expenditure. This had a particularly dramatic effect in backward regions like the South. By 1939 1.9 million individuals were in receipt of OAA, many times more than benefited from the puny state pension programmes in existence in 1935; 1 million in receipt of ADC, three times the number supported by widows' pensions in 1935; and 1.7 million in receipt of general assistance. An estimated 46 million people, over a third of the population, received public assistance of some kind over the course of the New Deal years. Welfare expenditure of all kinds amounted to $4.9 billion in 1939, compared with $208 million in 1932.

Yet most historians still conclude, like Leuchtenburg, that this was an opportunity only partly seized. The political situation created scope for further advances towards the establishment of national standards of minimum subsistence and a more comprehensive system of social insurance. Roosevelt's fiscal conservatism imposed a narrow conception of social insurance, as well as starving the WPA

23. Katz, *In the Shadow of the Poorhouse*, p. 235.
24. Quoted in Achenbaum, *Social Security*, p. 19.

of funds. Too often the Administration followed the line of least resistance, refusing to challenge Southern congressmen over minimum standards and racial discrimination or the AMA over medical insurance, deferring to local sensibilities and devolving responsibilities to local officials. In the words of the social work historian Frank J. Bruno, 'The Social Security Act can only be called a measure to furnish such means of security as do not arouse serious opposition'. The deficiencies of the resulting 'semi-welfare state' seriously constrained possibilities for the future. 'Nothing', says Patterson, 'had a greater long-range impact on the structure of the American welfare state than the jerry-built structure with which it began.'[25]

The Social Security Act of 1935 was the cornerstone of the American welfare state. It was not the fault of its authors that the edifice was not completed. Only minor extensions were possible in the late 1930s. The Fair Labor Standards Act of 1938 set a maximum working-week and a (low) minimum wage. To supplement a small number of low-cost housing projects built by the PWA, the United States Housing Authority, established in 1937, extended loans to municipal authorities for the construction of public housing. But the programme proceeded on a very limited scale. The sums available were small, much less, significantly, than was available for the financing and refinancing of mortgages for prospective home-owners by agencies like the Home Owners Loan Corporation and Federal Housing Administration, whose efforts did so much over time to transform the face of urban America. Fewer than 200,000 units of public housing had been constructed by 1941. The indifference of the Administration, the conservatism of Congress and the hostility of powerful real estate lobbies militated against a more effective attack on the longstanding problem of slum housing.

The end-product of the New Deal, then, was a 'semi-welfare state'. Radical critics of the New Deal, then and since, have commented on its failure to cure poverty and social injustice. They note that the plight of slum-dwellers, sharecroppers, blacks and other deprived groups was little changed, whereas New Deal social policy hardly altered the distribution of income. According to the New Left historian Howard Zinn, 'What the New Deal did was to refurbish middle-class America . . . to restore jobs to half the jobless, and to give just enough to the lowest classes (a layer of public housing, a minimum of social security) to create an aura of good

---

25. Bruno quoted in Patterson, *America's Struggle against Poverty*, p. 75; ibid., p. 56.

will'.[26] In other words, it did just enough to shore up a social system in serious danger of collapse. But the welfare state also fell short of what many of the more liberal New Dealers had desired. The implementation of their plans was held back by the power of interest groups like the American Medical Association and real estate dealers; by the structure of the American political system, which required important, and in some ways damaging, sacrifices to the spirit of localism and states' rights, particularly in the South; and, perhaps, by the underlying conservatism of the American people, with their belief in limited taxation, limited government and self-reliance and their tendency to regard poor people as morally deficient. As the emergency of the early Depression years receded, partly as a result of New Deal policies, such attitudes tended to reassert themselves. For social policy the early New Deal years offered a window of opportunity for dramatic changes of direction that would open with great infrequency.

After the New Deal

During the Second World War the National Resources Planning Board, in what could be seen as a kind of American Beveridge Report, produced a plan for a comprehensive 'American standard' of 'minimum economic security' for all citizens. Its report on *Security, Work, and Relief Policies*, published in 1943, proposed that old age, unemployment, disability and health insurance should be combined in a common system, federally administered and financed on the same basis as OAI, while public assistance should be nationalised. Social insurance should be coordinated with policies to ensure employment for all who were able to work. Their proposals were ignored, except, significantly, for veterans, through the GI Bill. Thus the war brought a comprehensive welfare state for one section of the population. Apart from that, in contrast to Britain, the war had barely any discernible effect on American social policy.

During the postwar decades the welfare state expanded considerably, building on the template created during the 1930s. Partly owing to the determined efforts of the Social Security Board to promote it at the expense of rival schemes, OAI was transformed from a Cinderella programme which supported fewer people than

26. Howard Zinn, ed., *New Deal Thought* (Indianapolis, 1966), p. xvi.

OAA, and which in most states paid less, to an almost universal system of old-age support whose benefits greatly exceeded welfare. As the number of contributors and beneficiaries grew, its political position was strengthened until by the 1960s it had attained a status of invulnerability. Year after year the Board came back to Congress with proposals for incremental improvements, many of which were accepted. Congressmen enjoy taking the credit for generosity to deserving senior citizens. Social security was repeatedly extended, both in terms of the number of individuals covered and in the size of benefits. In 1939 the Social Security Act was amended to allow benefits to be paid to the survivors (usually widows) of insured persons, so that what had been OAI now became Old Age and Survivors' Insurance (OASI). In 1950 many of the excluded categories of employees were brought under the terms of OASI, and the remainder a few years later. Whereas in 1949 only 1.3 million individuals received benefits under OASI, by 1960 the number had grown to 14.8 million. In 1956 disability insurance was added. In 1965 free medical treatment, known as Medicare, was made available to those drawing benefits under OASI, greatly enhancing the value of government assistance to the elderly. On several occasions the scale of contributions was increased, and benefits, with the help of the mountainous surplus that was accumulating, were made more generous. In 1972 social security benefits were protected against inflation. By this time social security could be regarded as a genuine 'retirement wage', one which for many people offered a modestly comfortable standard of living.

Programmes for the poor were also expanded, especially during the late 1960s and early 1970s. Aid to Dependent Children, or, as it now became, Aid to Families of Dependent Children (AFDC) in recognition of the obvious fact that those who cared for young children also required support, was substantially liberalised by relaxing standards of eligibility and raising the value of benefits. In 1965 Medicaid, that is free medical treatment for families on public assistance, was made available, a programme which had a dramatic impact on the medical treatment of the poor. By 1975 its cost had risen to $9.1 billion a year. Perhaps the most striking increases took the form of grants in kind, such as food stamps, housing subsidies and energy assistance. For example, the food stamp programme expanded a hundredfold between 1965 and 1975, by which time $4.3 billion was being spent on 17.1 million individuals.

Most of the welfare expansion occurred in the 1960s and early 1970s, which saw an increased public interest in the problem of poverty and a series of government programmes to eradicate it. The so-called War on Poverty, which was, initially at least, more concerned with the prevention than the alleviation of poverty – with extending opportunity rather than income security – had little direct impact on welfare expenditure. Yet its indirect effect was remarkable. By dramatising the issue of poverty and placing it firmly on the public agenda, the War on Poverty facilitated the acceptance of other programmes, such as Medicaid. Meanwhile, existing programmes were administered in a more generous fashion. In 1960, for example, local regulations and unwelcoming administration ensured that only about one-third of those eligible for ADC received assistance. By 1971 the take-up was close to 90 per cent. The reasons for this are not altogether clear. Supreme Court decisions struck down some of the more restrictive state regulations, like the 'employable mother' and 'absent father' rules; liberal federal officials in the Bureau of Public Assistance and the Department of Health, Education and Welfare put pressure on local administrators; and the laws of some Northern and Western states were liberalised. But no less important was a new attitude of mind among welfare clients, who exhibited an enhanced sense of entitlement, applying for grants more frequently and asserting their rights more aggressively in the face of sometimes hostile and indifferent officials. They were encouraged in this new intransigence by civil rights activists, by bodies like the National Welfare Rights Organization, and in some localities by organisations set up under the Community Action Program of the War on Poverty.

Thus total government spending on the poor increased from 7.7 per cent of GNP in 1960 to 16 per cent in 1974. The sum expended in the form of payments to the elderly, including OASI and Medicare, had reached $54 billion by 1974. By 1989 it had reached $236 billion, which was 7.4 per cent of GNP, and 38.9 million individuals were in receipt of social security benefits. There were 11 million AFDC recipients, as against under a million in 1939. These developments brought about a significant decline in poverty, especially among the elderly. Between 1960 and 1980 the number living in poverty, according to one estimate, fell from 18 per cent to under 8 per cent, largely as a result of government transfer payments. Whereas about a half of the elderly population could be classed as 'poor' in the 1930s, by the 1970s the proportion had fallen to a sixth. The level of assistance to female-headed families and other recipients of public assistance ensured that most remained in poverty, but they were at least provided, through food stamps, with a minimum diet and, through Medicaid, with adequate health-care.

Yet the American welfare state remained decidedly incomplete. The absence of health insurance, except for the elderly, and the limited stock of public housing, which amounted to only 4 per cent of housing units in 1970, most obviously attested to its limitations. The fact that social insurance was linked to an individual's work record means that many were still dependent on public assistance, with all the means testing, humiliation and harassment that that entailed. As in the 1930s, the expansion of welfare programmes was held back by the opposition of powerful interest groups, like the AMA. In contrast, the poor were unorganised and largely voiceless. Thus the War on Poverty of the 1960s was described as 'a movement of reform in search of a constituency'. Traditional ideas about the role of the state and the character of the poor continued to hamper reform. Opinion polls repeatedly revealed that a majority of Americans held unflattering views of welfare recipients, variously referred to as 'chiselers' or 'welfare mothers'. Much less sympathy was shown towards the victims of poverty than in the 1930s, when destitution was identified with large-scale cyclical unemployment. Now, in the affluent society of postwar America, it was widely associated with shiftlessness and moral degeneracy.

The major category of welfare by the 1960s was AFDC, a programme whose impact and social implications had changed dramatically since the 1930s. Originally, ADC was designed to assist widowed mothers, but with the introduction of survivors' insurance most such persons were brought under the more generous rubric of social security. In any case, the number of widows of child-rearing age had greatly decreased since the early twentieth century, when the idea of widows' pensions was first advanced. On the other hand, for a variety of cultural and demographic reasons, the number of young women who bore children out of wedlock expanded enormously, especially from the 1960s. A majority of clients were now women who had never married. Critics of the programme argued that the availability of aid to single mothers actually encouraged young women to have children without bothering to go through the formalities of wedlock, or even to form a stable relationship with a man. Rather than protecting the family, as was originally intended, the programme seemed actually to weaken it. It so happened that a large proportion of 'welfare mothers' were black, 44 per cent in 1979, although a majority, of course, were not. Whether the disproportionate incidence of single-parent families among African-Americans was due to cultural factors, or, as is far more likely, to poverty, deprivation and high levels of male unemployment, has been the subject of angry controversy since the publication of the Moynihan Report in 1965. However, it added a racial dimension to an already angry discourse and fuelled demands that the programme be terminated or cut back.

While attacks on the welfare state sputtered away throughout the postwar decades, during the 1970s and 1980s criticism of what was called the 'welfare mess' intensified. On the one hand, critics pointed to the horrifying expense of the welfare state, as the numbers dependent on AFDC and general assistance appeared to rise exponentially and as the lengthening life-span of senior citizens threatened to overturn the balance between contributions to and payments from the Social Security Fund. By a bitter irony, the 'welfare explosion' of 1965–74 immediately preceded the oil crisis of the mid-1970s, which, as it turned out, initiated a prolonged period of economic stagnation. Meanwhile, escalating medical costs drove the expense of Medicare and Medicaid far beyond expectations. Under more straitened economic conditions what had seemed like harmless benevolence now appeared reckless improvidence. The result was presented as a 'welfare crisis' which demanded a radical revision of American social policy. Conservatives demanded that social security be substantially restructured, even that it be made voluntary, and that welfare programmes be severely cut back. On the other hand, the welfare system was blamed by politicians like Ronald Reagan and sociologists like Charles Murray for eroding poor people's will to work and establish stable families. By effectively making welfare an entitlement, they argued, the woolly-minded liberalism of the 1960s had broken down the psychological barriers keeping people in the workforce and off the relief rolls and thereby created a condition of 'welfare dependency'. 'There is no humanity or charity in destroying self-reliance, dignity, and self-respect ... the very substance of moral fiber', complained Reagan, while Governor of California.[27] Such a critique, however, did not point to any alternative plan, beyond cutting welfare benefits, tightening eligibility and, despite clear evidence that only a small percentage of those on welfare were able to work, attempting to encourage or propel recipients into the labour market.

Such assaults were insufficient to dislodge the central pillars of

---

27. Patterson, *America's Struggle against Poverty*, p. 173.

the welfare state. Social security was too popular, with too many voters dependent upon it for their present or future security, to be eliminated, or even substantially revised – testimony perhaps to the political craft of its founders. Thus Reagan was forced to abandon his proposed reform of the social security system in the early 1980s and content himself with a modest amount of judicious tinkering. Social spending on the poor was an easier target. AFDC, for example, which had always been insufficient to lift families out of poverty, was allowed to fall by 35 per cent in real terms between 1970 and 1984 (unlike social security, AFDC was not index-linked), while during the early 1980s 408,000 claimants were taken off the rolls. Whereas social security was exempt from the spending cuts of the Reagan years, a variety of welfare programmes were severely pruned, despite the fact that they accounted for only 18 per cent of federal social spending. Changes in eligibility standards removed hundreds of thousands of disabled persons from the rolls, unemployment insurance benefits were reduced, and expenditure on food stamps, school lunches, energy assistance, housing subsidies and Medicaid was curtailed. Reagan seemed to be engaged in a systematic campaign to roll back the welfare state, at least that part of it added since the 1960s. Whereas during the 1960s and 1970s the federal government pushed the states towards what amounted to an entitlement to welfare, the 'war on welfare' of the 1980s and 1990s has tended to reverse that trend. The result is that the gap between social security and public assistance has widened still further. Thus recent welfare reforms, rather than radically changing the system, have confirmed its basic structure.

The American welfare state created by the New Deal was more effective in meeting the needs of middle-income groups, by establishing a system of social security and by mortgage assistance, than in providing sufficient resources for the poor. According to Michael Harrington, the 'welfare state benefits least those who need it most'.[28] In that sense what the New Deal undoubtedly did, as Zinn suggests, was to 'refurbish middle-class America'. The welfare revolution of the late 1960s and early 1970s went some way to raising the standard of living of the poor and reducing the gap between the social insurance and welfare components of the American welfare state, bringing it closer to its Western European counterparts. Even then it fell far short of a universal, consistent and comprehensive system. The conservative reaction of the last two

28. Quoted in Patterson, *America's Struggle against Poverty*, p. 162.

decades has, however, widened the gap still further and reinforced the fundamental chasm at the heart of the American welfare state. Its major defect has always been its disarticulated, uncoordinated structure. Rather than a comprehensive system of income support, it consists of a miscellaneous array of independent programmes, separately funded, separately administered, created on an *ad hoc* basis for different reasons under different political circumstances, and geared to the needs of different social groups. It is, argues Skocpol, difficult to defend, still less to arouse public enthusiasm for, a welfare state which lacks any vision of 'social compassion and collective solidarity'.[29] Without such a vision a truly adequate welfare state may never be achieved in America.

29. Skocpol, *Social Policy in the United States*, p. 225.

CHAPTER TEN

To the Great Society and Beyond

Introduction

The historian Eric Goldman in 1953 defined a liberal as one who 'measures politicians by the memory of Franklin Roosevelt'.[1] The New Deal set the agenda of American domestic politics for the next half-century. Apart from the emergence of civil rights, which grew in political salience during the 1950s and 1960s, its programmatic substance grew out of the restructuring of American politics during the 1930s. The New Deal set the template for American liberalism, which defined itself for over a generation in terms that would have made perfect sense to Franklin D. Roosevelt. Its task was to complete the New Deal project. Such, in particular, was the aspiration of Lyndon B. Johnson, himself a former New Dealer, who hoped in his 'Great Society' programmes not only to fulfil but to surpass the achievements of his political mentor. His failure, and the controversies that arose from the domestic and foreign policies of the Johnson years, did as much as anything to discredit liberalism and encourage the growth of a New Right which, breaking the boundaries of the postwar consensus, repudiated, and sought where possible to undo, the handiwork of the New Deal. Although, even at the peak of his popularity, Ronald Reagan was unable to dismantle the institutions of the New Deal state, he and the Republican Right did much to disable the handiwork of the Great Society. More seriously, confidence in the redemptive power of the state which had inspired progressives and liberals since the end of the nineteenth century deserted them at the end of the twentieth,

---

1. William E. Leuchtenburg, *In the Shadow of FDR: From Harry Truman to Bill Clinton* (Ithaca, N.Y., 1993), p. 57.

leaving them divided, confused and uncertain. How, from the confidence of the immediate postwar years, liberalism reached this pass is the subject of this chapter.

The politics of consensus

What emerged from the immediate postwar years was, in some ways, a constricted version of the New Deal vision. Imaginative plans for a postwar reconstruction dreamed up by the National Resources Planning Board had no hope of fulfilment. The Keynesian vision behind the Employment Act of 1946 was sadly diluted by the time of its passage. The act contained no real provision for economic planning, and, rather than conferring an individual's right to employment, it merely defined full employment as a desirable national objective. The frustration of organised labour's more imaginative strategies for tripartite control of industry and an expanded welfare state narrowed its focus to the particularistic bargaining and private negotiation of security coverage which came to characterise industrial relations during the postwar era, at least for the privileged minority of union members. Thus labour became a special interest group, rather than a force for radical change. Finally, the growing strains of Cold War confrontation fractured the seamless linkages between liberals and the broader Left, and with it any lingering hopes that the Democratic Party might be forged into a 'left-liberal' or social democratic party. As writers like Nelson Lichtenstein, Robert Griffith and Ira Katznelson have argued, the immediate postwar settlement set the parameters for modern American liberalism. Any broadly focused intention to reshape the capitalist economy was replaced by a commitment to fiscal policies that would keep the engine running at full capacity and welfare state programmes that would tend its casualties.

The Second World War and its immediate aftermath, marked by shortages, wage controls and inflation, gave added fuel to the conservative counter-attack against the New Deal which had smouldered since the late 1930s. The forces of organised business, in alliance with groups like the American Farm Bureau Federation and the American Medical Association, were mobilised with renewed vigour to contend against the expanded authority of the post-New Deal state. Conservative Republicans and Southern Democrats issued demands that Congress 'repeal the New Deal'. However, apart from the enactment of Taft-Hartley, the postwar conservative backlash brought few substantive results. Rather than succumbing to the apparent Republican resurgence, Roosevelt's successor Harry Truman fought back to secure re-election in 1948. He achieved this principally by affirming his commitment to the New Deal, now repackaged as the 'Fair Deal'. The Democratic platform called for extensions of social security, particularly the addition of health insurance, substantial spending on urban renewal and public housing, a higher minimum wage, repeal of Taft-Hartley and (a new component of postwar liberalism) a civil rights law. While calling for further reforms, he reminded voters of the past achievements of the Democratic Party – of their debt to the New Deal. 'Think it over when you go into the voting booths next month', he urged. 'Think of the gains you've obtained in the last sixteen years – higher wages, social security, unemployment compensation, federal loans to save your homes and a thousand other things.'[2] What they had gained, above all, was a measure of security, a safety net, which even in the affluent society of the postwar years many voters were reluctant to dispense with. It appears that Truman's evocation of the New Deal was successful, as, by the thinnest of margins, he carried the election and with him a Democratic Congress pledged to reform.

During the next few years Truman secured enactment of some of his reform proposals. In particular, the Housing Act of 1949 provided federal funds for public housing projects and much more generous funds for mortgage guarantees to middle-income home-buyers, while the Social Security Act of 1950 significantly extended the coverage and increased the benefits of OASI and liberalised ADC payments. These measures represented the first significant enlargement of the New Deal welfare state. Equally notable was what Truman could not achieve, including health insurance, federal aid to education, the Brannan Plan for farm income supports, repeal of Taft-Hartley and civil rights legislation. The ultimate outcome was a political stalemate that was to characterise most of the postwar decades.

The stalemate continued during the Eisenhower years. General Dwight D. Eisenhower was elected president in 1952 on the Republican ticket as a testament to his own enormous personal popularity, and as a consequence of public frustration with the Truman Administration's foreign policy, heightened during the period of the Korean War, not because a majority of the American

2. Leuchtenburg, *In the Shadow of FDR*, p. 32.

electorate wished to reverse the reformist policies of the Fair Deal. Although Eisenhower, had a profound distaste for many aspects of the New Deal, he did little to carry out his 'mandate for change'. Although it secured some tax cuts, some modifications of farm subsidies and some reductions in welfare spending, the first Republican Administration in twenty years left the legacy of the New Deal virtually intact. Indeed, rather than rolling back the welfare state, Eisenhower began to advocate further extensions of the social security system, including disability insurance and limited medical care for the indigent elderly, liberalisation of ADC, and further expenditure on public housing projects. As a pragmatic conservative, Eisenhower accepted that the programmatic liberalism of the New Deal was too deeply woven into the fabric of American life for its essentials to be challenged. The 'New Republicanism' had to assimilate elements of the New Deal, while seeking to eliminate its excesses. Thus the Republicans accepted the basic delineaments of the New Deal, or, at least, some Republicans did – for the most part those who, representing the urban-industrial states of the Northeast and Midwest, were obliged to come to terms with urban problems and challenge for urban votes. For nearly a generation the dominant voice in the party, at a national level, was that of New Republicans like Nelson Rockefeller of New York and Charles Percy of Illinois, who sought, like Eisenhower, to compete with the Democrats on the middle ground of American politics.

Though Eisenhower was by no means the weak and bumbling president that liberal journalists liked to depict, nor was he a crusading leader committed to counter-revolution. Indeed, his restrained conception of the presidential office was, according to his speechwriter, Emmet Hughes, almost deliberately designed as a studied retort to Roosevelt. Ike was an 'organization man' *par excellence*. His wartime record was built, as much as anything, on a talent for compromise and reconciliation, rather than confrontation, and he continued to exhibit similar skills in civilian life.

Above all, after his first two years in office, Eisenhower faced large Democratic majorities in both houses of Congress, which made more than incremental change impossible. His election in 1952 and his re-election in 1956 have been categorised as 'deviating elections', which departed from, but did not permanently alter, the underlying partisan distribution of the vote. In congressional elections the 'normal' Democratic majority reasserted itself. But for a Republican president to confront Democratic majorities in at least one chamber is not an abnormal condition; it has applied for roughly half of the postwar period. It would almost be fair to say that the conjunction of a Republican president and a Democratic Congress represents a 'standing decision' on the part of the electorate. Rarely in the postwar years has either party controlled the White House and enjoyed a sufficient majority in both houses of Congress to overcome the inertia, the obstacles to action, built into the system and to compensate for the presence of dissident minorities within their own ranks. Thus the dynamics of American politics make it difficult either significantly to extend or contract the New Deal.

Kennedy and Johnson

By 1960 the politics of equipoise embodied by the benign figure of Dwight D. Eisenhower was beginning to lose its charms. A modest, but still uncomfortable, recession during the late 1950s seemed to demand a more vigorous response than Ike was prepared to offer. The disciples of Keynes, who included most liberals, favoured the application of reflationary measures, particularly in the form of a generous tax-cut. The problem of civil rights, of racial injustice, was beginning to imprint itself on the nation's conscience. Above all, Americans were becoming concerned that in its competition with the Soviet Union for world supremacy the United States was losing ground. The successful launching of the space satellite Sputnik in 1957 seemed to indicate that the nation had relinquished the technological supremacy which it had taken for granted. More seriously, it cast doubt on the intrinsic superiority of American institutions. Many leading Americans complained of a loss of 'National Purpose' and an absence of strong leadership. They began to call for urgent action to improve educational standards, to address social problems and to restore the nation's vigour and self-belief.

John F. Kennedy in 1960 promised to 'get America moving again'. Though physically frail, he cultivated an image of youthful activism and vigour, quite unlike that of the elderly Ike. Kennedy represented a younger generation of Americans, 'the best and the brightest', which now assumed control of the nation's destiny. Highly telegenic, he was the first president of the television age, the first really to master the peculiar qualities of the medium, and possessed not so much a traditional political charisma as a 'star quality', a glamour and a cool, self-mocking charm that was very much of the modern era. His victory was one for political style and highly effective political organisation, rather than political substance. Kennedy offered the nation a change in approach, rather than a change in direction. Moderate and cautious in his political views, he was more pragmatist than idealist, but he inspired a generation with hope and, in his tragic death, transcended the limitations of worldly politics, leaving friends and admirers to construct a narrative of noble intentions and unfulfilled promise. Yet, in inspiring so many hopes and expectations, Kennedy contributed to the disenchantment that was to follow.

Preoccupied with foreign policy, Kennedy barely mentioned domestic issues in his inaugural address. His major economic proposal was a massive tax-cut, a purely reflationary measure that had no significant structural consequences, and, apart from proposing an increase in the minimum wage and raising a brief storm over steel prices, he did little to antagonise the business community. Towards the end of his life he was, as we shall see, drawn to support civil rights legislation. Shocked by conditions in Appalachia while campaigning for the White House, Kennedy supported various anti-poverty programmes which laid the groundwork for the later War on Poverty, but he was unable to get more than a few limited proposals past Congress before his assassination, including aid to depressed areas, an increased minimum wage, housing legislation and job training.

Lyndon B. Johnson, Kennedy's successor, was, in contrast, a crude, arrogant, overbearing figure. Deeply insecure, he yearned for approval and was desperately eager to make a record for himself, down to an almost obsessive score-keeping of bills proposed and laws passed. In his 'striving for hyperaccomplishment', as Alonzo Hamby puts it, he simply tried to do too much.[3] Johnson's project was to continue the work of Franklin Roosevelt, under whose tutelage his political career had begun, and construct a 'second New Deal' which would complete the work of the first and, indeed, go further by raising up the underprivileged, those at the very bottom whom the original New Deal had hardly touched, and tackling problems of racial discrimination which the original New Deal had ignored. His goal, says biographer Paul Conkin, was 'to perfect every institution, to solve all pressing problems, to eliminate glaring inequalities and injustices, to realize the old, even if opaque, dream of equal opportunity for all'. He was confident that 'no

3. Alonzo Hamby, *Liberalism and Its Challengers: From F.D.R. to Bush* (New York, 1992), p. 231.

problem, in principle, was uncorrectable, given time and enough effort'.[4] Johnson promised to build a 'Great Society' free from poverty, illiteracy and discrimination which would be fit to lead the world – and glorify the name of LBJ. This would be his legacy: to raise the underprivileged and remove poverty once and for all from the land.

It seemed for a while as if conditions were highly propitious for the execution of Johnson's project. Johnson himself was a master politician. Having spent most of his adult life on Capitol Hill, as congressional assistant, then as congressman and senator, and finally as Democratic leader in the Senate, he had acquired an acute understanding of the procedures and habits of Congress and the personal foibles of congressmen. He was on familiar personal terms with most of the leading figures in both parties, including the Republican Senate leader Everett Dirksen, with whom he shared a regular glass of bourbon. Many members remained in his debt from his time as Majority Leader; others were won over by promises of patronage or other favours. All were subjected to the 'Treatment', as described by Rowland Evans and Robert Novak:

> It came enveloping its target. … Its tone could be supplication, accusation, cajolery, exuberance, scorn, tears, complaint, the hint of threat. It was all of these together. It ran the gamut of human emotions. Its velocity was breathtaking, and it was all in one direction. Interjections from the target were rare. Johnson anticipated them before they could be spoken. He moved in close, his face a scant millimeter from the target, his eyes widening and narrowing, his eyebrows rising and falling. … Mimicry, humor, and the genius of analogy made the Treatment an almost hypnotic experience and rendered the target stunned and helpless.[5]

Individual legislators found the force of the Johnson personality, backed by the resources of the White House, hard to resist.

The political situation was also favourable. Enactment of the Kennedy programme seemed to be a necessary tribute to the assassinated president, while a buoyant economy encouraged the belief that the costs of reform could easily be borne. After the 1964 election, Johnson was blessed with overwhelming Democratic majorities in Congress. The right-winger Barry Goldwater who captured the Republican nomination gave the electorate the

4. Paul Conkin, *Big Daddy from the Pedernales: Lyndon Baines Johnson* (Boston, 1986), pp. 189, 193.
5. Rowland Evans and Robert Novak, *Lyndon B. Johnson: The Exercise of Power* (London, 1967), p. 104.

impression that he would start a Third World War, send American troops to Vietnam, launch a full-scale attack on Cuba, repeal the progressive income tax, sell off TVA, dismantle social security and block the progress of civil rights. For the 1960s (although it is remarkable how many of his ideas would later look like mainstream Republicanism) he was right off the political map. Johnson was therefore comfortably re-elected. Along with the huge majority in the presidential election (though not huge enough to please Johnson, who was aggrieved that anybody should vote against him), his party won majorities in Congress sufficient to break the congressional log-jam. For example, it commanded the two-thirds majority in the Senate which would enable passage of a motion to close debate in the face of delaying tactics by a determined minority. For the first time since the mid-1930s, one party held the presidency and sufficient majorities in both houses of Congress to get most of its programme through. This was a rare window of opportunity which Johnson, all too aware how rapidly his political credit could be expended, was determined to exploit.

The legislation of 1964–66 reflected both the unusual receptivity of Congress and the magnitude of Johnson's ambitions. It included the Civil Rights and Voting Rights Acts, the Economic Opportunity Act which formed the statutory basis of the War on Poverty, economic development of the Appalachian region, funds for slum clearance and mass-transit programmes, the Model Cities programme, federal aid for education, increases in farm subsidies, a higher minimum wage and the long-promised tax-cut. Congress enacted wide-ranging consumer and environmental protection laws that initiated a new 'social regulation' of business, motivated by public interest considerations, rather than the reconciliation of private interests, as in the past. In his eagerness to make a record, Johnson avoided confrontation by incorporating as many proposals and placating as many interest groups as possible. But, in trying to do everything and in refusing to order his priorities, he committed his Administration to an unwieldy and unmanageable legislative programme that eventually fell under its own weight. In particular, as we shall see, the civil rights and anti-poverty programmes raised expectations that they could not fulfil. The political fallout jeopardised both the Administration and the future of postwar liberalism.

In the end, Johnson turned out to be a tragic figure. His determination to carry all before him in Vietnam – not to yield, not to be the first American president to lose a war – brought him to disaster. He was deeply hurt by the character of the opposition to the war, and this contributed to his decision, after the Tet Offensive of February 1968, not to seek re-election.

Two significant features of American liberalism in the 1960s, building on the New Deal tradition, contributed to its special character and played a part in the frustration and discrediting of liberalism that was to come. One was a confidence in the solubility of the major problems in American society. Liberals retained a faith in the productive capacity of American corporate capitalism and in the essential verities of the American social and political system. They believed that problems such as poverty and racial discrimination were not structural problems arising out of the fundamental nature of American society, but anomalies which could be eradicated by a measure of fine-tuning. The enormous surplus wealth created by postwar American capitalism would ensure that their correction need not be a zero-sum game. The anticipated economic growth, engineered by the sophisticated application of Keynesian tools of demand management, would provide the resources for wide-ranging social programmes designed to eradicate poverty and equalise opportunity, so that the life-chances of the disadvantaged need not be improved at the expense of other elements of the population.

Liberals were confident also that the expertise and scientific knowledge at the disposal of modern government would contribute to the finding of solutions. By investing resources in systematic research to analyse social problems and design appropriate programmes, the errors of the past would be avoided. Liberal reform was essentially elitist in character. For all their faith in democracy, for all their eagerness to help the underprivileged, liberals expected reform to work from the top down. The experts would construct and administer programmes on behalf of the underprivileged. Thus the 1960s, like the 1930s, was a period in which university experts poured into Washington to advise the government, in which the worlds of academic research and policy-making intersected. Academics and policy intellectuals staffed the innumerable study groups and task forces that Kennedy and Johnson delegated to study almost every conceivable problem and to prepare the hundreds of bills that eventually went to make up the Great Society. Liberal administrations maintained a close, though often quarrelsome, relationship with the intellectual and academic communities, which provided them with much of their natural constituency. This close, sometimes incestuous, relationship was to prove one of liberalism's Achilles' heels.

Whereas New Deal liberalism had rested on the support of powerful economic interest groups and a mass popular vote, bound to the Democratic Party by ties of self-interest as well as belief, the liberalism of the 1960s was to a greater degree motivated by a sense of moral obligation, a desire to help the helpless and protect the politically powerless, to seek out social problems and solve them, regardless of political calculation. Its adherents were not the traditional Democratic interest groups, like the unions, most of which showed faint interest in the programmes of the Great Society, but a 'New Class' of radical intellectuals, well-educated and well-heeled, located in the media, the universities, the policy institutes and the welfare bureaucracy, and detached from any particular economic or social interest. Their spokesmen were leaders like Eugene McCarthy, George McGovern and Gary Hart who, for a while, wielded great power in the counsels of the Democratic Party, at the expense of old-style organisation politicians. This had the effect, not only of weakening the organisational structure of the party, but also of alienating many of its traditional supporters.

Civil rights

In his celebrated 'I have a dream' speech, which expresses much of the spirit of the civil rights movement in its classic phase, Martin Luther King was at pains to locate the demands of African-Americans within the mainstream of American political culture. His was a dream that was 'deeply rooted in the American dream'. He asked for no more than equal treatment under law and equal access to opportunity. King did not challenge mainstream American values; he merely asked that they be applied equally to African-Americans. His call for 'freedom' purposefully aligns the civil rights movement with the emancipation of the slaves a century earlier, an emancipation that turned out to be only partial, asking that the 'promissory note' given then should be redeemed now, so that his people might be 'free at last'.[6] In some ways, however, this was a dangerously misleading metaphor to apply to the problem of racial injustice in twentieth-century America. It glossed over the problematic nature of the concept of civil rights, especially when

6. Martin Luther King, 'I have a dream', in Richard Hofstadter, ed., *Great Issues in American History: From Reconstruction to the Present, 1865–1969* (New York, 1969), pp. 485–8.

applied to a section of the population whose status was determined not only by legal discrimination but also by a pervasive structure of economic disadvantage and social deprivation. This made civil rights an exceedingly thorny field for government action.

The 'Second Reconstruction' was made necessary by the failure of the first. After the Civil War the Constitution had been amended to guarantee full legal and political equality for black Americans. The Fourteenth Amendment demanded equal treatment in law for all citizens of the United States, while the Fifteenth Amendment stated that they could not be denied the right to vote on the grounds of 'race, color, or previous condition of servitude'. These amendments had important implications for the role of the federal government. They laid out certain rights that followed from American citizenship and placed an obligation on the federal government to enforce those rights. In practice, the federal government failed to meet that obligation, at least until the second half of the twentieth century. Southern states were permitted to disfranchise black voters by setting certain non-racial criteria for voting, such as literacy tests or poll taxes, which had the effect of disqualifying most blacks, thereby contravening the spirit, if not the letter, of the Fifteenth Amendment. They were allowed to enact the so-called Jim Crow laws, which segregated almost all public facilities, including not only schools, restaurants and railroad cars but also telephone booths, water fountains and cemeteries. In the absence of slavery, segregation served as a new way of ordering race relations and maintaining white supremacy. In *Plessy* v. *Ferguson* (1896), the Supreme Court sanctioned the principle of segregation, asserting that 'separate but equal' facilities were not discriminatory within the meaning of the Fourteenth Amendment. For half a century or more the fiction of 'separate but equal' served as justification for Jim Crow, even though, in practice, the facilities provided for black and white, while always separate, were hardly ever equal.

African-Americans, then, were very much second-class citizens with distinctly limited social opportunities. Legal discrimination was only the tip of an iceberg of social and economic deprivation. Most Southern blacks continued to work the land as tenants, share-croppers or labourers, trapped in conditions of the direst poverty. During the twentieth century, drawn by the attractions of higher wages and shaken loose from the land by the transformation of Southern agriculture that began in the 1930s, millions abandoned the cotton-fields of the South for the factories of the North. By 1967 half the black population lived outside the South. In the cities of the North, although there were no Jim Crow laws, African-Americans encountered an informal pattern of segregation and discrimination different from, but equivalent to, that which operated in the South. Consistently barred from prestigious, well-paid employment, African-Americans were confined to a limited range of low manual occupations, which in the mid-twentieth century typically accommodated over three-quarters of all black workers. Prevented by restrictive covenants, discrimination on the part of real estate and savings and loan companies, and the overt, sometimes violent, hostility of white residents from securing accommodation outside certain clearly defined neighbourhoods, like Harlem or the so-called 'Black Belt' on the South Side of Chicago, African-Americans inhabited tightly packed inner-city ghettos, highly segregated and racially homogeneous. The ghetto stood as a clear demonstration of how institutional racism shaped the lives of African-Americans, in the city as on the plantation.

Truman was the first twentieth-century president seriously to address the cause of civil rights. He asked Congress for civil rights legislation which would ban the poll tax, prohibit segregation in interstate transport and give legislative sanction to the Fair Employment Practices Commission (FEPC) set up by Roosevelt in 1941 to monitor discrimination in war industries. For reasons of military efficiency as much as racial justice, he also ordered the desegregation of the armed forces. Although Truman had shown up to that point no prior sympathy for the cause, a number of factors combined to place civil rights fairly and squarely on the political agenda.

At this critical juncture in American history domestic racism proved a continuing embarrassment in the conduct of foreign policy. During the Second World War and then the Cold War the United States claimed to be fighting on behalf of certain democratic ideals, certain values of fairness and equality which were clearly at odds with the pervasive practice of racism in the United States. It is evident from the results of opinion polls after the Second World War that, outside the South at least, the racist beliefs that had pervaded early twentieth-century American culture were losing some of their hold. That is not to say that prejudice had been eliminated entirely from American life – it clearly had not – but that racist views had lost some of their cultural hegemony, leaving the institutional structure of racism more vulnerable to attack. Most compelling was the growing influence of the black vote. As African-Americans moved north they acquired the right to vote, and by locating themselves in populous states like New York, Pennsylvania, Michigan and Illinois they acquired additional leverage. Because these states carried large blocks of electoral college votes and because they were closely contested, the black vote acquired great strategic importance, weighing heavier in the balance than the whole of the white South, which remained solidly Democratic. The curious, and highly propitious, mathematics of presidential politics did not, of course, apply to Congress, where Southern votes punched above their numerical weight. This meant that presidents, from Truman to Carter, tended to be more responsive to civil rights than Congress.

One branch of government with particular freedom of action was the Supreme Court. For years the National Association for the Advancement of Colored People (NAACP), the premier civil rights organisation, had mounted a series of legal challenges to test the constitutionality of Jim Crow. From the 1930s it began to win favourable decisions against Southern voting laws, restrictive covenants (agreements by the purchasers of property not to sell to members of specified minority groups), segregation in interstate transport and school segregation. Remember that the composition of the Supreme Court had been transformed by Roosevelt's appointments during the late 1930s and early 1940s. The Roosevelt Court, while more restrained than its predecessors in adjudicating questions of economic policy, was far more interventionist in its defence of individual liberties. In doing so, it transformed the nature of the American Constitution from a set of negative restraints on government action to a positive set of commitments to human rights. This interventionist, law-making tendency aroused the ire of conservatives as surely as the disposition of an earlier set of justices had enraged liberals.

In the most important of these decisions, *Brown* v. *Board of Education* (1954), the Court reversed *Plessy* v. *Ferguson* by declaring that 'separate but equal' educational facilities were, in effect, 'inherently unequal' because they 'generated a feeling of inequality' among black pupils.[7] School segregation therefore contravened the Fourteenth Amendment, and so, by implication, did the whole Jim Crow system. In a later decision the Court required that desegregation be carried out 'with all deliberate speed'. However, in the face of 'massive resistance' by Southern school districts, which resorted to all manner of expedients to forestall de-

7. Henry S. Commager, ed., *The Struggle for Racial Equality: A Documentary Record* (New York, 1967), pp. 49–54.

segregation, in some cases closing schools rather than integrating them, Eisenhower took no steps to enforce a decision of which he made it clear he did not approve. Only in the face of actual violence, as at Little Rock, Arkansas, did he send federal troops to enforce integration. As late as 1961 only 7 per cent of Southern black children were attending integrated schools.

Disenchanted with the fruits of the NAACP's legal strategy, newer civil rights organisations like the Southern Christian Leadership Conference (SCLC) and the Student Nonviolent Coordinating Committee (SNCC) and the older Congress of Racial Equality (CORE) turned to 'mass action' by blacks themselves to challenge the Jim Crow system. The leading figure in this phase of the civil rights movement was Martin Luther King. King articulated a strategy of 'non-violent direct action', that is passive resistance: 'One who breaks an unjust law must do so openly, lovingly and with a willingness to accept the penalty. I submit that an individual who breaks a law that conscience tells him is unjust, and who willingly accepts the penalty by staying in jail in order to arouse the conscience of the community over its injustice, is in reality expressing the highest respect for law.'[8] By their redemptive suffering blacks would change the hearts and minds of their oppressors and bring about changes in the law. Such a strategy was clearly modelled on that of Gandhi, although it also had precedents in the American labour movement and, more immediately, in the traditions of Southern black Christianity. Its appeal was that it offered a strategy for converting rage and frustration into a form of practical action that was consistent with the Christian tradition in which Southern blacks had been raised.

Such methods of non-violent resistance were successfully employed in the Montgomery bus boycott of 1955–56; the student 'sit-ins' at lunch-counters and other segregated facilities during 1960, which gave renewed impetus to the whole civil rights movement; the 'freedom rides' of 1961 in which groups of black and white protesters challenged segregation at bus terminals in the Deep South; the voter-registration drives of the early 1960s; and the demonstrations against segregation and job discrimination organised in cities like Birmingham and Selma, Alabama. In each case blacks took direct action against the Southern caste system. In each case they met with arrests, often violence, from law-enforcement agencies and white mobs – violence which was carried

8. Martin Luther King, 'Letter from Birmingham Jail', in ibid., p. 152.

out not only in the presence of newspaper reporters but television cameras. National television audiences were presented with images of a burning bus, a burning church, the arrest of schoolchildren, water cannons and police dogs turned on unresisting demonstrators. Like the Vietnam War, these events produced a series of searing images which burned themselves on to the national conscience. There is no doubt that the media played a crucial role in bringing a national public face-to-face with racism in its ugliest form – not the polite forms of racial exclusion practised by middle-class Northern whites but blatant and violent prejudice. By such means the public conscience was aroused and pressure placed upon federal officials. By such means federal officials were compelled to act to avoid the embarrassment of further such scenes being enacted before a national, not to mention an international, audience. This, then, was how non-violent action worked: not by influencing the hearts and minds of Southern whites, but by influencing the hearts and minds of Northern whites. Nor was it, in the fullest sense, non-violent. It involved, indeed required, acts of violence to achieve its desired effect – not by black protesters, of course, but by racist whites. It involved a deliberate orchestration of violence, which became more deliberate as time went on. King was well aware of how the strategy worked. So was James Farmer, the director of CORE. As he explained, 'We planned the Freedom Ride with the specific intention of creating a crisis. We were counting on the bigots of the South to do our work for us. We figured that the government would have to respond if we created a situation that was headline news all over the world, and affected the nation's image abroad. An international crisis, that was our strategy.'[9] The whole point of the exercise was to create incidents that would embarrass the federal government into taking the desired action.

John F. Kennedy was another late convert to civil rights. Having shown little interest in the subject before he became a presidential candidate, Kennedy realised that he would need the black vote to secure victory (as, indeed, in a closely fought election, turned out to be the case). But he also realised that he would need Southern votes in Congress to get his legislative programme through. To a tough-minded pragmatist like Kennedy, it appeared senseless to expend political capital in pursuit of unattainable goals. His strategy was to seek, in Harris Wofford's words, 'a minimum of civil rights

---

9. Irving Bernstein, *Promises Kept: John F. Kennedy's New Frontier* (New York, 1991), p. 63.

legislation and a maximum of executive action'.[10] Therefore he made a few conspicuous appointments of African-Americans. He set up an Equal Employment Opportunity Committee (EEOC) to monitor employment practices, a descendent of Roosevelt's FEPC which, like its predecessor, in the absence of legislative approval, had limited powers. Although in theory it could recommend the cancellation of federal contracts with companies that practised racial discrimination, it was reluctant to test its flimsy legal powers in the courts, preferring to proceed through negotiation and compromise, in the form of agreed 'Plans for Progress', which, however, had little discernible effect on minority-group employment in the companies concerned. Kennedy ordered the integration of all housing projects dependent on federal funds, including the large number of private homes financed with the help of the Federal Housing Administration. This, too, had little impact. The FHA, deeply committed to racially segregated housing patterns, simply declined to put it into effect. Finally, the Justice Department, under the urgent leadership of the president's brother Robert Kennedy, brought actions for violation of voting-registration laws, but, under existing legislation, which necessitated a case-by-case approach, progress was painfully slow.

Kennedy had no strong personal commitment to civil rights. Underestimating the moral imperative of racial equality and the radical zeal of the civil rights movement, he tended to look upon King and his colleagues as troublemakers and extremists (especially when systematically misinformed by J. Edgar Hoover and the FBI). But he could not avoid responding to the dramatic and vivid racial confrontations in the South. He could not ignore the state of public opinion, evident in opinion polls which showed 63 per cent approval for a civil rights bill similar to that which he eventually introduced; the prospect of losing the votes of blacks and liberals, much more damaging than the probable leakage of Southern white votes to a conservative Republican candidate in 1964; and the threat of black radicalism, evident for a few days on the streets of Birmingham, where an uncontrolled outbreak of rioting followed the carefully controlled demonstrations organised by the SCLC. Kennedy's efforts to straddle the issue – to promote integration without disturbing the political equilibrium, to appease militant blacks without alienating the white South – had, under the pressure of persistent and insistent civil rights agitation, transparently failed.

10. Ibid., p. 48.

As Burke Marshall explained, the president was anxious 'to deal with what was clearly an explosion in the racial problem that could not, would not go away'.[11] Otherwise, he would forfeit any claim to leadership on the issue.

Therefore, in July 1963, Kennedy finally called publicly for civil rights legislation. As he had feared, Southern Democrats were able, by filibustering, to block the bill's progress. However, it was passed after his assassination as a result of the superior legislative skills of his successor, Lyndon B. Johnson, who was, for a Southerner, more positive in his commitment to civil rights than Kennedy. To Johnson the issue offered an opportunity to prove his liberal credentials and his fitness to succeed the martyred Kennedy. The Civil Rights Act of 1964 required equal access to all public accommodations; authorised the Attorney-General to institute suits enforcing the desegregation of schools; prohibited discrimination in any programme that received federal assistance, which placed powerful financial incentives behind the drive for integration; and gave the EEOC statutory powers to prevent discrimination in employment on the basis of race and, as a result of an amendment mischievously thrown into the hopper by a conservative Southerner, on the basis of sex also. The following year, in the wake of the racial disturbances at Selma, Johnson secured passage of a Voting Rights Act, which strengthened national control over elections by authorising federal officials to keep a register of electors, and banned the devices like the poll tax and the literacy test by means of which Southern states had for three-quarters of a century kept black voters away from the polls. Three years later, against a backcloth of recurrent race riots, particularly following the assassination of Martin Luther King, Congress passed a Fair Housing Act which outlawed discrimination in private housing markets.

Together these measures constituted a major victory for the civil rights movement. By abolishing the Jim Crow system, they brought about a massive change in the conduct of Southern race relations. Schools and other facilities were integrated within a fairly short period of time, and blacks could soon vote freely in every state of the former Confederacy, dramatically changing the atmosphere of Southern politics. It seemed, on the face of it, that the descendants of the slaves were 'free at last'.

By what seemed like a bitter irony of fate, the triumphant climax of the civil rights movement coincided with the onset of race riots

11. Ibid., p. 101.

in the ghettos of the North. In 1965, with the ink hardly dry on the Voting Rights Act, a riot broke out in Watts, a black suburb of Los Angeles, at the end of which thirty-four lives had been lost and $40 million dollars worth of property destroyed. The years 1964–68 saw 400 serious racial disturbances. Though usually occasioned by clashes between ghetto inhabitants and the police, the riots provided evidence of the discontentment of ghetto blacks and their deep frustration at the failure of alternative methods of expressing their grievances. As Nicholas Lemann reminds us, in discussions of public policy during the early 1960s, 'the idea that an important national problem was brewing in the black slums of the Northern and Western cities was not at all a part of the conventional wisdom'. The very notion 'caused the whole consensual vision of American society to crumble'.[12] The civil rights movement, after all, made little difference to the prospects of ghetto blacks. The poverty, the social deprivation, the restricted opportunities that framed their lives were hardly alleviated. As John F. Kennedy explained in his civil rights address of June 1963:

> The Negro baby born in America today ... has about half as much chance of completing a high school as a white baby ... one-third as much chance of completing college; one-third as much chance of becoming a professional man; twice as much chance of becoming unemployed; about one-seventh as much chance of earning $10,000 a year; a life expectancy which is seven years shorter; and the prospects of earning only half as much.[13]

Yet Northern blacks were not disfranchised, nor segregated by law. They faced not public but private discrimination, which was much harder to eradicate by government action.

The Civil Rights Act contained a fair employment clause, as did many parallel state statutes. But these were notoriously difficult to enforce, in view of the many considerations that influenced the selection and promotion of employees, especially in smaller firms. In 1971 the Supreme Court pronounced 'neutral' tests of suitability for employment to be invalid unless they took account of past discrimination. A quota might be set, as in the so-called 'Philadelphia Plan' applied to the construction industry, but, in view of the likely shortage of qualified minority-group applicants, for historic reasons, filling the quota would require the exercise of 'positive

12. Nicholas Lemann, *Promised Land: The Great Migration and How It Changed America* (New York, 1991), p. 117
13. Commager, ed., *The Struggle for Racial Equality*, pp. 164–5.

discrimination' on their behalf. Such policies, not surprisingly, were deeply objectionable to other groups in the population.

It was similarly difficult to police the private housing market, to monitor the millions of private deals between buyer and seller, buyers and real estate agents, buyers and lenders. The Fair Housing Act, until its amendment in 1989, provided no effective mechanism for enforcement, leaving it to private individuals to bring suit, which was beyond the means of most victims of discrimination. Later studies showed discrimination to be pervasive, with realtors carefully 'steering' black customers away from white neighbourhoods and savings and loan associations refusing finance. Even if it was sometimes possible to open white neighbourhoods to minority-group families, it was impossible to prevent white families, or at least the more affluent white families, from moving away – the phenomenon known as 'white flight' – especially as the process was expedited by the provision of finance on generous terms by federal agencies like the Federal Housing Administration. How was integration possible if whites just kept running away? Their persistence in doing so betrayed a profound lack of enthusiasm for racial integration in so far as it impinged on their own neighbourhoods.

Northern schools were not formally segregated by law, but the persistence of residential segregation made for a pervasive pattern of informal segregation. The principle of neighbourhood schooling meant that ghetto schools were overwhelmingly black. Indeed, by 1970 schools in Boston, a city which prided itself on its liberal tradition, were more segregated than those in the South, where desegregation was well under way. The Supreme Court decided in a number of cases after 1968 that segregation violated the Constitution even where it was not mandated by law but was produced by social and economic factors, as was the case in much of the urban North. Federal courts in some cities ordered the 'busing' of white children to black schools and *vice versa*. Busing, which was condemned as an assault upon community institutions and local democracy, formed the basis for a number of vituperative and divisive local battles.

These forms of 'affirmative action' aroused the opposition of many Northern whites because they impinged directly on their lives, by, for example, busing their children to ghetto schools, introducing black families to their neighbourhoods or giving preference to blacks in job applications or college entry. This made a really effective attack on racial discrimination and black poverty politically impossible. Most Northern whites, according to opinion polls, continued to approve of the goals of housing integration and school integration but resented what they saw as the extreme measures used to achieve them. They were angered by the behaviour and the violent tone of the Black Power movement and by the actions of urban rioters, made all the more menacing by their proximity to working-class white neighbourhoods. The onset of rioting brought about a precipitous drop in white approval for the civil rights movement. Whereas in 1964 only 34 per cent of Americans believed that blacks were asking for too much, by 1966 the proportion had leapt to 85 per cent. The resultant 'white backlash' was an increasingly potent force in electoral politics. Federal policy dealt effectively with the morally unambiguous and politically isolated target of Southern racism, which was expressed in a form of statutory discrimination that was clearly at odds with the Fourteenth and Fifteenth Amendments. Despite the political leverage of Southern congressmen, this was a relatively easy target. It dealt much less effectively with the subtler forms of extra-legal discrimination practised in the North (and also in the South) and with the cumulative effects of black poverty.

The period during which race was a dominant issue in domestic politics had passed by the early 1970s. Richard Nixon believed that race relations would benefit from 'a period of benign neglect' on racial issues, which in most cases meant an easing of pressure against discrimination. Wedded to the promotion of a 'Southern strategy' as a road to electoral success for the Republican Party, he favoured caution on the issue of school desegregation, took a firm stand against busing and did nothing to improve enforcement of the laws against discrimination in housing and employment. His judicial appointments began a transformation of the Supreme Court that would in time replace the liberalism of the Warren Court with a much less interventionist spirit. As in other aspects of policy, however, the Nixon years saw not so much a reversal as a lessening of the reformist drives of the 1960s. Ronald Reagan was far more emphatic in his dislike of civil rights enforcement. He called for an effective moratorium on racially sensitive programmes, and agencies involved in affirmative action programmes were among the targets of his spending cuts, which also hit those urban and poverty programmes which especially benefited inner-city blacks.

Since the 1960s many African-Americans have enjoyed the fruits of the 'civil rights revolution'. The gap between whites and blacks in educational attainment, according to such indicators as years of schooling and proportions in higher education, has narrowed. White-collar jobs, especially in government service, have opened up for qualified black applicants, who are now able to enjoy standards of comfort and social opportunities unimaginable to their parents. But the ghetto remains. The reforms of the 1960s did little to transform the nature of ghetto existence. Indeed, since the 1960s, those conditions have deteriorated. Recession and the decline in blue-collar employment have, as always, hit blacks especially hard. Rates of unemployment for African-American males reached stratospheric levels, as did the incidence of one-parent families. Many of the inhabitants of the inner city appear to be trapped in a vicious circle of poverty and unemployment, family breakdown, delinquency and drug abuse, while the public and private agencies fighting against such forces have become seriously debilitated. The conjunction of residential segregation, neighbourhood deterioration and a lack of employment opportunity have created new forms of concentrated poverty and deprivation that have frightening implications for the future of American cities. Contemporary discussion of the 'underclass' reflects the desperation of those who seek to understand and remedy the situation.

The War on Poverty

Among the 'unfinished and neglected tasks' facing the nation was the alleviation of poverty. It was not that there was any more poverty in the 1960s, or that there was any measurable increase in public sympathy towards the poor, or that anti-poverty programmes were likely to attract votes, or that well-organised social movements were committed to its eradication. Obviously, the civil rights movement generated an interest in black poverty. Policy-makers were becoming aware by the mid-1960s that the removal of legal obstacles was insufficient in itself to equalise the opportunities and life-chances of African-Americans. For a while, an attack on poverty sold itself as a way of buying off ghetto unrest. Although conscious efforts were made, by drawing attention to the harrowing effects of white poverty in places like Appalachia, to disconnect the issues of poverty and race, it was apparent that, for many of its commanding officers, the War on Poverty commended itself as an attempt to address the appalling social problems of the black ghetto. Nevertheless, for most of the founding fathers of the anti-poverty programme the racial problem was not uppermost. In the last analysis, liberals believed, like J.K. Galbraith, that Americans were wealthy enough to eliminate poverty and that therefore they were under a moral obligation to do so. 'Having the power', said Johnson, 'we have the duty.'

Without the interest of Kennedy and, to a much greater degree, Johnson, the War on Poverty would never have been declared. It was Johnson's eagerness to confound liberal suspicions that led him to seize upon the sketchy pilot programmes that had been incubated under the Kennedy Administration and convert them into a much larger, more comprehensive and more ambitious programme. This was to be a project that would surpass his predecessor's achievements. It would form the 'centerpiece of his administration' and his main claim to historical recognition. Johnson aspired to be no less than the 'patron to all lowly Americans', the bringer of hope and opportunity to the humble and down-trodden.[14]

Therefore, Johnson in 1964 formally declared 'unconditional war on poverty'.[15] This largely involved extensions of existing social security and welfare programmes. As we have seen, total federal spending on the poor doubled between 1960 and 1974. Huge sums went to urban renewal and public housing projects, while federal aid to education, from nursery schools to universities, was expanded enormously. However, the foundation charter of the War on Poverty was the Economic Opportunity Act of 1964, an omnibus bill which incorporated a remarkably diverse collection of anti-poverty programmes, including job training, the Job Corps (a distant echo of New Deal public works programmes), loan and assistance programmes for small businesses, the Head Start scheme to furnish nursery education for socially deprived children, Upward Bound to improve their access to higher education, and the controversial Community Action Program (CAP). Too many programmes were implemented in far too hasty a fashion, with sometimes disastrous results.

The Community Action Program was only part of the whole anti-poverty package, but by its explosive political impact it coloured public reaction to the whole enterprise. The CAP originated in a commendable effort to involve local communities in the programmes designed to assist them. But precisely what that

14. Conkin, *Big Daddy from the Pedernales*, p. 220.
15. David Zarefsky, *Lyndon Johnson's War on Poverty: Rhetoric and History* (University, Ala., 1986), p. 21.

entailed was unclear. Although the law's authors probably envisaged the CAP as no more than a mechanism for channelling resources and services to communities and coordinating the various anti-poverty programmes, the stated goal of 'maximum feasible participation' suggested a wider involvement on the part of poor people themselves. Some of the intellectual progenitors of the War on Poverty, like the sociologists Lloyd Ohlin and Richard Cloward or the social activist Richard Boone, hoped that the CAP might serve to restore a sense of competence to disorganised local communities. Poor people, by organising, would be able more effectively to articulate their own demands and take control of their own lives. Poverty, Boone believed, was essentially a condition of powerlessness, and this the CAP was designed to remedy. The mobilisation of the poor was likely to mean the radicalisation of the poor. Especially where black militants and radicals like Saul Alinsky took control, local Community Action Agencies gave the poor an opportunity to express their grievances. They fought for better schools and more generous administration of welfare, against urban renewal projects that threatened their neighbourhoods and against police brutality. In such localities they challenged the authority of the institutions of local government – police, education and social welfare departments, highway authorities – and engaged in angry confrontations with the local political establishment. More generally, programmes were organised to ensure that the poor would not have much real influence, as against the middle-class professionals and local politicians who in most cases took charge. At the urging of powerful political chieftains, the rules were changed so as to disable the more radical forms of community organising. The CAP gave an impression of a more radical programme than actually existed and, in doing so, helped fuel a political backlash against the anti-poverty policy.

Nevertheless, the Community Action Program was not without effect. The services associated with the programme were beneficial in themselves, including neighbourhood health centres and legal services, which greatly assisted poor people in their struggles with the educational and welfare bureaucracies, enabling them to secure entitlements that they had previously been denied. In the broadest sense, the CAP, for all its inadequacies, did something to stimulate grass-roots political activity among the poor, one immediate off-shoot of which was the establishment of a National Welfare Rights Organization which continued to campaign on behalf of welfare recipients. Ironically, the most important outcome of a project designed to bypass traditional forms of poor relief was a massive enlargement of welfare programmes.

The job training programmes proved to be highly costly in relation to the benefits gained. The Job Corps, which with the CAP was one of the two spearheads of the War on Poverty, was supposed to remove ghetto youths from their slum environments and expose them to skills training and work experience that would enhance both their self-respect and their employability. At an estimated per capita cost of $8,000 a year – sufficient, as critics pointed out, to put trainees through Harvard – the Job Corps provided only basic training which did little to boost their job prospects. Training, in any case, was futile without reasonable hope of worthwhile employment.

In fact, the anti-poverty programme as a whole was too conservative, too limited in conception, to do the job for which it was designed. Its authors assumed that structural change was unnecessary; what was required was a transformation of the values and behaviour of the poor themselves. Poverty, it was contended, was essentially a problem of attitude. One of the reasons why poverty was turning out to be so intractable a problem, persisting even during periods of relative affluence, was because a 'culture of poverty' had grown up – an adaptation to poverty, involving crime, juvenile delinquency, drug abuse, single parenthood, negative attitudes to work and education, and a hedonistic lifestyle – which, while it might help poor people to cope with their immediate circumstances, deterred them from acting constructively to improve their situation. They were trapped, it was believed, in a cycle of poverty. The task of government, said Johnson, was 'to break that cycle by raising the educational, skill, and health levels of the younger generation, increasing their job opportunities, and helping their families to provide a better home life'.[16] Government programmes should give the poor a degree of education and training and inculcate appropriate behavioural traits that would enable them to climb the ladder of opportunity. This was the point of job training, the Job Corps, Head Start and Upward Bound. What the anti-poverty programme offered, as the title of the enabling legislation suggested, was not welfare but opportunity: 'a hand up, not a hand-out'. Therefore Johnson vetoed proposals for income maintenance, which would establish a minimum standard of living and provide income supplements for families which fell below that

16. Ibid., p. 41.

standard. There would, he insisted, be 'no doles'. He was also hostile to job-creation schemes which would have provided real economic opportunity for the poor but which would have trodden on too many toes, upset too many interests and been far too expensive. Still less would the Administration accept that poverty was a product of structural deficiencies in American society requiring a more drastic redistribution of wealth and power. The War on Poverty, notes Allen Matusow, was to be a war without casualties. Perhaps for that reason, it was also to be a war without substantial victories.

Poverty appeared to be at least as intractable an enemy as the Viet Cong. The problem seemed too deeply rooted to respond to government programmes. Frustration with the lack of results brought disenchantment. By drastically overselling the programme, the Administration aroused expectations that could not possibly be met. But, as David Zarefsky points out, it was only by appealing to 'abstract, transcendental symbols', only by promising an absolute, rather than a partial, triumph, that liberal enthusiasm could be aroused for a campaign that had no powerful interest groups or voting blocs behind it. In the words of Harold Weismann, 'Great societies are first believed in, then made'.[17] Johnson had to promise the moon to get anything. Although the gains were not trivial, objectives were stated in terms that made victory in the last analysis unattainable. Moreover, the precipitate fashion in which programmes were designed and implemented, in order to seize a fleeting political opportunity, left no room for pilot projects, for a learning process that would have avoided some of the grosser errors and inefficiencies that brought the War on Poverty into disrepute. The resulting loss of faith extended not only to the immediate impact of the anti-poverty programme itself but also to the possibility of any such policy succeeding in the future. It became an article of faith among conservative social thinkers like Charles Murray, but also among some liberals, that the experience of the War on Poverty proved the impracticability of any such enterprise. Ronald Reagan claimed that 'In the 1960s we fought a war on poverty, and poverty won'.[18] In fact, this was not true. The government never committed enough resources to the anti-poverty programmes – never more than $1.7 billion a year, or 1 per cent of the federal budget – for them to bear significant fruit. Sadly, however, the experience was not built upon as a basis for future policy.

17. Ibid., p. 203.
18. Lemann, *Promised Land*, p. 200.

In fact, transfer payments to the poor were more effective than the programmes administered by the Office of Economic Opportunity in lifting people out of poverty. According to one estimate, the percentage of the population living in poverty fell from 19 per cent in 1964 to 12 per cent in 1974, and this, according to Jonathan Schwartz and Mark Stern, was substantially due to the impact of government transfer payments. In the last analysis, the most important contribution of the War on Poverty might well have been to confer legitimacy upon the grievances of the poor, opening the way to more effective programmes, such as food stamps or Medicaid. The 'welfare revolution' of the late 1960s and early 1970s was therefore an indirect consequence of the War on Poverty. The apparent failure of the service strategy embodied in the War on Poverty convinced many liberals, especially under pressure from black activists and with the smoke of the burning ghettos fresh in their nostrils, that the only way to raise people out of destitution was to give them more money. They became convinced that poverty, especially black poverty, was a consequence, not of individual deficiencies, but of imperfections in American society, and that therefore the poor were entitled to some form of income support.

Building on the pioneering activities of the New Deal, the federal government in the postwar era financed public housing projects designed to provide satisfactory low-cost housing for the inhabitants of the inner city. In 1949, 1954, 1961 and 1968 Congress appropriated substantial sums for public housing programmes – and larger sums to subsidise private house purchase. As in the 1930s, public housing projects met fierce opposition from real estate interests and conservative politicians. Middle-class resistance ensured that they would be located in the slums and that black projects would be located in the ghetto. Budgetary and other restraints limited the number of projects that could be undertaken. By 1970 only 893,000 units of public housing were in existence, sufficient to house no more than 4 per cent of families. So inadequate was the supply of low-cost housing that it became, in effect, a perquisite of the poorest, most disadvantaged families. Rather than accommodating a representative cross-section of the urban working class, the projects housed those with the severest social problems. They became, in effect, a 'warehouse' for problem families, with rates of unemployment, crime, delinquency and drug abuse far higher than in the surrounding private dwellings. Rather than allowing their residents to transcend the problems of the inner city, the projects rapidly became a quintessence of urban blight in themselves.

Indeed, the public housing projects of the postwar decades were offset by other urban programmes. Much more government money – federal, state and local – went on highway construction than on public housing, and each new highway required the condemnation of acres of residential accommodation, mostly in working-class neighbourhoods alongside older railway lines, rivers and industrial complexes. Between 1949 and 1961 urban renewal programmes destroyed 126,000 units of housing, displacing an estimated half-million people, and built a mere 28,000. In other words, the slums were being knocked down faster than they were being replaced. Still more federal money was absorbed by mortgage assistance programmes managed by the Federal Housing Administration and the Veterans' Administration, which went principally to finance the purchase of new, single-family dwellings in the suburbs, thereby accelerating the exodus of middle-class and better-paid working-class families, but mostly white families, to the suburbs. In contrast, many inner-city neighbourhoods, particularly those with large minority-group populations, were 'red-lined' and denied loans. Thus federal housing policy encouraged the flight of white middle-class families to the suburbs, discouraged renovation of the inner city and promoted segregation. Far from demonstrating the futility of urban policy, Arnold Hirsch argues, postwar experience has shown how effective it can be, albeit to the benefit of private corporations, real estate interests and middle-class home-owners rather than the inhabitants of the inner city.

The War on Poverty was another victim of the conservative 'backlash' of the late 1960s. Increasingly seen as catering primarily to the black ghettos, where the most conspicuous programmes were located, it was relatively unpopular among white voters, especially low-income white voters who resented paying taxes for the benefit of families which appeared little worse off than their own. It fell foul of public hostility to the poor blacks who were regarded as its major beneficiaries and the conservative attitudes to the poor expressed by majorities of respondents in opinion polls. The programme never really enjoyed popular support.

The Vietnam War diverted resources from the anti-poverty programme, especially as Johnson ruled out the possibility of a tax increase in order to finance both his obsessions for fear that it would open a debate in Congress on their relative priority, causing conservatives to demand savage cuts in social spending and liberals to complain of the impact of the war. His attempt to finance both 'guns and butter' in the budget for fiscal 1966 opened the door to the inflation which did as much as anything to alienate middle-income voters from liberal reform. More seriously, the Vietnam War divided the nation. The growing peace movement became more and more heated in its denunciation of LBJ and all his works. Instead of a friend of the poor and the oppressed, he was now presented as an evil, tyrannical monster, an ogre, a bringer of death and destruction. The anti-war movement embraced many liberals and radicals, the very people who Johnson would have expected to support his domestic policies. Many, like Robert Kennedy, broke with the Administration, forcing the president to rely on the support of conservatives, who loyally backed the war. Along with the ghetto riots, the war 'destroyed the mood of triumphant liberal comity' that had fuelled reform.[19] In the end, the Vietnam War disabled the Johnson Administration and went a long way to destroy the liberalism of the 1960s.

The election of 1968, which was scarred by assassinations, rioting and a great deal of bitterness, resulted in the election of Richard M. Nixon. Although it appeared both at the time and in retrospect to signify a dissolution of both the Democratic coalition and the anti-poverty movement, Nixon's accession to the presidency by no means marked a reversal in social policy. Too preoccupied with foreign relations to engage in confrontations over domestic policy, Nixon mostly acquiesced in liberal initiatives emanating from Congress. Hence the extraordinary expansion of social spending that began under Johnson continued for several years. Indeed, the Nixon Administration was responsible for what was perhaps the most radical and comprehensive welfare reform proposal in the nation's history, namely Daniel Moynihan's Family Assistance Plan, which proposed to replace miscellaneous welfare programmes with a unified national system of income support. Objectionable to conservatives on account of its expense and to liberals on account of its provenance, the Family Assistance Plan failed to win the assent of Congress. Nevertheless, the increased levels of welfare and social security payments went some way to implementing Moynihan's 'income strategy' in a piecemeal fashion.

Liberalism in decline

The New Deal collapsed in the 1960s. Boldly put, in need of qualification, this is the key truth, the essential condition, of our

19. Ibid., p. 172.

recent political life', observes Jonathan Rieder.[20] The New Deal coalition formed in the 1930s was seriously fractured in 1968, leaving Hubert Humphrey a full 12 million votes behind Johnson's 1964 total. In retrospect, 1968 clearly marks the end of an era of liberal politics. Nixon certainly was no liberal. Indeed, he hated liberals (especially Kennedys) and the so-called 'liberal establishment' – intellectuals and the media. His successor (after the brief post-Watergate interregnum of Gerald Ford), the Democrat Jimmy Carter, was far from willing to commit himself to a full-blown liberal agenda. Carter in 1976 claimed that he did not approve of large-scale government spending and wished to decentralise political power and encourage private enterprise. One of his principal advisers, in tones of humility quite unlike that of the Johnson White House, admitted that 'we realize Washington does not have all the answers or possess all the resources or have the power to solve every problem plaguing society'.[21] Carter sought to rejuvenate the Democratic Party by reorientating it towards a 'neoliberalism' that was liberal on social issues and conservative on the economy, but failed to define it with sufficient clarity to convince traditional liberals that he was not at heart a conservative and conservatives that he was not a closet liberal. The many setbacks of his Administration – 'stagflation', the oil crisis, the Iran hostage affair – provided grist to Republican charges of liberal incompetence.

The central reason for the decline of liberalism after the 1960s was the erosion of its core constituency, namely the white working class. Since the 1960s the blue-collar working class has been hit by a series of economic disasters. The inflation of the late 1960s and 1970s, fuelled by the Vietnam War, led to a stagnation, then a decline, of real wages. The oil crisis of 1974 intensified the problem and initiated a lengthy period of 'stagflation' in which GNP per capita began actually to decline. So did industrial employment, as the declining competitiveness of American industry produced a wave of lay-offs and plant closures. The many new service jobs created in the 'Reagan boom' of the 1980s were mostly low-paid, part-time and temporary – scant compensation for the decline in traditional manufacturing employment. Thus many families were forced to live on tighter budgets under conditions of increased insecurity. This had a devastating impact on public morale and on the nation's confidence in the future. A by-product of these economic trends

20. Jonathan Rieder, 'The rise of the "silent majority"', in Steve Fraser and Gary Gerstle, eds, *The Rise and Fall of the New Deal Order* (Princeton, N.J., 1989), p. 243.
21. Leuchtenburg, *In the Shadow of FDR*, p. 193.

was the decline of organised labour, formerly a key component of both the Democratic Party and postwar liberalism but now sadly diminished in both numbers and influence. The labour movement, which had once formed a valuable link between the Democratic Party and the industrial working class, now played a much less important role in bringing out the vote in blue-collar neighbour-hoods.

Members of the white working class became less tolerant of programmes to help the poor when they imagined their own incomes to be only a little above those of welfare recipients. Spiralling welfare costs increased the tax burden on lower-income families. Their own more straitened circumstances drove home the real, or imagined, costs of social reform. They resented African-Americans' apparent claim to privileged treatment. 'Positive discrimination' offended against both their interests and their sense of fair play, the ethic of hard work and self-reliance according to which they had lived their lives. They welcomed Nixon's promise to delay school desegregation, prevent busing and maintain 'law and order', a phrase which in the semiotics of the Right came to stand for the suppression of racial unrest. Similarly, members of the white working class were offended by the cultural radicalism of 'women's libbers', hippies and student protesters, and outraged by the actions of anti-war demonstrators, which deeply offended their strong sense of patriotism and duty.

The alienation of the working class from the Democratic Party and from liberal politics, though precipitated by the interposition of race and the 'social issue', reflected a perceived change in the character of American liberalism during the 1960s. Liberalism, which used to signify social security and trade union rights, now, in their eyes, meant taking the side of blacks against whites, of criminals against the police, rationalising rioting and crime as understandable responses to deprivation and oppression, taxing working people for the benefit of the shiftless poor, support for feminists, student radicals and other dissidents. It meant neglect of the 'forgotten Americans', as Nixon called them, the 'silent majority' who worked hard, went to church, paid their taxes and sent their sons to fight in Vietnam. 'In the popular mind', notes Rieder, liberalism no longer suggested 'a vision of transcendent justice or the support of vulnerable working-class people. ... Liberalism appeared to them as a force inimical to the working and lower-middle classes, assaulting their communities, their sense of fairness, their livelihood, their children, their physical safety, their values.'[22] As Senator Morris Udall wryly commented in 1976, the word 'liberal' was now 'associated with abortion, drugs, busing, and big-spending, wasteful government'.[23] It was not that such people had necessarily become conservatives. Most continued to believe in the welfare state and the traditional values of New Deal liberalism, but aspects of the 'New Liberalism' of the 1960s and 1970s severely tested their loyalties.

A haemorrhaging of white working-class votes critically weakened the Democratic Party in the North and created the potential for a partial electoral realignment. More serious was the fracturing of the Solid South. The civil rights revolution of the 1960s broke the Democratic Party's hold on the region, allowing many white Southerners to follow their innately conservative inclinations. They were, says Rieder, "natural" Republicans, awaiting release'.[24] Starting with Goldwater in 1964, Republican presidential candidates competed on equal terms in the states of the former Confederacy. The 'Southern strategy' urged on Nixon by Republican strategists like Kevin Phillips sought to drive home this advantage, as well as forcing a wedge through the Democratic Party's constituency in the urban North, by subtly exploiting the issue of race. Having lost its hold on its core constituencies, the party looked more and more like a collection of fringe groups – special interests, racial minorities, intellectuals and radicals – especially after the triumph of the 'New Politics' in the rules reforms of 1972.

At the same time, many potential Democratic supporters simply were not voting. The proportion of the electorate turning out to vote declined again after the 1960s, with the poor, members of minority groups and working-class voters disproportionately represented in 'the party of non-voters'. Voter turnout in the presidential election of 1980 was 53 per cent of the potential electorate (itself a sad declension from nineteenth-century levels), but around 20 per cent in ghetto neighbourhoods like the South Bronx and Bedford-Stuyvesant, a measure of the alienation and disaffection from government shared by many residents who sensed that the system of government was beyond their control and that formal political institutions no longer represented their interests. There was a 25 per cent difference between the turnout among white-collar and blue-collar voters. As it moved to the right in the

22. Rieder, 'Rise of the "silent majority" ', p. 258.
23. John J. Broesamle, *Reform and Reaction in American Politics* (Westport, Ct., 1990), p. 7.
24. Rieder, 'Rise of the "silent majority"', p. 245.

1970s and 1980s the Democratic Party made little effort to mobilise this vote. In effect, these groups no longer had a party. Thus the conservative victories of the 1980s were due not only to the expansion of the conservative vote but the alienation of members of the Democrats' natural constituency.

As many political scientists have noted, the shifts in party fortunes since 1968 have not produced a permanent realignment in the partisan allegiance of the electorate, such as contributed to the making of the New Deal order in the 1930s. Instead, they have been associated with a dealignment, a decline in the significance of party as an agent of political action, either at a popular level, in the form of voting behaviour, or at an elite level, in the form of congressional behaviour and the organisation of presidential campaigns. The decline of political parties has tended to weaken the political influence of lower-income groups. In contrast, business lobbies and special-interest groups have gained more influence through the development of techniques of computer-assisted direct mailing and through Political Action Committees, on which, in the wake of reforms in campaign finance during the 1970s, candidates for office have been increasingly dependent for funding. Although such techniques are equally available to right and left, right-wing groups, under the leadership of people like Richard Viguerie, have been especially effective at using them to mobilise support and influence policy.

As liberals lost confidence and conviction, conservatives gained in strength. Whereas during the immediate postwar decades the dominant force in the Republican Party was the New Republicanism of Eisenhower and Rockefeller, the 1970s and 1980s saw the rise of what has become known as the New Right, which sought to reverse America's perceived decline since the 1960s – an apparent deterioration in morality and faith, in prosperity and power. The New Right, however, was by no means a homogeneous force and contained a number of very diverse, sometimes mutually hostile, elements.

Most striking was the impact of evangelical Christianity. The 1970s and 1980s saw a significant religious revival. A school of successful TV evangelists, like Pat Robertson, Jerry Falwell and James Robison, utilised the most modern tools of mass persuasion to present a traditional religious message. The tele-evangelists had huge audiences and raised enormous sums of money. By 1980 30 million Americans claimed to have been 'born again', that is to have undergone the conversion experience expected of evangelical

Protestants. Although not all 'born-again' Christians were political conservatives, most of their preachers were. Several, notably Robertson, a recurrent candidate for the Republican presidential nomination, were active in politics. The Religious Right organised predominately around social issues. It expressed, and gathered strength from, a revulsion at recent trends in American society and politics. Its adherents sought, in Gillian Peele's words, 'to defend their life-style and values against the onslaughts of a secular humanism which had seemed to acquire establishment status in the 1960s'.[25] The so-called Moral Majority demanded the restoration of prayer in public schools and control of school textbooks, condemned pornography and unorthodox forms of sexuality, fought bitterly against the feminist campaign to pass an Equal Rights Amendment to the Constitution, and, above all, demanded the prohibition of abortion. As Peele explains, 'The theme of 'protecting innocent life' drew religious leaders and their followers into politics in a way which was more analogous to a crusade than to ordinary politics'.[26] Abortion was the key moral issue of the late twentieth century, carrying with it all the emotional force and cultural significance carried by prohibition in the 1910s and 1920s. Since the Supreme Court in *Roe* v. *Wade* (1973) called into question state laws controlling termination, the Religious Right, in alliance with Catholic groups, has contended fiercely against abortion and called upon the government to make it illegal.

The other major component of the New Right was an intellectual critique of liberalism, at least in its twentieth-century version. Pointing to the failure of Keynesian economics to prevent inflation during the 1960s and economic stagnation during the 1970s, free market economists like Milton Friedman and George Stigler criticised the programmes of the Great Society and, indeed, the entire liberal project. They demanded a reduction of government interference and a release of individual energies. They urged the deregulation of industry and cuts in public spending and taxation that would free resources for private enterprise. Some economists advocated a large across-the-board tax-cut in order to stimulate enterprise and investment. High taxes, it was believed, acted as a disincentive to individual effort and wealth creation. Although the proposed tax-cut would be regressive in its effects, showering relief on those in the highest-income brackets, it fed off the frustrations

25. Gillian Peele, *Revival and Reaction: The Right in Contemporary America* (Oxford, 1985), p. 11.
26. Ibid., p. 94.

of lower-income taxpayers at rising tax demands. This was the basis of what became known as 'supply-side economics' or 'Reaganomics' (or, as the erstwhile moderate Republican and later Reagan disciple George Bush put it, 'voodoo economics').

Although his actions turned out to be more moderate, less ideologically consistent, than his rhetoric, much of this economic programme was put into effect by Ronald Reagan at the beginning of his term. Congress went some way to dismantling environmental controls on the private development of resources, while airlines and other industries were subject to substantial deregulation. Eligibility for AFDC, food stamps and Medicaid was tightened, the Job Corps abolished, and job training, Head Start and other educational programmes severely cut back. Since social security programmes were sacrosanct, these cuts fell almost wholly on the poor and on the newer Great Society programmes, rather than those dating back to the New Deal. Between 1980 and 1987, social spending as a share of the federal budget fell from 25.5 to 18.3 per cent, whereas defence spending rose from 22.7 to 28.4 per cent. Despite the fact that increases in defence expenditures in order to fight off the 'evil empire' of world communism greatly outweighed the savings on domestic programmes, Reagan persuaded Congress to make massive cuts in taxes, amounting to 23 per cent on income tax over three years. The rationale was that the resultant economic growth would generate increased tax revenues more than sufficient to cover the deficit. This did not happen. The result was instead a mounting deficit, reaching over $200 billion a year by the early 1990s, which had a powerfully distorting effect on government finance, the US economy and the patterns of international trade.

Reagan was able to enact only part of his programme. The spending cuts were, as Reagan's Director of the Budget David Stockman revealingly described, frustrated by both liberal and conservative congressmen's devotion to any government spending that was directed to their own districts. Congressional resistance also prevented significant cutbacks in 'social regulation' relating to the environment, consumer protection and occupational health and safety. The forces of liberalism remained strong. Too many interests were committed to the maintenance of the liberal state; conceptions of economic rights and social entitlements had embedded themselves too deeply in American thinking about government. For all its media exposure, the New Right could at no time command majority support in the American electorate. Successive opinion polls showed majorities opposed to reductions in government spending on social security, education and other social programmes. The popularity of Reagan was greater than the popularity of the Right. Many of those who voted for Reagan in 1980 and 1984 did so because they thought he was a nice man or because, after the domestic and international humiliations of the Carter presidency, they felt that it was 'time for a change', not because they shared his conservative views. The so-called 'Reagan Democrats' mostly remained Democrats when Reagan himself was not a candidate. The politics of stalemate, characteristic of the postwar era, continued into the 1980s and 1990s. Reagan achieved neither an ideological revolution nor a political realignment. The 'Reagan Revolution' turned out to be little more than an exercise in containment, holding back rather than reversing the growth of the post-New Deal liberal state.

More striking, perhaps, than the power of the Right was the lassitude of the Left. Liberalism had evidently lost its way. No longer confident that problems could be solved by generous government spending, anxious about the unpopularity of high taxes, unable to cope with the divisive issue of race, liberals were uncertain of their direction. The false steps, the vacillations of the Carter and Clinton presidencies, though a product in part of the incumbents' personalities and the fluctuating political situation in which they found themselves, were rooted fundamentally in an uncertainty about the validity of the liberal project itself. The lesson of the 1960s, shouted from the rooftops by conservative theorists but quietly conceded by many liberals, was that 'throwing money at a problem' did not work and that Big Government was not the answer. As the political scientist Everett Ladd noted in 1988, 'The New Deal era now seems as remote as the age of McKinley'.[27] But if the fundamental tenets of twentieth-century liberalism no longer command respect, no alternative formulation has taken its place.

27. Iwan Morgan, *Beyond the Liberal Consensus: A Political History of the United States since 1965* (London, 1994), p. 228.

CHAPTER ELEVEN

State and Society in Twentieth-Century America

Liberalism and its discontents

Liberalism as a political ideology had its roots in the Enlightenment. It embodied a belief in individual freedom, the sanctity of private property, equality of opportunity, rationalism, progress, the elimination of private and corporate privilege, and the diminution of the arbitrary power of the state. Towards the end of the nineteenth century liberalism underwent a metamorphosis. On one hand, concentrations of private power came to seem still more menacing to individual liberty than the power of the democratic state. On the other hand, inequalities of fortune created inequalities of opportunity, and ultimately class divisions, that appeared to threaten the very integrity of society. Social life was now perceived as producing a variety of problems for which government might offer solutions.

Modern American liberalism first emerged at the beginning of the twentieth century under the guise of progressivism, which was, in John J. Broesamle's words, 'the exploratory phase of twentieth-century American reform'.[1] The Progressive Era, broadly defined, saw the first major confrontation with the problems of the new industrial society. Progressivism represented a version of the *via media* sought by liberals and social democrats across Europe and the industrialising world around the turn of the century, between on one hand the dogmatic certainties of *laissez-faire*, once described as liberalism but now labelled conservatism, and on the other hand the equally dogmatic, and equally dangerous, certainties of socialism. In a general sense, progressivism was a response to the

1. John J. Broesamle, *Reform and Reaction in Twentieth-Century American Politics* (Westport, Ct., 1990), p. 46.

311

problems caused by industrialisation and the growth of the city. It seemed evident to the founder members of the American Economic Association, as to many other American intellectuals, that such problems required the firm hand of government. Two in particular preoccupied the progressive generation: the economic and political power of the newly formed giant corporations; and the social problems of the inner city, such as poverty, overcrowding, juvenile delinquency and prostitution. But such issues as labour relations, conservation, temperance and the rights of women also engaged its attention. Progressivism was highly diverse, even contra-dictory in its substantive concerns.

A wide variety of reform movements marched forth under the banner of progressivism, but what they had in common was a strong sense of moral commitment. Progressive reform was animated by an apostolic fervour that was rooted in evangelical Protestantism (although not all of its proponents were, or ever had been, evangelical Protestants) but sometimes translated into a faith in the capacity of applied science to solve social problems. Reasoned intelligence would point the way to a correct answer – to the solution that best represented the public interest, rather than some narrow selfish interest, and which ought to command the support of right-minded citizens. Although progressive legislation almost invariably emerged from a process of hard-nosed bargaining between competing interests, it was characteristically invested with a moral significance that either disarmed or irritated its opponents. Such an admixture of idealism and pragmatism remained, in varying degrees, characteristic of American liberalism throughout the century. Progressivism was a political style, not an ideology. It entailed, whatever the issue, a process of organisation, investigation, education and systematic lobbying. It entailed a reliance on expert agencies, staffed by enlightened bureaucrats, to resolve social and economic conflicts, and therefore a fundamental change in the character of the state. Much of the character of American liberalism, as of the twentieth-century American state, was set in the Progressive Era.

The New Deal built in many respects upon the progressive tradition. Many prominent New Dealers had come of age during the Progressive Era, and, for all their hard-boiled manner, they retained much of the idealism of the earlier generation. Several New Deal reforms built directly upon progressive antecedents, including the Tennessee Valley Authority, social insurance, banking reform and pure food and drug laws. However, there were important changes of emphasis, important enough to alienate a substantial number of former progressives – possibly a majority, according to Otis L. Graham's calculations – from the New Deal. Richard Hofstadter regarded the New Deal as marking a 'drastic new departure . . . in the history of American reformism'.[2]

Most importantly, whereas progressive reform mostly took the form of regulation of undesirable behaviours, the New Deal involved a much greater recourse to government spending power to achieve its ends. It was, to use Theodore J. Lowi's categories, largely 'redistributive' in character. Take, for example, the New Deal's approach to the problem of slum housing. Whereas progressive housing reformers like Lawrence Veiller advocated strict housing codes which would set standards for the private housing market, New Deal agencies like the US Housing Authority funded public housing projects to accommodate low-income families. Instead of a negative strategy of prohibiting bad housing, they provided money for the construction of good housing. New Deal farm policies likewise relied on the spending power of government. So, of course, did New Deal welfare policies. The result was a vast increase in government activity measured in terms of expenditure (the extension of government authority during the Progressive Era did not require massive increases in spending), as well as in the degree to which the arm of government extended into the lives of ordinary Americans. That is why the New Deal marks so significant a turning-point in the growth of American government. This is illustrated in Figure 11.1, which reveals, especially once the anomalous effects of military spending during the two world wars have been smoothed out (by following the line ABCD), a significant discontinuity in the growth of government expenditure during the 1930s.

As Thorstein Veblen had observed earlier in the century, 'the classic phrase is no longer to read "life, liberty and the pursuit of happiness"; what is to be insured to every free born American citizen under the new dispensation, is "life, liberty and the *means* of happiness"'.[3] In one of the earliest statements of the developing philosophy of the New Deal, the Commonwealth Club Address of 1932, Roosevelt promised to supplement the original constitutional settlement with 'an economic declaration of rights, an economic constitutional order'. In like vein, the 1936 Democratic Party platform declared that 'government in a modern civilization has

2. Richard Hofstadter, *The Age of Reform: From Bryan to F.D.R.* (New York, 1955), p. 301.

3. Broesamle, *Reform and Reaction in Twentieth-Century American Politics*, p. 38.

FIGURE 11.1   *Federal Outlays per capita at Constant (1958) Prices, 1900–1994*

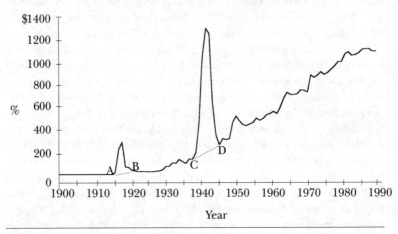

Note: AB and CD indicate probable levels of spending in the absence of the two world wars.

Sources: US Bureau of the Census, *Historical Statistics of the United States: Colonial Times to 1970* (Washington, D.C. 1975), Series F1, 5, A7, Y457, 462–3; *Statistical Abstract of the United States, 1980* (Washington, D.C., 1980), nos 2, 436, 531, 725; *Statistical Abstract of the United States, 1995* (Washington, D.C., 1995), nos. 2, 517, 699.

certain inescapable obligations to its citizens', which included protection of home and family, 'a democracy of opportunity for all the people' and 'aid to those overtaken by disaster'.[4] To the traditional rights of the citizen, as enumerated in the first ten amendments to the Constitution, were added new rights: such things as the 'rights' to employment, economic security, collective bargaining, housing and education. Liberalism came to represent a series of demands to use government authority to reduce risks in an increasingly unpredictable world. It was therefore highly malleable and almost infinitely extensible. There was no end to the number of individual and collective complaints that might be identified for which government might find a cure or against which it might offer security. This 'Second Bill of Rights' offered an almost inexhaustible charter for claims on the state.

The Second New Deal took on a distinctly social democratic

4. 'Commonwealth Club Speech', in Richard Hofstadter, ed., *Great Issues in American History: From Reconstruction to the Present, 1865–1969* (New York, 1969), p. 349; Donald B. Johnson, ed., *National Party Platforms* (Urbana, Ill., 1978), p. 360.

tinge. Definitely pro-labour in its sympathies, relying on a largely working-class constituency, New Deal liberalism bore some similarity to British Labourism. However, the state that Roosevelt built was also a 'broker state' which offered to deal with any organised interests in society. Another legacy of the New Deal was a kind of 'interest-group liberalism' that was morally neutral and indiscriminate in doling out its favours.

Postwar liberalism built upon the New Deal tradition. Liberals supported organised labour, defended farm subsidies and advocated the expansion of the welfare state. The Democratic coalition of the 1930s remained their (increasingly shaky) electoral base. Nevertheless, there were important modifications which, in the long run, decisively changed the character and, some might say, the viability of the liberal project. The first was the development after 1945 of a 'Cold War liberalism', wholeheartedly committed to the worldwide struggle against communism. In the face of cross-fire from the anti-communist Right, liberals severed the links with the domestic Left which had contributed so fruitfully to the New Deal. Whatever social democratic character New Deal liberalism had possessed was dissipated in the postwar settlement, which relied upon a tough-minded application of 'commercial Keynesianism' to keep the private-enterprise economy sailing at full steam ahead. However, the Vietnam War broke 'Cold War liberalism' into its component parts. The liberal coalition, like the Democratic Party, ran aground on the angry controversies over the war that culminated in the 1968 campaign.

The major adjunct to postwar liberalism was civil rights, but in the long run this turned out to be a problematic one. It was not that most Democrats outside the South did not support the goals of Martin Luther King and the civil rights movement, but that, when the enforcement of minority rights moved beyond legal equality to 'affirmative action' and anti-poverty programmes which appeared to pour money into the ghettos, large sections of the Northern white electorate became alienated. Thus liberalism lost much of the support of the white working class, which was the core of the Democratic Party. Their defection left the party in the hands of a new liberal coalition of intellectuals and minority groups, which was, in both political and electoral terms, highly vulnerable. The 1960s saw an enormous expansion of the programmatic liberalism of the New Deal, which now included educational opportunity, job training, urban renewal, public housing, and much else besides, vastly overextending the fiscal and administrative resources of government. It also saw the creation of a new 'social regulation' in defence of environmental and consumer interests which massively increased the level of federal interference with the activity of business.

The 1960s was, of course, the decade of the youth revolt, the counterculture, student protest, the Peace Movement and a revived feminism. A new cultural politics came to the fore, whose main issues were gender roles, sexuality, the legalisation of abortion, and the use of drugs, which, in Bruce Miroff's words, 'explod[ed] the categories of American group politics'.[5] These issues generated a new set of political divisions, very different to the modified class politics of the New Deal era, and helped fuel the conservative 'backlash' of the 1970s and 1980s. As of 1996 it seems difficult to see how the liberal project can be revived, nor even what it is.

The natural history of Leviathan

Conservative efforts to cut back the enfolding tendrils of the state enjoyed their greatest success during the Reagan presidency. Yet even then, with a popular and charismatic president, with, for a while, Republican majorities in Congress and broader cross-party support, with a conservative mood at large in the nation, and with liberals seemingly in disarray, the fruits of deregulation and down-sizing were paradoxical indeed. While not denying the damage that was inflicted on particular programmes, especially those of interest to the poor, others were either increased, like the defence budget, or took the form of entitlements that were, in effect, invulnerable to the parer's knife. Federal government outlays in 1980 stood at $590,947 million and in 1990 at $1,252,705 million, an increase in real terms by just over a third. Federal expenditure as a proportion of GNP rose slightly. The result of the vaunted Reagan cuts, then, was merely to retard, rather than reverse, the growth of the federal government. Indeed, most of the slack was taken up by subnational units, whose spending rose faster than that of the national government, with the result that public spending as a percentage of GNP rose as rapidly during the 1980s as in any postwar decade (see Table 1.2).

Government, it seemed, is like some great Leviathan which can only grow but never contract. The engine that cranks up state

5. Sidney Milkis, *The President and the Parties: The Transformation of the American Party System since the New Deal* (New York, 1993), p. 182.

spending is, as Robert Higgs sadly remarks, equipped with a ratchet that allows for progress in only one direction. Government programmes, once started, are rarely terminated. Many of them, accounting for 60 per cent of federal spending in 1980, take the form of entitlements, protected by statutory law and enforceable in the courts, which are immune to short-term financial adjustment. The most obvious example is social security, whose privileged status was established in the 1930s, but others include farm price-supports, defence contracts and a variety of grants-in-aid. Established programmes enjoy more than legal protection. Around each of them has grown, like barnacles upon the hull of an ageing freighter, a network of supportive political relationships. Organised interest groups, whether representing defence contractors, farmers, senior citizens or schoolteachers, lobby persistently for the maintenance, if not the enlargement, of the programme from which they benefit, forming close alliances with federal administrators, who themselves have a personal interest in its fate, as well as the congressional committees or subcommittees responsible for monitoring performance and appropriating funds. These so-called 'iron triangles' – of pressure groups, federal agencies, and congressional subcommittees – form tight communities of interest and expertise which are almost impermeable to outside interference. In a more general sense, congressmen, while often heartily in favour of general retrenchment, find it difficult to oppose specific expenditures from which their constituents benefit. They like to be seen in the guise of benefactors, sponsoring and taking credit for the distribution of federal largesse. The same ambivalence is evident, from opinion polls, in the general public, majorities of which endorse both tax-cuts and generous public spending on specific programmes like social security, education and defence. Voters have become used to a pervasive government presence, accustomed to turning to the state for solutions to their problems. As the crusty Social Darwinist William Graham Sumner warned a century ago, 'the experiment enters into the life of the society and never can be got out again'.[6]

Political scientists have offered a bewildering range of theories to explain the growth of government in industrialised societies over the last century or so. Many of these are variants of what has been called Wagner's Law, after the nineteenth-century German social scientist Adolf Wagner, which holds that industrialisation generates

6. Robert Higgs, *Crisis and Leviathan: Critical Episodes in the Growth of American Government* (New York, 1987), p. 72.

an expansion of the public sector at a rate higher than the growth of national income. One reason for this is that increased affluence enables a society to afford more 'public goods' like education and health-care. Another is that the concentration of population in industrial communities creates 'negative externalities' such as pollution and traffic congestion which can only be corrected by the hand of government. The greater interdependence of individuals and social groups creates more points at which social conflict can occur, solution of which may require the mediating authority of the state. The clash of interests in an industrial society stimulates the formation of a variety of organised pressure groups, each of which seeks to bend the actions of government to its needs. Only the state, it is believed, can check the power of the big business corporations which are so dominant a feature of modern industrial society. Finally, modernisation theorists regard the growth of the state as a necessary consequence of functional specialisation, differentiation and the growth of an 'organisational society'.

All such theories suggest a kind of inevitability about the growth of government, and there is little reason, on historical grounds, to question that the social and economic forces that have shaped the modern world do, among other things, create conditions which require government intervention on a growing scale. However, they do not provide any guide to the historical processes by which such intervention occurs in particular nations or the variations between them. Nor do they specify the human agents of change, something which is an essential component of any satisfying historical explanation.

Another variety of explanation is founded upon the relationship between capitalism and democracy. There is in any capitalist democracy a pronounced discrepancy between the distribution of wealth and the distribution of votes, creating temptations for the relatively deprived majority to use its electoral influence upon government to improve its life-chances. Socialist or social democratic parties emerge, representing predominately working-class constituencies, to campaign for redistributive measures, and these, in time, exert an influence on government. Government grows therefore as a result of the extension of the franchise. There is little firm evidence to support such an interpretation, certainly for the United States, either in the results of attitudinal surveys or in the history of individual policies, such as the Social Security Act. There is, of course, no unequivocally social democratic party in the United States. Although the voting public lent its support in the broadest terms to the expansion of government activity, certainly during the New Deal and perhaps the 1960s, it is much harder to discern any direct electoral influence on policy-making. In any case, the 'regime imperatives' of democratic government are more complicated than that. On one hand, it must satisfy the needs of a popular electorate, in terms of education, welfare and other social spending. On the other hand, it must maintain conditions under which private enterprise can flourish. The business community forms, in effect, a 'second constituency' for government officials.[7] This explains some of the inconsistencies in twentieth-century policy-making, the odd mixture of pro-business and redistributive policies that has emerged. Yet these broad imperatives leave considerable space within which policy-makers could operate.

There is no doubt that in many cases the growth of government has been inspired by the demands of business or other interest groups. A close examination of the history of almost every major piece of twentieth-century domestic legislation, as well as many minor ones, will reveal the important role played by organised pressure groups, which have worked tirelessly to turn to their advantage the regulatory, the adjudicative and the spending power of the state. Such an examination, however, will also reveal that such influences were rarely determining. The very complexity of interest-group pressures creates space for autonomous action on the part of policy-makers, who themselves act to define the issues, generate solutions and assemble coalitions in support of them. As Ballard C. Campbell has shown, administrative entrepreneurs like J. Edgar Hoover of the FBI and Wilbur Cohen of the Social Security Administration were able, by exploring the limits of their authority, by building political coalitions, by carefully cultivating the media, to build up the size and importance of their agencies. A still more critical role in state-building has been played by successive presidents.

One of the principal lessons to be drawn from the history of progressivism and liberalism in the twentieth century seemed to be the importance of the presidency as a motivating force in American politics. Only the president could claim to represent all the people and take responsibility for the overall public interest, whereas Congress represented an aggregation of parochial concerns. Only the president, standing apart from the immediate, particularistic

7. Ellis Hawley, 'Social policy and the liberal state in the twentieth century', in Donald T. Critchlow and Ellis W. Hawley, eds, *Federal Social Policy: The Historical Dimension* (University Park, Pa., 1988), p. 124.

concerns of congressmen and departmental officials, could engage
in long-term planning. From what Theodore Roosevelt called the
'bully pulpit' of the presidency, he could attempt to establish a
rapport with the people and, using the tools of the modern media,
speak to them directly. Since Theodore Roosevelt, but especially
since Franklin Roosevelt, presidents have sought to influence
Congress to secure passage of their legislative programmes, using
their own persuasive powers, the cajolements of patronage and
appeals to the wider electorate beyond the District of Columbia.
The presidency is the main locus of innovation in the American
political system, the principal source of change. It is, suggests
Stephen Skowronek, by its very nature an 'order-shattering'
institution. Each president is expected to define a project for his
Administration, if he wishes to be remembered by posterity, and is
judged in accordance with his success in achieving it. Successive
presidents have found it increasingly difficult to shift the
cumbersome machinery of American government and turn it in a
new direction, but there have been moments when imaginative and
determined national leaders, most notably Franklin D. Roosevelt
and Lyndon Johnson, have been able to exploit particularly
propitious conditions for state-building.

As we have seen, a number of obstacles to positive action are
built into the American constitutional structure, with its separations
of powers and divided sovereignty, which the political parties can
only partially mitigate. The Democratic Party in particular has, since
the presidency of Woodrow Wilson, consistently offered a more
sympathetic medium for liberal reform. With the possible exception
of the early years of the century, when Theodore Roosevelt pulled
elements of the Republican Party some way towards acceptance of a
progressive programme, reform eras have been periods of
Democratic control of the national government. However, the
Democratic Party itself contains a diversity of groups, some of
which, particularly white Southerners, were conservative over a wide
range of issues. The South has exerted a restraining influence on
the party's reforming instincts for much of the century. Thus the
successful fruition of any major reform initiative requires, in effect,
that the Democratic Party controls the White House and enjoys a
sufficient majority in both houses of Congress to overcome the
inertia, the obstacles to action, built into the system and to allow for
the possibility of resistance from the party's Southern wing. Such
moments of political opportunity have been rare in this century.
The dynamics of American politics make it difficult to achieve more

than incremental change except under unusually favourable political circumstances.

Robert Higgs argues, with some plausibility, that national emergencies call forth extensions of government control which are rarely thereafter reversed. Certainly, the depressions of the 1890s and the 1930s compelled a reassessment of the role of the state. The New Deal, which represented the most important turning-point in the growth of the American state, bore the marks of the national emergency during which it was created. Both of the century's major wars have left a legacy of extended government. The Second World War, in particular, accustomed the public to mass payment of the federal income tax, to the maintenance of a swollen defence establishment and to federal economic controls. However, the nature of the political response in each case was not entailed by the nature of the crisis. It was shaped by the actions of individuals, the programmes of political parties and the political structures in which they operated. The growth of government is 'path-dependent'. It results from the particular sequences of institutional growth and the particular decisions made at critical junctures.

In fact, the growth of government has been largely incremental in character. Although there have been one or two explosive moments, like the periods of the New Deal and the Second World War, expansion has mostly taken the form of the augmentation of existing programmes – a modest increase in scope, a marginal enlargement of powers, a slightly more generous appropriation – year after year or Congress after Congress. Cautious by nature, legislators prefer to authorise incremental changes to an established policy rather than to initiate a strikingly new departure. Social security is a vivid example of this. After the initial 'big bang' of 1935, the programme has grown at a steady rate from a fairly small to a gargantuan enterprise.

The process of state-building in itself constitutes a partial explanation for the growth of government. Whether in particular instances the initiative came from the demands of private interest groups, the designs of public servants or the crusading activities of reform movements, whether it arose in response to a social crisis such as the Great Depression or some other specific historical conjuncture, the outcome was a cumulative process of state-making. Once a particular policy had been initiated, a locus was created in government for further expansion: pressure groups were created, if they did not exist already, to lobby for the maintenance and enlargement of the programme; the bureaucrats entrusted with its administration came up with further plans for its enhancement, and with it the aggrandisement of their own role; both interest groups and civil servants forged profitable links with legislators eager to serve constituency interests; and the public became just a little more accustomed to the intervention of the state. Its fruits became accepted by the beneficiaries as an entitlement. Each accretion of state power to advance the welfare of some segment of the population lowered the resistance to further grants of power for somebody else's benefit. The result was the gradual acceptance, particularly since the 1930s, of what Campbell calls a 'claimant philosophy': 'Each round of policy development expanded people's expectations about the purpose of civic action, reestablishing the context in which subsequent decisions were made. This process gradually undermined the foundations of the republican polity and crystallized into a claimant outlook.' There was, agrees Bernard Wishy, a 'growing conviction … that American society … presented a vast series of unspecifiable needs for which there were satisfactions devisable by experts and depending for success on government actions and funding'.[8] Citizens were encouraged to seek relief from government from the conflicts and uncertainties of modern life. Once the principle was accepted, it was difficult to refuse new demands. The interaction between public expectations, interest-group pressures and bureaucratic imperatives fuelled a continuing cycle of expansion.

The outcome was a sprawling monster of a state, virtually beyond the comprehension, never mind the control, of any one individual. Americans have shown in the twentieth century a strong preference for delegating important governmental powers to executive agencies, partly as a result of a lack of respect for the decision-making capacity of their legislative representatives, partly out of a recognition of the sheer technical complexity of most of the issues that came within the purview of the state. In the absence of an established administrative core, the enforcement of policies was mostly entrusted to independent agencies, which were allowed enormous discretion. The statutes creating them usually outlined their powers in very general terms, leaving them, in effect, substantially to define their own role. They were permitted such wide discretion by virtue of their expertise, because of lax and often friendly oversight by congressional subcommittees, and because of

8. Ballard C. Campbell, *The Growth of American Government: Governance from the Cleveland Era to the Present* (Bloomington, Ind., 1995), p. 53; Bernard Wishy, *Good-bye Machiavelli: Government and American Life* (Baton Rouge, La., 1995), p. 219.

their success in forging political alliance with client groups. As Theodore Lowi has complained, they prefer to adjudicate disputes on a case-by-case basis rather than laying down firm rules, and they allow considerable scope to interest groups in the formulation of policy, even to the extent of a virtual delegation of authority, as, to some extent, in the administration of farm subsidies. The new bureaucracy works like a patronage system, delivering goods and services to a range of clients, but it is hardly less decentralised than the patronage system of old.

The outcome is 'a hapless confusion of institutional purposes, authoritative controls, and governmental boundaries', an administrative state which is as disarticulated and uncoordinated, and in the last analysis as uncontrollable, as the 'state of court and parties' of the nineteenth century. 'Beyond the state of courts and parties', says Skowronek, 'lay a hapless administrative giant, a state that could spawn bureaucratic goods and services but that defied authoritative control and direction.'[9] Presidents who were once constrained by the practices of party organisation are now constrained by the practices of the administrative state. The structure of the American state seems no better fitted to meet the demands of a new century than was the early American state to meet the challenges of the twentieth.

---

9. Stephen Skowronek, *Building a New American State: The Expansion of National Administrative capacities, 1877–1920* (Cambridge, 1982), pp. 287, 290.

Glossary

Adkins v. *Children's Hospital* (1923): a Supreme Court decision which invalidated a District of Columbia law setting minimum wage-rates for women workers.

Agricultural Adjustment Act of 1933: was designed to reduce surpluses of farm produce by paying farmers to take land out of production. A later Agricultural Adjustment Act (1938) allowed for the imposition of compulsory quotas, authorised price-support loans on crops in storage and provided incentives for the cultivation of soil-conserving crops.

Agricultural Adjustment Administration (AAA): created to administer the Agricultural Adjustment Act *(q.v.)*.

Aid to Dependent Children (ADC): established by the Social Security Act *(q.v.)*, provided matching federal funds to support state programmes of assistance to single mothers and their children. Later renamed *Aid to Families of Dependent Children* (AFDC).

American Association for Labor Legislation (AALL): a body set up in 1905 by a group of social scientists interested in labour legislation. It was the most prominent advocate of social insurance during the early twentieth century.

American Farm Bureau Federation (AFBF): the most powerful pressure group representing American farmers, especially large producers.

American Federation of Labor (AFL): a federation of trade unions established in 1885, the principal national organisation representing organised labour until the creation of the Congress of Industrial Organizations *(q.v.)* in the 1930s. Its members were mostly craft unions *(q.v.)*.

American Medical Association (AMA): an organisation representing the professional interests of American doctors. From the 1920s it lobbied effectively to block health insurance proposals.

Anti-Saloon League (ASL): an organisation formed in 1895 to coordinate the efforts of various temperance movements in the campaign for prohibition *(q.v.)* legislation.

antitrust describes political movements and government programmes seeking either to break up industrial consolidations or to regulate their activities.

Brown v. *Board of Education of Topeka* (1954): one of a group of cases in which the Supreme Court decided that racial segregation *(q.v.)* in education was 'inherently unequal' even if the facilities provided were of equal standard.

charity organization society (COS): a type of organisation formed in many cities during the late nineteenth century to coordinate philanthropic activities and promote the practice of 'scientific philanthropy' *(q.v.)*.

Children's Bureau: a federal agency set up in 1912 to investigate child welfare and later entrusted with the administration of programmes relating to children. Predominantly staffed by women, it also provided a focus for women's social reform activities.

Civil Rights Act of 1964: required equal access to all public facilities, expedited the desgegregation of schools, prohibited discrimination in federally funded programmes, and barred discrimination in employment on the grounds of race or sex.

Civil Works Administration (CWA): a temporary work relief agency created in the autumn of 1933 which provided temporary employment for up to 4 million workers. It was disbanded the following spring.

Clayton Act (1914): attempted to make the Sherman Act *(q.v.)* more effective by specifying the business practices which were proscribed by law. It also provided trade unions with limited and, as it turned out, ineffective, immunities against prosecution under the antitrust laws and against labour injunctions *(q.v)*.

Committee on Industrial Organization: see Congress of Industrial Organizations

Communist Party (CP): formed out of those elements of the Socialist Party of America *(q.v.)* which elected in 1919 to follow the party line laid down by the Communist International in Moscow.

Community Action Program (CAP): established in 1964 to involve local communities in the anti-poverty programmes initiated by the Economic Opportunity Act *(q.v.)*.

Congress of Industrial Organizations (CIO) was created by leaders of industrial unions *(q.v.)* within the American Federation of Labor *(q.v.)* who formed a Committee on Industrial Organization in 1935 and then the independent Congress of Industrial Organizations in 1938. The two labour federations amalgamated in 1955 to form the AFL-CIO.

Congress of Racial Equality (CORE): a civil rights organisation formed in 1942 which was active during the freedom struggle of the 1960s.

craft unions: labour organisations whose prospective membership was defined by possession of a common trade or craft. Each craft union was held to have sovereign jurisdiction over workers in a particular trade. Cf. industrial unions *(q.v.)*.

Danbury Hatters case (Loewe v. *Lawlor)*: a 1908 decision in which the Supreme Court declared a labour boycott to be an illegal restraint of interstate trade and confirmed the application of the Sherman Act *(q.v.)* to labour organisations.

Economic Opportunity Act of 1964: set up a number of programmes designed to reduce poverty by providing education and training, including the Job Corps, Head Start, loans for small businesses, and the Community Action Program *(q.v.)*.

Eighteenth Amendment to the US Constitution: ratified in 1919; prohibited the manufacture, transportation or sale of alcoholic beverages. Repealed by the Twenty-first Amendment in 1933.

Equal Employment Opportunities Commission (EEOC): an agency set up by President Kennedy in 1961 to monitor racial discrimination in employment on federally funded programmes.

Farm Security Administration (FSA): created by the Bankhead-Jones Tenancy Act of 1937 to carry on the work of the Resettlement Administration *(q.v.)*.

Farmers' Holiday Association: a movement of Midwestern farmers during the early 1930s to fight bankruptcy and foreclosure by direct action, including attempts to place an embargo upon the movement of food to local towns.

Federal Emergency Relief Administration (FERA): created in May 1933 to provide emergency relief through matching grants to the states and direct grants to areas of special need. Its operations were wound up in 1936.

Federal Housing Administration (FHA): established in 1934 to promote home ownership and stimulate the construction industry by providing federal guarantees for mortgages. It contributed to the great expansion of housing construction after the Second World War, particularly in the suburbs.

Federal Reserve System: a network of regional reserve banks created by the Federal Reserve Act of 1913 in order to provide a more elastic currency and a more effective mobilisation of banking reserves in times of financial stringency, under a measure of government supervision which was increased by the banking legislation of the New Deal.

Federal Reserve Board (FRB): the agency responsible for supervising the operation of the Federal Reserve System *(q.v.)*.

Federal Trade Commission (FTC): created in 1914 to administer the antitrust *(q.v.)* laws and police 'unfair methods of competition'.

Fourteenth Amendment to the US Constitution: ratified in 1868; was designed to protect American citizens, including newly emancipated African-Americans, from discriminatory treatment. Until the 1930s it was more often interpreted as a check on the power of state governments to pass regulatory legislation which interfered with the freedom of contract of individual businesses and employees.

General Federation of Women's Clubs (GFWC): an association of women's clubs founded in 1891 which in the early twentieth century gave considerable support to movements for social reform.

Hepburn Act: an act passed in 1906 amending the Interstate Commerce Act *(q.v.)*, particularly by investing the Interstate Commerce Commission *(q.v.)* with the power to set maximum railroad rates on the complaint of a shipper.

industrial unions: labour organisations which enrolled workers according to the industry in which they were employed rather than the skill which they possessed. Cf. craft unions *(q.v.)*.

Industrial Workers of the World (IWW, also known as 'Wobblies'): a radical anarcho-syndicalist union formed in 1905 which recruited mainly among migrant workers in the West and unskilled factory workers in the East.

Interstate Commerce Act (of 1887): required that railroad rates be 'just and reasonable' and prohibited various forms of discrimination against shippers and localities.

interstate commerce clause of the US Constitution: authorises Congress to regulate commerce 'with foreign nations, and among the several States' and forms the legal basis for federal regulation of industry, commerce and labour.

Interstate Commerce Commission (ICC): created to administer the Interstate Commerce Act *(q.v.)* and later laws regulating railroads as well as other forms of interstate transportation and communication.

Jim Crow: a name commonly given to the system of racial segregation *(q.v.)* in the Southern states.

judicial review: the practice by which the federal judiciary determines whether legislation by either federal or state governments lies within the powers conferred upon them by the US Constitution.

Keynesianism: a strategy of economic management which requires the government to adjust the balance between its revenues and its expenditures so as to provide a stimulus to the economy during periods of recession and apply a brake during periods of inflation.

labour injunction: a court order enjoining persons engaged in a labour dispute to desist from actions which were regarded as likely to cause 'irreparable' damage to the property interests of an employer or of third parties.

Lochner v. *New York:* a 1905 decision of the Supreme Court in which a New York maximum-hours law was held to contravene the Fourteenth Amendment *(q.v.)* by interfering with the contractual liberty of adult male workers.

Loewe v. *Lawlor: see Danbury Hatters case.*

Mann-Elkins Act of 1910: gave the Interstate Commerce Commission *(q.v.)* power to suspend increases in railroad rates and to investigate rate schedules on its own initiative.

McNary-Haugen Bill: a scheme to eliminate farm surpluses, passed twice by Congress in 1927 and 1928 but vetoed by President Coolidge. The government would buy up surplus produce in order to raise prices to 'parity' *(q.v.)* levels and dispose of it on overseas markets.

Medicaid: a programme created in 1965 which provides matching federal funds to provide free medical treatment to families on public assistance.

Medicare: a programme created in 1965 which provides free medical treatment to recipients of social security benefits.

Mugwump: a Republican who declined to support the party's candidate, James G. Blaine, in 1884 on account of his alleged record of political corruption. The term was used more generally to describe an attitude of gentlemanly disgust with Gilded Age politics.

Muller v. *Oregon:* a 1908 Supreme Court decision which approved of a state law imposing maximum hours for women workers on the grounds that their physiology and social role warranted restrictions on their employment which would be unwarranted for men.

National Association for the Advancement of Colored People (NAACP): the oldest of the principal civil rights organisations, founded in 1909, brought the actions leading to many of the key court decisions in favour of racial equality.

National Association of Manufacturers (NAM): an organisation formed in 1894 which largely represented small and medium-sized firms.

National Child Labor Committee (NCLC): formed in 1904 to campaign for the regulation of child labour.

National Civic Federation (NCF): formed in 1900, though intended to combine the points of view of business, labour and the general public, largely represented the interests of large corporations.

National Consumers' League (NCL): formed in 1899 to campaign for the protection of working women and children.

National Industrial Recovery Act: passed in June 1933, allowed firms to draw up code agreements covering wages, hours and competitive practices. It also set up a large-scale public works programme under the Public Works Administration *(q.v.)*.

National Labor Relations Act: see Wagner Act.

National Labor Relations Board (NLRB): created in 1934 to mediate labour disputes arising out of the National Industrial Recovery Act *(q.v.)*. A reorganised NLRB, with augmented powers, was entrusted with enforcement of the Wagner Act *(q.v.)*.

National Recovery Administration (NRA): established to administer code agreements under the National Industrial Recovery Act *(q.v.)*.

National War Labor Board (NWLB): established in 1918 to arbitrate labour disputes in war industries. An agency with the same title and similar powers was created during the Second World War.

NLRB v. *Jones & Laughlin*: a 1937 case in which the Supreme Court confirmed the constitutionality of the Wagner Act *(q.v.)*.

Northern Securities Co. v. *US*: in which the Supreme Court in 1904 ordered the dissolution of a combination of railroads in the Northwest, demonstrating that the Sherman Act *(q.v.)* covered mergers as well as 'loose' combinations in restraint of trade.

Office of Economic Opportunity (OEO): administered programmes established by the Economic Opportunity Act *(q.v.)*.

Old Age Assistance (OAA): a programme of state assistance to the elderly poor supported by matching grants under the Social Security Act *(q.v.)* of 1935.

Old Age Insurance (OAI): a federally administered programme of insurance established by the Social Security Act *(q.v.)* of 1935. In 1939, when benefits were extended to the spouses, mostly widows, and dependent children of deceased contributors, it was renamed *Old Age and Survivors' Insurance* (OASI).

open shop: a workplace in which union membership was not required of employees or, more often, from which unions were debarred altogether.

parity: a term used to describe the level of agricultural prices, in relation to the prices of manufactured goods, which was held to give farmers a fair return on their products. The ratio of prices in the immediate pre-First World War years was usually taken as the basis for calculating parity.

Plessy v. *Ferguson*: an 1896 Supreme Court decision which declared that segregated public facilities did not contravene the equal protection clause of the Fourteenth Amendment *(q.v.)* if the facilities provided for the two races were 'separate but equal'.

Populist Party: a radical farmers' party that flourished in the South and West during the early 1890s. Its platform included a national paper currency, free coinage of silver and government ownership of railroads.

prohibition: commonly referring to the prohibition of the liquor traffic.

Public Works Administration: created by the National Industrial Recovery Act *(q.v.)* of 1933 to administer a programme of large-scale public works projects.

Pure Food and Drug Act of 1906: required truthful labelling of food and drug products and prohibited certain harmful ingredients.

Reconstruction Finance Corporation (RFC): an agency established in 1932 to furnish loans to key private-sector institutions. It continued to play a major role in the economic policy of the New Deal.

Resettlement Administration (RA): an agency established in 1935 to provide assistance to migrant farmers and rehabilitation and resettlement loans to tenant farmers. It was succeeded by the Farm Security Administration *(q.v.)* in 1937.

Schechter Poultry Corporation v. *US*: 1935 decision of the Supreme Court which found the National Recovery Administration *(q.v.)* unconstitutional on the grounds of excessive delegation of powers and interference with intrastate business.

scientific philanthropy: a movement which arose during the late nineteenth century to make charitable provision more 'efficient' by better record-keeping, systematic investigation of cases and coordination of the activities of separate agencies.

Securities and Exchange Commission (SEC): an agency established in 1934 to regulate stock exchange dealings.

segregation: the requirement, mandatory by law in Southern states between the 1890s and the 1960s, that separate facilities be provided for black and white. It refers more generally to separation on the basis of race.

sharecropping: a type of agricultural relationship in which the landlord and the person who worked the land agreed to share the crop.

Sheppard-Towner Act of 1921: provided matching federal funds to supplement expenditures by the states on preventive health-care programmes designed to reduce rates of infant mortality.

Sherman Act: the original antitrust law passed in 1890. It declared illegal 'every contract, combination . . . or conspiracy in restraint of trade or commerce' between the states.

social security: usually refers to Old Age Insurance *(q.v.)* and related programmes.

Social Security Act of 1935: the foundation-stone of the American welfare state. It initiated programmes of unemployment insurance, Old Age Insurance, Old Age Assistance and Aid to Dependent Children *(qq.v.)*.

social settlements: residences in slum neighbourhoods inhabited by social reformers, most of whom were female. They provided a variety of social and cultural facilities, while also offering a focus for reform activities and social research.

Socialist Party of America (SPA): formed in 1901 by a number of socialist parties and factions, by far the largest party of the Left during the early twentieth century.

Southern Christian Leadership Conference (SCLC): a civil rights organisation formed in 1958 under the leadership of Martin Luther King Jr.

Standard Oil of New Jersey v. US: the 1911 decision that proclaimed the so-called 'rule of reason': a large corporation was not illegal under the Sherman Act *(q.v.)* unless it engaged in 'unreasonable' competitive practices (as, however, Standard Oil was found to have done).

Taft-Hartley Act of 1947: made a number of amendments to the Wagner Act *(q.v.)* which adjusted the legal balance in favour of employers.

United Automobile Workers (UAW): the CIO *(q.v.)* union which organised auto workers during the late 1930s and 1940s and became one of the most powerful labour organisations in the country.

United Mine Workers (UMW): one of the few industrial unions *(q.v.)* in the American Federation of Labor *(q.v.)*, a founder member of the Congress of Industrial Organizations *(q.v.)*.

US v. Butler et al.: a 1936 Supreme Court decision that ruled the

Agricultural Adjustment Act unconstitutional because of the discriminatory character of the tax levied to finance it and because agriculture was held to be a local activity subject to state, not federal, regulation.

US v. *E.C. Knight Company*: an 1895 Supreme Court decision which called into question both the applicability of the Sherman Act to mergers and the power of Congress to regulate manufacturing.

Volstead Act of 1919: the legislation drawn up to enforce the Eighteenth Amendment *(q.v.)*.

Wabash, St. Louis and Pacific Railway Company v. Illinois: an 1886 Supreme Court decision which, by ruling out state regulation of interstate railroad operations, accelerated the movement towards federal supervision.

Wagner Act: the National Labor Relations Act of 1935, which gave workers the right to be represented by a union of their choice and compelled an employer to recognise and bargain in good faith with that union.

War on Poverty: a collective description of the antipoverty programmes of the Johnson Administration, particularly those initiated by the Economic Opportunity Act *(q.v.)*.

welfare capitalism: a movement among a number of large corporations before the First World War, and still more in the 1920s, to improve labour relations and workforce loyalty by instituting private welfare programmes.

Women's Christian Temperance Union (WCTU): a women's organisation formed in 1874 to campaign for prohibition of the liquor traffic.

Women's Trade Union League (WTUL): an association established in 1903 by female reformers to support women workers in their attempts to organise trade unions and to campaign for laws regulating their wages and hours of work.

Works Progress Administration (WPA): the largest work relief agency of the New Deal, established in 1935. It set up work programmes for writers and artists as well as a variety of projects for manual workers.

'yellow-dog contract': a contract signed by a worker as a condition of his employment which debarred him from membership of a trade union.

Further Reading

This is by no means an exhaustive listing of the works that have been consulted in the course of writing this book, still less of the voluminous literature on the subject of twentieth-century American politics and government. It is intended to serve as an indication of the books and articles to which the reader might most usefully refer for the purpose of further study.

1. General

BLUM, JOHN M. *The Progressive Presidents: Roosevelt, Wilson, Roosevelt, Johnson.* New York: Norton, 1980.

BROESAMLE, JOSEPH J. *Reform and Reaction in Twentieth-Century American Politics.* Westport, Ct.: Greenwood, 1990.

BURNHAM, WALTER DEAN. *Critical Elections and the Mainsprings of American Politics.* New York: Norton, 1970.

CAMPBELL, BALLARD C. 'Federalism, state action and "critical episodes" in the growth of American government' *Social Science History* 16 (1992), 561–82

CAMPBELL, BALLARD C. *The Growth of American Government: Governance from the Cleveland Era to the Present.* Bloomington: University of Indiana Press, 1995.

DAWLEY, ALAN. *Struggles for Justice: Social Responsibility and the Liberal State.* Cambridge, Mass.: Harvard University Press, 1991.

GALAMBOS, LOUIS and JOSEPH PRATT. *The Rise of the Corporate Commonwealth: United States Business and Public Policy in the Twentieth Century.* New York: Basic Books, 1988.

HAYS, SAMUEL P. *American Political History as Social Analysis.* Knoxville, Tenn.: University of Tennessee Press, 1980

HIGGS, ROBERT. *Crisis and Leviathan: Critical Episodes in the Growth of American Government.* New York: Oxford University Press, 1987.

HOFSTADTER, RICHARD D. *The Age of Reform: From Bryan to F.D.R.* New York: Random House, 1955.

KLEPPNER, PAUL, ed. *The Evolution of American Electoral Systems.* Westport, Ct.: Greenwood, 1981.

LEUCHTENBURG, WILLIAM E. 'The pertinence of political history: reflections on the significance of the state in America' *Journal of American History* 73 (1986), 585–600.

MCCRAW, THOMAS K. *Prophets of Regulation.* Cambridge, Mass.: Harvard University Press, 1984.

MCCRAW, THOMAS K. ed. *Regulation in Perspective: Historical Essays.* Cambridge, Mass.: Harvard University Press, 1981.

SKOCPOL, THEDA. 'State formation and social policy in the United States' *American Behavioral Scientist* 35 (1992), 559-84.

WISHY, BERNARD. *Good-bye, Machiavelli: Government and American Life.* Baton Rouge, La.: Louisiana State University Press, 1995.

2. State and society in late nineteenth-century America

BROCK, WILLIAM R. *Investigation and Responsibility: Public Responsibility in the United States, 1865–1900.* Cambridge: Cambridge University Press, 1984.

GOODWYN, LAWRENCE. *Democratic Promise: The Populist Moment in America.* New York: Oxford University Press, 1976.

HAYS, SAMUEL P. *The Response to Industrialism, 1885–1914.* Chicago: Chicago University Press, 1957.

HOLMES, WILLIAM F. 'Populism: in search of context' *Agricultural History* 64 (1990), 26–58

HURST, JAMES WILLARD. *Law and the Condition of Freedom in the Nineteenth-Century United States.* Madison, Wis.: University of Wisconsin Press, 1956.

KELLER, MORTON. *Affairs of State: Public Life in Mid-Nineteenth Century America.* Cambridge, Mass.: Harvard University Press, 1977.

MCCORMICK, RICHARD L. 'The party period and public policy: an exploratory hypothesis' *Journal of American History* 66 (1979), 279–98.

MCFARLAND, GERALD W. *Mugwumps, Morals, and Politics, 1884–1920.* Amherst, Mass.: University of Massachusetts Press, 1975.

McMATH, ROBERT, JR. *American Populism: A Social History, 1877–1898.* New York: Hill & Wang, 1993.

MORGAN, H. WAYNE, ed. *The Gilded Age.* Revised edn. Syracuse, N.Y.: Syracuse University Press, 1970.

PAINTER, NELL I. *Standing at Armageddon: The United States, 1877–1919.* New York: Norton, 1987.

POLLACK, NORMAN. *The Just Polity: Populism, Law and Human Welfare.* Urbana, Ill.: University of Illinois Press, 1987.

SKOWRONEK, STEPHEN. *Building a New American State: The Evolution of National Administrative Capacities, 1877–1920.* Cambridge: Cambridge University Press, 1982.

SPROAT, JOHN G. *The 'Best Men': Liberal Reformers in the Gilded Age.* New York: Oxford University Press, 1968.

WIEBE, ROBERT H. *The Search for Order, 1877–1920.* New York: Hill & Wang, 1967.

WILLIAMS, R. HAL. *Years of Decision: American Politics in the 1890s.* New York: Wiley, 1978.

3. *Capital, labour and the state, 1890–1920*

CHANDLER, ALFRED D., JR. *The Visible Hand: The Managerial Revolution in American Business.* Cambridge, Mass.: Harvard University Press, 1977.

DICK, WILLIAM M. *Labor and Socialism in America: The Gompers Era.* Port Washington, N.Y.: Kennikat, 1972.

DUBOFSKY, MELVYN. *Industrialism and the American Worker, 1860–1920.* 2nd edn. Arlington Heights, Ill.: Harlan Davidson, 1985.

DUBOFSKY, MELVYN. *The State and Labor in Modern America.* Chapel Hill: University of North Carolina Press, 1994.

FINK, LEON. 'Labor, liberty and the law: trade unionism and the problem of the American constitutional order' *Journal of American History* 74 (1987), 904–25.

FONER, ERIC. 'Why is there no socialism in America?' *History Workshop Journal* 17 (1984), 57–80.

FORBATH, WILLIAM E. *Law and the Shaping of the American Labor Movement.* Cambridge, Mass.: Harvard University Press, 1991.

FRISCH, MICHAEL H. and DANIEL WALKOWITZ, eds. *Working-Class America.* Urbana, Ill.: University of Illinois Press, 1983.

GORDON, DAVID M. *et al. Segmented Work, Divided Labor: The Transformation of Labor in the United States.* Cambridge: Cambridge University Press, 1982.

GUTMAN, HERBERT. 'Work, culture and society in industrializing America, 1815–1919' *American Historical Review* 78 (1973), 531–87.

HATTAM, VICTORIA C. *Labor Visions and State Power: The Origins of Business Unionism in the United States.* Princeton: Princeton University Press, 1993.

LASLETT, JOHN H.M. and SEYMOUR M. LIPSET, eds. *Failure of a Dream: Essays on the History of American Socialism.* New York: Anchor Press, 1974.

LIVINGSTON, JAMES. 'The social analysis of economic history and theory: conjectures on late nineteenth-century development' *American Historical Review* 92 (1987), 69–95.

MONTGOMERY, DAVID. *The Fall of the House of Labor.* Cambridge: Cambridge University Press, 1987.

OESTREICHER, RICHARD J. 'Urban working-class political behavior and theories of American electoral politics, 1870–1940' *Journal of American History* 74 (1988), 1257–86.

ORREN, KAREN. *Beyond Feudalism: Labor, the Law and Liberal Development in the United States.* Cambridge: Cambridge University Press, 1991.

PORTER, GLENN. *The Rise of Big Business, 1860–1910.* Arlington Heights, Ill.: AHM, 1973.

SALVATORE, NICK. *Eugene V. Debs: Citizen and Socialist.* Urbana, Ill.: University of Illinois Press, 1982.

WEINSTEIN, JAMES. *The Decline of Socialism in America, 1912–1925.* New York: Monthly Review Press, 1967.

ZUNZ, OLIVIER. *Making America Corporate, 1880–1920.* Chicago: University of Chicago Press, 1990.

4. Progressivism: the new political order and the regulation of business

BLUM, JOHN M. *The Republican Roosevelt.* Cambridge, Mass.: Harvard University Press, 1954.

BUENKER, JOHN D., JOHN C. BURNHAM and ROBERT CRUNDEN. *Progressivism.* Cambridge, Mass.: Schenkman, 1977.

COOPER, JOHN M. *The Warrior and the Priest: Woodrow Wilson and Theodore Roosevelt.* Cambridge, Mass.: Harvard University Press, 1983.

CRUNDEN, ROBERT. *Ministers of Reform: The Progressives' Achievement in American Civilization, 1889–1920.* New York: Basic Books, 1982.

FILENE, PETER G. 'An obituary for the progressive movement' *American Quarterly* 22 (1970), 20–34.

FREYER, TONY. *Regulating Big Business: Antitrust in Great Britain and America, 1880–1990.* Cambridge: Cambridge University Press, 1992.

GOULD, LEWIS L., ed. *The Progressive Era.* Syracuse, N.Y.: Syracuse University Press, 1973.

HAYS, SAMUEL P. *Conservation and the Gospel of Efficiency: The Progressive Conservation Movement, 1890–1920.* Cambridge, Mass.: Harvard University Press, 1959.

HOVENKAMP, HERBERT. *Enterprise and American Law, 1836–1937.* Cambridge, Mass.: Harvard University Press, 1991.

KELLER, MORTON. *Regulating a New Economy: Public Policy and Economic Change in America, 1900–1933.* Cambridge, Mass.: Harvard University Press, 1990.

KLOPPENBERG, JAMES T. *Uncertain Victory: Social Democracy and Progressivism in European and American Thought, 1870–1920.* New York: Oxford University Press, 1986.

KOLKO, GABRIEL. *The Triumph of Conservatism: An Interpretation of the Progressive Movement.* New York: Free Press, 1963.

LETWIN, WILLIAM. *Law and Economic Policy in America: The Evolution of the Sherman Antitrust Act.* New York: Random House, 1966.

LINK, ARTHUR S. and RICHARD L. MCCORMICK. *Progressivism.* Arlington Heights, Ill.: Harlan Davidson, 1983.

LIVINGSTON, JAMES. *Origins of the Federal Reserve System: Money, Class and Corporate Capitalism, 1890–1913.* Ithaca, N.Y.: Cornell University Press, 1986.

MARTIN, ALBRO. *Enterprise Denied: Origins of the Decline of American Railroads, 1897–1917.* New York: Columbia University Press, 1971.

MCCORMICK, RICHARD L. *The Party Period and Public Policy: American Politics from the Age of Jackson to the Progressive Era.* New York: Oxford University Press, 1986.

MOWRY, GEORGE E. *The Era of Theodore Roosevelt and the Birth of Modern America, 1900–1912.* New York: Harper, 1958.

RODGERS, DANIEL T. 'In search of progressivism' *Reviews in American History* 10 (1982), 113–32.

SKLAR, MARTIN. *The Corporate Reconstruction of American Capitalism: The Market, the Law, and Politics, 1890–1916.* Cambridge: Cambridge University Press, 1988.

SKOWRONEK, STEPHEN. *Building a New American State: The Evolution of National Administrative Capacities, 1877–1920.* Cambridge: Cambridge University Press, 1982.

WEINSTEIN, JAMES. *The Corporate Ideal of the Liberal State, 1900–1918.* Boston: Beacon, 1968.

YOUNG, JAMES HARVEY. *Pure Food: Securing the Federal Food and Drug Act of 1906.* Princeton: Princeton University Press, 1989.

5. Patterns of social reform, 1890–1920

BERKOWITZ, EDWARD and KIM MCQUAID. *Creating the Welfare Study: The Political Economy of Twentieth-Century Reform.* New York: Praeger, 1988.

BOYER, PAUL. *Urban Masses and Moral Order, 1820–1920.* Cambridge, Mass.: Harvard University Press, 1978.

BREMNER, ROBERT. *From the Depths: The Discovery of Poverty in the United States.* New York: New York University Press, 1956.

DAVIS, ALLEN F. *Spearheads for Reform: The Social Settlements and the Progressive Movement.* New York: Oxford University Press, 1967.

FRANKEL, NORALEE and NANCY S. DYE, eds. *Gender, Class, Race and Reform in the Progressive Era.* Lexington, Ky.: University Press of Kentucky, 1991.

GORDON, LINDA. *Pitied But Not Entitled: Single Mothers and the History of Welfare.* New York: Oxford University Press, 1994.

GORDON, LINDA, ed. *Women, the State and Policy.* Madison, Wis.: University of Wisconsin Press, 1990

KATZ, MICHAEL B. *In the Shadow of the Poorhouse: A Social History of Welfare in America.* New York: Basic Books, 1986.

MUNCY, ROBYN. *Creating a Female Dominion in American Reform.* New York: Oxford University Press, 1991.

ORLOFF, ANN S. 'Gender in early U.S. social policy' *Journal of Policy History* 3 (1991), 249–81.

ORLOFF, ANN S. and THEDA SKOCPOL. 'Why not equal protection? Explaining the politics of public social spending in Britain, 1900–1911, and the United States, 1800s–1920' *American Sociological Review* 49 (1984), 726–50.

ROBERTSON, DAVID B. 'The bias of American federalism: The limits of welfare state development in the Progressive Era' *Journal of Policy History,* 1 (1989), 261–91.

SKLAR, KATHRYN KISH. *Florence Kelley and the Nation's Work: The Rise of Women's Political Culture, 1830–1900.* New Haven, Ct.: Yale University Press, 1995.

SKOCPOL, THEDA. *The Politics of Social Policy in the United States.* Princeton: Princeton University Press, 1995.

SKOCPOL, THEDA. *The Protection of Soldiers and Mothers: The Political Origins of Social Policy in the United States.* Cambridge, Mass.: Harvard University Press, 1992.

TRATTNER, WALTER I. *From Poor Law to Welfare State.* 5th edn. New York: Free Press, 1994.

WARD, DAVID. *Poverty, Ethnicity and the American City, 1840–1925: Changing Conceptions of the Slum and the Ghetto.* Cambridge: Cambridge University Press, 1989.

6. The 1920s

BERNSTEIN, IRVING. *The Lean Years: A History of the American Worker, 1920–1933.* Boston: Houghton Mifflin, 1960.

BLOCKER, JACK S. *American Temperance Movements: Cycles of Reform.* Boston: Twayne, 1989.

BRAEMAN, JOHN, ROBERT BREMNER and DAVID BRODY, eds. *Change and Continuity in Twentieth-Century America: The 1920s.* Columbus, Ohio: Ohio State University Press, 1968.

BURNER, DAVID. *Herbert Hoover: A Public Life.* New York: Knopf, 1979.

CLARK, NORMAN. *Deliver Us from Evil: An Interpretation of American Prohibition.* New York: Norton, 1976.

DEGLER, CARL. 'The ordeal of Herbert Hoover' *Yale Review* 52 (1963), 563–83.

FAUSOLD, MARTIN L. *The Presidency of Herbert Hoover.* Lawrence, Kan.: University Press of Kansas, 1985.

FAUSOLD, MARTIN L. and GEORGE T. MAZUZAN, eds. *The Hoover Presidency: A Reappraisal.* Albany, N.Y.: State University of New York Press, 1974.

HAWLEY, ELLIS W. *The Great War and the Search for a Modern Order.* New York: St Martin's Press, 1979.

HAWLEY, ELLIS W. *et al. Herbert Hoover and the Crisis of American Capitalism.* Cambridge, Mass.: Schenkman, 1973.

HAWLEY, ELLIS W., ed. *Herbert Hoover as Secretary of Commerce, 1921–1928.* Iowa City: University of Iowa Press, 1981.

HAWLEY, ELLIS W. 'Herbert Hoover, the Commerce Secretariat, and the vision of an 'associative state', 1919–1928' *Journal of American History* 61 (1974), 116-40.

HICKS, JOHN D. *Republican Ascendancy, 1920–1933.* New York: Harper, 1960.

KARL, BARRY D. *The Uneasy State: The United States from 1915 to 1945.* Chicago: University of Chicago Press, 1983.

KERR, K. AUSTIN. *Organizing for Prohibition: A New History of the Anti-Saloon League.* New Haven, Ct.: Yale University Press, 1985.

LINK, ARTHUR S. 'What happened to the progressive movement in the 1920s?' *American Historical Review* 64 (1959), 833–51.

MCELVAINE, ROBERT S. *The Great Depression: America, 1929–1941.* New York: New York Times Books, 1984.

MOORE, LEONARD J. 'Historical interpretations of the 1920s Klan' *Journal of Social History* 24 (1990), 341–57.

MURRAY, ROBERT K. *The Politics of Normalcy: Governmental Theory and Practice in the Harding-Coolidge Era.* New York: Norton, 1973.

PARRISH, MICHAEL E. *Anxious Decades: America in Prosperity and Depression, 1920–1941.* New York: Norton, 1992.

ROMASCO, ALBERT U. *The Poverty of Abundance: Hoover, the Nation, the Depression.* New York: Oxford University Press, 1965.

WILSON, JOAN HOFF. *Herbert Hoover: Forgotten Progressive.* Boston: Little, Brown, 1975.

7. The New Deal and the political economy of twentieth-century America

ALLSWANG, JOHN M. *The New Deal and American Politics.* New York: Wiley, 1978.

AUERBACH, JEROLD S. 'New Deal, Old Deal, or Raw Deal: some thoughts on New Left historiography' *Journal of Southern History* 35 (1969), 18–30.

BADGER, ANTHONY J. *The New Deal: The Depression Years, 1933–1940.* London: Macmillan, 1989.

BELLUSH, BERNARD. *The Failure of the NRA.* New York: Norton, 1975.

BILES, ROGER. *The South and the New Deal.* Lexington, Ky.: University Press of Kentucky, 1994.

BRAEMAN, JOHN. 'The New Deal and the "Broker State"' *Business History Review* 46 (1972), 409–20.

BRAEMAN, JOHN, ROBERT BREMNER and DAVID BRODY, eds. *The New Deal.* 2 vols. Columbus, Ohio: Ohio State University Press, 1975.

BRINKLEY, ALAN. 'The antimonopoly ideal and the liberal state: the case of Thurman Arnold' *Journal of American History* 80 (1993), 557–79.

BRINKLEY, ALAN. *The End of Reform: New Deal Liberalism in Recession and War.* New York: Knopf, 1995.

CONKIN, PAUL. *The New Deal*. London: Routledge & Kegan Paul, 1968.

HAMBY, ALONZO, ed. *The New Deal: Analysis and Interpretation*. 2nd edn. London: Longman, 1981.

HAWLEY, ELLIS W. *The New Deal and the Problem of Monopoly*. Princeton, N.J.: Princeton University Press, 1966.

JEFFRIES, JOHN W. 'The "new" New Deal: FDR and American liberalism, 1937–1945' *Political Science Quarterly* 105 (1990), 397–418.

KARL, BARRY. 'Constitution and central planning: The Third New Deal revisited' *Supreme Court Review* 1989, 163–201.

LEUCHTENBURG, WILLIAM E. *Franklin D. Roosevelt and the New Deal, 1932–1940*. New York: Harper, 1963.

LEUCHTENBURG, WILLIAM E. 'The New Deal and the analogue of war', in John Braeman, Robert Bremner and David Brody, eds, *Change and Continuity in Modern America* (Columbus, Ohio: Ohio State University Press 1964), 81–143.

LEUCHTENBURG, WILLIAM E. *The Supreme Court Reborn: Constitutional Revolution in the Age of Roosevelt*. New York: Oxford University Press, 1995.

MERTZ, PAUL E. *New Deal Policy and Southern Rural Poverty*. Baton Rouge, La.: Louisiana State University Press, 1978.

MILKIS, SIDNEY. *The President and the Parties: The Transformation of the American Party System since the New Deal*. New York: Oxford University Press, 1993.

PATTERSON, JAMES T. *Congressional Conservatism and the New Deal*. Lexington, Ky.: University Press of Kentucky, 1967.

PATTERSON, JAMES T. *The New Deal and the States*. Princeton: Princeton University Press, 1969.

SALOUTOS, THEODORE. 'New Deal agricultural policy: an evaluation' *Journal of American History* 61 (1974), 394–416.

SCHLESINGER, ARTHUR M., JR. *The Coming of the New Deal*. Boston: Houghton Mifflin, 1958.

SCHLESINGER, ARTHUR M., JR. *The Politics of Upheaval*. Boston: Houghton Mifflin, 1960.

SITKOFF, HARVARD, ed. *Fifty Years Later: The New Deal Evaluated*. New York: Knopf, 1985

SKOCPOL, THEDA and KENNETH FINEGOLD. 'State capacity and economic intervention in the early New Deal' *Political Science Quarterly*, 97 (1982), 255–78.

8. *The rise and fall of organised labour*

BRODY, DAVID. *Workers in Industrial America: Essays on the Twentieth-Century Struggle.* New York: Oxford University Press, 1980.

COHEN, LIZABETH. *Making a New Deal: Industrial Workers in Chicago, 1919–1939.* New York: Oxford University Press, 1990.

DAVIS, MIKE. *Prisoners of the American Dream.* New York: Verso, 1986.

FINEGOLD, KENNETH and THEDA SKOCPOL. 'Explaining New Deal labor policy' *American Political Science Review* 84 (1990), 1297–315.

FRASER, STEVE. *Labor Will Rule: Sidney Hillman and the Rise of American Labor.* New York: Free Press, 1991.

GERSTLE, GARY. *Working-Class Americanism: The Politics of Labor in a Textile City, 1914–1960.* Cambridge: Cambridge University Press, 1989.

GOLDFIELD, MICHAEL. *The Decline of Organized Labor in the United States.* Chicago: University of Chicago Press, 1987.

GOLDFIELD, MICHAEL. 'Worker insurgency, radical organization and New Deal labor legislation' *American Political Science Review*, 83 (1989), 1257–82.

LICHTENSTEIN, NELSON. *Labor's War at Home: The CIO and World War II.* Cambridge: Cambridge University Press, 1982.

MOODY, KIM. *An Injury to All: The Decline of American Unionism.* New York, Verso, 1988.

NELSON, DANIEL. 'The CIO at bay: labor militancy and politics at Akron, 1936–1938' *Journal of American History* 71 (1984), 565–86.

ORREN, KAREN. 'Organized labor and the invention of modern liberalism in the United States' *Studies in American Political Development* 2 (1987), 317–36.

ORREN, KAREN. 'Union politics and postwar liberalism in the United States' *Studies in American Political Development* 1 (1986), 215–52.

TOMLINS, CHRISTOPHER L. *The State and the Unions: Labor Relations, Law, and the Organized Labor Movement in the United States, 1880–1960.* Cambridge: Cambridge University Press, 1986.

ZIEGER, ROBERT H. *American Workers, American Unions, 1920–1985.* Baltimore: Johns Hopkins University Press, 1986.

ZIEGER, ROBERT H. *The CIO, 1935–1955.* Chapel Hill, N.C.: University of North Carolina Press, 1995.

9. *The making of the welfare state*

ACHENBAUM, W. ANDREW. *Social Security: Visions and Revisions.* Cambridge: Cambridge University Press, 1986.

BERKOWITZ, EDWARD. *America's Welfare State: From Roosevelt to Reagan.* Baltimore: Johns Hopkins University, 1991.

BROCK, WILLIAM R. *Welfare, Democracy and the New Deal.* Cambridge: Cambridge University Press, 1988.

COLL, BLANCHE D. *Safety Net: Welfare and Social Security, 1929–1979.* New Brunswick, N.J.: Rutgers University Press, 1995.

CRITCHLOW, DONALD T. and ELLIS W. HAWLEY, eds. *Federal Social Policy: The Historical Dimension.* University Park, Pa.: Pennsylvania State University Press, 1988.

GORDON, LINDA. *Pitied But Not Entitled: Single Mothers and the History of Welfare.* New York: Oxford University Press, 1994.

JACOBY, SANFORD M. 'Employers and the welfare state: the role of Marion B. Folsom' *Journal of American History* 80 (1993), 525–56.

JENKINS, J. CRAIG and BARBARA G. BRENTS. 'Social protest, hegemonic competition, and social reform: a political struggle interpretation of the origins of the American welfare state' *American Sociological Review* 54 (1989), 891–909.

LEFF, MARK H. 'Taxing the "forgotten man": The politics of social security finance in the New Deal' *Journal of American History* 70 (1983), 359–81.

LUBOVE, ROY S. *The Struggle for Social Security, 1900–1935.* Cambridge, Mass.: Harvard University Press, 1968.

PATTERSON, JAMES T. *America's Struggle against Poverty, 1900–1985.* Cambridge, Mass.: Harvard University Press, 1986.

ORLOFF, ANN S., ed. *The Politics of Pensions: A Comparative Analysis of Britain, Canada and the United States, 1880–1940.* Madison, Wis.: University of Wisconsin Press, 1993.

QUADAGNO, JILL S. *The Transformation of Old Age Security: Class and Politics in the American Welfare State.* Chicago: University of Chicago Press, 1988.

SKOCPOL, THEDA. *Social Policy in the United States.* Princeton, N.J.: Princeton University Press, 1995.

WEIR, MARGARET, ANN S. ORLOFF and THEDA SKOCPOL, eds. *The Politics of Social Policy in the United States.* Princeton, N.J.: Princeton University Press, 1988.

10. To the Great Society and beyond

BERMAN, WILLIAM C. *America's Right Turn: From Nixon to Bush.* Baltimore: Johns Hopkins University, 1994.

BERNSTEIN, IRVING. *Guns and Butter: The Presidency of Lyndon Johnson.* New York: Oxford University Press, 1996.

BERNSTEIN, IRVING. *Promises Kept: John F. Kennedy's New Frontier.* New York: Oxford University Press, 1991.

BLUM, JOHN MORTON. *Years of Discord: American Politics and Society, 1961–1974.* New York: Norton, 1991.

BRAUER, CARL M. 'Kennedy, Johnson and the War on Poverty' *Journal of American History* 69 (1982), 98–119.

BRUCE, STEVE. *The Rise and Fall of the New Christian Right.* Oxford: Oxford University Press, 1988.

CONKIN, PAUL K. *Big Daddy from the Pedernales: Lyndon Baines Johnson.* Boston: Twayne, 1996.

DAVIES, GARETH. *From Opportunity to Entitlement: The Transformation and Decline of Great Society Liberalism.* Lawrence, Kan.: University Press of Kansas, 1996.

DIVINE, ROBERT, ed. *The Johnson Years: Vol. 1. Foreign Policy, the Great Society and the White House.* Lawrence, Kan.: University Press of Kansas, 1981.

DIVINE, ROBERT, ed. *The Johnson Years: Vol. 3. LBJ at Home and Abroad.* Lawrence, Kan.: University Press of Kansas, 1994.

FRASER, STEVE and GARY GERSTLE, eds. *The Rise and Fall of the New Deal Order, 1930–1980.* Princeton: Princeton University Press, 1989.

GRAHAM, HUGH D. *The Civil Rights Era: Origins of National Policy.* New York: Oxford University Press, 1991.

GREENSTEIN, FRED I. *The Hidden-Hand Presidency: Eisenhower as Leader.* New York: Basic Books, 1982.

GRIFFITH, ROBERT. 'Dwight D. Eisenhower and the Corporate Commonwealth' *American Historical Review* 87 (1982), 87–122.

HAMBY, ALONZO. *Beyond the New Deal: Harry S. Truman and American Liberalism.* New York: Columbia University Press, 1973.

HAMBY, ALONZO. *Liberalism and Its Challengers: From FDR to Reagan.* New York: Oxford University Press, 1992.

KATZ, MICHAEL B., ed. *The 'Underclass' Debate: Views from History.* Princeton, N.J.: Princeton University Press, 1993.

LACEY, MICHAEL J. ed. *The Truman Presidency.* Cambridge: Cambridge University Press, 1989.

LADD, EVERETT C., JR. 'Liberalism upside down: the inversion of the New Deal order' *Political Science Quarterly* 91 (1976), 577–600.

LAWSON, STEVEN F. *Running for Freedom: Civil Rights and Black Politics since 1941.* Philadelphia: Temple University Press, 1991.

LEMANN, NICHOLAS. *The Promised Land: The Great Black Migration and How It Changed America.* New York: Knopf, 1991.

LEUCHTENBERG, WILLIAM E. *In the Shadow of FDR: From Harry Truman to Bill Clinton.* Ithaca, N.Y.: Cornell University Press, 1993.

LOWI, THEODORE J. *The End of Liberalism: The Second Republic of the United States.* 2nd edn. New York: Norton, 1979.

MATUSOW, ALLEN J. *The Unraveling of America: A History of Liberalism in the 1960s.* New York: Harper, 1984.

MORGAN, IWAN. *Beyond the Liberal Consensus: A Political History of the United States since 1965.* London: Hirst, 1994.

PEELE, GILLIAN. *Revival and Reaction: The Right in Contemporary America.* New York: Oxford University Press, 1985.

SCHLESINGER ARTHUR M., JR. *Robert Kennedy and His Times.* London: Deutsch, 1978.

STEIGERWALD, DAVID. *The Sixties and the End of Modern America.* New York: St. Martin's Press, 1995.

STERN, MARK. *Calculating Visions: Kennedy, Johnson and Civil Rights.* New Brunswick, N.J.: Rutgers University Press, 1991.

Index